Path Of
The Bodhisattva Warrior

THE THIRTEENTH DALAI LAMA

Path Of
The Bodhisattva Warrior

The Life and Teachings of the Thirteenth Dalai Lama

Compiled and Translated by Glenn H. Mullin
Biography by Glenn H. Mullin

Foreword by Professor Thub-ten Nor-bu

Illustrations by Namkhah Tashi
Edited by Christine Cox

WITHDRAWN

Snow Lion Publications
Ithaca, New York, USA

College —

BQ
7935
.T482
1988
c.1

Snow Lion Publications, Inc.
P.O. Box 6483
Ithaca, New York 14851
USA

Copyright © 1988 Glenn H. Mullin

Library of Congress Catalog Number

ISBN 0-937938-55-6

Library of Congress Cataloging-in-Publication Data

Thub-bstan-rgya-mtsho, Dalai Lama XIII, 1876-1933
    [Selections. English]
    Path of the Bodhisattva warrior ; with a Life of the thirteenth Dalai Lama by Glen H. Mullin ; foreword by Thub-ten Nor-bu ; compiled and translated by Glenn H. Mullin ; illustrations by Chris Bannigan ; edited by Christine Cox.
        p.   cm.
    At head of title: The thirteenth Dalai Lama.
    Includes index.
    ISBN 0-937938-55-6
    1. Dge-lugs-pa (Sect)—Doctrines 2. Buddhism—Doctrines.
3. Thub-bstan-rgya-mtsho, Dalai Lama XIII, 1876-1933. 4. Dalai lamas—Biography. I. Cox, Christine. II. Mullin, Glenn H. Life of the thirteenth Dalai Lama. 1988. III. Title.
BQ7935.T482   1988
294.3'923'0924—dc19
[B]   88-18300
                                                        CIP

Contents

The Bodhisattva is like
   the mightiest of warriors;
But his enemies are not
   common foes of flesh and bone.
His fight is with the inner delusions,
   the afflictions of self-cherishing
      and ego-grasping,
Those most terrible of demons
That catch living beings in the
   snare of confusion
And cause them forever to wander
   in pain, frustration and sorrow.
His mission is to harm ignorance and delusion,
   never living beings.
These he looks upon with kindness,
   patience and empathy,
Cherishing them like a mother cherishes
   her only child.
He is the real hero,
   calmly facing any hardship
In order to bring peace, happiness
   and liberation to the world.

—The Thirteenth Dalai Lama
from his "Discourse on the Great *Lam Rim*"

Acknowledgements

The work of compiling the various translations in the *Path of the Bodhisattva Warrior* was not accomplished alone, and I would like to thank the various spiritual mentors and friends who provided me with guidance and assistance.

I began reading the Great Thirteenth's *Sung-bum* during the winter of 1985-86 with the Ven. Ar-tsa Tul-ku, a professor at Magadha University, Bihar, India. At the time I was in Bodh Gaya to attend a discourse being given by His Holiness the Dalai Lama; Rin-po-che kindly took time from his busy life to read through with me the five poems that constitute chapter four of the present volume. I later published one of these in *The Middle Way*, and another in *Bulletin of the Tibet Society*, Indiana (Vol. 18, Dec. 1986), and I would like to thank the editors of these two publications for their permission to reuse them here.

Ven. Chom-dze Ta-shi Wang-gyal, a wonderful *ge-she* of Dre-pung Monastery who these days is in the employ of the Library of Tibetan Works and Archives, Dharamsala, India, read through the brief text of chapter one with me, as well as the short guru yoga prayer of chapter six. As always, his commentary was lively and insightful.

The material in the remaining chapters—which in fact constitutes the bulk of this book—was read with two very wonderful tul-kus: Ven. Am-chok Rin-po-che of Gan-den (who recently returned to Tibet to rebuild Am-chok Tsen-nyi Dra-tsang, his monastery in Am-do

Province); and Ven. Shar-pa Rin-po-che of Se-ra, who presently serves in H. H. the Dalai Lama's Private Office. These two young lamas have been extremely kind to me over the years; in particular, they both dedicated several hours a day over a period of almost six months to this project, and without their generous and learned inspiration my efforts would have been like those of a blind man trying to find his way over a dangerous mountain pass.

After the preliminary draft translations had been completed I rechecked all difficult passages with two of my favorite gurus: Ven. Denma Lob-chu Rin-po-che and Ven. Do-boom Tul-ku, both of whom were educated in Dre-pung Lo-sel-ling Monastery. The former of these lamas is now serving as the abbot of the Dalai Lama's private monastery, Nam-gyal Dra-tsang; the latter is the Director of Tibet House, New Delhi.

A number of Tibetan friends, who helped me in the work of researching the historical background within which the Thirteenth Dalai Lama lived and wrote, are also deserving of mention: Acharya Ta-shi Tse-ring of the Library of Tibetan Works and Archives, a never-ending source of information on Tibetan literature; Mr. Tub-ten Sang-gye, also of the Tibetan Library, who had worked for many years in the Great Thirteenth's government; and the Ven. Lo-dhi Gya-ri, who provided me with many interesting oral traditions concerning the Great Thirteenth's magnificent deeds.

As always my thanks go out to Mr. Gya-tso Tse-ring, Director of the Tibetan Library in Dharamsala, who helped me in countless ways by granting me access to the facilities of his institution and listening patiently for many long hours to my dreams and schemes. He has been a constant friend and support to me in my work for more than fifteen years now, and my debt to him can never be repaid.

Finally I would like to thank the Ven. Tak-tser Rin-po-che, who recently retired his professorship at Indiana University, for providing me with the Foreword; and the very talented Mr. Chris Bannigan, a Canadian artist well trained in the Tibetan tradition, who provided the marvelous illustrations.

And, of course, Christine Cox, my editor at Snow Lion Publications; Jeff Cox, my publisher; Sidney Piburn, senior editor and the book designer; and Hilary Shearman, who helped me throughout the work with proofreading and by offering numerous suggestions.

Preface

In the chapter on the life of the the thirteenth Dalai Lama, I have principally drawn the materials directly relating to His Holiness' life from the three main Tibetan biographies of him (see Bibliography). As for the Western sources used, I naturally have referred to the two earlier English biographies of the Great Thirteenth—those by Sir Charles Bell and Tokan Tada—but as these are more personal accounts of their authors' travels and experiences in Tibet than they are formal biographies, and were written at a time when Tibetan studies were at a pioneer state, I found them to be of limited value. As often as not they also proved to be misleading when it comes to actual historical facts.

Most useful in drawing up an historical perspective were the writings of Mehra, Fleming and Richardson. The works of the first of these scholars proved to be especially relevant to this study. Although I do not agree with his perspective, his attention to detail is most laudable.

I greatly enjoyed reading through all the travelogues of the early adventurers, missionaries and entrepreneurs who visited Tibet between the years 1875 and 1935. Although the information given in such sources is often superficial and the impressions conveyed usually prejudiced, one nonetheless can glean a wealth of folk culture and common anecdotes.

Rather than bury the biography in piles of footnotes I have simply listed my sources in the Bibliography (provided at the end of the biography).

I have tried to keep footnotes to a minimum throughout the actual translations. The volume has already become thicker than initially projected. Consequently the notes are largely restricted to identifying the various persons quoted by the Great Thirteenth, so as to give the reader an historical perspective on the scope of his thought. As for technical points, I have contented myself to refer the reader to where these are touched upon in some of my earlier books with Snow Lion.

As for the treatment of Tibetan names and textual titles, I have tried to follow as simple and unostentatious a policy as possible. Personal Tibetan names are given phonetically as they sound, not by formal transliteration (i.e., Ten-dzin rather than the unwieldy bsTan-'dzin). I generally hyphenate the individual syllables because of the unusual manner in which Tibetans use consonants; although with shorter and somewhat familiar place names (e.g., Lhasa) I dispense with the hyphen. This rather personalized approach may irritate some Tibetologists, but I beg their indulgence. I am attempting to present my books on the selected writings of the early Dalai Lamas as literature, not as dry grist exclusively for the academic mill. Serious scholars should easily be able to work out the Tibetan forms, if they so desire; these are of no value to the casual reader, to whom they merely appear as eyesores.

When texts are quoted by the Great Thirteenth I first give the titles in English translation, followed by the Tibetan counterpart in transliteration (within parentheses). Most of these titles actually refer to Tibetan translations of Indian Buddhist scriptures; if anyone is interested in taking them back to the original Sanskrit all they have to do is check the Tibetan forms against the Sanskrit counterparts as given in any of the standard catalogues of the *Kan-gyur* and *Ten-gyur* collections. I recommend the catalogues of either Suzuki (Tokyo) or Tarthang Tulku (California).

To understand where the Great Thirteenth is coming from as an author it helps to have a basic understanding of the general structure of Tibetan Buddhist thought. To establish a basic perspective I usually recommend that novices to Tibetology read one of my earlier books with Snow Lion Publications, *Essence of Refined Gold*; this work, which contains a modern commentary by the present Dalai Lama to the Third Dalai Lama's classical presentation of the path, is an excellent primer.

Foreword

by the Ven. Tak-tser Rin-po-che, Prof. Thub-ten Jig-me Nor-bu

Even though I never met the Thirteenth Dalai Lama personally, I nonetheless owe him a tremendous debt of gratitude. Everything in my life was touched by his kindness, and even my name came to me from him.

The reason for my intimate connection with him has its roots in the life of the previous Tak-tser Lama, of whom I am said to be the reincarnation. Myself I'm not sure if I am or not, but Tibetans believe that I am.

The story of the friendship between the Thirteenth Dalai Lama and the previous Tak-tser Lama has its origins in the Great Thirteenth's second visit to Kum-bum Monastery in Am-do, which was built by the Third Dalai Lama at the birthplace of Lama Tsong-kha-pa. At the time His Holiness was returning from China, and decided to spend a couple of months in Kum-bum. During this period the previous Tak-tser Lama hosted and served him as best he could, and they became very close.

The Thirteenth Dalai Lama wanted to make a pilgrimage to a number of places in the area that were associated with events in the early life of Tsong-kha-pa. One of these involved a short outing to Shar-chong Monastery, where Tsong-kha-pa as a child had received his novice ordination. The previous Tak-tser Lama accompanied him on this pilgrimage. Moreover, he himself had a small hermitage, Shardzong Ri-tro, that lay on the road between Kum-bum and Shar-chong, and he thought that this would be a good opportunity to invite the Great Thirteenth to visit and bless his hermitage.

During this visit the Great Thirteenth and the previous Tak-tser took a walk in the adjoining area and had lunch beside a stupa overlooking Tak-tse, a tiny village of ten or twelve farm houses. During the meal the Great Thirteenth commented on the picturesque serenity of Tak-tse. Afterwards he and the previous Tak-tser Lama walked through the village. He examined each of the houses individually, inquiring about the house names and the names of the residents. He then returned to the stupa and sat in meditation for some time. Later he commented that one day he would like to return to Tak-tse.

Shortly after that outing the Great Thirteenth and his entourage continued on their return journey to Lhasa.

Two years later the previous Tak-tser Lama died. The attendants and disciples of the Lama waited a couple of years for him to take rebirth and the baby to grow to childhood, and then formed search committees to look for the reincarnation. Because of the friendship that had existed between the Great Thirteenth and the previous Tak-tser, they thought to approach His Holiness directly on the matter. With this in mind they compiled a list of children recently born with auspicious signs, and sent it to the Dalai Lama. He examined it, but commented that the correct name was not on it.

The party returned to Am-do and compiled a second list. Again this was presented to the Great Thirteenth, and again he rejected it. And so on for a third attempt.

This all took considerable time, for only two caravans a year travelled between Kum-bum and Lhasa: one in the summer, that was comprised of horses and yaks; and one of camels in the winter. The road passed through many barren and desolate regions, and many parts of it were inhabited by tribes of bandits. Thus it was necessary to travel with one of these two large caravans. So the compilation of each new list meant considerable time and effort on the part of the search committees.

Finally a fourth list was drawn up and presented to him, and this time my name was included. The Great Thirteenth put his seal on my name, and declared that I was the reincarnation of the Tak-tser Lama. He gave the committee a complete set of monk robes and a longevity painting of White Tara to carry back to Am-do for me. He also chose four large mastiffs from his palace and sent them for my monastic house in Kum-bum; these remained with me as I grew up in the monastery and were a constant source of joy to me.

The Great Thirteenth also sent me a new name, Tub-ten Jig-me Nor-bu, which has remained with me throughout my life.

Then many years later when he himself passed away his reincarnation was discovered in the same family in Tak-tse Village in which I myself had been born. He had become my younger brother!

This was something our household had never even dreamed possible. Our village was very small and was located far from Lhasa, and our home extremely humble. But all of this came to pass because of the special mystical arrangements that the Great Thirteenth had made that day in 1909 when he and the previous Tak-tser Lama had picnicked together in the hills of Am-do.

I do not relate this story to you in order to prop myself up in the eyes of the world, but to demonstrate what a very special person the Great Thirteenth was. As for me, anything good that can be said about my life is due solely to his exceptional kindness. He truly was my *Kyabgon*, my "Protecting Lord." Because of his blessings, deeds and compassion my life took the direction that it did.

But he was not kind to me alone. His wisdom and compassion touched upon all Tibetans, and spread throughout all those regions where Tibetan Buddhism is practiced. His greatness has been recorded by all historians of modern Tibet.

Nor were the benefits that he brought to Tibet limited to the spiritual side of life. Politically he managed to free our country from the stranglehold that China was attempting to exert over us; from 1913 until after his death in 1933 he succeeded in maintaining a free and independent Tibet. Moreover, in his 'Final Testament' of 1932 he outlined how we should proceed if we were to remain free from China. Unfortunately after his death those who followed were unable to live up to his vision; but this was our fault, not his.

He also contributed tremendously on the social level. For example, he abolished capital punishment and other forms of harsh criminal justice. He struggled to introduce modern ways and ideas to Tibet, sending students to British schools in India and England, and also opening a British school in Gyang-tse. He imported technology for electricity, updated the postal and minting systems, and attempted to modernize Tibet in other such ways.

His work in tightening the system of monastic education is also well known. In particular, he significantly upgraded the methods of testing candidates for the highest degrees. He went so far as to have the final tests conducted in his summer palace, where he and the top scholars of the country could oversee them.

As for his literary activities, here too he was very active, composing treatises on many different philosophical and devotional subjects, as well as on poetry, meditation, history, and so forth.

Also he seemed to be constantly engaged in teaching students and transmitting various lineages. He gave sutra discourses and Tantra initiations to tens of thousands of disciples throughout Central Asia. Merely the number of monks and nuns that he ordained reached into the thousands.

The fact that all of these things were done by one man is amazing. Each one of these spheres of activity would require a complete lifetime for an ordinary person. His accomplishments were like those of ten great people.

Actually, the tradition of the Dalai Lamas is really something very fantastic. We choose a young child to be a Dalai Lama, and always he turns out to be really wonderful. This is amazing. For example, with our own children we all try to bring them up to be good, responsible human beings; but somehow they go their own way, regardless of our efforts. But each of the Dalai Lamas has turned out so perfectly. This really says something about the tradition.

All the Dalai Lamas have been very special human beings; but somehow for me it was as though the Great Thirteenth was special among the specials. I am extremely delighted to see this study of his life and works come out in English. Glenn's project with Snow Lion Publications, which makes available to the Western world selected writings of the early Dalai Lamas, as well as accounts of their lives and deeds, is a noble and important endeavor. I offer my prayers that it may reach fulfillment, and that this volume on the Great Thirteenth may increase the West's understanding of Tibetan Buddhism and the Tibet situation.

TAK-TSER TUL-KU, TUB-TEN JIG-ME NOR-BU

Life of the Thirteenth Dalai Lama

To date there have been fourteen Dalai Lamas. But of them all, two stand out above the others: the Fifth and the Thirteenth. It is only to them that the title of *Chen-po*, or "Great," is traditionally applied.

The Great Fifth, lovingly remembered for both his prose and poetry, was a prolific writer, an excellent historian, an inspired artist and architect, a patron of medicine and the dramatic arts, and a skilled statesman. He was the first Dalai Lama to become both the spiritual and the secular leader of Tibet, uniting the three provinces of the country under his rule in 1642. He was truly the guru and father of Classical Tibet.

The Great Thirteenth was very much born from the same mold, making tremendous contributions to the spiritual, cultural and political life of the country. His was the task of introducing his people to the Western world and of guiding them through the turbid waters of the power struggle in which Britain, Russia and China were locked, a struggle in which Central Asia had become an object of prey. He was the guru and father of Modern Tibet.

A. DEATH OF THE TWELFTH AND REBIRTH OF THE GREAT THIRTEENTH

When the Twelfth Dalai Lama Trin-le Gya-tso passed away in the third month of the Wood Boar Year (1875) at the tender age of nineteen, Central Asia was plunged into sorrow. Tibet had not had a strong Dalai

Lama for some time now, and the absence was becoming deeply felt. The first eight in the line of incarnations had all lived full and active lives, serving as central pillars in the spiritual and cultural development of Tibet; indeed, from the time of the Third Dalai Lama the line had become the country's foremost reincarnate lineage. Then suddenly the Ninth, Tenth and Eleventh all had died prematurely; and now the Twelfth had followed suit.

Most Western scholars suspect foul play in the untimely death of the Twelfth. Some suggest intrigue on the part of expansionist China, for whom a weak Lhasa government would mean greater Chinese influence in Tibet. Others have pointed a suspicious finger at ambitious political factions within Tibetan society itself, factions that would benefit from the creation of a vacuum in the Lhasa arena.

However, Tibetan authors make a clear distinction between *gyu*, or inner causes, and *kyen*, which is a mere cooperative condition. We see this differentiation being clearly drawn in the writings of the Tibetan historian Pur-chok-pa Tub-ten Jam-pa, who composed the standard biography of the Thirteenth Dalai Lama, *Ngo-mtsar-rin-po-chei-phreng-ba*, or *A String of Wondrous Gems*.

He provides us with a far more colorful and romantic explanation: "The peerless spiritual master and omniscient protector of living beings His Holiness Je-tsun Khen-rab Trin-le Gya-tso (i.e., the Twelfth Dalai Lama) did not live beyond childhood. The sentient beings on earth simply did not have sufficient meritorious karma to deserve the presence of such an enlightened being. Moreover, he wished to inspire thoughts of Dharma and the reality of death in the minds of the trainees of this world who grasp at the idea of permanence, and he saw that there were other world systems with trainees in need of his attention. For these and many other special reasons he decided that it would be useful to enact the drama of passing away while still in his youth. Thus on the twentieth day of the third month of the Wood Boar Year he sat in meditation and withdrew his physical manifestation from the world, absorbing himself temporarily into the *dharmadhatu* sphere of highest reality." (Tibetan text, page 7.)

Pur-chok-pa goes on to say, "However, the great Bodhisattvas have no time to rest in the personal bliss of individual nirvana. The force of great compassion is strong within them, like the king of mountains at the center of a ring of golden hills, and like the sun and moon in a sky of stars. Hence it was not long before he once again cast his compassionate glance toward this world and reflected upon how, where and when he should take rebirth in order to increase the legacy of happiness and enlightenment on earth."

The biography states that when the Twelfth Dalai Lama was considering taking rebirth his attention turned to the tiny village of Langdun, or "Elephant View," located a few hundred kilometers to the southeast of Lhasa. It was known by this name because it lay at the foot of a magnificent mountain shaped like a charging elephant. Situated in Lower Dvak-po between the holy Heruka pilgrimage site of Tsa-ri and the sacred mountain of Shan-ta, the entire area was adorned by many naturally-formed mystical signs, such as the eight auspicious emblems, the seven royal symbols, and so forth. Pur-chok-pa informs us, "When the Twelfth Dalai Lama was preparing to take rebirth he observed this site with admiration, and felt that it would be ideal."

Next the appropriate parents had to be chosen. "In Lang-dun there lived a peasant farmer by the name of Kun-ga Rin-chen," Pur-chok-pa writes. "By nature he was sincere and non-deceitful, and had faith in the spiritual masters and the Three Jewels of Refuge. He was a naturally good man, known to all for his wise counsel, stable mind, steadfast devotion, and fearlessness in the face of danger. Physically he was both handsome and strong. His wife Lob-zang Dol-ma was equally noble in spirit. She was unassuming and gentle, with an instinctive sense of respect and compassion for all living beings. Throughout her life she had dedicated all her spare time to spiritual practice, and had a deep aspiration to one day give birth to a Buddha. It was this humble peasant family that the Omniscient Master chose for his next rebirth. . . . He flew forth from the pure Buddhafields like a falling star and, amidst countless extraordinary signs, entered into this world once more."

On the night of his conception the Lang-dun region was struck by an earthquake, ". . . for the humans and divinities of the world were unable to sustain the joy of the birth of a *mahatma*." The walls of the room in which the child was conceived cracked open and the roof shifted a handspan in distance. However, the altar in the room remained undisturbed. And although many buildings in the area collapsed, no harm whatsoever befell any living being. The next day rainbows filled the sky, seeming to emanate from the tiny house of the peasant family.

At first the local people were filled with apprehension. They approached the sage Dvak-po Tul-ku Jam-pal Lhun-drub with the request to perform a divination and to interpret the nature of the many strange phenomena that were occurring. "When the earth shakes," he told them, "either bad or good can be indicated. Often the birth of a high Bodhisattva is accompanied by signs such as these. Indeed, it is not impossible that the recently deceased Gong-sa Chok-trul [i.e., the Dalai Lama] has himself chosen to take rebirth here in the Dvak-po region. Many of the events that have occurred are very similar to those that manifested when Gyal-wa Gen-dun Drub-pa [the First Dalai Lama] completed construction of the main temple of Ta-shi Lhun-po Monastery." (Tibetan text, page 9.)

On the night of the child's conception the mother dreamed that a young female dressed in Lhasa-style apparel came to her, offered her a white silk scarf and said, "A great lamp of the world is about to take rebirth as your son. Watch over him carefully." Later the same evening she dreamed that she found a white conch-shell, the sound of which reverberated with the melodious Dharma teaching that awakens fortunate beings from the sleep of ignorance and points out the path leading to peace and liberation.

On another occasion she dreamed that a string of prayer flags reached from the Potala of Lhasa to the pillar of the conception room of her house at Lang-dun. A Lhasa monk and a girl dressed in exquisite ornaments appeared to her and gave her a beautiful vessel studded with jewels. "This cup belongs to Kyab-gon Rin-po-che [i.e., the Dalai Lama]," the girl told her. "Please keep it for him."

These and many other such dreams came almost nightly to the expectant mother during the course of her pregnancy.

Many unusual physical phenomena also occurred. In the seventh month of the year the family began to prepare the winter's supply of butter. One morning they half-filled several containers, and then took a break for lunch. When they returned, the containers had miraculously filled and overflowed by themselves. Then in the middle of the winter a pear tree outside the family's house blossomed. The flowers stayed in bloom for several weeks, and were unaffected by the snow and the freezing weather.

Another event that caused considerable talk occurred on the evening of the sixth day of the tenth month of the year. An apparition of a pagoda-style building appeared over the farmhouse and remained in full visibility to all for much of the evening. Eventually it transformed into a multicolored rainbow, and then became a pure, white luminous sphere and melted into the sky.

From the beginning of Lob-zang Dol-ma's pregnancy a large white bird took up residence in a walnut tree beside the family's house. Ev-

ery morning it would fly off in the direction of Lhasa and return in
the evening, circumambulating the house clockwise three times before coming to rest in its nest.

Also, elders and shepherds in the area noted the appearance of a
new star directly over the nearby Gam-po Mountain.

All of these omens generated considerable excitement. Everyone suspected that a high teacher was soon to incarnate amongst them.
However, few dared to think that this would be none other thanthe
Dalai Lama himself. Lob-zang Dol-ma had not spoken to anyone about
the content of her many dreams, not wanting to cause unnecessary
gossip. She knew well enough that almost every pregnant mother in
the country was praying that the child being carried in her womb was
the reincarnation of the Dalai Lama. But Tibet has more than a thousand incarnate lamas, and at any one time several dozen of these are
in the state between death and rebirth; Lob-zang Dol-ma, as well as
most other people in the region, simply thought that the Lang-dun
area was about to be blessed by the birth of one of these, perhaps one
that had been close to the recently deceased Dalai Lama.

At dawn of the fifth month of the Fire Mouse Year (1876) Lob-zang
Dol-ma painlessly gave birth to a baby boy. The first rays of the morning sun burst forth from behind the eastern peaks and flooded into
the room at the precise moment that the infant took his first breath.
A brilliant rainbow instantly appeared over the house in a sky that
was dotted with small puffs of cloud. A few moments later a light rain
fell, auspiciously purifying the land and coating everything with
diamond-like droplets that seemed to add to the magic of the occasion.

The biography (Tibetan text, page 13.) states, "Even at the moment
of birth the child was of an extraordinary appearance. The limbs of
his body were perfectly developed, and his forehead was broad and
full, like an opened umbrella. His hair was rich and lustrously black,
with a single strand of white curling out clockwise at the crown. The
pads of his fingers and toes were marked by tiny orbs of light, and
mystic wheels could be discerned in the lines on the soles of his feet.
His eyes were wide and elegant, and gazed with an expression of alert
compassion that seemed to be fully aware of everyone and everything
in the room. He bore every sign of being an incarnation of Avalokiteshvara, the Bodhisattva of Compassion, and those who beheld him instinctively experienced a strange and inexplicable sense of joy."

B. THE SEARCH FOR THE NEW INCARNATION

Meanwhile back in Lhasa a committee had been formed to search for the Twelfth Dalai Lama's reincarnation. Because the Dalai Lama is the country's foremost incarnate, the process would be a long and complex one and would involve dozens of people over the period of several years. A great deal of information would have to be gathered and analyzed. Numerous oracles and high lamas would be consulted, and visits made to Lha-moi La-tso, the mystical and visionary Lake of the Goddess. Then after the committee had narrowed the search to the two or three most likely candidates, the individual children would have to be submitted to a number of personal tests. This last stage would involve showing each of the children various items that had belonged to the late Twelfth Dalai Lama, together with similar objects that he had never seen or touched. The true incarnation should be able to select the correct articles from among the imitations.

The responsibility of the search committee was a grave one, for the selected child would be trained to become the spiritual and secular leader of the country. Having completed his studies, he would one day become supreme pontiff and king of Tibet. In addition, he would become an important spiritual leader to the tens of millions of peoples inhabiting the many countries and regions of Central Asia where Tibetan Buddhism predominates.

The Twelfth Dalai Lama had passed away while sitting in meditation in the Joyous Sunlight Chamber, a small chapel located in the south wing of the Potala. At the time of his passing he had been facing directly south; but by the following evening his head had turned toward the southeast. The body was later placed to dry in a casket of salt, as part of the mummification process. Once more it was faced in a southerly direction, but when the lid of the casket was removed to change the salt it was noticed that again the head had turned toward the southeast. Each time the salt was changed the position of the head was corrected, but each time it automatically turned back toward the southeast. All those in charge of the funeral rites witnessed this phenomenon.

The elderly Fifth Pan-chen Lama, who was considered to be the second highest reincarnate lama in Tibet (only the Dalai Lama incarnations are held in higher regard), was approached by the committee and asked to perform a divination to determine the direction of the Twelfth's rebirth. He confirmed that it would take place to the southeast of Lhasa.

The two oracles of Sam-ye Monastery were then invoked and questioned. Both of them stated that the reincarnation would manifest to the southeast.

During the summer the State Oracle of Ne-chung Monastery performed a trance in the presence of the Twelfth Dalai Lama's mausoleum. When asked for information on where the new incarnation would take place he replied, "The auspicious fruit of your aspirations will take rebirth to the southeast of Lhasa. A mountain shaped like an umbrella rises from behind the house of his birth, and a waterfall flows in front. . . ." He went on to describe in detail the layout of the place in which the rebirth would occur.

Again in the seventh month of the Fire Mouse Year (1876) the Ne-chung Oracle was invoked. This time he informed the committee, "The Emanation of Great Compassion, our supreme arya master, has already taken rebirth in the place that previously I described to you. The flower of his body, speech and mind even now has begun to blossom." (Tibetan text, page 15.)

At dawn of the twenty-sixth of the tenth month, which is the day after the national butter-lamp festival, a brilliant rainbow appeared in the sky above Lhasa. One of its tips seemed to emanate from the Potala and the other reached out to the southeast, coming to rest over the Dvak-po region. This was visible to all. The sky was adorned with small white clouds, almost solid in appearance, shaped like victory banners and other auspicious symbols.

The committee was now preparing to send out search parties to the southeast, with instructions to gather the names of children recently born under auspicious conditions. The Ne-chung Oracle was again invoked, this time in front of the Regent Ta-tsak Rin-po-che, various government officials, and the teachers, incarnate lamas and administrators of Dre-pung Monastery. The Oracle spoke to them as follows, "Hrih!!! O Regent who serves the land so well, monk and lay officials of the government, elders of Ne-chung Monastery, lamas and administrators of Dre-pung Monastery, I will fulfill your wishes to know where the [Dalai Lama] reincarnation is located. The Three Jewels of Refuge bear witness to the truth of what I say. Our sky-like teacher, the mere sight of whom brings benefits in both this and future lives, has been reborn to the southeast. I have already described the landscape to you. His father's name is Kun-ga and his mother's is Dolma. You should immediately appoint a holy guru to go to the Lake of the Goddess and to make an observation there. I will offer my assistance in the search." (Tibetan text, pages 16-17.)

"Whom should we send?" the committee asked.

"Appoint the former abbot of the Upper Tantric College, Gyu-to Khen-sur Lob-zang Dar-gye. Have him go to Cho-khor-gyal Monastery beside the waters of the visionary Lake of the Goddess. Meanwhile, you should draw up a list of all villages to the southeast of Lhasa, and send this list with him. While at Cho-khor-gyal Monastery, Gyu-to Khen-sur should perform a hundred thousand invocations of Pal-den Lha-mo. When this has been done he will definitely receive clear signs of the reincarnation's exact location."

Consequently the Former Abbot of Gyu-to, together with a small number of hand-picked ritual assistants, left for Cho-khor-gyal Monastery and the Lake of the Goddess. They took up residence there and began the lengthy invocations and meditations that had been recommended by the Ne-chung Oracle.

At the time of the group's arrival it was the middle of winter and the lake's surface was covered with snow. However, after they had completed their spiritual practices a forceful wind arose and cleaned away the snow, until "...the surface of the lake became as clear as a crystal mirror polished a hundred times."

Then slowly from within the lake various images began to form. First they saw a farm with neatly kept terraces above to the east. An ancient stupa (reliquary) stood to the northeast. To the southeast was an old farmhouse, two or three storeys in height, with a courtyard surrounded by a metal fence.

After these scenes had passed, a picture of a small village appeared. The village seemed to lie between the house and the stupa. These and many other images came and then faded. The group also saw the shape of the mountains in the area, as well as the nearby villages, grazing lands and meadows, and a long strip of farmland.

As Pur-chok-pa puts it in *A String of Wondrous Gems*, all of this appeared to them "...as clearly as though reflected in a mirror, or as though perceived in a crystal ball."

The details of the scenes in their visions were carefully written out and sent to the central committee.

Gyu-to Khen-sur then entered into intense prayer and meditation. Just before dawn of the third day of the tenth month he dreamed that he stood in the center of a village. Walking eastward to the outskirts of the village he came to the household of a peasant farmer. The verandah of the house faced south, and on it sat a couple with a small child in their arms. "This is Kyab-gon Rin-po-che (the Dalai Lama)," they said to him. He took the child in his lap, whereupon the boy lovingly touched him on the forehead and cheeks and said, "It is now more than five months since I took birth. But for the moment do not reveal my true identity to my parents or to the local people."

Toward the end of his retreat Gyu-to Khen-sur again dreamed of the child. This time he was told, "The reincarnation has taken place to the southeast of Lhasa in the region of Dvak-po Lang-dun. Go there and you will easily locate him." (Tibetan text, page 19.)

Gyu-to Khen-sur communicated all of this information to the Lhasa authorities and then left for Dvak-po Lang-dun. Because in the dream the child had advised him to be secretive, he traveled in the guise of a simple pilgrim and did not announce his purpose. In Dvak-po Lang-dun he recognized the many landmarks that he had perceived in the Lake of the Goddess and in his dreams, and was easily able to locate the peasant household that had appeared to him. When he arrived at the house, the parents and child were seated on the verandah just as they had been in his dream.

Later Gyu-to Khen-sur wrote, "As for the child, he was slightly thinner than I remembered him from my dreams, but was otherwise identical. And how delightful he was to behold! His body was simply exquisite, with every sign of being that of a high incarnation. When I saw him I could easily imagine what it must have been like for those who had met Buddha as a child in Lumbini Gardens. And when I picked him up and placed him in my lap he touched my face as though blessing me, just as had occurred in my dream. From that moment on I didn't have the slightest doubt that this was the child for whom we had been searching."

Gyu-to Khen-sur had come to the house informally and, although he sent a hurried message back to Lhasa to inform the authorities of his discovery, did not yet reveal his purpose to the parents or villagers. Nonetheless, he could not bring himself to leave the child's side. Therefore he asked the parents to permit him to stay in their guestroom for awhile. The request was not unusual; Tibet had no hotels, and so most households kept a room to rent to pilgrims and travelers. In this way he managed to keep an eye on the child's well-being without attracting undue attention to himself.

Gyu-to Khen-sur's letter generated considerable excitement in Lhasa. The committee had compiled a list of promising children who had been born with auspicious signs. Further tests narrowed the list to three names, with that of the child from Lang-dun at the top.

Soon two special officials were sent to perform tests on the child's memory. With them they carried various items that had belonged to the late Twelfth Dalai Lama. These included a vajra and bell set, a rosary, a hand-drum, and some articles of clothing. One by one the articles, mixed in with a number of similar objects, were placed on a tray and held up to the boy, and he was asked to take what he wanted. In each case he chose only those that had belonged to the previous Dalai Lama.

This same test had been conducted on the other two candidates, but only the boy from Lang-dun was able to correctly separate the authentic articles from the imitations. The search for the new Dalai Lama had come to an end. The results were clear and final.

During the search for the Dalai Lama a slightly comical episode took place in Lhasa. The wife of Ku-chok Do-ring, who hailed from a powerful aristocratic family, was pregnant at the time and was convinced that the child in her womb was the precious incarnation, and told everyone of her convictions. Every morning and evening she would hold an incense pot under her dress for a few moments, "...to consecrate the passage whereby the incarnation would enter the world." When the real Dalai Lama was discovered in a peasant family far to the southeast, a popular folk song appeared on the streets of Lhasa,

> The radiant sun of Tibet
> Has taken birth in Dvak-po.
> As for Lady Do-ring,
> All she has is ash on her ass.

C. RECOGNITION AND PRELIMINARY ORDINATION

On the full moon of the ninth month of the Fire Ox year (1877) a delegation was sent from Lhasa to Lang-dun, bringing with it lavish gifts from the Regent, the government and the principal monasteries. A throne was constructed in the living room of the tiny house, and the child was placed on it. The dozen or so officials sat around him on carpets laid out on the floor. The many presents that they had brought with them were offered to the child and his family, including numerous religious statues and articles, sacred medicines, three pouches of silver coins, a number of gold bars, large sacks of various foods, and so forth. Although merely an infant, the child behaved with perfect decorum throughout the proceedings. This was an unofficial enthronement, and his identity as the true incarnation was now made known to all.

The following month the child and his family were asked to come to Central Tibet. Crowds of pious devotees lined the road as the procession moved along, hoping to catch a glimpse of the young lama and to receive his blessings. He was carried on a golden palanquin at the center of a line of high monks, officials and devotees. The spectacle was magnificent, with a large escort of horsemen dressed in traditional Mongolian outfits, monks in rich yellow brocades, dignitaries in various ethnic costume, and so forth. Occasionally the procession would stop for the child to give blessings to the crowds that had gathered.

Eventually they arrived at Gun-tang Monastery, located across the Kyi-chu River to the south of Lhasa. It was the day before the full moon of the eleventh month, and an elaborate reception had been arranged for him in the De-wa-chen Temple. Here he met with the Regent Ta-tsak Rin-po-che for the first time, as well as with all the high lamas and government officials of the Lhasa area. Numerous foreign dignitaries were also permitted to be present, including the Chinese ambans and the ambassadors of Nepal, Kashmir, Sikkim and so forth. All who came received the traditional hand-blessing, which the child performed without shyness or intimidation. The Regent formally welcomed him to Central Tibet, and the monks of the principal monasteries offered prayers for his long life.

Two weeks later, on the fourth day of the new year (i.e., the Earth Tiger Year, or 1878), the child met with the (Fifth) Pan-chen Lama and prepared to receive the hair-cutting rite and preliminary ordination of a monk. The Pan-chen, whose advice had been instrumental in the search for the new incarnation, had come all the way from Shigatse, Southern Tibet, in order to perform the ceremony and to give the young lama his ordination name.

The Dalai and Pan-chen Lamas had for centuries shared a unique relationship. Often called the "Father and Son" (*yab-sres*) of Tibet, they were the two highest reincarnates in the country. The First Pan-chen had been the guru of the Fifth Dalai Lama, and later, after the aged Pan-chen had passed away, the Fifth Dalai Lama became the guru to his reincarnation, the Second Pan-chen. In turn, when the great Fifth died and was reborn as the Sixth, the Second Pan-chen Lama again became the guru. As the Sixth was short-lived, this same Pan-chen had also served as guru to the Seventh Dalai. When the Second Pan-chen died and his reincarnation was located, the Seventh Dalai acted as the guru to the Third Pan-chen. And so it went over the centuries, with whichever of the two was elder serving as guru to the younger. Sometimes the Dalai Lama would be the guru, or "father," and the young Pan-chen would be the student, or "son"; in other centuries the situation would be reversed. Now it was the Pan-chen who was the 'father' and the young Dalai who was the 'son.' Consequently the former had come many hundreds of miles in order to ordain and name the latter.

The Thirteenth Dalai Lama's ordination ceremony took place a week later, on the eleventh day of the new year. Here the Pan-chen Lama gave him the name by which he would henceforth be known: Je-tsun Nga-wang Lob-zang Tub-ten Gya-tso Jig-trel Wang-chuk Chok-le-nam-gyal Pal-zang-po, or "The Most Venerable Lord of the Teachings, He of Sublime Mind, Ocean of Buddhist Doctrines, Fearless and Power-ful One, Glorious Guru Victorious in All Ways." The name was in-timidatingly lengthy, and in fact the Tibetans were generally to use only the fourth and fifth parts of it, or Tub-ten Gya-tso. Because all the Dalai Lamas are known as Gyal-wa Rin-po-che, or "Precious Master," the Great Thirteenth was to become known to history as Gyal-wa Tub-ten Gya-tso.

The young lama and his family remained in Gun-tang for approxi-mately two months. They were then taken across the Kyi-chu River to Sam-ten-ling, a monastery located on a hill three miles to the north of Lhasa commanding an excellent view of the Lhasa plains. The child lama would remain here for the next year, undergoing preparation for his formal enthronement and entrance into the Potala.

This was the beginning of the many years of study that would fol-low. The Regent Ta-tsak Rin-po-che was appointed as his Senior Tu-tor, and Pur-chok-pa Jam-pa Gya-tso as Junior Tutor. This latter master had in fact served as the principal guru of the previous Dalai Lama (the Twelfth) and had led the funeral services following the Twelfth's death, as well as overseeing the mummification of the body. The elderly Regent in his capacity as Senior Tutor would give the Thirteenth a number of initiations, precepts and transmissions; but the actual job of day-to-day teaching would fall on Pur-chok-pa, the Junior Tutor. And when the Regent passed away some seven years later, Pur-chok-pa would be given the position of Senior Tutor.

Later on we will see the tremendous love and respect with which the Thirteenth Dalai Lama was to regard Pur-chok-pa Jam-pa Gya-tso. It is interesting to note that after Pur-chok-pa's death the Great Thirteenth took time from his busy schedule to compose a major biography of him. In turn, the reincarnation of Pur-chok-pa Jam-pa Gya-tso in the person of Pur-chok-pa Tub-ten Jam-pa was to become the chief disciple and biographer of the Great Thirteenth.

D. ENTHRONEMENT

Life in Sam-ten-ling Monastery was a period of transition for the young incarnation. Certainly it was more disciplined than the way he had lived as a farmer's son in Lang-dun; but it was far less austere than that lying before him after his entrance into formal training in the Potala. In Sam-ten-ling he was allowed to spend several hours with his family every day, and his schedule was informal. Once in the Potala, visits from his parents would become far less frequent. His days would be crowded with spiritual study and practice, and with a constant flow of visitors from all over Central Asia coming in search of his blessings.

But all of that was still far in the future. For the moment a more down-to-earth reality was at hand. He had to be introduced to the extraordinary role of a Dalai Lama. He may well be regarded as the reincarnation of the twelve previous Dalai Lamas, yet there was much to be "re-learned."

The great guru Pur-chok-pa Jam-pa Gya-tso also took up residence in Sam-ten-ling Monastery, and began to give him instructions on a daily basis. In particular, Pur-chok-pa was charged with the task of preparing his ward for the elaborate ceremony of enthronement scheduled for the following year. At that time the child would have to appear in front of tens of thousands of people, with his every move being carefully studied by all.

Preparations for the enthronement had already begun. News of the discovery of the new Dalai Lama had been communicated to the Chinese Emperor Kuang Hsu via the Chinese ambans stationed in Lhasa, with requests for the Emperor's approval of both the enthronement of the child and the appointment of Ta-tsak Rin-po-che and Pur-chok-pa as the two tutors.

This was a necessary step in the process; for although Tibet was not officially a province of China, the Tibetans certainly respected Manchu power. To recognize and enthrone a Dalai Lama without first showing the courtesy of asking the Emperor's blessings could have drastic consequences.

It is impossible to speak about the life of the Thirteenth Dalai Lama in any depth without first looking at the complex relationship that existed between Tibet and China in the late nineteenth century.

The word most often used by Tibetan historians to describe this relationship is *cho-yon*, or "Priest/Patron." During the Thirteenth's early life this term was used almost exclusively in context to Tibet's friendship with (and later entrapment by) Manchu China; but in fact it far predates the Manchu Empire, having its roots in the unusual interchange that occurred between Tibet and Mongolia many centuries earlier.

The concept of *cho-yon* came into vogue in Central Asia during the thirteenth century with the friendship established between the Tibetan lama Sa-kya Pan-di-ta and the Mongolian Prince Goden, who was the grandson of Genghis Khan. It further developed half a century later with the Mongolian emperor Kublai Khan and his spiritual preceptor the Tibetan lama Sa-kya Pak-pa. We see it used again in the sixteenth century with the Third Dalai Lama and his Mongolian disciple Altan Khan of the Tumed nation; and also in the seventeenth century with the Great Fifth Dalai Lama in his relationships with both the Mongolian king Gushri Khan of the Qoshot nation, and the Chinese Ching Emperor Shunzhi.

In these early days the basic idea was that the "Priests," or Tibetan lamas, would provide spiritual instruction, act as mediators and peacemakers, and perform rituals for the well-being of the "Patrons." In return for these services the "Patron country" was expected to protect the "Priest country" from foreign invasion, internal upheavals, and so forth.

As Michael van Walt van Praag puts it in *The Status of Tibet* 1987, page 12, "Two principal elements made up the *cho-yon* (Priest/Patron).... The first element is that of the Lama as *cho-ne*, the object of worship and offerings, and the respective Khans and Emperors as *yon-daq*, the patron, the worshipper, and the giver of alms.... The second element is that of protection. The Patron in the *cho-yon* relation is bound to protect his Priest and Spiritual Teacher.... The Lama, in turn, sees to the spiritual well-being of the Patron and his subjects, and he prays and conducts religious services for their benefit...."

Thus the tradition began simply enough, with an arrangement perhaps somewhat similar to that of the Vatican and the various countries in which Roman Catholicism held sway at certain periods of Western history.

Things became more complicated in the early eighteenth century.

Relations between Tibet and the Mongols became strained when Mongolia's Qushot and Dzungar tribes began warring with one another, and the conflict spilled over into Tibet. Both sides became rather heavy-handed in their religious zeal, resulting in intense Tibetan resentment of their presence in Lhasa. Meanwhile to the east the Manchu Empire was rising, and when the Tibetan patriot Polhanas asked for support in his attempt to clear Tibet of Mongol armies, the Kangxi Emperor cooperated. Later when the Sixth Dalai Lama's reincarnation was discovered at Li-tang near the Chinese border, the Kangxi's request to provide the child with an escort for the long and dangerous trip to Lhasa was not considered to be inappropriate. This marked the end of Tibet's traditional political alliance with Mongolia. Tibetan Buddhism continued to be the predominant form of religion in Mongolia, and Mongolian monks continued to come to Tibet for higher studies; but the Tibetans would no longer trust the Mongolians to the extent of the *cho-yon* marriage. The divorce was final, and the new "Patron" was Manchu China.

The *cho-yon* arrangement was never to work out as well with the Manchu rulers as it had with the various Mongolian khans. Whereas the Mongolians had been sincerely interested in Tibet for religious reasons, the Manchus seem to have been much more politically motivated. They realized that Tibet was the spiritual and cultural fountainhead of Central Asia, the "Jerusalem" of millions of Central Asian Buddhists, and that whoever had influence over Tibet would have a voice in affairs extending far beyond the borders of Tibet itself.

The Manchu Emperor also expected to have more of a say in things Tibetan than had the Mongolian khans. An official Chinese resident, or "amban," was stationed in Lhasa with the twofold task of communicating to the Emperor any events that would be of significance to him, and of lobbying for the Emperor's wishes and policies as concerned Tibet. In the beginning the ambans were not much more than silent witnesses to the drama of Lhasa's many activities, but by the mid-eighteenth century they had become more like foreign advisors in Tibet's political life.

The relationship took a more serious turn in 1788, with the Nepali Gurkha invasion of Tibet. Tibet put up a fierce resistance, and when a Manchu force arrived to assist her the Gurkhas were easily routed. But even though Tibet had won the war, her political status was damaged. From this time on, the Lhasa government was expected to submit all matters of importance to the ambans for the approval of the Emperor. Tibet had not fully become a part of the Manchu Empire, but it had become a fairly close satellite.

The Manchu Emperor also wanted to play a direct part in the choosing of the Dalai Lama reincarnations. In 1793 he sent a large golden urn to Lhasa, with the request that it be employed in the selection process. The idea ran something like this. After the search for the reincarnation of the Dalai Lama had been narrowed down to the two or three most promising candidates, the names of these should be written on scrolls of paper and placed in the golden urn. The lamas should then do prayers for divine intervention, and a representative of the Emperor blindly draw forth one of the scrolls. The child named on the scroll should be the one recognized as the true reincarnation.

Needless to say, the proposal did not go over particularly well in Lhasa, and there is no historical evidence to substantiate that the urn was ever used. The Tibetans were not about to leave the final decision of the selection of their Dalai Lama in the hands of a game of chance. They had far more confidence in their high lamas, oracles and mystical "Lake of the Goddess" than they did in prayers for divine intervention. However, the urn did remain in Lhasa, and with each new Dalai Lama an excuse had to be sent to the Emperor to explain why it had not been considered necessary to use the thing.

This was certainly the case in the selection of the Thirteenth Dalai Lama. Only after his discovery had been officially accepted by the Lhasa authorities was the Emperor informed of the development of events and his "approval" of the enthronement requested.

Pur-chok-pa writes, "The information given by the oracles and high lamas, the images seen in the Lake of the Goddess, and all of the tests performed on the candidates pointed decisively to the child from Langdun as being the true reincarnation. The Pan-chen Lama, Regent Ta-tsak Rin-po-che, the high lamas and officials of Gan-den, Dre-pung, Se-ra and Ta-shi Lhun-po monasteries, and all the monk and lay officials of the Lhasa government unanimously agreed with the results and were satisfied that the correct choice had been made. Therefore it was decided that there was no need to resort to the golden urn. The Manchu ambans were informed, and were asked to communicate this information to the Emperor, together with the request for his approval of the scheduled enthronement and the appointment of the Regent Ta-tsak Rin-po-che and Pur-chok-pa Jam-pa Gya-tso as the senior and junior tutors." (Tibetan text, page 25.)

In fact at this point in history the process of asking the Emperor's approval was merely a diplomatic formality. It was little more than a courtesy owed to him for his Patron role. In no way could he ever risk refusing to give this "approval," for to do so would be to jeopardize his position as Patron. Consequently approval was soon forthcoming, and the Tibetans set about the task of readying themselves for the gala event.

Astrologers were asked to choose an auspicious date for the enthronement ceremony. The thirteenth day of the sixth month of the Earth Hare Year (i.e., July 1879) was deemed to be most appropriate, and the preparations began.

The entire city of Lhasa was cleaned and polished for the occasion, and banners were hung from every rooftop. On the day of the enthronement thousands of monks, nuns and lay devotees lined the sides of the road that the young lama would travel from Sam-ten-ling Monastery to the Potala. The Regent led the procession, followed by the Lhasa government officials, the chief monks from the various monasteries, various other leaders from around the country, and also the Chinese ambans and other foreign dignitaries resident in Lhasa. The sound of monastic trumpets and the aroma of rich incense filled the air as the spectacle of exotic pageantry unfolded. The crowd following behind increased in size as the procession passed and the devotees lining the streets joined in.

The first stop was the Jo-khang, Tibet's oldest and holiest temple. Here the Dalai Lama descended from his palanquin and offered prostrations in front of the sacred statue of Buddha Shakyamuni that was housed inside. The procession then went on to the Potala, ascending the many steps leading to the Avalokiteshvara chapel on the roof. This chapel housed a statue of the Bodhisattva of Compassion that was said to have self-manifested thirteen hundred years earlier during King Song-tsen Gam-po's construction of the Red Fort, from which the Potala itself was later built. The image was believed to possess miraculous qualities, and many of the previous Dalai Lamas had performed meditation retreats in front of it.

Everyone then proceeded to the Potala's main assembly hall and the actual enthronement began. The Regent and other high-ranking lamas presented the Dalai Lama with offering scarves as a sign of their devotion, as did the Lhasa government officials and principal leaders from around the country, as well as the Chinese ambans and other foreign representatives. The Regent delivered a proclamation officially declaring the enthronement, and the Chinese amban read a letter of congratulations from the Emperor. Although only four years old, the young Dalai Lama sat through the lengthy proceedings with a natural dignity that deeply inspired all those who were present.

From that day on the Dalai Lama took up residence in the traditional four-room apartment located on the roof of the Potala. His new life had officially begun.

E. THE LONG PERIOD OF TRAINING

Over the weeks that followed, each day brought a new celebration. First the Pan-chen Lama held a welcoming banquet in his honor, and then in turn similar receptions were sponsored by lamas and representatives of the major monasteries, various secular dignitaries from around the country, and numerous foreign officials. Each of these celebrations served to show off the young Dalai Lama to his people, and to introduce him to the principal spiritual and social leaders with whom he would have to work in his later years.

These must have been overwhelming times for the child lama. He was expected to sit and receive a constant stream of visitors, and to participate in long, arduous ceremonies. But gradually the pace of his life began to slow down somewhat and to become less public, as the emphasis shifted from celebration and ritual to study and learning.

Pur-chok-pa Jam-pa Gya-tso took up residence in the Potala with the boy and was placed in charge of his basic education. The Pan-chen Lama and the Regent Ta-tsak Rin-po-che would also give him a number of precepts and instructions, as would many other teachers; but Pur-chok-pa would remain his closest preceptor.

On the sixth day of the first month of the Water Horse Year (1882) the young scholar took the ordination of a novice monk, with the Regent Ta-tsak acting as the ordaining master and Pur-chok-pa as the *acharya*.

Again the Chinese Emperor sent a letter of congratulations written in gold ink, together with numerous gifts. "We rejoice at the news that the Oceanic Teacher has begun to engage in his learning more diligently than ever," he wrote. "We offer our prayers that, through this, the Yellow Hat tradition may thrive and flourish in the world, and that Buddhism may endure on earth as long as possible. In honor of the occasion of the novice monk ordination of the Oceanic Teacher we present an emerald rosary, a ricebowl made of jade, various silk brocades...."

This was the first year that the Thirteenth Dalai Lama presided over the Great Prayer Festival of Lhasa. As can be seen from the translated selection of his works included in chapter one of this volume, his participation in the Great Prayer Festival was to become a major part of his annual schedule. *A String of Wondrous Gems* points out that through the energy he dedicated to this festival he restored it to the level of grandeur and prestige it had enjoyed during the era of the early Dalai Lamas.

The young scholar's studies now began to intensify, and several additional tutors were appointed to assist in his progress. These included Ge-she Lob-zang So-nam from Se-ra Monastery and Ge-she Zang-po Pun-tsok from Gan-den. A number of scholars from the principal Lhasa monastic colleges were also appointed as his *tsen-zhab*, or special assistants in debate and philosophical training.

Over the years that followed he engaged in disciplined study and practice under these and other high lamas. Every day he would rise at four in the morning and begin his day with several hours of prayer and meditation. Then would come lengthy periods of instruction, interspersed with heated discussions with the special assistants. Many times the debates would continue long into the night.

At the age of twelve the Great Thirteenth made a tour of the seven colleges that constitute the three principal monastic universities: Gan-den, Dre-pung and Se-ra. His visit caused considerable excitement among the monk scholars of these institutions, for it was announced that he would join in the debates on the open courtyards. For the young lama this would be his first opportunity to publicly test the progress of his studies; and for the monks of the monastic colleges it would be an opportunity to see their chief incarnate engage in an open competition of wits. And for a fortunate few it would provide an opportunity to debate with him personally.

The eager monks were to be more than satisfied, for in each of the colleges the young lama agreed to sit before the congregation and take up debates from the floor. No doubt his tutors were somewhat apprehensive at his bold offer; but he was not to fail them. The Junior Tutor Pur-chok-pa Jam-pa Gya-tso, who was present during all the encounters, later commented, "Watching how easily and skillfully the youthful incarnation handled the debates thrown at him simply caused the hair on my body to stand on end. His maturity and understanding simply astounded everybody. No one who was there had the slightest doubt that he was truly the incarnation of Avalokiteshvara, the Bodhisattva of Compassion. All we could do was look on in awe."

The elderly Pan-chen Lama, from whom the Dalai Lama as a child had received his preliminary ordination and his name, had passed away a few years earlier, and his reincarnation had been discovered and was brought to Lhasa. Now it was the Dalai Lama's turn to be the one bestowing blessings and a name. To the baby Pan-chen he gave the name Pan-chen Lob-zang Cho-kyi Nyi-ma, "Mighty Sage of Sublime Mind, Veritable Sun of Dharma Knowledge."

In total the Great Thirteenth received teachings, initiations, oral transmissions and assorted precepts from almost a hundred different gurus during his lifetime. The majority of these were of the Ge-luk-pa, or Yellow Hat School; but like all the earlier Dalai Lamas he combined his Ge-luk-pa training with a strong dose of teachings and practice of the Nying-ma, or Old School. It should be remembered that the Ge-luk-pa itself was a fusion of the Ka-dam, Sa-kya and Kar-gyu Orders, so by approaching his training in this way he was able to gain a thorough understanding of all four sects of Tibetan Buddhism.

The tradition of combining Ge-luk-pa and Nying-ma studies had been popularized by the Second Dalai Lama. Since then it had become the trademark of every Dalai reincarnate. The Great Fifth had perhaps most completely embodied the approach, and the Great Thirteenth followed closely in the footsteps of the Fifth.

He dedicated tremendous energy to studying and practicing the various Nying-ma doctrines. In fact, the annals of Dzog-chen Monastery describe him as an important *Ter-ton*, or "Nying-ma-pa Treasure Revealor", the treasures he revealed including several important scriptures on the mandala meditation known as Vajra Kilaya, 'Lord of the Mystic Dagger.' Many people also believe that the Great Thirteenth bore the secret tantric name Drak-den Ling-pa, whose magnificent deeds had been prophesied by Guru Padma Sambhava in the mid-eighth century. He is alleged to have written numerous secret texts under this alternative name; these treatises, of course, are not included in his standard *Collected Works*.

There is no need to list the names of the many gurus under whom the Great Thirteenth trained, nor to outline all the lineages that he received. These are given in full detail in Pur-chok-pa's biography of him. Also, the Great Thirteenth lists them all himself in his *Sunlight on the Blossoming Garden of the Buddhadharma*, in which he provides a detailed account of the teachings, initiations and so forth that he received, as well as the names of the teachers from whom he received them. In the Yellow Hat lineages his four favorite gurus seem to have been the Regent Ta-tsak, his Junior (and later Senior) Tutor Pur-chok-pa, Lama De-yang Tul-ku from Am-do, and the renowned Ling Tul-ku. His three closest Nying-ma lamas seem to have been Las-rab Ling-pa, Rang-rig Ling-pa, and So-gyal Tul-ku.

We can perhaps learn more from the Great Thirteenth's attitude toward his studies than we can from a list of subjects. In his *Sunlight on the Blossoming Garden of the Buddhadharma* he writes, ''Very early in my life I understood that the Buddhist path leading to liberation and enlightenment is comprised of a threefold process: listening to the teachings, reflecting on their meaning, and meditating on the essence. And as Sa-kya Pan-di-ta put it, without establishing a level of competence in the first of these three steps there is not much value in taking up the second and third. Without a firm basis in learning, the activities of contemplation and meditation are rendered impotent. Therefore at a very young age I decided to dedicate myself with all my strength to a thorough study of the teachings under the guidance of qualified gurus.'' (Tibetan text, folios 2-3.)

He goes on to say, ''However, my teachers were quick to point out to me that the Buddhist path is not accomplished merely through intellectual means. They advised me to bear in mind the song of Lama Drom Ton-pa in which it is said, 'When I study I also apply contemplation and meditation. When I engage in contemplation I maintain the practices of study and meditation. And when I meditate I continue to study and contemplate. This is the Ka-dam-pa way.' I took this precept as an essential advice spoken especially for me, and tried to apply it throughout my period of training. None of the three steps by itself brings enlightenment; only when the three are adopted in a balanced way are maximum results achieved. To study and contemplate without applying the teachings to one's mindstream through meditation is of little spiritual significance.''

The Great Thirteenth's *Sunlight on the Blossoming Garden of the Buddhadharma* is a fascinating work of considerable historical interest. Not only does it give us all the various lineages that the Thirteenth received during his many years of study and practice, in many cases it lists the complete line of historical gurus through whom the individual traditions were transmitted from generation to generation over the centuries. The text is some 427 pages (214 folios) in length, and the list of teachings that he studied is most impressive. Thousands of scriptures had to be read and understood. The study included numerous *Sung-bum* collections, or *Complete Collected Works* of renowned masters of the past, as well as all the most important literary works of both India and Tibet. The index of merely the tantric empowerments and initiations that he received would by itself constitute an encyclopedia of Tibetan Buddhism. Yet of the dozens of gurus under whom he studied during his lifetime, he remained most close to Pur-chok-pa Jam-pa Gya-tso. The Japanese monk Tada Tokan, who lived in Tibet from 1913 to 1923 and personally studied under the Dalai Lama during that time, records that the Great Thirteenth several times commented to him of the deep affection in which he held Pur-chok-pa.

A rather touching reference to Pur-chok-pa appears in a transcript of a talk that the Great Thirteenth gave in the late 1920s, as recorded in his *Complete Collected Works*. His guru Pur-chok-pa Jam-pa Gya-tso had passed away many years ago; in the interim the new reincarnation had been discovered and re-trained, and was just about to appear in the public debates held in Lhasa during the Great Prayer Festival. The Thirteenth was delivering a general discourse to the congregation of the Festival, when suddenly he broke off from his theme and began to speak about how kind the previous Pur-chok-pa had been to him. He went on to describe the many lineages of the teachings that he had received under Pur-chok-pa's guidance, and concluded by asking the crowd to pray that the new incarnation of Pur-chok-pa would turn out to be as great as his predecessor.

I thought that it would be useful to quote the passage in full. Not only does it describe the depth and scope of the Great Thirteenth's studies under his principal guru, it also shows us something of the Dalai Lama as a man. An elderly lama friend of mine who was present as a child during this very discourse informed me that as the Dalai Lama spoke his voice became soft and rich, vibrating with an emotion that touched everyone in the audience. When he had concluded, there was hardly a dry eye left in the assembly.

He spoke as follows. (*Collected Works*, Tibetan text, vol. 2, pages 198-199.)

"Today in the audience we have the young reincarnation of my late guru Yong-dzin Pur-chok-pa Rin-po-che. This youthful reincarnate has now come of age and is about to stand and be tested for his *ge-she* (Doctor of Philosophy) degree in front of a sea of sages and scholars from the three monastic universities and two tantric colleges. I would like to offer my prayers for his success.

"His predecessor was my principal spiritual teacher and showed me tremendous kindness. When I was but a child he taught me how to read and write, and as I grew up he led me through study and practice of the vast branches of Buddhist knowledge. Under him I read all the major Buddhist treatises coming from India, together with numerous Tibetan commentaries and monastic textbooks. He guided me through the five major Buddhist topics—*prajnaparamita, madhyamaka, vinaya, abhidharma,* and *pramana*—together with all the principal commentaries. He led me through this entire corpus of Buddhist literature, not just casually but guiding me line-by-line with a pointed finger, teaching me logic and dialectics, and testing my understanding like a caring parent watches the growth of a child.

"He also gave me my final monastic ordination and transmitted to me all the various oral tradition teachings, such as the *Lam Rim* and *Lo-jong* lineages coming from Atisha and Lama Tsong-kha-pa, the Fifth Dalai Lama's *The Sacred Instructions of Manjushri,* the First Pan-chen Lama's *The Path to Joy* and *Offering to the Guru,* the Second Pan-chen Lama's *The Quick Path,* the root text and commentaries to the *mahamudra* tradition, the ear-whispered oral transmission teachings from Gyal-wa Wen-sa-pa that point the mind to the correct view of emptiness, and also the various tantric commentaries. Each of these transmissions he enriched with the living freshness of his own inner realization.

"On top of this he gave me my most important tantric initiations, including those for the tantras of Guhyasamaja, Heruka Chakrasamvara, Vajrabhairava, and Kalachakra. He also transmitted to me several of the large collections of tantric lineages, such as 'The Hundred *Zurka* (Zur-bka) Traditions', the *Vajramala* Set, 'The Hundred Lineages of Mai-tri-pa,' and so forth.

"With all of these tantric lineages he generously gave me the initiations that ripen and mature the mind, the explanations that produce liberation, and the scriptural transmissions that act as firm supports. These he delivered in all their completeness, without holding anything back, like pouring nectar from one vase into another.

"Moreover, he never allowed my training to become one-sided, always watching to see that my practice of contemplation and meditation kept a proper balance with my efforts in study. He revealed the entire path of enlightenment to me, like teaching a child how to walk and talk. His kindness to me was inconceivable, and there is no way I could ever hope to repay it.

"Let us all offer our prayers that the new incarnation of that great guru will in some small measure be able to live up to the legacy established by his predecessor."

Having said this, the Great Thirteenth then returned to his discourse and continued with the theme he had been discussing.

The above description by the Dalai Lama of his personal studies under Pur-chok-pa is very concise and in no way fully covers the many facets of his education. But it does point out the four principal types of spiritually orientated subjects that every Dalai Lama was expected to master.

Firstly there is the philosophical training comprised of the five genres of literature: *prajnaparamita, madhyamaka, pramana, abhidharma,* and *vinaya* (perfection of wisdom, emptiness theory, higher logic, metaphysics and ethics). The many years of debate training characteristic of the principal monasteries in Tibet centered around the study of these five. In the Ge-luk-pa School to which the Dalai Lama traditionally belongs, the manner of studying these had been adopted from the Sa-kya Order.

The second genre focusses on the oral transmission teachings dealing with the various Sutrayana meditations. The main kinds of texts here are those known in Tibetan as *Lam Rim* and *Lo-jong.* The Ge-luk-pa School had adopted this system of training from the Ka-dam-pa Order.

The third genre involves the Vajrayana, or the tantric tradition, which bridges both philosophical and meditational trainings. Tibetan spirituality is basically a combination of the Buddhist sutra and tantra legacies coming from India, with the emphasis on the sutra doctrines during the early phases of training and on the tantras during the later phases. The Great Thirteenth combined these in his education much in the same way as had the early Dalai Lamas. Here under Pur-chok-pa Jam-pa Gya-tso he studied the *Sar-mai-gyu,* or "tantras of the New Schools' that the Ge-luk had absorbed from the various *Sar-mai-cho-luk,* or New Schools: Kar-gyu, Sa-kya, Ka-dam, Ra-lug, and so forth. He studied the *Nying-mai-gyu* or 'Tantras of the Old Schools' under various of his Nying-ma teachers, the most significant of these being Ngak-pa Las-rab Ling-pa.

The fourth category of studies is generally known in Tibetan as "the ten branches of knowledge," and involves subjects like grammar, poetry, prose, art, medicine, history, and so forth. This tradition had come into the Ge-luk-pa School from the Sa-kya sect.

Another way of breaking down the Tibetan tradition of studies is into the threefold branch system of *Kan-gyur, Ten-gyur* and *Bod-zhung,* or Translated Word (Sutras and Tantras) of Buddha, Translated Commentaries (by later Indian Buddhist Masters), and Indigenous Tibetan Literature. The Great Thirteenth received a thorough training in all three of these branches. This threefold manner of approaching spiritual training had been developed in Tibet by the Zha-lu School established by Bu-ton Rin-chen Drub-pa in the thirteenth century. The Great Thirteenth was a strong admirer of Bu-ton, and at one point in his life composed a long poem in praise of him and his work.

Training in this multifaceted manner the Great Thirteenth achieved the level of learning and understanding expected of a Dalai Lama.

On the eleventh day of the first month of the Wood Sheep Year (February 1895) he took the full ordination of a monk, with his guru Pur-chok-pa Jam-pa Gya-tso presiding as the ordaining master. The ceremony took place in the Jo-khang Temple at Lhasa, and was attended by thousands of monks from the three monastic universities and two tantric colleges. The Manchu Emperor Kuang Hsu sent him a letter of congratulations: "We have been informed that the Oceanic Teacher has taken the complete precepts of a monk, and are most delighted at the happy news. We offer our prayers that the Oceanic Teacher will strive to complete his studies, so that the sublime teachings of the Yellow Hat tradition may be disseminated throughout the world. We take pleasure in offering him a number of gifts, which accompany this letter...."

In the Earth Dog Year (1898), when he was in his twenty-third year, he announced that he would appear in each of the three principal monastic universities for public debate, and would stand for his *geshe* exam. This is the highest examination in the Tibetan academic tradition, being somewhat equivalent to our Doctor of Philosophy degree, and to win it the Dalai Lama would have to debate with the best scholars in the country in front of some twenty thousand monk spectators, with his every word being carefully scrutinized by all. This was the traditional manner in which every Dalai Lama marks the end of his long period of study.

As *A String of Wondrous Gems* puts it, "Although nobody doubted the high level of his wisdom and understanding, he wished to uphold the tradition of proving oneself in open public debate before all the greatest sages in the land, a tradition that had been maintained by all the early Dalai Lamas." He remained for more than two weeks in each of the three monastic universities, every day debating with the best scholars of the generation. Pur-chok-pa writes, "And he met them like a mountain that is undisturbed by wind and thunder. . . . The lion's roar of his wisdom burst the bubble of pride of the many jackals who came to challenge him."

Thus he ascended to the highest pinnacle of learning known to the Tibetan Buddhist world.

As the Great Thirteenth wrote in *Sunlight on the Blossoming Garden of the Buddhadharma*, from his youth he had been made aware of the necessity to combine study with the practice of meditation. It is not possible therefore to speak of his studies without saying something about his meditational training.

In the Tibetan tradition meditation is practiced in three principal ways: firstly there is *tun-zhi-gi-nal-jor*, or the training of developing the habit of engaging in meditation four times daily; secondly there is the practice of *las-rung*, or performing short retreats from time to time; and thirdly there is the *nyen-chen*, or "great retreat" that lasts from three to four years, and should be accomplished at least once during one's lifetime.

The Great Thirteenth upheld all three of these modes of meditational training. From childhood he developed the habit of sitting in meditation four times each day, with Pur-chok-pa Jam-pa Gya-tso overseeing his progress. In the beginning his sittings were comprised largely of chanting the sutras and various prayers; but as his maturity increased the process became less one of recitation and more an opportunity to pursue contemplation and meditation.

As for the second mode, or the practice of occasionally making short retreat, this too he honored from childhood. Every year he would engage in two or three brief *las-rung* lasting a week or two each, and before reaching his teens had performed one retreat of three months' duration. As the years passed, the time that he dedicated annually to *las-rung* gradually increased.

The third tradition is that of the *nyen-chen*, or 'great retreat.' He entered his first *nyen-chen* during the fourth month of the Water Hare Year (i.e., spring of 1903); but unfortunately this was not to be completed. The retreat had to be abandoned fourteen months later, during the sixth month of the Wood Dragon Year (1904) due to the looming possibility of a British invasion. The British had amassed a large force on the Indo-Tibetan border, and the Ne-chung Oracle while in trance advised the Lhasa government to request the Dalai Lama to break his retreat and go to Mongolia until the conflict was resolved.

However, the Great Thirteenth was to make another attempt at the "great retreat" a decade later, after the problems with Britain (and as a consequence also with China) had been resolved. On the thirtieth day of the tenth month of the Fire Dragon Year (late autumn 1916) he entered into seclusion and began the extensive preliminary practices of the Vajrabhairava (Yamantaka) tantric system. Over the twelve months that followed he completed vast numbers of the traditional preliminaries that purify the mind and accumulate the merit necessary for success in the actual practice. Included here were mini-retreats on Refuge, Vajrasattva, Samayavajra, Vajradaka, and so forth.

The formal Vajrabhairava retreat itself began on the thirteenth of the tenth month of the Fire Snake Year (autumn 1917), and continued for almost two-and-a-half years. As Pur-chok-pa puts it, "Here he first applied himself to the generation stage yogas practiced in four daily sessions, cultivating clear appearance in the mandala meditations and making firm the divine tantric pride, thus purifying the basis of ordinary perception of death, intermediate state and rebirth. When this had been made firm he went on to the completion stage yogas that fulfill the experiences originally aroused through the generation stage practices...."

Having completed the major part of the "great retreat", he appeared at the Great Prayer Festival of the Earth Sheep Year (spring 1920), leading the festival and overseeing the public debates of the monks standing for their *ge-she* exams. But it was a short appearance, and the full retreat was not concluded until the twenty-fourth day of the eighth month, for he still had to perform the process known as the "retreat-concluding practices." This refers to the extensive fire rites and special mantra practices usually done at the end of the *nyen-chen*.

Thus over a period of almost four years he fulfilled the tradition of 'the great retreat,' complete with the time-honored threefold approach of preliminaries, main body of yogas, and the concluding practices.

Pur-chok-pa writes, "In this way he gained complete inner experience of the essence of the Vajra Vehicle, and upheld the legacy established by the early Dalai Lamas."

F. EMPOWERMENT AND "THE CASE OF THE ENCHANTED SHOES"

The Regent Ta-tsak Rin-po-che had passed away during the fourth month of the Fire Dog Year (1886), when the Great Thirteenth was only eleven years old. Consequently the Lhasa government had to appoint another Regent to serve until the Dalai Lama came of age.

The position was given to De-mo Tul-ku Trin-le Rab-gye of Ten-ge-ling Monastery. Unfortunately, time was to prove him to be a poor choice. In the beginning of his term of office he seems to have been a good enough man; but power has its dangers, and this adage would soon apply to De-mo Tul-ku. Having become Regent, he proceeded to appoint his brothers Nor-bu Tse-ring and Lob-zang Don-den to assist him in his administrative duties. The former of these turned out to be corrupt and power-hungry, playing on the innocence of his brother the new Regent for his personal gain.

In 1893 the Great Thirteenth entered his eighteenth year, the age at which a Dalai Lama normally is empowered as active ruler of the country. However, the Regent and his brothers were reluctant to relinquish authority. Consequently the empowerment was postponed for two years, the reason given being that the Dalai Lama should complete his religious studies before becoming involved in the affairs of state.

As described earlier, two years after the initial postponement of his enthronement the Great Thirteenth took his final exams in the three monastic universities, thus officially concluding his studies. After that it became impossible for the Regent to delay the transference of power any longer.

The empowerment ceremony took place four months later, on the eighth day of the eighth month of the Wood Sheep Year (September 1895). As on the occasion of his enthronement many years ago when he was still a child, the ceremony began with prayers in front of the sacred Shakyamuni Buddha statue in the Jo-khang Temple in downtown Lhasa, and then moved to the Avalokiteshvara Chapel on the roof of the Potala. After this he was welcomed in the main assembly hall of the Potala by the foremost spiritual and secular personalities of the land, and was enthroned as supreme leader of the Land of Snows. To symbolize his new position as a *Chakravartin-raja*, or "Wheel-Turning Emperor," he was given a finely engraved wheel made of pure gold almost two pounds in weight with a radius of thirty centimeters. He was also given four similarly shaped rings of silver, and one made from an alloy of silver and gold.

Things went well enough for the next few years. Even though the Great Thirteenth had completed his principal philosophical studies and passed his exams with flying colors, he continued to pursue his training with vigor, concentrating largely on tantric subjects that lay outside the mainstream of the general curriculum. In particular he spent a great deal of time studying the Hayagriva tantric system that had come down from the Fifth Dalai Lama; and also the *Dor-je Pur-pa* (Vajrakilaya, or 'Diamond Dagger') system, which he received from his Nying-ma-pa guru Las-rab Ling-pa.

The Earth Boar Year (1899) got off to a bad start. During a trance at the Great Prayer Festival the Ne-chung Oracle warned of dangers to the Dalai Lama's life. Nonetheless the Great Thirteenth continued to preside over the festival, and also over the *ge-she* exams.

However, soon afterwards he began to complain of physical discomfort, nausea, and dizziness. The Ne-chung Oracle was again invoked. This time he warned of a pair of shoes that had been given to the Dalai Lama's friend and tutor So-gyal Tul-ku. So-gyal was questioned on the matter, and informed the committee that indeed Sha-od Tul-ku, a young *ngak-pa* lama from his homeland of Nya-rong in Eastern Tibet, had given him a pair of exquisite shoes with the express request that he present them to the Dalai Lama as a gift. So-gyal admitted to accepting the shoes, but had never gotten around to passing them on to the Dalai Lama, considering that to do so would be out of place. In addition, So-gyal announced, he had had a bad feeling about the shoes from the beginning, and that once when he had tried them on he had experienced a nosebleed.

The shoes were brought forth and torn apart. Inside the soles were discovered various substances used in black magic, including a mystical diagram with the Dalai Lama's name written on it. Sha-od Tul-ku was arrested and questioned, and confessed that he had been hired by the ex-Regent and his brothers to destroy the Dalai Lama through occult means in an attempt to win back the throne for them. Some Tibetans suspect that slow-acting poison had been slipped into the Dalai Lama's food (a stronger potion would be detected by the food-taster), with the idea that in this weakened condition he would be vulnerable to the black magic when he put on the enchanted shoes.

The ex-Regent and his brothers were arrested. Nor-bu Tse-ring confessed to instigating the plot; he admitted that during his period of serving as minister to the Regent he had made many enemies through the abuse of his position, and that after he had fallen from power some of the Lhasa authorities had sought to punish him by making his life difficult.

The Lhasa parliament was enraged and asked that the death penalty be administered. The Dalai Lama, however, intervened on the behalf of the unhappy culprits, declaring himself to be totally opposed to capital punishment for any crime whatsoever. However, it is said that the black magician Sha-od Tul-ku was quietly put to death by government officials who were fearful that if he were permitted to live he may weave his evil spells from behind bars, and would bring vengeance down on the heads of those responsible for his imprisonment.

Most works on modern Tibetan history give us very little information on the mysterious life of the magician and would-be occult murderer Sha-od Tul-ku, even though they all mention this bizarre plot in which he was involved. While doing research on the present volume I happened to interview a lama friend from Nya-rong, the area in Eastern Tibet from whence hailed both the Great Thirteenth's friend and tutor So-gyal Tul-ku and the evil Sha-od.

The story begins in the early nineteenth century with a renowned Nying-ma-pa yogi by the name of Nya-lo Pe-ma Don-drub. He was an eminent teacher who had thirteen principal disciples, later known to history as 'the thirteen Ling-pas.' This great guru lived a simple nomadic life, his only home being his tent. Amongst his disciples were both So-gyal Tul-ku and Rang-rig Dor-je (later known as Ku-sum Ling-pa).

It so happened that on one occasion someone in a village near Nya-lo's camp died. The family approached him with the request that he perform prayers for the deceased, as well as *po-wa*, or "the transference of consciousness." Nya-lo called the consciousness of the deceased into a cup, sealing the lid with his *vajra*. He invited each of his thirteen disciples to try and lift the *vajra*, saying that whoever could do so would become his chief successor. All thirteen tried, but none were successful. Then all tried together. The *vajra* came off and flew out through the air vent in the roof of the tent. It was later found by Rang-rig Dor-je, indicating that he would become the foremost of Nya-lo's disciples.

Shortly after this episode a child by the name of Sha-od was born in Nya-rong. Rumored to be the reincarnation of the person for whom Nya-lo Pe-ma Don-drub had performed the consciousness transference ritual, he exhibited many unusual characteristics. It was prophesied that he would one day become a man of power. But a warning came with the prophecy: he would achieve occult abilities, but whether he would use these for good or evil was undecided, and those around him must take special care to see that he was not tempted to follow the path of darkness.

Some years later when Rang-rig Dor-je was preparing to go to Central Tibet the child's mother approached him and requested that he take Sha-od with him. Rang-rig Dor-je performed a divination, and then refused the woman's application. "If he stays in Nya-rong he will become a great yogi," he told her. "But if he goes to Central Tibet he will become seduced by power and will meet with disaster."

The boy's mother was not to be dissuaded. She approached So-gyal Tul-ku, who also was about to leave for Lhasa, and requested that he accept the boy as his ward. So-gyal was greatly impressed by the boy's innate magical abilities, and agreed to take responsibility for him.

In Central Tibet things went much as Rang-rig Dor-je had prophesied. Sha-od Tul-ku's power and magical abilities were developed far in excess of his integrity and wisdom. The ex-Regent and his evil brother perceived this and, with the plan to corrupt him and then employ him in their devious plot to regain their lost privileges, they befriended the young magician.

When the plot was eventually uncovered it proved to be quite embarrassing to So-gyal Tul-ku, who had brought Sha-od to Central Tibet with him and who thus shared in the responsibility for the near-disaster. So-gyal himself had become a close friend and spiritual advisor to the Great Thirteenth, and thus nobody suspected that he personally was involved in the plot. Consequently he was not directly punished, and was allowed to remain close to the Dalai Lama. However, his prestige was certainly diminished in the eyes of the Tibetan people.

As mentioned above, even though the Dalai Lama opposed the motion for capital punishment Sha-od died mysteriously soon after his arrest. It is said that he became a malevolent spirit, and that So-gyal Tul-ku, who had brought him to Lhasa against Rang-rig Dor-je's advice, was appointed by the government to perform an exorcism to release the demon from his mind-set.

So-gyal, however, was not able to accomplish the task. Therefore he requested Rang-rig Dor-je to assist him in the ritual. But Rang-rig was extremely displeased at the turn of events and refused to cooperate. Years ago he had warned So-gyal against bringing the impressionable Sha-od to Central Tibet. "You brought him here," he snapped at the distraught So-gyal, "so you can bury him."

Tibetans believe that still today Sha-od remains a tormented ghost as retribution for his evil deed, and that sometimes late at night his lamentations can be heard in the hallways of the Potala.

G. TIBET'S "CLOSED DOOR" POLICY

The Thirteenth Dalai Lama was born into a Tibet known to the Western world primarily for its geographical inaccessibility and its attitude of studied political isolationism. His country had watched with apprehension as British power grew in India, seeming to gnaw steadily at Tibet's southern and western frontiers.

Curiously enough, the first political exchange between Tibet and the British had come about through the former's efforts. The incident had occurred more than a century before the Great Thirteenth's birth. In 1772 Bhutan had attacked Kuch Behar, a small state adjoining British-run Bengal, and the British retaliated by sending a punitive expedition into Bhutan. At the time Bhutan was more or less a vassal state of Tibet, and the Bhutanese appealed to the Pan-chen Lama of nearby Shi-ga-tse to mediate on their behalf. Accordingly in 1773 the Pan-chen Lama wrote a letter to Warren Hastings, the Governor-General of Bengal, apologizing for the Bhutanese aggression and requesting him to show leniency. (Younghusband, 1910, pages 4-5.)

Hastings saw the occasion as a wonderful opportunity to break the ice with Tibet and perhaps even open trade with her. He replied positively to the Pan-chen, and recalled the British forces from Bhutan.

The following year he delegated George Bogle, a young Scot, to visit Shi-ga-tse with the mission of attempting to win the Pan-chen to the idea of lobbying in Lhasa for a trade agreement with British India. Bogle seems to have been successful enough at Shi-ga-tse itself; but the Pan-chen was not able to convince the Lhasa authorities that the British could be trusted. The Regent at Lhasa wrote him a scathing letter, warning of the dangers inherent in the foreign overtures. "The English," he stated in no uncertain terms, "are well known to be fond of war and conquest, with little concern for our religion. In the beginning they will ask to trade with us, but soon after entering the country will search for ways to dominate us politically and to undermine our culture."

Bogle himself reported, "The Government at Lhasa considered me sent with a mission to explore their country, which the ambitions of the British might afterwards prompt them to invade, and their superiority of arms render them successful." (Lamb, 1960, page 11.)

Thus it appears that even as early as the 1770s Lhasa's closed-door policy was firmly in place.

Tibet had reason enough to be shy towards the British. Most Western writers of the period tend to act rather indignantly over this early rejection, but there was some fire in the British smoke. Many were the Asian, African and American kingdoms that had casually allowed an initial exchange with the British, only to later find themselves under British administration.

It may safely be said that Lhasa's isolationist policy came about from two basic causes. The first was a suspicion that the British, if allowed to enter the country, would attempt to destroy the Tibetan religious tradition and replace it with Christianity. The second was a fear that the British wanted to colonize Tibet. It may be added that the first of these—the religious apprehension—was born from personal experience; the second was acquired by hearsay, coming about largely due to the advice of the Manchu Chinese.

Tibet's first political intercourse with Britain may have been the above exchange with Warren Hastings, but this was not her first experience of Europeans. No doubt these earlier contacts had aroused her suspicions, for they had almost exclusively been with extremely bigoted missionaries who had come in the age of European religious intolerance, narrow-minded men driven by the hope of gaining a few Tibetan converts, of replacing Tibetan Buddhism with one brand or another of Christianity.

There had been the Jesuit mission founded in Tsa-pa-rang, Western Tibet, in 1625 by Father Antonio de Andrade and a handful of Portugese, who preached to the Tibetans on "...the errors of their faith, and the reality of the One True Faith of Jesus Christ." Then there was Johannes Grueber and Albert de Dorville, who visited Lhasa in 1661 and wrote of the Fifth Dalai Lama, "He is a devilish God the Father...." And Ippolito Desideri, who lived in Lhasa from 1716-1721 and tried in various ways (quite unsuccessfully) to convince the Tibetans of "...the superiority of the Christian faith." Other important names include Horace de la Penna, who arrived in 1719 and established a Capuchin mission; the Dutchman Van der Putte, who referred to the Tibetans as "savages"; the Protestant zealot Gutzlaff, who urged a mass effort to convert the Tibetans by force from their devotion to Buddhism and the Dalai Lama, whom he called, "...a Moloch in human shape—a worthless, abject being." It should be noted that most of these missionaries enjoyed considerable hospitality while in Tibet; their manner of returning the kindness shown to them lacked both grace and tact. It certainly did not speak well for the European attitude, nor did it win many friends in Tibet.

Of the above, it was perhaps the ill-timed advent of the Italian Jesuit missionary Ippolito Desideri that best stereotypes the religious snobbery and insensitivity characteristic of almost all the early European visitors to Lhasa. He may well have played the most significant role in the formation of Lhasa's negative attitude toward European religious motives.

Desideri arrived in Lhasa from Tsa-pa-rong on March 18th, 1716, a decade after Lha-zang Khan of the Qoshot Mogols had invaded Tibet and deposed the Sixth Dalai Lama, resulting in the latter's death. Desideri attempted to befriend the unpopular Khan and his ministers, appearing frequently at the court in order to try to win him over to the cause of his mission. According to Desideri's own account, the Khan enjoyed receiving the attentions of a European, and promised to seriously consider the Christian case. "If after mature discussion and examination he should be convinced of having lived in error, he, his family, his court and all his people would become followers of the word of Jesus Christ," Desideri tells us. (Fillipi, 1932, page 98.)

We should not underestimate the contempt that any foreigner in the court of the hated invader Lha-zang Khan would arouse, an invader who on his assumption of power had put many of the traditional Tibetan leaders to death and who now ruled as a ruthless dictator. The fact that the foreigner in question was attempting to convince the evil Khan to order Tibet to convert to Christianity could hardly be expected to win Desideri the love and affections of the Tibetans.

But Desideri was not to be daunted. He proceeded to compose a book in Tibetan, the first portion of which he publicly presented to the Khan at an oppulent ceremony, wherein he outlined "the falseness of the Tibetan religion" and the superiority of Catholic dogma, "the one and only true religion." While writing his literary bombshell he was housed first in the Ra-mo-che Temple and then in Se-ra Monastery under the direct patronage of the Khan. His account of Tibet (written later when he was back in Italy) bears chapter headings such as, "The False and Peculiar Religion prevailing in Tibet," "Reasons Why the Alleged Incarnation of the Grand Lama must be the Work of the Devil," "The Colossal Error of the Tibetans in Denying that there is any Absolute Uncreated Being," "How the False Religion was Brought to Tibet," and so forth. These, of course, are headings intended for an Italian audience; but judging from his notes it would seem that he did not express himself to the Tibetans with any greater tact or open-mindedness. But time was not on his side.

The Dzungar Mongols were jealous of Qoshot activities in Central Tibet, and were enraged at the way Lha-zang had deposed the Sixth Dalai Lama and his viceroy De-si Sang-gye Gya-tso. They attacked Lhasa with a large body of troops and quickly took the city. Lha-zang Khan himself died in the fighting, and Tibet fell into Dzungar hands. Desideri had lost his patron and the source of his hopes. Even worse, as a friend to the deposed Khan his life was no longer safe. He therefore left Lhasa and took up residence in Dvak-po Khyer, eight days to the southeast. Coincidentally the following year Rome held a council to decide the jurisdictions of various missionary works, and it was concluded that Tibet was within the territory of the Capuchins, not the Jesuits. A letter to this effect reached Desideri in 1721, whereupon he took the road south out of the country.

The experience of these early European missionaries undoubtedly left the Tibetans with an unpleasant after-taste. Yet the strongest cause of their formal adoption of an isolationist policy was to come not from religious quarters, but from political considerations and the connection with the Chinese Manchus that was soon to form.

The presence of the Dzungar Mongols in Tibet was short-lived. Although they had succeeded in removing Lha-zang Khan from power they proved to be unpleasant saviors, and their victory was followed by a period of pillage and vandalism. Fanatical adherents to the Yellow Hat School of Tibetan Buddhism, they showed a complete intolerance of the older sects. In particular, their intense persecution of the Nying-ma monasteries in Central and Western Tibet caused them to lose the popularity they had won by displacing Lha-zang Khan.

In 1719 Khang-chen-ne of Western Tibet formed an alliance with Po-lha-ne of Southern Tibet with the objective of ousting the Dzungars. The Manchu Emperor Kang-hsi saw in this union the opportunity to gain an influence in 'the land of the lamas,' and came to their support. The Dzungars were quickly defeated, and in 1720 the young Seventh Dalai Lama was placed in the Potala. The Manchus were allowed to establish a residence in Lhasa for the purposes of communicating with the Emperor, and the basis for the Manchu-Tibetan relationship that endured for almost two hundred years (and that was inherited by the Thirteenth Dalai Lama) was established. In 1728 Po-lha-ne of Tsang emerged as the principal secular ruler; it was he who allowed the Manchu Emperor to appoint two ambans to the Lhasa residence. In all probability it was the advice of these two ambans that played the greatest role in formally closing Tibet to the British.

The closed-door policy was to remain in effect from then until 1913, when the Great Thirteenth ordered all Chinese officials out of Tibet and terminated the traditional 'Patron/Priest' relationship that China and Tibet had shared for almost two centuries.

H. A PAWN IN "THE GREAT GAME"

The close of the eighteenth century saw the end of the power struggle between Mongolia and Manchu China, a struggle that had dominated East Asian life for almost five hundred years and from which the Manchus clearly emerged as the victors. The nineteenth century, however, was to bring an entirely different scenario into the picture. Mongolia and China no longer were to be the principal players in the Asian power structure. Instead, Czarist Russia and the British Empire stepped forth as the new rising stars.

Russia's Asiatic policy had been strikingly successful for several hundred years now, and it was estimated that Russian territories in Asia had been expanding at a rate of 20,000 square miles a year since the 1500s. The change in Russian fortunes had come at the end of the fifteenth century, when the Tartars turned from their constant attacks on Russia and made India their target of aggression. Russia moved from the defensive to the offensive. The pace of things picked up with Peter the Great at the end of the eighteenth century, and became something of an avalanche in the nineteenth century under the rules of Alexander I, Nicholas I, and the two Alexanders to follow (II and III). One after another the Khanates were absorbed into the swelling Russian Empire. Railways began to spring up over the length and breadth of Northern Asia, carrying Russian troops and supplies wheresoever the Czar dictated. The completion of the Trans-Siberian Railway in 1891 was particularly alarming to the other colonial powers, for now Russia had the ability to reach into the very heart of the Far East.

Britain, on the other hand, was expanding by means of the sea. Her navy carried her diplomats, merchants and soldiers far and wide, and began to envelop Asia from the south and southeast. Tibet, a large land mass with a small population, was strategically important as the key to Central Asia both culturally and geographically. Wedged between the Russian and British 'spheres of interest,' she came to be caricatured in the European media as a tiny llama standing alone under the hungry stares of the Russian bear to the north and the British lion to the south.

The Tibetans first began to feel the colonialistic pinch from the British, whose activities and power in India greatly increased during the eighteenth century, and who saw Tibet as an alternative trade route to Western China, Mongolia and Turkestan. British India was also very interested in Tibet's legendary gold mines, which she saw as a commercial buffer in trade with the East.

Tibetan mistrust of the British in India became pronounced with the rumored presence of the latter in Nepal in the 1760s when the Hindu Gurkhas attacked and subdued the Buddhist Newaris. They also suspected them of having played a silent part in the Gurkha attacks on Southern Tibet in 1788-9, and again in 1792. When "the Company" (i.e., the East India Trading Co., who represented the British Government in India) signed a trade agreement with the Gurkhas in 1792 almost at the same time that Tibet (with Manchu help) managed to expel Gurkha forces from within Tibetan territory, Tibetan suspicions soared.

And then there was the Bhutanese incident of 1772 related earlier, in which the Pan-chen was asked to mediate. It is possible that Bhutan initiated this conflict with the British; but Bhutan lay within the Tibetan cultural region, and its invasion by British forces was not inclined to find sympathy with the Lhasa authorities.

In February of 1817 the British forced a treaty with Sikkim in which the latter agreed to place their foreign relations under the former's control. In return, the British agreed to protect the latter from Gurkha incursions. Again, Sikkim was traditionally a cultural satellite of Tibet; its annexation by the Company did not pass unnoticed.

British attentions then turned to the Western Himalayas. Events of 1816 and 1817 saw Kumaon and Garwhal fall under British influence, the former by outright annexation and the latter, including the regions around Simla and the Sutlej Valley, by turning them into "protectorates." All of these areas traditionally had strong ties with Lhasa both culturally and commercially.

To the north of these states lay Ladakh and its dependencies of Lahoul and Spitti. Ladakh was then known to the West as "Little Tibet," and also "Second Tibet" (for it was the second Tibetan region on the India side of the mountains to have had a Christian missionary outpost, the first being Tsa-pa-rong in Gu-ge). Here too Tibetan culture dominated.

Of particular interest to the British was Gartok, the capital of Western Tibet, a smallish town through which all trade between Tibet and

Ladakh (as well as its principalities) passed. The British were especially interested in the fine shawl wool coming from Tibet through Gartok for resale in Kashmir, which in 1816 was estimated to comprise a quarter of Tibet's trade with Ladakh. This wool, they surmised, would be very well received on the European markets.

But the Tibetans were unwilling to trade with the enterprising newcomers, nor even to communicate with them. When Captain Alexander Gerard wrote to authorities in Gartok in 1821 requesting permission to visit the holy Lake Manasarowara he was stopped at the Tibetan frontier and informed that ''. . .orders had been received from Lhasa to make no friends with the Europeans, and to furnish them neither with food nor firewood. Nor could letters for forwarding to points in Tibet be accepted, but must be returned unopened.'' Clearly, the Tibetans were both aware of and displeased with British encroachment upon her frontiers. (Lamb, 1960, page 62.)

In 1834 the Raja of Jammu, a Dogra ruler by the name of Gulab Singh, sent Zorawar Singh into Ladakh with an army. The expedition, which had a tacit British approval, also took parts of Western Tibet. The Tibetans counterattacked in 1841, expelling the Sikhs from their own territory as well as from Ladakh. The following year the Sikhs returned and a treaty was signed, with the British acting as witnesses.

Until this time Britain had been trying to deal with Tibet directly, largely through overtures to the Pan-chen and the Ta-shi Lhun-po authorities. But this was soon to change. Their many attempts to bring Lhasa to the bargaining table had failed, and another tactic was now in the making.

As stated earlier, the Tibetans had inherited their isolationist policy largely from the Manchu government, and believed that by means of it the British could be held at bay. Whenever pressed, they would reply that their ''Patron/Priest'' arrangement with China did not allow them to enter into separate agreements with foreign powers; and when the Chinese were approached they would state that they had no authority to speak for Tibet. As Younghusband put it, ''So the same old story goes on year after year, til centuries are beginning to roll by, and still the story is unfinished.'' (Younghusband, 1910, page 18.)

But Russian advances in the north and the growth of ''Russiaphobia'' throughout India no longer permitted the luxury of a casual approach. It may be more expedient, Col. Browne Wade conjectured, to deal directly with China and thus get at Tibet ''through the back door." (Lamb, 1960, page 129.) This marked a clear departure from earlier British policy, which generally tried to keep its Indian interests separate from those she held in the Far East. But fear of Russian assimilation of Tibet demanded a new and more bold approach.

The new policy took shape in the form of the Chefoo Convention, signed by the British and Chinese on Sept. 13, 1876, and ammended in July of 1886 amid considerable controversy.

The Chefoo Convention was to the Tibetans a betrayal. What it meant to them in real terms was Britain and China privately agreeing with one another to the former's acquisition of Burma and the latter's authority over Tibet. The "patron" had sold out the "priest." In terms of Britain's greater plan of containing Russian expansionism, by giving Tibet to China the Czar would effectively be kept out of Lhasa and away from the northern borders of British India.

Coincidentally, this most important treaty was signed in the same year that the Thirteenth Dalai Lama took birth. He was to make resistance to this agreement one of the main political themes of his life.

In particular, the Chefoo Convention agreed to permit British trade missions to pass through Tibet. In November 1885 the Chinese issued the British with special passports granting them authority to take a trade mission to Lhasa from India. The mission assembled in Darjeeling in early 1886 under the direction of Colman Macauley, but it produced such a controversy in England that it was disbanded. The main objective of the day had been accomplished: Tibet had been placed safely outside the Russian sphere of influence, and now lay within the jurisdiction of China, with whom Britain held close ties.

But then a curious turn of events transpired. The young Thirteenth Dalai Lama, furious at the Chinese for presuming the right to sign a treaty on Tibet's behalf, decided to send a clear signal to both London and Peking. Although only ten years of age, he seems to have clearly realized the implications of the Sino-British agreement. In July of 1886 he dispatched an army to the Chumbi Valley and into Sikkim by a distance of thirteen miles, setting up fortifications on a hilltop at Ling-tu.

The episode was embarrasing to the British in India, but there was no consensus on how to react. Macauley suggested that he proceed to Ling-to and request Tibet, Sikkim and Bhutan to negotiate a treaty. London did not agree; there was no need to aggravate the situation by drawing attention to it and thus endanger the recently concluded Chefoo Convention. It would be better, Lord Dufferin decided, to ignore the incursion altogether and hope that the Tibetans would eventually retire of their own accord from a position that was undoubtedly difficult to maintain with supplies. (Lamb, 1960, page 167.)

In October the Chinese protested to the Tibetans over this violation of the Chefoo Convention. In return the Tibetans responded by reinforcing their position at Ling-tu and closing the area to British and Chinese alike.

The biography of the Great Thirteenth comments, "The young incarnation took time from his important studies to oversee the building of a sizeable army. Many of his advisors recommended that he distance himself from the events, but he felt it to be crucial that Tibet make known her independence from both China and the English. He therefore blessed the four officials in charge of recruiting the army, and later gave his blessings as well as protection strings to the many soldiers who were dispatched to the south.... Because involvement in wrathful activities can shorten one's lifespan, three high Nying-ma-pa lamas and fifteen ritual assistants were requested to perform long life rituals for him day and night during this period, as was the entire Nying-ma monastery of Min-dro-ling."

Britain's studied inactivity did not seem to be having the desired effect. In December of 1887 a letter was sent to the Tibetans at Ling-tu informing them that if they did not withdraw voluntarily they would be forcibly removed in the spring. A similar letter was sent to the Dalai Lama in February. The Tibetans did not reply to either.

Meanwhile the Chinese were in a frenzy. In an attempt to delay affairs they recalled their amban from Lhasa and appointed a new one.

But the case was perhaps best described in Peking by Li Hung-chang in a conversation with Edwin Goshen, in which the former commented, "People talk of China's influence in Tibet, but it is only nominal, as the Lamas are all powerful there...." (Lamb, 1960, page 184.)

In March 1888 the British sent a force of 2,000 well-equipped soldiers under Brigadier Graham to expel the Tibetans. In May the poorly equipped Tibetans launched a surprise attack, and almost succeeded in capturing the Governor General of Bengal, who at the time was visiting the frontier. However, the attack eventually was repelled. In September a further Tibetan attack was launched, this time from Nadong. It too was unsuccessful, and marked the end of the Tibetan initiative.

Tibet had lost its first war with the British Empire, but she had succeeded in letting the British know her feelings and attitudes regarding Chinese authority within her borders.

Britain had unwittingly opened something of a can of worms with China by creating the 1876 Chefoo Convention. By "giving" Tibet to China she brought into question her own position in the many Himalayan states, such as Sikkim and Bhutan, that traditionally were Tibetan satellites. And because of the complex situation she had created, she could not now sign a treaty directly with Tibet but rather had to do so through a Chinese intermediary.

Therefore the treaty that followed the Anglo-Tibetan conflict on the Sikkimese border was slow and painstaking in the making, and was to further alienate the Tibetans from both the Chinese and the British. Signed at Darjeeling in 1890 by A.W. Paul for England and both Ho Chang-jung and James Hart for China, in effect it was a mutual agreement by these two parties recognizing British control over Sikkim and Chinese control over Tibet, without the Tibetans being consulted on the matter. This was the political implication of the treaty; commercially (as amended by the Trade Regulations of 1893) it allowed Britain to open a trade mart at the border town of Ya-tung and to carry on commerce there with the Tibetans.

Not having been allowed to participate in the negotiations, Tibet refused to acknowledge the treaty. The British border markers that were erected on the frontiers of Tibet and Sikkim were removed by the Tibetans; and as for the trade mart at Ya-tung, the Tibetans walled off the only road leading from Ya-tung into Tibet, thus effectively rendering the enterprise impotent.

Another problem created by the treaty and resented by Lhasa was that the British now for the first time formally had agreed not to talk directly to the Tibetans, but rather to refer all Tibet-related matters to the Chinese government.

1895 saw the Sino-Japanese War, in which the Chinese were thoroughly defeated. Chinese authority in Tibet, already minimal, lost all credibility.

While all of this had been going on to the south and east of Tibet, the Russian Empire had been steadily growing in the north. Russian strength was well known in Lhasa, mainly because of the large number of Mongolian principalities that had fallen under Russian sway. Many of the Mongolians of these areas continued to pursue their studies in the great monastic universities of Lhasa, bringing with them stories of the Russian activities.

One man in particular was to play an important role in building communications between Lhasa and the Czar: Tsan-zhab Nga-wang Lob-zang, a Mongolian monk who had graduated with high honors from the Go-mang department of Dre-pung Monastery, and who was one of the seven "assistant tutors" (*Tsan-zhab*) to the Dalai Lama. Popularly known to the Tibetans as Tsen-nyi Khen-po, or "Master of Dialectics," he became famed to both the British and the Russians by the simpler name of Dorjieff (from the Tibetan *Dor-je*). Born in the Buryat region of the Mongolian territories that had in recent times been acquired by the Czar, Dorjieff was therefore a Russian citizen.

On October 22 of the year 1900 a dispatch reached the Foreign Office in London from H. M. Charge d'Affairs in St. Petersburg, informing the British Government that not only was the Mongolian lama Dorjieff in Russia, but that the *Journal de Saint-Petersburg* had carried a lengthy article outlining Dorjieff's reception by the Emperor (Czar Nicholas II) in the Lividia Palace at the Black Sea resort of Yalta. British intelligence also learned that Dorjieff had carried a letter of greetings to the Czar from the Dalai Lama. (Fleming, 1961, page 39.)

In June of 1901 Dorjieff was back in Russia (clandestinely via British India, a further irritation to the English) as the head of what the Russian press described as "...an extraordinary mission of eight prominent Tibetan statesmen." The Tibetan envoys were given audiences by both the Emperor and Empress, to whom they presented gifts and a letter from the Dalai Lama. As Peter Fleming puts it, Dorjieff and the Tibetans "...were a nine day wonder in the Russian capital, where the newspapers drew the obvious conclusions from their unheralded but gratifying visit." The Russian paper *Novoe Vremye* mused, "Under the circumstances, a *rapprochement* with Russia must seem to the Dalai Lama the most natural step, as Russia is the only power able to counteract the intrigues of Great Britain..." (Fleming, 1961, page 40.)

Needless to say, the British were extremely alarmed at the turn of events. Here they had taken such pains to insure Tibet's distancing from Russia by signing her over to China, only to see the looming possibility of bungled British policy combined with China's increasing weakness resulting in a Tibeto-Russian pact.

Ekai Kawaguchi, a Japanese monk who lived and studied in Tibet for three years just after the turn of the century, speaks of a short treatise written by Dorjieff that had gained wide popularity in Tibet. The treatise, Kawaguchi states, set forth the proposition that Russia was none other than the mythological Shambala, the mystical kingdom that was prophesied to emerge one day as the great patron and defender of Buddhism. Kawaguchi writes, "I knew several priests who undoubtedly possessed copies of this pamphlet.... The one from whom I confidentially obtained the drift of the writing told me that he found in it some unknown letters. I concluded that the letters must be Russian.... Tsan-nyi Khen-po's artful scheme has been crowned with great success, for today almost every Tibetan blindly believes in the ingenious story.... and holds that the Tsar will sooner or later.... found a gigantic Buddhist Empire." (Kawaguchi, 1909, pages 499-500.)

Kawaguchi also reports seeing two large caravans of gifts from the Czar arriving in Lhasa, the first comprised of 200 camels loaded with various wares and the second of 300 camels. He makes particular reference to the golden brocades that were a personal present to the Dalai Lama, a gift that symbolically meant more than the many hundreds of lesser items. (Kawaguchi, 1909, page 505.)

These exchanges between Tibet and Russia inspired near-panic in British India. The new Viceroy, Lord Curzon, had arrived in 1898 and was determined to set the British Empire's relationship with Tibet on a proper footing. He had grown up in the school that saw Russia as the greatest menace to British supremacy and to Western civilization as he knew it. He looked with mistrust on the policy of leaving Tibet in China's care, and was not at all convinced that such a course of action (or rather, inaction) would be sufficient to check the Russian advance.

On the 24th of May, 1899 he wrote to Hamilton, the Secretary of State for India, "The lamas have found out the weakness of China. At the same time they are being approached by Russia. There seems little doubt that Russian agents, and possibly even someone of Russian origin, has been at Lhasa, and I believe that the Tibetan Government is coming to the conclusion that it will have to make friends with one or the other of the two great Powers. That our case should not be stated in these circumstances, and that judgement should go against us by default, would be a great pity." (Lamb, 1960, page 241.)

Again in October of 1901 he wrote to the Foreign Office, "As a student of Russian aspirations and methods for fifteen years, I assert with confidence—what I do not think any of her own statesmen would deny—that her ultimate ambition is the dominion of Asia. She conceives herself to be fitted for it by temperament, by history, and by tradition. It is a proud and a not ignoble aim, and it is well worthy of the supreme moral and material efforts of a vigorous nation. But it is not to be satisfied by piecemeal concessions, neither is it capable of being satisfied save at our expense. . . . Acquiescence at Kashgar will not divert Russian eyes from Tibet. Each morsel but whets her appetite for more, and inflames the passion for a pan-Asiatic dominion. If Russia is entitled to these ambitions, still more is Britain entitled, nay compelled, to defend that which she has won, and to resist the minor encroachments which are only a part of the larger plan." (Lamb, 1960, pages 239-240.)

Britain had maneuvered herself into a difficult position with Tibet, firstly by nibbling away at the Himalayan kingdoms to the south and west of Tibet and secondly by signing treaties with China recognizing Chinese authority over Lhasa. In 1898 Calcutta sent presents to the Dalai Lama via the Bhutanese diplomat Kazi Urgyen, with the request that Kazi discretely investigate the possibilities of establishing a closer relationship between Tibet and British India. He reported that the Dalai Lama had asked him to act as an unofficial peacemaker between Lhasa and Culcutta, and that Tibetan attitudes seemed to be favorable to a British overture. However, he added, the Tibetans were not agreeable to Chinese authority in their country and would only talk to the British provided that it did not appear they were doing so at the orders of China. Kazi Urgyen informed the British that ". . .the Dalai Lama is doing his utmost to lessen Tibetan dependence on China, and has established an arsenal in Lhasa as part of his plan to build up the Tibetan army."

In 1899 the British had Kazi Urgyen draft letters to the Dalai Lama proposing trade. The Tibetans declined to accept the correspondence due to the fear that a dialogue of this nature could be interpreted to mean that they accepted the Anglo-Chinese trade regulations of 1893, to which the Tibetans had not been allowed as a participant.

Lord Curzon decided on an alternative route of communication. In July of 1900 he dispatched a letter to the Dalai Lama via Western Tibet. However, the letter was returned a few months later; nobody wanted to take responsibility for delivering it.

Kazi Urgyen was scheduled to visit Lhasa the following year with two elephants, two peacocks and a leopard for the Dalai Lama. Lord Curzon gave him a revised form of the earlier letter. If the Tibetans did not soon start negotiating with the British, Curzon wrote, ". . .my Government must reserve the right to take such steps as may seem to them necessary and proper to enforce the terms of the Treaty, and to ensure that the Trade Regulations are observed." (Mehra, 1961, page 117.)

Kazi Urgyen returned to India in October, claiming that the Dalai Lama had refused to accept the letter. However, Sarat Chandra Das, the famous lexiconographer who for several decades had been an advisor of Tibetan affairs in the pay of British India, commented that in all probability the former did not have the courage to present the letter directly to the Dalai Lama as instructed, but instead had followed the traditional protocol of first discussing the matter with the Lhasa ministers. The ministers would undoubtedly have been against the idea, and once Kazi had asked their advice he would be unable to go over their heads by approaching the Dalai Lama directly.

The timing of these events was to be significant in their interpretation by the British. The Buryat monk Dorjieff happened to be in Russia bearing greetings from Lhasa the same year that the Viceroy attempted to send his first letter to the Dalai Lama. The Viceroy's second letter was sent and returned the following year, when Dorjieff and the delegation of "eight Tibetan statesmen" were in St. Petersburg with the Czar, having gotten there by traveling through British India. The British had suffered a distinct loss of face.

Soon thereafter popular rumors began to abound in both London and British India, rumors that spoke of a "secret pact" between Russia and Tibet, and also of a "Sino-Russian agreement." According to this latter theory, China and Russia had signed a treaty in which the former agreed to allow Tibet to orientate toward Russia in return for Russia allowing various parts of Chinese Turkestan and Eastern Mongolia to be left open for a Chinese takeover.

This latter agreement was reported to have been signed in Lhasa on Feb. 23rd, 1903 by a Russian agent named Licoloff and the Chinese Amban Ho. British intelligence in China concurred that five Russians had visited China in 1903 and then gone on to Lhasa, thus giving credence to the rumor. The *North China Herald* went so far as to publish a story outlining the main clauses of the supposed agreement.

Lord Curzon personally believed that something was underfoot to which the British were not privy. In November of 1902 he wrote that he was ". . .a firm believer in the existence of a secret undertaking, if not a secret treaty, between China and Russia about Tibet. . ." and that he considered it his ". . . .duty to frustrate this little game while there is still time."

The idea of a secret Sino-Russian pact was not impossible. China's control over Tibet was questionable, so for her to relinquish her weak claims there for more tangible gains elsewhere was quite plausible. And as Alastair Lamb points out, there were hundreds of pieces of intelligence gathered by the British Service in support of the theory.

Lord Roberts, the Commander-In-Chief of the British army in India, was extremely concerned. In October of 1902 he wrote, "I consider it out of the question Russia being permitted to obtain a footing in Tibet; we have had, and shall still have, quite enough trouble owing to Russia being so near to us on the Northwest Frontier of India—that we cannot avoid; but we can, and ought to, prevent her getting a position which would inevitably cause unrest all along the Northeast Frontier." (Lamb, 1960, page 279.)

To Curzon there was only one possible solution: an Anglo-Tibetan treaty negotiated in Lhasa. He regarded the Russian threat as serious indeed, and wrote, "...unless we take steps promptly and effectively to counteract it, we shall rue the day for years to come."

The problem for Lord Curzon was that London did not see Tibet as being as important as China in the overall scheme of things in the British Empire, and in no way wished to risk the lucrative China trade by violating the Chefoo Convention through an invasion of Tibet. A compromise was struck: the British would meet the Tibetans at Khamba-jong, just inside Tibetan territory, and negotiate a trade agreement from there. J. C. White and Major Francis Younghusband were appointed to lead the British delegation, with an escort of two hundred soldiers. But, the Home Government insisted, on no account was there to be an advance beyond Kham-ba-jong without direct permission from London.

The British force crossed the Tibetan border without resistance on July 1903. However, the Tibetans did not dispatch anyone with sufficient authority to carry on discussions. Days became weeks and months, with no progress in the situation.

Lord Curzon now had to build up a case to convince London to allow the party to advance further into Tibet. The issue was a sensitive one, for the project had to be executed without unduly alarming either China or Russia. Trade with China could not be sacrificed; and a direct encounter with Russia could easily lead to a conflict that could escalate out of control. Nobody was certain whether or not Russia had pledged assistance to Tibet, nor even if Russian troops were present in Lhasa.

In November a cautious note of permission to advance arrived. J.C. White was recalled and Younghusband became the sole political head of the expedition, with Brigader-General MacDonald as commander of the military escort (which had by now increased to over 8,000 men). In December they crossed the Je-lep-la Pass into the Chumbi Valley and Phari. In January they proceeded to Tuna, where they set up camp for three months and waited in vain for a delegation from Lhasa.

In March the expedition moved toward Gyang-tse, meeting its first resistance at Guru. Here the Tibetans were easily defeated, albeit with heavy casualties on the Tibetan side. The expedition reached Gyang-tse on April 11th, after a number of further clashes but with no serious setbacks.

May saw an unsuccessful Tibetan attack on the expedition at Gyang-tse, but still no delegation arrived from Lhasa to negotiate a treaty. Finally the British force reached Lhasa on August 3rd. The Lhasa Convention was signed on September 7th by both the British and the Tibetans (the Chinese amban refusing to participate).

On the 22nd of September Younghusband and his expedition left to return to India. But they did not return as heros. The invasion of Tibet had been intensely controversial, being initially conceived solely as a trade mission. News that more than a thousand Tibetans had died in the skirmishes did not go over well in London. Younghusband was accused of going above and beyond the mandate that had been given to him.

As problematic as his methods were several clauses of the Lhasa Convention that he had forced. Article seven, for example, allowed for the British occupation of the Chumbi Valley for a period of seventy-five years, which was tantamount to annexation, a move that would cause considerable international consternation. Article nine asked the Tibetans to agree to have no dealings with any foreign power whatsoever without British consent, an arrangement that undoubtedly would enrage both the Russians and the Chinese. An appended seperate article allowed for the British trade agent at Gyang-tse to visit Lhasa at will, a clause more or less creating a British Resident in Lhasa. This was something that London and Russia had agreed that neither of them would do.

Probably all would have gone well had Curzon been in India at the time. Unfortunately for Younghusband, Curzon was on an extended leave, and his replacement, in the person of Lord Ampthill, was not of a similar disposition. Whereas both Curzon and Younghusband had felt that the only way to guarantee Tibetan freedom from a Russian presence was the establishment of a permanent British influence in Lhasa, London did not agree and had said so previous to the expedition and in no uncertain terms.

The debate and confusion that raged in London and India following the Younghusband expedition eventually led to the disgrace of
Younghusband and, to a lesser extent, Lord Curzon. Unfortunately
it also resulted in the treaty of Great Britain and China, signed in Peking in April of 1906, in which all that Younghusband had gained was
thrown away and Tibet was handed over once more to Chinese control. This policy was later further strengthened by the Anglo-Russian
treaty of 1907, in which Russia agreed to Tibet's going to China in
return for British recognition of the Czar's presence in Mongolia; and
also by the Simla Convention of 1913-14, where once again misguided British politics were to tie Tibet to China.

In the "Great Game of the British Empire" it may accurately be
said that England thrice sold Tibet to China. In the beginning the
British in India chose to call Tibet a part of China in the hope of gaining favor with the Manchu Emperor and of using Tibetan soil as an
alternative trading route to the Far East; in the middle she re-sold Tibet
to China in order to validate her own colonialism of Burma and the
Indian Himalayas, and also to keep Tibet out of the Russian sphere
of interest; in the end, having invaded Tibet and rendered her help-
less she handed her over to China in order to maintain the *status quo*
and to cover up her own bungled policies.

The Thirteenth Dalai Lama seems at a very young age to have perceived the delicacy of the Tibetan predicament, and to have attempted to negotiate a middle ground between British India, Russia and
China. The path he followed was perilous, and perhaps it may be argued that it did not meet with tremendous success. However, the fact
that he never buckled under the pressure, and that he inspired his
tiny country to challenge the might of these three superpowers in Asia,
is one of the many reasons that the Tibetan's remember him as the
"Great Thirteenth."

I. A PILGRIMAGE OF CONVENIENCE

The manner in which the Great Thirteenth dealt with the British
throughout this period has been criticized by many Western scholars.
Even Sir Charles Bell, who later became a close friend to him and was
to be his main Western biographer, felt that he had made many
mistakes.

Certainly the Dalai Lama had not dealt with matters in the way the
British had hoped he would, and his ostensible stubbornness with them

precipitated the Younghusband invasion. But on the other hand, it must be admitted that the British were not particularly accomodating to the Tibetan position. With the Chefoo Convention they had insisted on dealing with Tibet as though she were a suzerain of China, and this was a platform from which the Tibetans did not wish to work. As early as 1899 the Great Thirteenth had sent a message to Calcutta (through Kazi Urgyen) stating that he was willing to open a dialogue with the British provided that it was on an equal footing and that it did not appear that he was doing so in acquiescence to Britain's Chefoo Convention with China. It may well be argued that, if any mistake was made here, it was created by the British for insisting in all their communications that Tibet accept the Anglo-Chinese pact. In the end, the British claimed that they were invading Tibet because the latter refused to accept the Trade Regulations of the Chefoo Convention, to which the Tibetans themselves had not been a signing party.

Sir Charles Bell, however, as a diplomat concerned with the preservation and expansion of the British Empire in Asia, could hardly be expected to take this view. Nor could he be expected to interpret favorably the Great Thirteenth's overtures to Russia, the principal enemy of the British in Asia. Bell writes, "The Dalai Lama was now twenty-six years old. . . . He had to some extent made good in matters of internal administration, for in that he was dealing with his own people, and their religious devotion to him carried him through. But in foreign politics he had to stand on his own two feet. His ignorance led him astray; and his impetuosity and unyielding will, which were always strong ingredients in his character, pushed him still further on the road to disaster." (Bell, 1946, page 61.)

The "disaster" to which Bell is referring is, of course, the British invasion. Somehow it never occurred to him that responsibility for this invasion should have been attributed to the British themselves and to their misguided policy.

It must also be kept in mind that the goings-on with the British were but one of many concerns of the Dalai Lama, and it did not seem at the time to be a pressing issue. While British minds were buzzing with thoughts of what to do in Tibet, life in Tibet continued to proceed at a typically casual pace. Contacts had been established with Russia; the Chinese amban in Lhasa seemed happy enough; and the British seemed to be bumbling along in India much as they had been for the last century or so. There was nothing in the Tibetan air to suggest that a few British hot-heads were secretly working toward an outright invasion. Sir Charles Bell may call the Dalai Lama impetuous, but history reveals that if anyone was impetuous at the time it was Lord Curzon and Francis Younghusband. The fact that both of them landed in trouble back in London because of their handling of the Tibet incident tends to confirm this interpretation.

It would appear that in 1903 the Dalai Lama was convinced Tibet's foreign relations were basically stable, for in the early summer of that year he entered into the *nyen-chen*, the "great retreat" that lasts for a period of three to four years.

And in all probability he had interpreted the general political atmosphere correctly, at least as far as the overall British policy was concerned. London in no way wanted to see a military invasion of Lhasa, for to do so was to risk grave consequences in her relationships with both Russia and China.

As Alastair Lamb points out, the invasion really occurred more as a freak accident of fate than anything else. The high-strung Curzon was peeved that his two letters to the Dalai Lama had been rejected; he interpreted the rejection as coming from the Dalai Lama himself, whereas in all probability neither communication ever reached the Great Thirteenth, but was intercepted and turned back somewhere along the line. Another wild card in the game was Younghusband, an immature officer eager to please Lord Curzon and to make for himself a reputation as a daring man on the field. London had only authorized him to take a small trading mission a few miles into Tibet with the objective of bringing the Tibetans to the bargaining table; these two rather headstrong statesmen took the occasion as an opportunity to launch a full scale invasion to Lhasa, with the hope of winning fame and glory for themselves.

While Younghusband sat on the borders of Tibet sending messages back and forth to Lhasa, the Thirteenth Dalai Lama was engaged in his retreat. The Tibetans, therefore, attempted to stall the British, hoping to postpone the making of any important decisions until the Dalai Lama's retreat was over. To them it was only a matter of delaying things for two or three years, when their leader would again be out and around in public; to the British the delays seemed endless and inexplicable. Younghusband wrote, "Never have I met so obdurate and obstructive a people." It seemed that his every attempt to bring discussions to a head met with delays and obstructions.

Younghusband, of course, was completely unaware of the fact that the Dalai Lama was in a closed retreat. Nor do later British writers seem to have known of it. Even Bell fails to mention the fact in his *Portrait of the Dalai Lama.* The situation may best be described as the collision of two radically different cultures: the one intensely spiritual and the other both militant and secular. Younghusband had determined to settle a trade agreement with the Tibetans by the summer of 1904; but with the Dalai Lama in a three year retreat, the Tibetans were in a state of temporary political *incommunicado.*

Fourteen months after the Great Thirteenth had entered into meditation the British left Gyang-tse and began the final stage of their invasion of Lhasa. The Tibetan Government, unsure of what course of action to follow, invoked the Ne-chung Oracle and asked his advice. The Oracle recommended that the Dalai Lama be requested to discontinue his retreat and leave for Mongolia until a settlement with the British could be achieved.

A famous Tibetan book of prophecies, *A Lamp of Prophecies Clearing Away Darkness (Lung-mun-sel-sgron-me)* states,

> There will come a [Dalai Lama] incarnation
> By the name of Tub-ten, who will be
> Born in the land of Lang [i.e., Lang-dun]...
> During his rule foreign armies will come to Tibet
> And he, the ruler, will travel to China.

Typical to its style, *A String of Wondrous Gems* provides us with a non-worldly account of the Dalai Lama's reasons for leaving the Tibetan capital at that time: "The Great Thirteenth realized that there were countless trainees in Mongolia and China in need of his attentions. Also, he had a long-standing wish to visit the holy places of the northeast, particularly the birthplace of Lama Tsong-kha-pa in Am-do and the holy Five-Peaked Mountain [i.e., Wu-tai-shan] of Manjushri in Western China. He especially wanted to spend some time on the Five-Peaked Mountain, for he felt it to be important for him to reconsecrate the site for the spiritual inspiration of future generations and as a power spot for the release of mystical energies conducive to world peace. He also realized that he was destined to rediscover several important religious treasures there that would be important to the future of Buddhism. Therefore when the British appeared at the bridge south of Lhasa he decided that the time had come for him to leave the Potala and travel to these faraway regions." (Tibetan text, page 283.)

Thus it came to pass that when Younghusband arrived in Lhasa the Dalai Lama was nowhere to be found. He had departed for Mongolia, leaving instructions with his Cabinet and the Gan-den Tri Rinpo-che to work out a treaty with the British. The tactic was an ancient one: The invaders would be placed at a distinct disadvantage by having to deal with minor officials, and if a bad treaty were agreed to it could later be repudiated on the basis that it had not been signed by the Dalai Lama himself.

One of the most intimate first-hand accounts of the Younghusband expedition comes from the pen of Edmond Candler, who had participated in the mission and relates his experiences in *The Unveiling of Lhasa* (London, 1905). Discovering the Dalai Lama gone was a distinct anticlimax. No one would even tell them anything of the Lama's whereabouts. Candler writes, "We had spies and informers everywhere, and there were men in Lhasa who would do much to please the new conquerors of Tibet. There were also witless men, who had eyes and ears, but it seems, no tongues.... For all we knew, the Dalai Lama may be still in his palace in some hidden chamber in the rock, or maybe he had never even left his customary apartments, and still performed his daily offices in the Potala.... We had been in Lhasa almost three weeks before we could discover where he had fled.... To us, at least, his flight has deepened the mystery that envelops him, and adds to his dignity and remoteness; to thousands of mystical dreamers it has preserved the effulgence of his godhead unsoiled by contact with the profane world..." (Candler, 1905, pages 255-6.)

Candler adds, "I cannot help dwelling on his flight.... To my mind, there is no picture so romantic and engrossing in modern history as that exodus, when the spiritual head of the Buddhist church, and temporal ruler of six million Tibetans, stole out of his palace by night and was borne away in his palanquin, no one knows on what errand.... A month later I followed on his track and stood on the Phembu Pass twelve miles north of Lhasa, whence one looks down on the huge belt of mountains that lie between the Brahmaputra and the desert, so packed and huddled that their crest looks like one continuous undulating plain stretching to the horizon. Looking across the valley, I could see the northern road to Mongolia winding up a feeder of the Phembu River. They had passed along here and over the next range, and across range after range, until they reached the two canonical snow-peaks that stand out of the plain beside Tengri Nor, a hundred miles to the north. For days they skirted the great lake...."

and then broke into the desert, across which they must be hurrying now toward the great mountain chain of Burkhan Buddha, on the southern limits of Mongolia.'' (Candler, 1905, pages 261-2.)

Candler's image was not far from the truth, although the Dalai Lama generally rode his horse for much of the early part of the journey (the palanquin being reserved for short outings when he was expected to give blessings to the crowds). The journey was not an easy one, being several months in duration and taking him through deserts and over many high mountain passes. The latter part of the trip was completed only in the early winter, by which time the Mongolian snows were upon him.

But it must have been very exciting both for him and for the peoples of those remote regions. News of his advent preceeded him wherever he went, and the roads were lined with devotees in search of his blessings. He stopped frequently in order to give short sermons to the people, and even though he was under the strain of considerable political upheaval never seems to have lost sight of his spiritual role. As he crossed the Chang-tang, or Northern Plains, where even the valleys are more than sixteen thousand feet in altitude, hundreds of nomadic tribes flocked to him for his blessings.

Finally after three months of hard travel he arrived in Urga (Kulon, or modern day Ulan Bator), the capital of Mongolia. More than ten thousand Mongolians stood in wait outside the city, prostrating themselves on the ground as he approached.

He was to remain in Urga for the next year, and during this time pilgrims came to him from all over Mongolia, Buryat, Siberia and the adjoining regions in order to make offerings and to receive his blessings. He also made numerous short excursions into the nearby countryside, giving teachings and initiations to the many Buddhists of the area. He celebrated the Great Prayer Festival here on the new year (February 1905), and also on the year to follow (1906), leading the prayers and giving teachings to the thousands who came.

In Urga he was the guest of the Je-tsun Dam-pa Lama, the head of Buddhism in Mongolia. Some authors (both Sir Charles Bell and W.D. Shakabpa being among them) have commented that the Je-tsun Dam-pa became jealous of the Dalai Lama due to the latter's extreme popularity with the Mongols and the tremendous reverence that he received. But there is nothing to indicate that this was really so; and in that the Dalai Lama was one of the Je-tsun Dam-pa's gurus (the latter as a child had received precepts from the former), it is unlikely.

More probably the rumor was created by British writers bitter at having allowed the Dalai Lama to escape and at the extravagant receptions accorded to him in Mongolia.

While in Urga the Dalai Lama received numerous visits from Russian diplomats, another factor that worried the British. The Czar personally sent him several presents and telegrams. The Dalai Lama's assistant tutor, the Mongolian Buryat monk Dorjieff (of whom we heard earlier), had helped arrange for his reception in Urga, and now the Dalai Lama sent him to St. Petersburg to discuss the situation with the Czar.

In 1906 the Great Thirteenth left Mongolia for Am-do and Kham Provinces of Eastern Tibet. Here he wished to visit the many monasteries that adorned the mountain ranges on the border between Tibet and China. He especially wanted to spend some time in Kum-bum Monastery, that had been built by the Third Dalai Lama at the birthplace of Lama Tsong-kha-pa, founder of the Yellow Hat School.

Two Englishmen were to witness the reception he received at Kum-bum: Lt. John Weston Brooke and the Christian missionary J. Ridley of the China Inland Mission. The former's travels have been recreated posthumously from his diary by W.N. Fergusson (*Adventure, Sport and Travel on the Tibetan Steppes*, London, 1911), which although somewhat distorted by the Christian and colonialist perception, gives us a vivid picture of the spectacle.

The pair watched the procession pass on the road, and then followed it into the town. "A crowd of horsemen drew near, surrounding a large yellow cloth-covered chair, which was carried by four horses led by four mounted Tibetans, two on each side, so that we only caught a glimpse of the occupant for a second. We followed with the crowd until we reached a large camp which was prepared for him outside of the monastery of Kum-bum. Here we found hundreds of tents, all pitched in a square, with one, a Mongol tent of rich yellow cloth, surrounded by a wall of the same material, where the Dalai Lama was to spend the night. Outside the square were crowds from many different nationalities from different parts of Asia: Mongol Princes with gaily-attired camels, bringing presents from the north; wild-looking Tibetans with matted hair hanging down their backs, riding equally wild-looking ponies, driving unyieldy yaks, thin from long travelling, perhaps from Lhasa or unknown regions in Southern Tibet; Chinese in gorgeous coloured silks; and muleteers with their galled mules."

The next day the Dalai Lama gave blessings and a sermon to the colorful crowd, and moved into a small apartment that had been prepared for him in the monastery. The Englishmen were given a private audience. Brooke's diary recalls, "He gave me a small image of Buddha. Mr. Ridley received a bundle of joss-sticks and a roll of Lhasa cloth.... The room was well-warmed, and a mysterious scent of incense pervaded the atmosphere. The Dalai Lama sat in front of us, cross-legged, on silk cushions which were placed on a table about four feet high.... His face did not show the slightest trace of expression; he greeted us with a slight forward movement of his body, but nothing like a smile ever approached his face as we conversed.... One could not help thinking that he must have trained his features to resemble the unsympathetic emptiness of the brazen images of the country.... After about half an hour's talk, which was mostly on our side, I asked if I might photograph him, but he refused. With a low bow we backed out of his presence; as we backed his features relaxed into a faint smile.... So ended our audience with the Dalai Lama, his first, I believe, with an Englishman." (Fergusson, 1911, pages 3-6.)

The Great Thirteenth remained at Kum-bum Monastery for several months, giving teachings and blessings to pilgrims and the people of the area. He also took the opportunity to make short trips into the adjoining regions, and to lead prayer gatherings in front of the mystical tree that had grown from the spot where Tsong-kha-pa's afterbirth had been buried.

While he was at Kum-bum a delegation of officials arrived from Lhasa requesting him to return to Central Tibet. An invitation also arrived from the Emperor and Empress at Peking, requesting him to visit the Chinese capital. The Russians then contacted him, advising him to return to Lhasa without visiting Peking; and the British gave him similar advice.

It should be noted here that the Dalai Lama's political predicament was extremely sensitive at this point in time. After the flight from Lhasa the Chinese Emperor had declared him deposed, and had had posters to this effect put up on the streets of Lhasa (though it is said that the Tibetans immediately took them down and smeared them with filth). The English had then attempted to set up the Pan-chen Lama as a replacement to the Dalai, but the former had declined the offer. While all this was going on, both England and China were carrying on secret discussions with one another and also with Russia on various schemes. The Dalai Lama seems to have been informed of these intrigues, and was well aware that for the moment he was in a position to do nothing other than continue with his spiritual activities and keep an eye on the developing situation.

Britain was in an awkward position again. As Parshotam Mehra points out in *Tibetan Polity, 1904-37* (Germany, 1976), she did not want to see the Dalai Lama return to Lhasa until her position there was more clearly resolved; nor did she want to see him visit China, where her intrigues with the Emperor could become an embarassment.

On Nov. 19, 1906, Sir. A. Nicolson wrote from St. Petersburg to Sir Edward Grey, informing him that the Russians were very much concerned over Chinese designs in Tibet and elsewhere in Central Asia, that Dorjieff was presently in Russia on behalf of the Dalai Lama, and that the Russian Government was monitoring the Dalai Lama's activities and was willing to provide him with a small armed escort for his return to Lhasa. (Mehra, 1976, page 15.)

Shortly afterwards Sir John Jordan, the British Minister to China, wrote to Grey, advising him that the Dalai Lama should not be allowed to visit Peking, where the weakness of his position as created by the British invasion could lead to a further and undesirable increase of Chinese power in Lhasa. It would be more in accordance with British interests, Sir John Jordan wrote, if he were to return to Lhasa directly, as "a useful counter-poise" to Chinese authority in Tibet. (Mehra, 1976, page 19.) From this and other similar correspondence between the various British offices it is obvious that the invitation from China was feared in both London and St. Petersburg, and that the British regretted their invasion of Lhasa. For although they wanted to see Tibet under China's suzerainty, they did not want to allow Peking complete control. The key word was suzerainty as opposed to sovereignty, a fine distinction but one that was becoming increasingly important in the British mind.

Of particular concern to England were the secret talks she was holding with Russian diplomats, and which eventually led to the Anglo-Russian treaty of 1907, in which London agreed to the Czar's claims in Mongolia, Turkestan and so forth, in return for Russia agreeing to England's stance on Tibet, i.e., to having Tibet set up as a buffer state between Russia and British India, under nominal Chinese administration, or suzerainty.

Now the Dalai Lama realized that both Russia and England were against his visit to China. His curiosity was aroused, and he determined to accept the Emperor's invitation.

But first he would visit Wu-tai-shan, the sacred Five-Peaked Mountain, China's holiest pilgrimage site. Here he took up residence in a temple that had been built several centuries earlier for the Fifth Dalai Lama. Politics were important, but spiritual concerns must take prominence.

For five months he remained on the Five-Peaked Mountain, immersed in prayer and meditation. And of course the throng of devoted pilgrims continued to come to him for his blessings and teachings.

A String of Wondrous Gems states that while at Wu-tai-shan he achieved many visionary experiences and performed a number of miracles.

Somewhat of note, W.W. Rockhill, the American ambassador to China who later mastered the Tibetan language and visited Lhasa, came to see him at this time, carrying greetings from President Roosevelt. Several Japanese delegations also arrived, including the Buddhist priest Sonya Otani, the Japanese ambassador Gonsuke Hayashe, and the military attache Masanoni Fufushima.

The Dalai Lama arrived in Peking in September, 1908, and was received with great ceremony. Here he stayed at the Yellow Palace, that had been built by the Ching Emperor Shun Chih for the Fifth Dalai Lama when the latter had visited Peking in 1653.

But when the Great Fifth had come he was treated as the leader of a foreign country. The Chinese Government knew that the Thirteenth was presently in a weakened position, and they planned to use this to their advantage. The Dalai Lama was told that he should *kowtow* at his audience, or bow in the manner of a visiting vassal, and that he would be given a seat lower in height that those of the Chinese rulers, again a symbol of Chinese authority over Tibet.

As Sir Charles Bell wrote of the Great Thirteenth, "Who that knew him intimately could ever forget him? There was a strong personality inside that small body, and he struggled manfully against all odds." The Dalai Lama objected to both conditions, and the audience had to be postponed. He would see the Emperor and Empress on equal terms, or he would not see them at all.

Eventually arrangements were made, and he received independent audiences with both Chinese rulers. The audiences went well, and in October he was entertained at the palace for a full week, officiating over various religious rites and leading prayers for peace in the land.

Then a most unexpected event occured. Suddenly on November 21st the Emperor passed away; and the following day the Empress followed suit. The nation was thrown into a state of shock. The Dalai Lama was asked to lead the funeral rites for both. Tibetans believe that his advice was also sought in choosing the new Emperor.

A month later the Great Thirteenth left Peking and began the long trek back to Lhasa. The journey would take him almost a year to complete, for he was expected to give sermons and initiations at every monastery along the route, and to give blessings to the crowds who lined the roads as he traveled. His *Collected Works* is filled with notes taken at discourses given on these occasions, and with small texts of advice written for the various monasteries. The two Hayagriva treatises included in the present selection of translations, and also a number of the poems, are examples of materials that grew out of these encounters.

He finally arrived at Lhasa in the middle of December, 1909, having been absent from the Potala for more than five years.

J. A SECOND FORCED PILGRIMAGE

The ancient Tibetan text *A Lamp of Prophecies Clearing Away Darkness (lung-mun-sel-sgron-ma)* reads,

> In the Year of the Male Iron Dog
> A war with China will occur.

The Tibetans believe that the Great Thirteenth was well aware of this prophecy, that he therefore had spent several months in Peking trying to deflect its fulfillment, and that he made certain to return to Lhasa before the Iron Dog Year (1910) arrived.

He originally had left Tibet because of the invasion of Sir Francis Younghusband, and in hopes of undoing the political web the British had spun around his country. Yet even though he succeeded in making known the Tibetan sentiment, the problem was a long way from being solved.

In all fairness it must be said that Sir Francis had been a kind invader, as invaders go. He was well intentioned in his mission, and was genuinely humane with the conquered Tibetans. Providing medical care to the wounded and compensating the local villagers for all food and services that he demanded of them, he left his victims with a general impression of his decency and fairness. The treaty that he struck with the Lhasa authorities would have served Tibet well, had London allowed it to stand; but unfortunately the Foreign Office undermined it two years later in the Anglo-Chinese Agreement signed at

Peking, where all that Younghusband had won for England was handed over to the Chinese, much to the chagrin of all who had intimate knowledge of the actual situation in Central Asia.

The real failure of London's policy in Tibet was its lack of consistency. The Younghusband expedition had effectively destroyed Tibet's defences, an act that perhaps would not have resulted in disaster had the British upheld their end of the bargain in the Lhasa treaty; but the new agreement signed in Peking in 1906 gave the Chinese a free hand in a now hamstrung Tibet.

Even as the Dalai Lama was returning from China the dangers began to become manifest in the form of General Chao Erh-feng, known to the Tibetans as "Butcher Chao" because of his habit of beheading all who stood in his way. The number of those he beheaded was said to reach into the tens of thousands.

Butcher Chao had begun carving away at pieces of Tibet's eastern border as early as 1905, merely a year after Younghusband's invasion. His activies steadily increased over the following years, and he decided to take the Tibetan capital shortly after the Dalai Lama's return. With Tibet stripped of its defences, the task was an easy one.

The Chinese army arrived in Lhasa on the third day of the first month of the Male Iron Dog Year, i.e., February of 1910. The ancient prophecy was made manifest. Tibet was once more prey to a foreign invader, and it was the Great Thirteenth's responsibility to come to the rescue.

The Ne-chung Oracle was again invoked. The Dalai Lama should flee to British India, he advised, and from there should work for Tibetan independence. The problem had been created by the British; it should be solved from British soil.

The Great Thirteenth's escape this time was even more dangerous and dramatic than it had been in 1904, for Lhasa was now in enemy hands and was surrounded by alien soldiers. Therefore the Dalai Lama, his chief ministers, and a small armed escort slipped out of the Potala in the dead of night, crossing the Ra-ma-gang River and heading westward.

The next day Butcher Chao learned of the flight and sent a cavalry in chase, offering a large reward to whoever would bring him "the head of the Dalai Lama."

One man stands out above all others in the events to follow: Chensel Nam-gang, a youth of peasant extract whom the Dalai Lama had taken into his bodyguard some years earlier and had cultivated as one of his main aides. When the Dalai Lama crossed the Chak-tsam Bridge and headed south toward India, Chen-sel Nam-gang remained behind with a small body of troops and for two days held off the large and highly trained Chinese forces, thus allowing the Dalai Lama time to make good his escape. This young hero then himself slipped off into the hills and followed after his master. As we shall see, Chen-sel Nam-gang was to play an important part in Tibetan history, firstly being appointed by the Dalai Lama as head of the Tibetan resistance movement in India, and later, after the Manchu Government had fallen and the Chinese had been pushed out of Tibet, becoming the famous Tsa-rng Da-zang Dra-dul, Commander-in-Chief of the Tibetan military. A separate book deserves to be written about the many glorious deeds of this wonderful hero, who so symbolizes all that was good in Old Tibet and that is good in the Tibetan character; but that must by necessity be the task of a different author than myself.

The Great Thirteenth was well received in India by the British, who were rightfully disturbed at how their Tibet policy had backfired on them. When the Dalai Lama first arrived, Sir Charles Bell was in Bhutan negotiating a treaty by which Bhutan would enter into the British Commonwealth. What a contrast the two situations must have made in the eyes of British diplomats: the one of an utterly bungled approach, and the other of a policy unquestionably successful. British hospitality was fully extended to the Dalai Lama, no doubt to a considerable extent inspired by a sense of guilt over the mess London had unwittingly made of things.

In Kalimpong the whole town came out to receive their famous and holy visitor. Hindus, Buddhists, Muslims and Christians alike lined the road to greet him.

A few days later the party was moved to Darjeeling, the summer capital of Bengal. It was to be housed here until the situation in Lhasa permitted their return.

As on the Dalai Lama's earlier trip to Mongolia and China, here again he was in a forced exile; but from outer appearances he seemed more like a sage on pilgrimage. Every day hundreds of devotees came to see him and receive his blessings, and he continued to give teachings and initiations as usual. The predicament in Tibet must have demanded much of his thought; but, as with the present Dalai Lama, the Great Thirteenth showed the ability to thoroughly compartmentalize his life, at any one moment living in that dimension expected of him. When British diplomats visited he was the diplomat; when

Tibetan ministers and resistence leaders approached him he responded as the secular chieftain; and when pilgrims and devotees came, he was the spiritual preceptor.

Shortly after the Great Thirteenth's arrival in Darjeeling he met with Sir Charles Bell, whom the British Government now placed in charge of the Tibetan dignitary's care. Over the years to follow, this sensitive and kind Englishman, who years earlier had acquired a flawless command of the Tibetan language, was to become the Dalai Lama's closest British friend. He was also to serve as one of the most important Western spokesmen for Tibet in those early days of "Tibetology," authoring half a dozen books on Tibetan culture.

Sir Charles arranged for the Dalai Lama to be settled in a vacant English mansion outside the town, and his ministers in a townhouse. The accomodations were simple enough, but adequate to the purpose. The British Government also provided a small grant for the provision of their new guests.

In March the Viceroy Lord Minto invited the Dalai Lama to Calcutta, where he was accorded a twenty-one gun salute. The Foreign Office, however, had ruled that England was to remain neutral in Tibet's conflict with China, and thus Lord Minto was in a position to do nothing more than grant hospitality and moral encouragement to the refugees, whose task it was to effect the liberation of their homeland.

The Dalai Lama therefore appealed to the Czar to come to Tibet's aid. Again, the reply was polite but negative; Russia's treaties with Britain did not permit her to intervene in Tibetan affairs.

As Sir Charles Bell points out, throughout this rather trying ordeal the Dalai Lama continued his religious practices and meditations as usual. Anyone passing near his house in the morning or evening would hear him chanting his prayers, to the accompaniment of his small handdrum and bell. And often when he traveled in India he would miss his meals rather than interrupt his meditations.

The departure of the Dalai Lama from Lhasa and his exile in Darjeeling caused severe problems for the Chinese in Tibet, who would have far preferred to use him as a puppet in their designs or to dispose of him altogether. As the latter course of action was now out of the question, they made overtures to him to return and take up office under Chinese supervision. A Manchu official with a letter to this effect arrived in India in September of 1910.

The Dalai Lama sent a stern reply to the amban: "I received your message asking me to return to Lhasa to help you in your administration of our country. . . . In the past the Manchu emperors had always shown great care for the welfare of the successive Dalai Lamas, and the Dalai Lamas had reciprocated these feelings of friendship. We always had each other's best interests at heart. . . . But now the situation has changed drastically. . . . Many Chinese troops were recently sent into Tibet, oppressing the people and the monasteries to such an extent that requests came to me from every quarter to give my permission for violent resistance. I refused this permission, feeling that it would be best first to attempt to work out a peaceful settlement. With this in mind, and at great personal hardship, I came to the Tibetan frontier and prepared to negotiate. But then many Chinese troops were sent after me to bring me back dead or alive. . . . Meanwhile back in Tibet many peaceloving people have been killed or illegally imprisoned. . . . It appears that the Emperor himself has stood behind all of this on the advice of the amban, without any considerations whatsoever for Tibetan independence or the ancient religious connection between our two countries. . . . Therefore I feel that there is no longer any point in talk. . . . It is not possible for Tibet and China to have the same relationship as before.'' (Shakabpa, 1967, pages 234-237.)

In March of the new year (1911) the Dalai Lama and his party took the opportunity to make pilgrimage to the four places in India that are holy to all Buddhists: where the Buddha had been born, where he had achieved his enlightenment, where he had delivered his first teaching, and where he had passed away. In each of these locations the Great Thirteenth meditated and engaged in intensive prayer. His visit to and re-consecration of these sites was to revive the interest of the many Himalayan Buddhists in them, giving them a new lease on life. It is interesting to note that the present Dalai Lama in many ways has continued the work that was then initiated by the Thirteenth, and that the revival of the Indian Buddhist pilgrimage places has to a large extent been due to these two incarnations.

Tibetans believe that the Patron/Priest arrangement that China had enjoyed with the Tibetan lamas over the past two centuries had provided her with much of the karmic fortune required for her peace and stability. Thus when the Great Thirteenth was in Peking and the Emperor and Empress had abused their patron role by trying to pressure him politically, it was no coincidence that they both passed away even while he was still in the city. They had destroyed the root of merit sustaining their positions; the karmic repercussions manifested almost instantly in their deaths.

But the Chinese error did not end there, for the new rulers almost immediately invaded Tibet in the hope of making it into a province of China. The entire Manchu Dynasty had now undermined its base of merit. The karmic result was the revolution of 1911, that broke out in China while the Dalai Lama was in exile in India. In November Manchu rule came to an end, replaced by Sun Yat-sen and his Nationalist Party. Butcher Chao was recalled from Szechuan and suffered death by beheading, the gruesome punishment he had inflicted on so many of his own victims. The wheel of fate had turned full circle.

When the Great Thirteenth heard news of the growing strength of the Chinese revolution he sent Chen-sel Nam-gang, the hero of Chak-tsam Bridge, back to Tibet to lead the underground forces. The tactic worked well. All over Tibet the Chinese garrisons were uprooted, until only the main army in Lhasa remained.

In June of 1912 the Great Thirteenth left Kalimpong for Tibet, having once again outlived the temporary successes of his enemies.

An anecdote told to me by a British friend seems relevant at this point. In the late 1970s my friend was traveling through the Tibetan refugee monasteries in India doing research for some documentary films on which he was working. His search led him to Gan-den Monastery, where he hoped to interview Zong Rin-po-che, an elderly lama famous for his immense knowledge and mystical personality. The interview was immediately granted, and Zong Rin-po-che provided a most unexpected explanation for his show of hospitality: "When the Great Thirteenth came to India (in 1910) I was in his entourage as a young disciple, being six years of age at the time. When I arrived in India I had an eye cataract; this ailment was brought to the attention of an English doctor in Darjeeling, who cured it for me. At the time we were in India as refugees fleeing a Chinese invasion; after I got my sight back, we managed to regain our country from the Chinese. Now I am an old man, again in India as a refugee fleeing a Chinese invasion. To me, the Englishman curing my eye problem symbolizes that it will be the British who are instrumental in our getting back our country. Therefore whenever a Britisher comes to see me I always treat him as best I can."

Zong Rin-po-che had said this with a mischevious smile on his lips. But there could certainly be some truth to it. If the Great Thirteenth had succeeded at anything in his struggles with Britain, Russia and

China, it was to make clear to everyone at a very early stage of modern history Tibet's interpretation of her own status. The British may sign secret treaties with Russia and China declaring China's "special interests" in Tibet; but he would tell one and all that Tibet was Tibet, and the property of no one but the Tibetans. Once again he had driven home his point.

K. AN IMPERFECT SOLUTION

In June of 1912 the Dalai Lama and his entourage crossed the border back into Tibet; but it was not possible for him to enter Lhasa yet. The Chinese were on the retreat, but there was considerable cleaning up to be done, and he wanted to oversee the final stages of this himself. In addition, he wanted to insure that bloodshed was kept to a minimum; the British had requested him to see that none of the Chinese leaders in Tibet who surrendered were executed by the Tibetans, and only his immediate presence could ensure against the occurrence of excesses. Finally, he wanted to be certain that the Tibetan forces did not let up before the job was complete; the policies and responses of the new Chinese rulers were still an unknown factor, and he wanted to see all Chinese out of Tibet before Peking's Nationalists had consolidated their power in China.

Back in Lhasa the Hero of Chak-tsam Bridge was successfully implementing the Great Thirteenth's policies. The final pocket of Chinese resistance was driven into a corner of Lhasa, where it could hold out for some time but could not pose a threat. Eventually it too surrendered, and the war was at an end.

To add insult to injury, the Great Thirteenth had all Chinese prisoners marched to India and handed over to the British, rather than have them transported directly to China by the overland route. Possibly the Dalai Lama's motivation here was one of compassion for the unfortunate soldiers, for many of those whom the British later shipped back to China were executed by their new rulers.

In January of 1913 the Dalai Lama finally returned to Lhasa. The entire city turned out to greet him and rejoice in the success of his adventures.

On the eighth day of the first month of the new year the Great Thirteenth issued his famous Declaration of Independence, with its five essential clauses defining Tibet's new direction. He wrote, "From the time of Genghis Khan and Altan Khan of the Mongols, the Ming Dynasty of the Chinese, and the Ching Dynasty of the Manchus, Tibet and China cooperated on the basis of the Patron/Priest relationship. But a few years ago the Chinese authorities in Szechuan and Yunnan provinces, using the pretext of policing the trade marts, sent large numbers of troops into our country and attempted to colonize us. Therefore I left Lhasa, taking my ministers with me, and hoped to set straight in the Emperor's mind that our relationship was and always had been one of Patron/Priest, and not one of the subordination of one by the other.... However, his reply was obstructed by corrupt Peking officials, and in the process of our dialogue the Manchu Dynasty collapsed. The Tibetans were encouraged by the turn of events, and expelled the Chinese from Central Tibet, and I returned safely to my sacred homeland. All that remains now is to drive out a few more Chinese troops from the eastern border areas, and the Chinese intent of colonizing Tibet will have faded like a rainbow in the sky." (Shakabpa, 1967, pages 246-248.)

The Great Thirteenth then went on to outline the five principal policies to be implemented in the immediate future: (1) everyone should strive to preserve Tibet's cultural traditions through rebuilding any of the institutions and monuments that had been destroyed by the recent period of conflict; (2) the various religious traditions should respect one another, and should look more to the maintenance of their spiritual and educational traditions and less to politics and business enterprises; (3) the civil and military government officials should act with fairness and justice toward all citizens, and should improve their human rights records. In particular, capital punishment was to be abolished in all parts of the country, as were all forms of harsh physical punishment of criminals; (4) more thought and effort must be given to the issue of national defense, "for although the Tibetans are a religious and independently minded people, safeguards must be put in place to ensure national survival"; and (5) the traditional methods of land distribution and taxation must be revised, and more modern social forms introduced.

A month after the Great Thirteenth's issuing of this declaration, Tibet and Mongolia signed an agreement recognizing one another's independence from China.

The Dalai Lama's next step was to attempt to bring the Chinese to the negotiating table, with the British as intermediaries. This took the form of the Simla Convention of 1913-14. Here he sent the Minister Shatra to negotiate for Tibet; Britain sent Sir Charles Bell and Sir Henry McMahon; and the Chinese sent Ivan Chen.

Shatra informed Bell that the Dalai Lama wanted four conditions to be met: Tibet was to manage her own internal affairs; she should also have control over her external affairs, although important issues could be decided in reference to Great Britain; no Chinese ambam, officials or soldiers would be stationed in Tibet; and Tibet's territory on the east would include the areas up to Tachienlu.

While in India the Dalai Lama had gained an understanding of the British love for legalities. Therefore the Tibetans went to the conference with extensive documentation in support of their claims, including all the old treaties that had been signed with China and other Asian countries, numerous tax records from disputed areas, documents of Lhasan appointments of officials in disputed areas, and so forth. In total they brought fifty-six thick volumes of legal documents. The Chinese came with very little other than verbal claims.

The British were in a difficult position. All legal evidence was on the side of the Tibetans; and, in addition, the Chinese had been expelled from Tibetan territories. But McMahon did not want to antagonize the new Chinese rulers. Thus the Tibetans were asked to accept a deal similar to that created by the imperialist powers in Mongolia: there would be two Tibets, one Outer and the other Inner.

The former, which would include all of western, southern and central Tibet, as well as much of the eastern provinces of Kham and Amdo, would be completely autonomous, though under the suzerainty of China. China would not be allowed to interfere with the internal administration of this region, which would remain under the Dalai Lama's direct rule; nor would China be allowed to send any troops into Outer Tibet, other than an ambassador and his private escort, which was not to exceed more than three hundred soldiers.

The arrangement did not please anyone. It was far less than the Dalai Lama had expected, and he did not at all like the idea of "two Tibets." Nor did he trust the provision allowing China special status; he had hoped that if a favored status as regards Tibet were given to anyone, it would be to either the British or Russians. Perhaps in her position as mediator in the discussions Britain did not feel it would be appropriate for her to be awarded this privilege; and she certainly was not about to see it be granted to Russia. The wording of the agreement was also alien to the Chinese, who therefore refused to sign it. In the end McMahon lost patience with them, and the treaty was signed bilaterally by Britain and Tibet, with the stipulation that China would not be privy to any benefits of the document until she added her signature to it (which in fact she never did).

It is sad to note here that one of the reasons the Tibetans agreed to endorse the Simla Convention and did not press more forcefully for the four conditions that the Great Thirteenth had stipulated, particularly those that defined Tibet's relationship with China, was the persuasive influence of Sir Charles Bell. The high regard which the Tibetans held for Sir Charles, and his friendship with the Dalai Lama, acted as factors that won the Tibetan negotiators over to McMahon's vision. No doubt Sir Charles played his part in good conscience, feeling that the deal was reasonable to the Tibetans; but he had a distinct conflict of interest, for his job primarily was to sell the British blueprint, and not to advise the Tibetans on what was best for them. The Tibetans did not fully understand this, and took his advice as being solely that of a friend of Tibet. Events in future years were to prove his influence at Simla to be most unfortunate, for the status given to Tibet at Simla was to keep her out of the League of Nations, and, later on, out of the United Nations. As a mere "autonomous region" she would not be allowed into these important international bodies. Of course at the time Sir Charles could not have forseen this problem, for no international tribunal of this nature had ever before existed; but the Great Thirteenth sensed the dangers inherent in the agreement, and was furious at the British for having forced it upon his representatives. He had just spent several years extracting his country from the Chinese noose; to have it handed back on a platter to them did not please him.

In the end the Simla Convention was just one more confusing event in Britain's ambiguous treaties with and about Tibet. Here McMahon had insisted that Tibet sign a treaty acknowledging herself as "an autonomous region of China"; but by signing the document directly with Tibet without Chinese consent, the legal implication was that Britain recognized Tibet as an independent nation with the authority to sign its own international agreements. For the third time, Britain had put her signature on a treaty with Tibet without the presence of China, although it was Britain herself who was pressing Tibet so hard to accept the concept of Chinese suzerainty.

But treaty or no treaty, the Dalai Lama was not having any Chinese diplomats or troops in his country; and because China had not signed the Simla Convention she could not call on the British to lobby for the right to do so. Thus from the time of the Great Thirteenth's declaration of independence in 1913 until after his death in 1933, no Chinese officials were allowed to live on Tibetan soil. Chinese individuals who had married Tibetans had their choice of adopting Tibetan nationality or leaving the country.

For the remainder of his life the Great Thirteenth continued to attempt to get Tibet's independent status accepted by the international community; yet even though he managed to keep all Chinese out of his country, nobody would listen to his plea. The jurisdiction was that of Britain, and Britain was too concerned with the struggle to maintain her rapidly disintegrating empire to cause waves over what to her was not a pressing issue.

Some years later Sir Charles Bell realized the gravity of the position he had influenced his Tibetan friends to accept at Simla. He commented bitterly, "Britain, while professing friendship [with Tibet], seems always to refuse assistance." Over the years that followed, he attempted to rectify his error by slowly changing Whitehall's attitude, firstly by his visit to Lhasa in 1920-21 and the subsequent British agreement to sell arms to Tibet; and then in 1930 by lobbying outright for recognition of Tibet's independence on the grounds that no Chinese official had been permitted in Tibet for over twenty-five years, and that the Chinese themselves had refused to endorse the Simla Convention and therefore were not legally in a position to claim any benefits from it. He suggested that Asia would in the future be far more secure if Tibet were established as an independent buffer state between India and China. Unfortunately the timing of his petition was bad, and met with no success.

L. A PERIOD OF HEALING AND REVIVAL

Of the five clauses attached to the Great Thirteenth's declaration of independence, the fourth (and perhaps most important) focussed on national defence.

From his childhood the Dalai Lama had demonstrated a strong interest in developing the military. Even as early as the mid-1880s he had begun to realize that Tibet's independence would never be secure until she was able to defend herself. The traditional arrangement of Patron/Priest, in which the former was expected to see to the security of the latter, may have worked well enough in the olden days of loose and informal foreign contracts; but it was not suited to the bureaucratic mentality of the twentieth century.

Perhaps the Simla Convention more than anything else had driven this idea home. It had become obvious that neither Britain nor Russia would do anything for Tibet, and that if China were to be kept out it would have to be by Tibet's own efforts.

Therefore not long after returning to Lhasa the Great Thirteenth arranged for an overhaul of the army, with the Hero of Chak-tsam Bridge, who now had been renamed Tsa-rong, as the Commander-in-Chief.

In Tibetan eyes the world's three most powerful nations were Russia, Britain and Japan, all of whom had had successful military encounters with China. The Great Thirteenth therefore arranged for each of these powers to train a Tibetan regiment. At the conclusion of the training period the three regiments had to demonstrate how well they could perform. It is said that the soldiers trained by the Japanese advisor Yasujiro Yajima most deeply impressed the Lhasa authorities, and that it was therefore decided to have the Tibetan military run along Japanese lines.

The decision could also have been linked to the fact that the various treaties Russia and Britain had signed with each other (and with the Chinese) placed them both in an unpredictable political stance as regards Tibet; they may help clandestinely, but neither could be counted on under pressure. Also, neither Britain nor Russia would supply her with armaments, whereas Japanese wares could easily be acquired via Mongolia. Finally, Japan had had several military incidents with both China and Russia, from which the Japanese had emerged victorious. Tibet's new international direction thus began to move toward Japan.

This was the case until a year or so after the Dalai Lama entered his great retreat, when pro-British forces in Lhasa used his absence to replace the Japanese with a British orientation. From then on the military followed British training methods. The transition was completed in 1920, when Sir Charles Bell officially visited Lhasa and managed to implement an arrangement with the British that would include the limited supply of armaments.

The period from 1913 to 1916 saw the Great Thirteenth busily engaged in revitalizing Tibet's cultural and spiritual institutions. He had been out of the country as a leader in exile for almost eight years because of the British and Chinese invasions, and there was much to be done. The monastic communities had to be revived and their educational facilities upgraded, as did those of the medical colleges and hospitals. The various schools of performing arts had to be seen to, and the fine arts stimulated. Then the political institutions, which for five years had been run by the Chinese invaders, had to be over-hauled; and, as mentioned above, the military had to be built up. In brief, a country had to be reconstructed from the ruins of the old.

It appears that by the spring of 1916 the Great Thirteenth felt that things had once more been set in order, for during the fourth month (June) of that year he temporarily retired from public life and entered into his great retreat, which was to last until the autumn of 1920. No doubt for him this was a welcomed period of inner peace and spiritual resuscitation; he had been under intense pressure for more than a decade, and the opportunity to do nothing but sit and meditate must have been tremendously uplifting.

After completing his retreat he once more dedicated himself thoroughly to the spiritual and cultural affairs of the country. As Sir Charles Bell points out, his work load was immense, and seemed to touch all aspects of Tibetan life.

One of the principal reasons for the greatness which the Tibetan people attribute to the Thirteenth Dalai Lama, and one of the causes of the love with which they remember him, is the manner in which he dealt with anyone who showed corruption or vanity. His courage in the face of the British and Chinese military forces proved him a man of independent spirit and insightful perception; but it was in his dealings with his own people that his personality shone most brightly.

An example reflecting his strong character in this regard is the manner in which he restructured the administration of the Great Prayer Festival of Lhasa, Tibet's largest national celebration. Traditionally the policing of Lhasa was handed over to two monk officials for the duration of this festival; this policing contract was awarded on a bidding system, with the winner of the concession being given the right to collect fines for any violations that occurred during the festival. The result was that whoever received the contract would attempt to fine whomever they could for as much as possible for the most insignificant infraction. It was a race with time; a set amount had been paid for the privilege of policing the city, and there was an opportunity to collect a fortune in fines during that brief period.

The original idea had been good enough. The festival was largely a gathering of monks—some fifty thousand of them—so it was only logical that it should be policed by monks. But over the centuries the emphasis changed from that of keeping the monks in line to that of harassing the Lhasan townspeople into paying indiscriminate fines for fabricated offenses. As a result, almost all laypeople deserted the city during the festival and went to visit relatives or friends in the country, often returning only to discover that their homes had been looted in their absence.

The Great Thirteenth stripped the festival magistrates of this power, making their position purely ceremonial. He arranged that, rather than have the concession awarded by a bidding system, each of the principal monasteries should send him the names of two monks, from which he would choose those to serve.

Tibetans like to tell the story of when he called in the monk administrators and let them know of the new plan. "But the tradition was established by the Fifth Dalai Lama himself," they argued. "And who is the Fifth Dalai Lama today?" was his reply. For indeed, according to Tibetan belief he was the officially recognized reincarnation of the Great Fifth. Because of his intervention the festival once more became an occasion of joy and celebration, and the lay people again began to attend it. In fact, one of the principal deeds of the Great Thirteenth was his revival of this festival. Throughout the later years of his life he always presided over it, and his presence gave it a sanctity it had not enjoyed since the days of the early Dalai Lamas.

Another popular story is his treatment of Se-ra Monastery when he learned that the Se-ra treasurers had been following questionable practices in the handling of monastic finances. It is said that a farm village had borrowed some money from Lower Se-ra, but when the time came to repay the loan it was unable to do so. Some monks from the monastery went to the village to forcibly collect, and when they were unsuccessful they instead seized various possessions as collateral. The farmers appealed directly to the Dalai Lama, whereupon he had the matter investigated. Later he summoned the abbots of the three departments of Se-ra and kept them standing in his antechamber for two full days before giving them an audience. He then fined them heavily, and warned that if in the future he ever again heard of such happenings they would be dismissed from their posts.

He was no less forthright with the aristocracy. This is well illustrated by the life of the Hero of Chak-tsam Bridge, who due to his personal talents surpassed any of the noblemen of the day and became one of the most influential men in the Dalai Lama's government. A similar case is that of the monk Kun-pel-la, a peasant by birth whom the Dalai Lama cultivated as his principal aide, and who also became one of the most powerful men in the land. These and other such events made the Great Thirteenth into a champion of the ordinary person and a symbol of mobility in Tibetan society.

Another pertinent story emerges from out of the Dalai Lama's efforts to publish the *Kan-gyur*, the Tibetan scriptural collection in one hundred and eight volumes containing the sutras and tantras ascribed to Lord Buddha. The project was extensive, for Tibetan printing is done by woodblocks, each of which must be individually carved by hand. The complete project would require the carving of approximately a hundred thousand blocks. Merely the editing work demanded the participation of several master scholars.

A problem arose during the printing. There are a number of conflicting interpretations of the philosophical doctrines contained in certain of the scriptures due to the ambiguity of some of the passages, ambiguities that Tibetan scholars traditionally have praised as contributing to the richness and non-dogmatic nature of Buddhist philosophy. But part way through the project the Dalai Lama discovered that the chief editor, Je She-rab Gya-tso, was rewriting some of the controversial passages so as to make them more closely agree with the viewpoint of his own monastery, Drepung Go-mang. There were also a number of contested scriptures accepted by the Nying-ma School but which Je She-rab Gya-tso did not personally regard as being the word of Buddha, and which he therefore attempted to omit altogether.

The Dalai Lama was furious, and dismissed him from the prestigious position of editor-in-chief. He had all of Je She-rab Gya-tso's work rechecked, and did the remainder of the editing himself.

Another important work of the Great Thirteenth's was his restoration of Tibet's oldest temples and monasteries, including the Jo-khang, the Ra-mo-che, and Sam-ye Monastery. The wall paintings in many of these were more than a thousand years old, and were badly in need of repair. Some of the more superstitious Tibetans objected to the restoration on the grounds that it required removing the old paint, which meant the temporary destruction of the consecrated images. The Dalai Lama mentions this criticism several times in his public sermons at the Great Prayer Festival, and scolds his people for holding such superstitious views. One year he commented, " It is rather sad that, when Buddha himself so strongly advocated the use of reason and the logical mind, so many of our people seem to still be stuck in the mire of superstition and primitive thinking." But he was not daunted, and the various restoration projects continued without interruption.

Tibetans also love to tell of how strict he was with his weather lamas, whose job it was to remain high on the mountains around Lhasa, making rain when rain was needed, and stopping hail when the crops and flowers were ripe and in bloom. His weather lamas were the best in the country, so they were generally successful in their rituals; but when they failed, the Great Thirteenth would call them to account. If after consideration he decided that the failure was not due to lack of effort on their part there was no punishment. But on one occasion after an unexpected hailstorm he learned that his four weather lamas had not been at their posts on the mountain when the storm had begun to form. He had them brought to his courtyard and whipped.

As Tak-tser Rin-po-che mentions in the Foreword to the present volume, the Great Thirteenth is also lovingly remembered for his effort to upgrade and standardize the examination process for those who would stand for the *ge-she* degree. It was rumored that corruption and bribery had crept into the process of obtaining this most coveted diploma, and that some who were allowed to enter the final tests were unfit. As the final examination was oral, and for ordinary monks took place on an open courtyard in the company of many other candidates, it was possible for an unqualified candidate to slip through without really being tested. This was because the most intensive tests were supposed to take place back in the individual monasteries, with each monastery sending only its top applicants for the public debates at the Great Prayer Festival. The Dalai Lama implemented a much more rigid screening process, so that unqualified candidates could not appear. He himself, together with his tutors and several carefully selected high lamas, then supervised the final stages of the testing.

Nor did he permit those who had attained the ge-she degree to rest on their reputations. It is said that he kept a close eye on all the top lamas, and often called them individually to debate with him, and to check up on what they were doing with their knowledge.

The Great Thirteenth's contribution to the Tibetan medical tradition was no less significant. He upgraded the training and testing of medical students in the two principal medical colleges at Lhasa, and revised the system of national "medicare" that the Great Fifth Dalai Lama had installed several centuries earlier. According to the new plan, the various districts of the country would send medical students to the Lhasa colleges for their final training, after which they would be returned to their native districts to set up clinics. The "medicare" system worked on a simple and straightforward basis: anyone who could not pay for treatment simply said so, and was then treated free of charge. Many hospitals operated on a dual schedule; those who could pay for their treatment should come in the morning, and those who couldn't pay should come in the afternoon. Because Tibet was a sparsely populated country, this "honor system" approach seems to have worked reasonably well.

Amidst all of these activities the Great Thirteenth lived a quiet but busy life. Every day he would rise long before sunrise and perform several hours of meditation. After breakfast he would personally carry out his correspondence with those who wrote to him from around the country. Many letters also came to him from the various Mongolian countries, as well as from India and China. Most of these requested private spiritual advice, his prayers for someone who had died, names and blessings for newborn children, and so forth. Some were from intimate disciples, others from distant devotees. He gave each his personal attention.

After lunch he would generally paint or meditate for an hour or so, before embarking on the long series of private and governmental audiences that would comprise the afternoon. On some days this would include meetings with his ministers or the parliament; on others he would be expected to give individual blessings or teachings to large groups who had come to see him. The various committees in charge of the numerous projects he had initiated would also report to him at this time.

It is said that he loved to garden for an hour or so in the early evenings, and to take a walk in the Nor-bu Ling-ka park at sunset. He would then retire to his chambers, to write or meditate, or to join his private monastery Nam-gyal Dra-tsang in prayers and rituals. The many compositions attributed to him were generally penned at this time of the day.

Sleep would not come until almost midnight; and it is said that when he was in the middle of giving an initiation ritual or teaching that required several days or weeks to complete, often he would sit up in meditation all night.

One of the more exhausting tasks required of him must have been that of giving group blessings. This could involve receiving a complete tribe of nomads from some part of the country, or from Mongolia or India. It could also involve receiving a complete monastery or nunnery. As Sir Charles Bell records, even if it were a group of ten or twenty thousand people he would be expected to bless each person individually. The crowd would pass before him in single file, and he would either place his hands on the head of each devotee in turn, or touch the devotee's head with his tasselled wand. This would be punctuated by brief vocal interchanges, in which he would ask a question of someone in the group, or someone would ask a brief question of him. With lay people the request was often for a name for a baby, or a sacred medicine pill, or a blessing to cure some illness. With monks and nuns it was more often a request to attend some initiation or teaching he was about to give, or for his blessings for a meditation retreat on which they were about to embark.

Tibetans also like to speak of the miraculous powers and psychic abilities of the Great Thirteenth. Generally a monk is not allowed to openly display these qualities; but sometimes even a Dalai Lama will slip in this regard. It is said that once when presiding over the Great Prayer Festival he noticed some monks performing their rites incorrectly. He immediately stood up in disgust and stamped his foot to draw their attention back to the ritual. An impression of his foot was left in the solid stone on the verandah of the Jo-khang Temple for all to see; it was more than a centimeter in depth and was perfectly shaped to the contours of his foot.

Another important function of every adult Dalai Lama is participation in the process of the discovery and certification of new reincarnate lamas. Whenever a high lama dies a committee is formed to search for the reincarnation. Often the Dalai Lama will be approached for clues as to where to begin the search. Some Dalai Lamas have shown a greater talent in this work than others, but it is said that the Great Thirteenth was amongst the best. From the time he reached maturity he played an instrumental role in the discovery of many of the incarnates who required "finding," including the reincarnations of his senior tutor Pur-chok-pa (who later became his chief disciple and biographer), his assistant tutor Ling Rin-po-che (who later became the senior tutor to the present Dalai Lama), and Ra-deng Rin-po-che (who after the Great Thirteenth's death became the Regent of Tibet).

For example, when the search for the reincarnation of the high lama of Ra-deng Monastery began, the committee first came to the Dalai Lama for advice. He watched his dreams for a few days, and then sent them a letter describing the landscape of the area, the direction from Lhasa, and the first names of the mother and father (neither of whom he had ever met). The information led the committee to the correct area, and eventually to the discovery of the incarnation.

In later years the Great Thirteenth showed a special fondness for this incarnation. He would often visit Ra-deng Monastery for a few weeks at a time, retreating to solitary meditation in a small house in the juniper forest above the temple complex. He gave many private initiations and teachings to the young lama, and carefully watched over his spiritual growth. Then a year before he died he gave the Ra-deng Rin-po-che his personal divination box, commenting that in the future he may need it to help decide matters of state. Later the Ra-deng Lama became one of the most important figures responsible for the discovery of the new Dalai Lama incarnation.

Indeed, after the Great Thirteenth passed away the dangerous job of serving as Regent was unexpectedly given to the reincarnate of Ra-deng. The decision was made by the cabinet and by a drawing of lots of the names of the various candidates that had been put forth.

The Tibetans regard this act of giving the divination box as a sign of the clairvoyance of the Great Thirteenth, for at the time there was no other way that he could have known that the Ra-deng Rin-po-che would be chosen to serve as Regent.

An important duty of every Dalai Lama is the ordination of those who want to embark on the religious life. Each person ordained by a lama will also receive a monastic name from him. The name is usually in two parts, the first being the first name of the ordaining lama and the second being specific to each individual. Because the Great Thirteenth's first name was Tub-ten, and he ordained thousands of monks and nuns, this became one of the most common names in monasteries throughout Central Asia in the early part of this century. In turn, each of these ordained monks and nuns later helped in the naming of the new babies in their own communities, also giving their own first name as the first name of the child. Because of the Great Thirteenth's tremendous popularity, the next best thing to meeting him was to receive a name from him or from someone whom he had ordained. In this way the name Tub-ten spread until it became the most widely used in the land.

But of all the things for which the Great Thirteenth is most fondly remembered, the most warmly recollected is his fiery temperament combined with his sense of justice and fair play. Almost all Westerners who met him commented on how dynamic and aggressive he was in his dealings with his own people. Some mistook this forcefulness as representing fits of bad temper, but those who knew him well saw it as a skillful means of effectively motivating a conservative and slow-moving society. Tibetans regard the line of Dalai Lamas as generally being incarnations of Avalokiteshvara, the Bodhisattva of Compassion; but in expression each of them embodies whichever of the three essential Bodhisattvas is most appropriate to the times: Avalokiteshvara, whose nature is compassion; Manjushri, embodiment of wisdom; and Vajrapani, who embodies power and wrath. In general the Great Thirteenth was the incarnation of Avalokiteshvara, the Bodhisattva of Compassion; but his mode of expression reflected the nature of Vajrapani, the Bodhisattva of Wrathful Activities.

We in the West tend to think of the Dalai Lamas as being remote figures locked away in the Potala, a combination of king and prisoner. But the Tibetans think of them as being far more resourceful and adventurous. When I was researching the present work in India in 1986, Ar-tsa Tul-ku told me that Tibetans believe the Thirteenth Dalai Lama would often don the dress of a nomad or farmer, and roam the streets of Lhasa in disguise in order to pick up gossip and learn the views of the ordinary people concerning the workings of his government officials. Whenever he would hear of corruption, he would immediately call the guilty parties to his court and question them on it, or would send his personal task force to investigate. It seemed that nothing could be done without his coming to know of it. And when there was evil or injustice afoot he seemed to be the first to learn of it, and to counteract it with force.

So widespread became this belief that the women of Lhasa used to sing a song,

> The Great Thirteenth is everywhere,
> And it seems that nothing escapes his eye.
> For his justice strikes like lightning,
> And his word resounds like thunder in the sky.

M. WRITTEN WORKS OF THE GREAT THIRTEENTH

Perhaps because of the colossal impact of his activities as a statesman, orator, religious teacher and social leader, the Thirteenth Dalai Lama is not particularly thought of as a important writer. His other activities seemed to totally eclipse this aspect of his life. Moreover, he did not compose standard monastic textbooks, a pastime to which most Tibetan authors were completely addicted, and the only form of literature that many Tibetans read; instead he turned his pen to whatsoever caught his fancy and seemed meaningful.

Yet he indeed was a talented author, and from amongst his previous incarnations only the First, Third, Fifth and Seventh match his literary output in both quality and quantity. And like so many writers, it is possible that his literary grandeur will not be appreciated by the general public until several generations after his death.

His *Sung-bum*, or *Complete Collected Works*, was printed in Tibet not long after his passing. More recently it has been republished in India by modern offset (from the original Tibetan woodblock prints) by Dr. Lokesh Chandra and his International Academy of Indian Culture (Sata-pitaka Series, 1981, Vol. 283-289).

The *Sung-bum* is arranged into seven volumes and comprises several hundred titles. The Tibetan compilers collected many of the shorter titles into anthologies, thus rendering the materials more accessible.

Vol. I contains three texts: a biography of his principal spiritual teacher Pur-chok-pa Jam-pa Gya-tso, which is approximately three hundred pages in length; his account of the building of the mausoleum for this same guru; and a detailed biography that he wrote on another of his gurus, the Red Hat incarnate lama Je Zha-mar Gendun Ten-dzin Gya-tso.

Thus this section of his *Collected Works* is quite personal, dealing with the lives of two of his most intimate teachers.

Vol. II, approximately eight hundred pages long, is mainly comprised of his "Sermons at the Great Prayer Festival," and of his tantric writings on various mandala meditations.

The full title of the collection of sermons is "Various Oral Discourses, including those given on the occasion of the Jataka Readings during the Great Prayer Festival at Lhasa and also at Kum-bum Monastery." There are approximately two dozen entries in this collection, from which I have translated the last eleven for the present volume.

The styles of the individual sermons vary considerably. They were created from notes taken during oral discourses, and different scribes seem to have been used on the various occasions. Of the eleven I have translated, it would seem that two different scribes were used: one for the first three of the discourses (i.e., the Water Dog to Wood Mouse Years), and another for the remaining seven.

I chose these particular discourses because they follow a distinct continuity from one year to the next. They cover the period beginning with the Great Prayer Festival a year and a half after the Dalai Lama completed his "great retreat", up to the final discourse on the year of his death. As a set they form a mosaic presenting a complete picture of the Great Thirteenth's spiritual vision. Moreover, because they were created from notes taken during his oral teachings they more strongly reflect his public personality than do many of his more formal writings. Tibetan literature tends to be quite formal, whereas Tibetan oratory is much more free. And because the Great Thirteenth was heard more than he was read, these sermons very much represent the impression he would have made upon the average Tibetan. The remaining works in vol. II, which include more than a dozen titles, are largely tantric in nature. The principal texts here are his commentaries to the tradition of meditation on the complex mandala known as the "Sixteen Ka-dam-pa Heartdrops," his *sadhana* for meditation on the mandala of Kurukulla, various Avalokiteshvara practices, longevity meditations, and other texts of this nature related to mandala divinities such as Kalachakra, Vajrabhairava, Hayagriva (two texts of which are included in this volume in English translation), Vajrakilaya, various Dharmapalas, and so forth.

Vol. III is mainly composed of minor liturgical works. Here we find the various prayers to be read in conjunction with meditation on the mandala of Sarasvati, an anthology of guru yoga meditations that he wrote at the request of various disciples (one of which is herein translated), numerous liturgies that he wrote for the Great Prayer Festival over which he presided, the collections of long life prayers that he composed for many of the most famous lamas of his era (intended to be read by the disciples of these teachers), the various "prayers for quick rebirth" that he wrote for disciples awaiting the reincarnations of their deceased gurus, several texts focussing on the Bodhisattva Manjushri that he wrote while residing on the Five-Peaked Mountain of Wu-tai-shan in China, and so forth.

Also included here are his notes on the encyclopedic mandala collections known as *The String of Diamonds* (i.e., *Dor-je-dreng-wa*), *The Collected Tantras of Maitri-pa* (*Mi-tra-gya-tsa*), and *The Collected (Tantras Called A) Source of Jewels* (*Rin-jung-gya-tsa*). This volume also contains his five poems of spiritual advice (that I have translated for the present selection, chapter IV).

Vol. IV is comprised of about a dozen titles. Several of these are collections of specific types of writings. One, for example, is his *cha-yig*, or letters of advice and instruction written to monasteries around the country. Many of these were in response to requests for his advice; others were composed because he thought the monastery in question needed guidance.

Another collection is called "Advice to Various Peoples in Tibet Proper and the Tibetan Cultural Areas on How to Act As Regards Both Spiritual and Worldly Matters." As the title implies, the item contains numerous treatises written to various groups of people in Central Asia who look to the Dalai Lama as their mentor.

A third collection is called "Verses Written for Publications and on Painted Scrolls." This anthology contains several hundred brief poems of prayer and praise written by the Great Thirteenth as prefaces to books that were published during his lifetime, and others that were written on the backs of religious paintings brought to him for this purpose by devotees throughout Central Asia. The individual pieces are extremely beautiful in the original, although they do not easily translate into any Western tongue.

The remainder of the volume mostly contains minor verse works of prayer to various Buddhas and Bodhisattvas. Many of these were written in front of some of the most famous religious images in Tibet and thus reveal profound inspiration. Again, they tend to be rather esoteric for Western literary tastes and thus do not translate easily.

Vol. V is comprised of an assortment of materials, much of which is quite personal.

The first item here is his *Sunlight on the Blossoming Garden of the Buddhadharma*, a text that I have referred to earlier in this Introduction (in the section on the Great Thirteenth's training). This is the Dalai Lama's own account of the numerous teachings, initiations and oral transmissions that he received during his youth, listing all of his main gurus and what he studied with them.

The second item includes all the principal letters that he wrote during his lifetime. These are of tremendous historical value. Most of them were written in response to particular inquiries or needs, so must be read in context to the specific situation which inspired them. Several are addressed to close disciples and consequently are in the nature of personal spiritual advice; I wish I could have included some of these pieces in the present study, but unfortunately space would not so permit.

This volume also contains a number of guidebooks that he wrote about various temples that he had had restored. Of particular note are those dealing with the art frescos in the Potala and the Ra-mo-che Temple.

The remainder of the volume is comprised of minor works, mostly written in verse form. Here we find his extensive biographical eulogy of the medieval Tibetan scholar Bu-ton Rin-chen Drub-pa, his short *vinaya* commentary, and so forth.

Finally, Volumes VI and VII make up *A String of Wondrous Gems*, the official biography of the Great Thirteenth that was compiled under the guidance of Pur-chok-pa Tub-ten Jam-pa primarily from the Dalai Lama's own notes and diaries (although, as Pur-chok-pa points out in the colophon, he also drew from other sources). In the Tibetan tradition the stylistic difference between biography and autobiography is that the former will tend to completely glorify the subject, whereas the latter will be exceedingly humble in tone. This is because a biography will usually be written by a chief disciple long accustomed to seeing every action of the guru as a teaching. An autobiography, on the other hand, is written by a lama about himself, and thus will follow the axiom of never speaking highly about oneself. We can presume that Pur-chok-pa drew an outline of the physical facts of the Dalai Lama's life from the master's personal notebooks, but the interpretation and import that he gives to them is largely his own.

In deciding on which of the Great Thirteenth's numerous writings to include in the present selection I followed the criteria that I have used in compiling earlier volumes on the previous Dalai Lamas. Basically, anything incorporated must be reflective of the character and style of the author, and must be meaningful in English translation (many Buddhist works are, in my opinion, too technical for translation at this stage in Buddhist studies). Also, the collection as a whole has to project something of the subject as author, thinker and teacher, and the scope of his literary efforts must to some degree be conveyed. And then finally, as the instrument of transmission I have to be fully confident that these diverse objectives have been satisfactorily achieved, and that I have done everything within my power to portray the subject and his works in as sympathetic and true a manner as is possible.

Sometimes a collection will come together reasonably easily and will seem complete even before the work of translation has begun, when the project is still a mere vision. This was the case with the *Selected Works of the Second Dalai Lama: The Tantric Yogas of Sister Niguma*. On other occasions more juggling will have to be done, the *Complete Collected Works* of the subject re-read a number of times, and several alternative strategies drawn up. This occurred with *Selected Works of the First Dalai Lama: Bridging the Sutras and Tantras*.

But generally somewhere in the process of compiling there comes a specific moment when the work of selection seems complete. Before that moment there is a sense of a vacuum, of something still to be done. The issue becomes a delicate one: where to place the next stroke of the literary brush, what tones to use, what to add or erase, and when to stop applying more paint.

With the present project the basic format came together quite quickly, with the sermons, the poems of advice, the Hayagriva texts, and so forth offering themselves as obvious choices. But when the first draft was complete I still had a sense of something missing. Therefore once again I scanned through the various titles of the *Sung-bum*, re-read several possible alternative texts, re-thought the format of the volume, and so forth; but still there remained a nagging feeling that something important had been overlooked.

It was time to call on the blessings of the Buddhas and Bodhisattvas. I recited several rounds of the name mantra of His Holiness as well as the heart mantras of my principal mandala practices, meditated for a while, and then came up with a unique strategy. Placing the seven volumes of the collected works of the Great Thirteenth on the table in front of me, I closed my eyes and began to pick up and put down the individual volumes until I no longer knew which was which. This went on for about half an hour, until suddenly I knew that the volume I held in my hands was the one for which I was searching. I then flipped back and forth through the pages of the volume for a few minutes, until the energies began to change. Then suddenly a rush of energy shot up my spine and the hair on my body trembled.

I opened my eyes and started slowly to read from the top of the page that lay open before me. The page number was 179 (folio 88, side A), the text the Great Thirteenth's biography of his guru Pur-chok-pa Jampa Gya-tso. Previously I had perused only the last sections of this work, which dealt with that period of Pur-chok-pa's life in which he had had contact with the Thirteenth Dalai Lama. I hadn't bothered to read through the early portions, which treat his youth and training. The text is quite long, and I had felt that there was very little chance of discovering anything relevant to my project in the first half of it.

But as I read I noticed that part way down page 179 the Great Thirteenth decided to digress a bit from his principal subject matter and to speak in a general way about Pur-chok-pa's tantric studies. By way of an introduction to these studies, he proceeds in the twenty-seven pages that follow to provide a wonderfully lucid and concise guide to the four classes of Buddhist tantras.

I was absolutely thrilled. The text was just what I was looking for: formal, tightly structured and with plenty of substance. It would work perfectly to balance the more informal materials I had chosen to use in the early chapters, and would add a rich perspective to the poems, Hayagriva materials, and the text on guru yoga meditation. In my heart of hearts I knew that the selection was finally complete.

I immediately set about translating the piece, which now serves as Chapter III, under the title "A Guide to the Buddhist Tantras."

The Thirteenth Dalai Lama was like a multi-faceted diamond, of which each individual facet could inspire a study of its own. His *Collected Works* is no less rich and diverse. It is not possible to convey the full import of his voluminous writings in a small selection of translations such as this; but if in this literary mosaic I have managed to capture a fraction of his spirituality and literary talents my time and efforts will have been well spent.

N. THE PAN-CHEN CONTROVERSY

The Great Thirteenth lived an extremely active and fruitful life, perhaps more so than any other Dalai Lama with the possible exception of the Great Fifth. He accomplished a tremendous amount for Tibet on both spiritual and secular levels, and most tasks that he took in hand met with success.

But there were also failures. In particular, two major thorns continued to plague him throughout his life. Both of these were inherited with his position as political chieftain; and, try as he may, he was never able to eliminate either of them.

The first of these was the British insistence on regarding Tibet as being under Chinese suzerainty. The second thorn emerged in the relationship between his government and the office of the Sixth Pan-chen Lama, the incarnate lama of Ta-shi Lhun-po Monastery. This also developed into a complex irritation that outlived both lamas. No account of the Great Thirteenth's life would be complete without at least a mention of this incident.

As described earlier, the various incarnations of the Dalai and Pan-chen Lamas had shared a close relationship, and generally whichever lama was the elder at any given point in history would serve as the guru to the younger. In terms of traditional hierarchy they were the two highest lamas in the country, with the Dalai Lama being regarded as the higher of the two.

It is said that the two were personally very close to one another, and that the problems that occurred during the lifetime of the Sixth Pan-chen arose from the intrigues of ministers and officials in their offices rather than from differences between the two lamas themselves. Then once the schism had been formed and the seed of mistrust planted, the rift became impossible to bridge.

Undoubtedly there is a grain of truth to this interpretation, but it is not the whole truth. The Ta-shi Lhun-po administrators were definitely both jealous and suspicious of the Lhasa officials, and *vice versa*. At certain points in time the British and then the Chinese exploited this rivalry, thus intensifying the confusion. Consequently communication between the two lamas became obstructed, particularly once the split had attained its apex, making it difficult to re-establish mutual understanding.

But the root causes of the wound lay in deeper soil. In one sense it was a natural outcome of the Tibetan home situation in confrontation with changing times. Tibet was a country of loosely affiliated kingdoms, districts and tribes joined together as a nation because of a common bond of language, religion and culture. The different parts of the country had for centuries been allowed to operate quite autonomously of the Lhasa government. But during the nineteenth and twentieth centuries this loose arrangement was replaced by a growing centralization brought about mostly because of the increased threat of foreign invasion, firstly by the British and then by the Chinese. In particular, strong centralization was one of the principal policies of the Thirteenth Dalai Lama, who saw it as the only possible method of safeguarding the country against Chinese expansion.

But the first appearances of the breach between the two offices began to manifest long before the Great Thirteenth came to power. They occurred during the final years of the life of the previous Pan-chen Lama (the Fifth), when the Dalai Lama was still an infant. These were the days of Tibet's closed door policy, when no one was allowed to visit from British India. In the late 1870s Ta-shi Lhun-po Monastery issued a travel permit to Sarat Chandra Das, a Bengali Indian who wished to map the Tibetan ranges. Das made two visits to Lhasa, even managing to gain an audience with the young Dalai Lama.

But then the Lhasa authorities learned that the pilgrim was in the employ of the British government. His so-called scientific visit became viewed as a spying mission, and an investigation followed. The Ta-shi Lhun-po officials who had issued him with travel documents were arrested, and then tried and convicted of treason. Among them was the eminent lama Seng-chen Dor-je-chang, a tutor to the Pan-chen Lama himself. The punishments were severe, and the death sentence was inflicted on Seng-chen Dor-je-chang, who was regarded as the principal person responsible for the breach of national security.

Mistrust intensified in the late 1880s with the conflict between Tibet and the British. Lhasa instituted a special tax to cover the costs of the new army that had been formed overnight. Because of the special status of the Pan-chen Lama, Ta-shi Lhun-po had traditionally been exempt from such taxes; this time, however, they were not spared. The Ta-shi Lhun-po administrators interpreted the change as a further punishment for their participation in the Das affair.

A third complication grew out of the fact that both the British and the Chinese saw the Pan-chen Lama and the Ta-shi Lhun-po administration as a possible alternative to the Lhasa government. This was natural enough, for the Pan-chen was hierarchically the second highest lama in the country; but both foreign governments exploited the situation in such a way as to put the Pan-chen in a compromised position with his own countrymen, and especially with the Lhasa authorities.

In all honesty it does not appear that the Sixth Pan-chen was altogether adverse to the idea of heading an alternative government. He never formally accepted the position, but seems to have toyed with it considerably.

The concept became an actual proposal in 1904, when Sir Francis Younghusband invaded Lhasa and the Dalai Lama was forced to flee to Mongolia and China. Having gained control, Younghusband wanted to leave the country with an administration that would represent British interests. He lobbied with his superiors to allow him to set up the Pan-chen Lama as the acting head. The Pan-chen's outright friendliness toward the British, in contrast to the Dalai Lama's uncooperative attitude, made the move seem logical to him.

But permission was never cleared, for Younghusband had fallen out of favor with the Home Office and also because it became obvious that the Tibetans would violently resist the move. Nor did the Pan-chen openly express interest in the proposal, although from records of his communications with the British it is obvious that his curiosity had been aroused. (Mehra, 1976, pages 28-33.)

In 1905 the British sent a message to the Dalai Lama informing him that he should not return to Lhasa until the situation there had calmed, and that if he were to disregard this advice he could expect the British to take military action against Lhasa once more. Meanwhile the Viceroy had invited the Pan-chen Lama to visit Calcutta during the winter of 1905-6, an event planned to coincide with the Prince of Wales' (later King George V) tour of India.

The Pan-chen cautiously accepted the invitation, knowing full well that such a visit to the camp of the enemy while the Dalai Lama was still in a state of forced exile would be regarded with extreme suspicion by Lhasa, and could even be construed as grounds for a charge of treason.

Arrangements were made by Fredrick O'Connor, trade agent at Gyang-tse, who wrote back that the Pan-chen had agreed to come only if he were granted ". . .a promise of help from us against any attempted retaliation on the part of the Lhasa government." (It was a mere twenty years since his tutor Seng-chen Dor-je-chang had been put to death for collaboration with the British, and he fully realized the dangers inherent in such a visit.)

Meanwhile in India the British administration was in a state of transition. By the time the Pan-chen arrived in Calcutta Lord Curzon, who had made the original invitation, had been replaced by Lord Minto. The new Viceroy informed the Pan-chen that he was not in a position to give him any support in the event of problems from Lhasa, and, that if Lhasa were to be challenged, the Ta-shi Lhun-po administrators would be on their own.

Had Lord Minto taken the opposite stance, it is hard to say what policy the Pan-chen would have adopted. He quite conceivably could have played directly into British hands. As it was, he returned to Shiga-tse a frightened man. He had stuck his neck out with the British on the oral guarantee from Lord Curzon, a pledge that Lord Minto was not prepared to acknowledge. Consequently he made a conscious attempt to maintain a low profile over the years to follow. When the Dalai Lama finally returned to Lhasa in 1909 the Pan-chen journeyed all the way to Nag-chu-kha to greet and speak with him. At this meeting the Great Thirteenth assured the Pan-chen that there was no need to worry about his India visit, and that no repercussions would come from Lhasa.

However, not long after the Dalai Lama's return to Lhasa the Chinese invasion occurred and he had to leave the country once more, this time for British India. Previously the Chinese had denounced the Pan-chen because of his communications with the British; but when it became obvious that the Dalai Lama was the man to be eliminated if Chinese designs were to succeed in Tibet, the Peking authorities made an immediate about-face and began to play up to the administrators of Ta-shi Lhun-po Monastery. In January of 1911, with the Dalai Lama still in exile in India, they invited the Pan-chen Lama to Lhasa. Here they housed him first in the prestigious Jo-khang Temple, and then in the Dalai Lama's own summer palace, the Nor-bu Ling-ka. He was lavishly entertained and was repeatedly shown off in public in the company of the amban.

But even more brazen, they had him and the amban carried around the city in golden palanquins, a privilege generally reserved for the Dalai Lama or, if allowed to others, only granted at the discretion of the Dalai Lama or his Regent. Thus to many Tibetans this violation of tradition was a sign of an attempt to fill the position made vacant by the Dalai Lama's forced absence. The Lhasans could not tolerate the insult, and as the palanquins passed along the narrow streets they went up to the roofs of their houses and threw down their dirty socks onto the procession.

The Pan-chen's stay in Lhasa was not to last for long, for shortly thereafter the revolution in China reached full strength and the Manchu government fell to the Nationalists. The Tibetans saw their opportunity for independence and seized the moment. Acting on instructions from the Dalai Lama's government in exile, they rose in rebellion from one end of the country to the other.

Early in 1912 it became obvious that the Dalai Lama would soon return to Tibet. Again the Pan-chen Lama began to show uneasiness at the way he had acted. The records of the British trade agents at Gyang-tse reveal that he approached them several times for assurances of British protection in the event that Lhasa should decide to punish him for collaboration with the Chinese. He also requested the British to press for him to be allowed "...to enjoy an independence equal to that which he had enjoyed prior to the departure from Tibet of the Dalai Lama." (Mehra, 1976, page 36.)

This move by the Pan-chen did not particularly help his case. The British were not prepared to grant him this assurance, and instead decided to discuss the matter directly with the Dalai Lama. The cat was out of the bag.

The Pan-chen and his ministers therefore hurried to Ra-lung to meet the Dalai Lama and his entourage, ostensibly to welcome them back to Tibet. In fact their principal concern was more probably to try and iron out any bad feelings before the Dalai Lama arrived in Lhasa and

set up his new government. The meeting seems to have been successful, and once again the Pan-chen was assured that he would suffer
no repercussions. The Ta-shi Lhun-po administrators, however, were
given a strong warning for the part they had played in the intrigue.

In particular, it was pointed out that when Tibet as a whole had
risen up in revolt against the Chinese invaders Ta-shi Lhun-po and
its forces had held back and remained inactive. There were even suggestions that some of the Ta-shi Lhun-po officials had helped the
Chinese. But the issue was not pressed, and once again the relations
between the offices of the two lamas had normalized.

This could easily have been the end of the conflict, but such was
not to be the case. Over the years that followed, the new Chinese
government continued to make overtures to the Pan-chen Lama, sending lavish gifts to both him and his administrators. The Dalai Lama
had cut off all direct ties with China, and would only communicate
with Peking through British mediation. Consequently the Chinese saw
the Pan-chen as their only hope for getting a foot in the Tibetan door.
They attempted to have the Pan-chen or at least one of his representatives present at the Simla Convention of 1913-14, a condition that
neither Lhasa nor Britain looked upon favorably.

Shortly after the Dalai Lama's return to Lhasa the Pan-chen Lama
began to speak about a potential visit to China. It was obvious that
he was not happy with his curtailed position. The visit would probably have occurred had Lu Hsing-chi not dissuaded it on the grounds
that it was too dangerous and would be strongly resented by the British, and possibly even militarily obstructed by them, for they now saw
the Pan-chen as precariously Sinofied. On April 15, 1913, the British
Secretary of State wrote the Viceroy in India, asking him to communicate British coolness in regard to the Pan-chen's proposed China visit,
and that in the event that the lama chose to go, ". . . if a collision between him and the Dalai Lama results from his intrigues, no protection can be looked for from us." (Mehra, 1976, page 41.)

This British scolding seems to have calmed down Ta-shi Lhun-po
for some time, and the correspondence between the Dalai and Pan-
chen Lamas from 1914 onwards suggests that the latter had decided
to relinquish his political ambitions. In 1915 he wrote the Dalai Lama
a very pleasant letter requesting the Dalai to give him a number of
initiations and teachings; the Dalai Lama's reply agrees to the request
in principal but suggests that because the Pan-chen is busy with construction of a large Maitreya statue and he himself is engaged in a pub-

lishing project, it may be better for the Pan-chen to come to Lhasa the following year. In fact the event did not materialize as planned, for the following spring the Dalai Lama entered into meditation for four years. Nonetheless, the sentiment was one of restored harmony.

But the quiet did not last for long. After the Dalai Lama completed his retreat he turned his attention to reviving various projects he had initiated years earlier but that had suffered from neglect during his long period of meditation. One of these was his attempt to build up the army.

This project took on a new energy following the Lhasa visit of Sir Charles Bell during 1920-21. Sir Charles strongly advised the Great Thirteenth to intensify his efforts to create an effective military, emphasizing that it was Tibet's only hope for maintaining its independence from China. Britain would help with arms and advisors, but would not become directly involved.

The Dalai Lama immediately implemented Sir Charles' advice. Again, to cover the costs of the increased numbers of soldiers a new tax was levied. This time Ta-shi Lhun-po was taxed particularly heavily, and the feud that had laid dormant for so long once again flared up.

On December 23, 1923, the Pan-chen Lama left Shi-ga-tse for Mongolia and China, ostensibly on a teaching tour but, in the eyes of the Lhasa ministers, more probably to rally support from his many important foreign devotees.

The Dalai Lama was devastated. For more than a decade he had restrained the Lhasa nobility from punishing Ta-shi Lhun-po for its many dubious activities during the wars with Britain and China. He fully appreciated the fact that the Pan-chen as Tibet's "second in command" had been placed in an awkward situation during and immediately following these periods, and for this reason had pushed his ministers to be as tolerant and passive as possible in their dealings with the Ta-shi Lhun-po officials. But now it was all thrown back at him; the Pan-chen had betrayed his trust, and Lhasa was in an uproar.

In January 1924 the Dalai Lama sent the Pan-chen a scathing letter. "You seem to have forgotten the sacred history of your predecessors," he wrote. "Like a moth attracted to a flame you have wandered away to the deserts and plains. Without even consulting or confiding in me, from whom you received your monastic ordination, you have raced away in the company of evil companions, like a mad elephant charging up a wrong path. . . . It is difficult to believe that a person such as yourself, who is regarded as a teacher and enlightened being by so many of the common people, can be motivated by petty self-interests and by the three psychic poisons. Selfishness is one of the greatest causes of harm in this world, and I implore you to abandon it. It is still not too late to change your mind and to turn back."

But the die had been cast. Bad went to worse, and before long the Pan-chen Lama found himself crossing the border from Mongolia into China. From that time onward the prospects of his return became infinitely complex. At a time when the national priority was disentanglement from the Chinese web, he had involved China in Tibetan affairs.

In the beginning the Pan-chen Lama seems to have enjoyed life in China. The attention and honor showered on him by the Chinese government certainly must have been flattering. But months soon began to turn into years. The "lecture tour" that he had originally planned as a short excursion and a means to exert pressure on Lhasa had become an extended exile. He began to regret the course of action that he had taken, and repeatedly appealed to the British to mediate his return for him.

The Dalai Lama too was distraught over the Pan-chen's long absence, and feared that it would cause unnecessary friction within the country at a time when he wanted to create a strong united front. He wrote several letters to the Pan-chen, requesting him to return and guaranteeing him safe passage.

However, the problem was not easily resolved. The Pan-chen's officials would not allow him to return unconditionally, and the conditions that they set were unacceptable to several of the most important Lhasa ministers. The dialogue went back and forth, mostly through British intermediaries, but to no avail.

Finally it appeared that a suitable arrangement had been struck, and the party prepared to return. Suddenly war broke out in China and, not wanting to enter Tibet on an unstable footing, the Ta-shi Lhun-po officials reneged on the contract.

Eventually in 1933 a new deal was struck and the Pan-chen began the long homeward journey. And then dramatic news arrived from Lhasa: The Dalai Lama had suddenly and mysteriously passed away. Again there was no way they could proceed, for in the Dalai Lama's absence the situation in Tibet would be volatile, and for them in particular would be extremely hazardous.

Consequently they turned back to China, where the Pan-chen Lama lived out the remainder of his life. He passed away a few years later, in November of 1937.

It is interesting to note that throughout the long years of their estrangement the Dalai and Pan-chen Lamas always spoke well of one another, and both of them placed the blame for the problem not on each other but on minor officials in their entourages. The Pan-chen felt that various Lhasa ministers were persecuting him and Ta-shi Lhun-po out of jealousy for the esteem in which the Shi-ga-tse administration was held by both the British and Chinese leaders. On the other hand, the Dalai Lama believed that the Pan-chen was being badly advised by several of his ministers thought to be in the pay of first the British and then the Chinese. No doubt both assessments were correct to some degree.

Earlier I mentioned the Pan-chen's 1915 request for a special teaching from the Dalai Lama, that the latter had postponed until the following year and then, because of entering into the "great retreat," even longer. After the Great Thirteenth completed his meditation the meeting did take place, and most people thought that it had settled the conflict with Ta-shi Lhun-po. The two lamas had sat in conversation throughout the day and long into the night. Their talk and laughter were heard echoing in the hallways of the Nor-bu Ling-ka, and they seemed to completely forget time. When the Pan-chen eventually did leave, the Dalai Lama picked up a lantern, took the Pan-chen by the hand, and walked him all the way to the front gate of the summer palace, something he had never done for any other visitor. (Taring, 1970, pages 66-67.)

It is also interesting to note that one of the final acts of the elderly Sixth Pan-chen Lama was the assistance he rendered to the Lhasa committees in their search for the Thirteenth Dalai Lama's reincarnation. The advice and information that he gave to them helped them greatly in their task of locating His Holiness the present Dalai Lama.

O. THE FINAL YEARS

Traditionally it is said that the three most essential deeds of a lama are *ched*, *tsod*, and *tsom*: teaching disciples, engaging in philosophical discussions, and composing spiritual treatises. For the last decade of his life the Great Thirteenth dedicated tremendous energy to these three endeavors.

His activities in cultural spheres have aready been touched upon. Here one of his most significant was that of restoring Tibet's classical institutions; merely the work on the Jo-khang and Ra-mo-che Temples involved the coordinated efforts of a hundred of the country's most talented artists. The overall effect was a total rejuvenation of the fine arts. He also commissioned the building of several new temples, including the magnificant chapel in the Nor-bu Ling-ka dedicated to the Three Essential Bodhisattvas. The publishing house that he founded printed many of the great literary classics, including the collected works of Bu-ton, most of the important writings of Taranatha, and so forth. The patronage that he gave to the various performing arts, both the religious *cham* dances and the classical *lha-mo* operas, completely revived the Tibetan dance tradition. As well as upgrading the traditional forms of education, in the hope of modernizing Tibet he arranged for a number of young Tibetans to go to English schools in India and England, and sponsored the creation of a British-run school in Tibet. The list goes on and on. And it should be noted that he did not merely appoint committees to execute these diverse tasks for him, but took a direct and personal interest in them himself. As a result, he deeply inspired the spiritural and cultural life of the country.

As a secular leader he also strove constantly for the political well-being of his people. Much of this had to be limited to internal affairs, for his wish to clarify Tibet's status *vis-a-vis* China was to a great extent foiled by Britain. The best he could do on the external front was physically hold the Chinese out of the country and hope that eventually a transformation would manifest in the British attitude.

From the time of the Bolshevik Revolution in Russia he showed an intense dislike for communism, and worked diligently to safeguard his country against it. He watched with distaste as the Red Soviets gradually absorbed and destroyed the spiritual cultures of the Buddhist republics of the Mongolian peoples to the north of Tibet, and worried that the wave of communism would one day wash over onto his own country.

During the New Year festivities of 1932 the Ne-chung Oracle warned the Tibetan government of dangers to the Dalai Lama's life, and advised that various long life prayers and rituals be performed. These were all done as prescribed. The government officials then approached His Holiness and asked for his advice on what more they could do.

Shortly thereafter the Great Thirteenth released what has come to be known as his "Final Testament," a short text in which he recounts the major themes of his life and advises his people on how they should proceed in the future. Because the text mentions several events that later came to pass, it is also known as *The Prophecies of the Great Thir-*

teenth, a title under which it has received several printings in the refugee camps of India. The work is only a few pages in length, so I will take the liberty of quoting it in full. It reveals the essence of the Dalai Lama's own interpretation of his life, the Tibet situation, and the future of his people.

"As is well known to all of you, it was considered to be unnecessary to utilize the Emperor's golden urn in the process of determining my incarnation. The prophecies that had been made by the oracles and lamas, and the tests performed upon me as an infant, were in themselves deemed to be sufficiently convincing. Therefore as a child I was recognized and enthroned as the true reincarnation of the previous Dalai Lamas.

"In accordance with tradition I was trained by numerous holy spiritual masters, including the Regent Ta-tsak Rin-po-che and Yong-dzin Pur-chok-pa Dor-je-chang. Under their guidance I studied in depth the nature of the Buddhist path, beginning with simple prayers and continuing up to the most obtruse subjects. From them I received the preliminary, novice and full ordinations of a monk, and was guided through the five principal subjects of Buddhist philosophy: *prajna-paramita, madhymaka, pramana, abhidharma*, and *vinaya*. I learned to debate the essential themes of all these teachings, thus being exposed to their inner meanings. My studies included the ocean of sutra and tantra lineages, and under these wonderful masters I received countless instructions, initiations, direct transmissions, and secret oral teachings. I applied myself ceaselessly day after day, year after year, to this vast corpus of spiritual lore, until my mind was completely saturated with it.

"Even though I was still quite immature, when I reached the age of eighteen I was called upon to accept the responsibility of serving as spiritual and secular head of the country. I considered myself unqualified for the position, but because both the political and religious leaders unanimously petitioned me to accept it, and the Chinese Emperor also urged me to do so, I felt that there was no alternative but to agree.

"From that time on I have had to sacrifice my personal wishes and individual freedom for the greater task of working day and night for the spiritual, social and political welfare of the country. The responsibility was by no means small, and it weighed heavily upon my mind.

"In the Wood Dragon Year the English armies began to build up on our borders and threaten an invasion. It would have been simple enough for me to have placated them by submitting to their demands, but such a course of action could easily have resulted in danger to our independence and sovereignty. Therefore, in spite of the difficult and hazardous journey I left for Mongolia and Manchu China, the two countries with whom the Great Fifth Dalai Lama had established Patron/Priest arrangements, and with whom Tibet shared relations of mutual respect and support.

"I was given wonderful receptions in both these countries, and in Peking the Emperor and Empress received me graciously and showed me great honor. I informed them of our situation, and they showed deep sympathy.

"But while I was there they both passed away and the new Emperor, Shon-ton, was installed. I held some talks with him, and then left to return to Tibet.

"Yet even as I traveled, the Chinese amban sent false reports to the Emperor and as a result a Chinese army under Lui Chan began to invade from the east.

"Once more as the person responsible for the welfare of the country I was forced to leave my homeland and struggle for the national interest. Again, without regard for the hardships incurred by such an undertaking, I took my ministers and officials and retreated into the holy land of India, where I appealed to the British government to mediate negotiations between China and ourselves. The British did attempt to do this, but the Chinese were totally unresponsive.

"Under these circumstances there was really nothing we could do, other than sit and pray for a favorable change in the nature of the situation. And our prayers were soon answered, for the profound power of truth is great, and the forces of karma infallible. Civil war broke out within China itself, and the picture in Tibet completely transformed. The Chinese troops stationed in our country were cut off from all assistance, and became stagnant like a pool from which the flow of water is terminated. Bit by bit we were able to rout them out and to expel them from our land.

"My government and I resumed control of the country in the Water Ox Year (1913), and from that time until the present day, the Year of the Water Monkey (1932), we have continued to rule without any trace of foreign interference. This has been an era of peace and prosperity for Tibet, and all the people have been able to live in harmony and joy.

"These events of our history are well documented, and are known to all of you. Therefore I do not have to go into them in detail. I have mentioned them in brief just to let you know how I perceived things as they happened. Throughout all that occurred I did my best to safeguard our spiritual, cultural and political identity, and if there has been any positive results from my efforts that alone will bring me satisfaction. I am not recounting these various deeds so that you will praise or thank me; the only reward I seek is for our land to remain strong and for our people to live in happiness. Other than this I do not want even a sesame seed for my efforts.

"I have now become rather old, and want to step down from the responsibility of serving as spiritual and secular leader of the country. I would like to dedicate the remainder of my time to meditation, and to think about my next life. This is something that we all must do in our old age.

"Unfortunately it appears that I am not to be allowed this luxury, and I dare not turn my back on the trust that has been placed in me by my meditational divinities and Dharma Protectors. Moreover, when I approached my spiritual preceptors with the request that they grant their blessings for my decision to resign from power they asked me not to do so; and also the majority of the Tibetan people seem to have faith in me alone these days, and have fervently petitioned me to change my mind on the matter and to remain at the helm of the country. Therefore there is really nothing I can do other than continue.

"However, I am now almost fifty-eight years old, and soon it will be impossible for me to serve you any longer. Everyone should realize this fact, and begin to look to what you will do in the future when I am gone. Between me and the next incarnation there will be a period in which you will have to fend for yourselves.

"Our two most powerful neighbors are India and China, both of whom have very powerful armies. Therefore we must try to establish stable relations with both of them. There are also a number of smaller countries near our borders who maintain a strong military. Because of this it is important that we too maintain an efficient army of young and well-trained soldiers, that is able to establish the security of the country. In the present age the five great degenerations seem to totally dominate life on earth, to the extent that fighting and conflict have become part of the very fabric of human society. If we do not make preparations to defend ourselves from the overflow of violence, we will have very little chance of survival.

"In particular, we must guard ourselves against the barbaric red communists, who carry terror and destruction with them wherever they go. They are the worst of the worst. Already they have consumed much of Mongolia, where they have outlawed the search for the reincarnation of Je-tsun Dam-pa, the incarnate head of the country. They have robbed and destroyed the monasteries, forcing the monks to join their armies or else killing them outright. They have destroyed religion wherever they've encountered it, and not even the name of Buddha-dharma is allowed to remain in their wake. I am sure you have heard the reports coming out of Ulan Bator and other such places.

"It will not be long before we find the red onslaught at our own front door. It is only a matter of time before we come into a direct confrontation with it, either from within our own ranks or else as a threat from an external [communist] nation.

"And when that happens we must be ready to defend ourselves. Otherwise our spiritual and cultural traditions will be completely eradicated. Even the names of the Dalai and Pan-chen Lamas will be erased, as will be those of the other lamas, lineage holders and holy beings. The monasteries will be looted and destroyed, and the monks and nuns killed or chased away. The great works of the noble Dharma kings of old will be undone, and all of our cultural and spiritual institutions persecuted, destroyed and forgotten. The birthrights and property of the people will be stolen; we will become like slaves to our conquerors, and will be made to wander helplessly like beggars. Everyone will be forced to live in misery, and the days and nights will pass slowly, and with great suffering and terror.

"Therefore, now, when the strength of peace and happiness is with us, while the power to do something about the situation is still in our hands, we should make every effort to safeguard ourselves against this impending disaster. Use peaceful methods where they are appropriate; but where they are not appropriate, do not hesitate to resort to more forceful means. Work diligently now, while there is still time. Then there will be no regrets.

"The future of our country lies in your hands. Whether you are a chief minister or simple government official, monk or lay person, teacher or disciple, secular leader or ordinary citizen, I urge you all to rise up together and work for the common good in accordance with your individual capacity. One person alone cannot ward off the threat that faces us; but together we can win out in the end. Avoid rivalry and petty self-interests, and look instead to what is essential.

"We must strive together with positive motivation for the general welfare of all, while living in accordance with the teachings of the Buddha. If we do this, then there is no doubt that we will abide within the blessings of the national protective divinity Ne-chung, who was appointed by the Acharya [Padma Sambhava] to assist the line of Dalai Lamas in the task of caring for Tibet.

"From my side, I too will do all that I can for the common good, and direct my blessings to those who do likewise. I offer them my prayers that their efforts may meet with every success.

"As for those who do not act correctly at this critical time, they will experience the fate they justly deserve. Their indulgent behavior may bring them comfort for a few moments, but in the end they will meet with disaster. Now they sit and lazily watch the time pass; but before long they will come to regret their apathy. And then it will be too late for remedies.

"I feel that the happiness and prosperity of Tibet will continue for the remainder of my life. After that there will be considerable suffering, and each of you will individually experience the consequences of your ways in the manner I have described above.

"My experiences and reason have convinced me that these things could come to pass, and that it would be useful for me to speak of them to you.

"Numerous external rituals have been and are being performed for my long life. But actually the most important thing people can do for me is to perform the inner ritual of holding this advice of mine in their hearts. If in the past mistakes have been made we should learn from them, and should resolve to change and to work hard from now on to the best of our abilities.

"From my side I will continue to do whatever I can to enhance the quality of our spiritual and cultural traditions, and to dedicate my energies to securing the Tibetan political situation. I encourage and will pray for all of you in positions of leadership who do likewise. Hopefully if we all work hard our people will be able to know peace and happiness in the end, and our country be able to survive long into the future.

"You have asked me to give you my advice, and therefore I have done so. Please take it to heart, and try to apply its essence day and night in all that you do. Think carefully about what I have said, for the future is in your hands. It is extremely important to overcome what needs to be overcome, and to accomplish what needs to be accomplished. Do not confuse the two."

The above short text is perhaps the most famous of everything the Great Thirteenth wrote, for much of what he said in it eventually became reality. His advice of building up a strong army to keep out the communists was ignored, and in the 1950s the Red Chinese invaded. In Tibet itself almost a fifth of the population was killed by the "liberators," and tens of thousands were put in concentration camps. Many more fled as refugees to India. They came to realize the truth of his words, "We will become like slaves to our conquerors, and will be made to wander helplessly like beggars. Everyone will be forced to live in misery, and the days and nights will pass slowly, and with great suffering and terror."

Tibetans believe that every Dalai Lama is born enlightened, and has complete power over how long he lives and when he will die. Any appearance to the contrary is merely an act for the sake of operating in the mundane world and training the minds of ordinary people.

In his last testament the Great Thirteenth mentions being "almost fifty-eight" in conjunction with the possibility of his passing away. Tibetans believe that this was a warning to them that he would die the following year, when he was fifty-eight.

The question might be asked: If the Great Thirteenth had power over his life and death, why did he choose to pass away at that particular time?

One theory that I heard from several learned Tibetans during my stay in the refugee camps in India was that he had given his people a map of how they could become militarily self-sufficient, and thus prepare themselves for the eventual communist invasion that he had foreseen. However, they were too lethargic and factionalistic to heed his words, and could not accept the idea of supporting a large army. It became evident that they would not be prepared for the invasion, and that if anything were to be done he would have to do it himself.

It was prophesied that his devotees had sufficient merits to be blessed by his presence for eighty-two years, provided that they acted correctly. But when they hesitated on following through on his advice to create a strong defence for the country, it put him in a difficult position. He could quietly live out the remainder of his life and when his twilight years arrived watch helplessly as the Red Chinese invaded; or he could pass away and reincarnate quickly, so that when the invasion occurred he would be a young, energetic man able to guide his people through the troubled waters, lead them into exile in India, and from there work for Tibetan independence and the preservation of Tibet's unique spiritual culture.

He chose the latter option.

There is also talk that events in the lives of the Twelfth, Thirteenth and Fourteenth Dalai Lamas were deeply linked. The Twelfth died early so as to allow the Great Thirteenth to be at a maximumly effective age to meet the challenges that would confront Tibet, Mongolia and China in the first half of this century; and the Thirteenth died early in order to make way for the Fourteenth, who would work for the preservation of Tibetan spirituality and the Tibetan identity, while at the same time serving needs on a global scale relevant to all of humanity, and bringing the healing energy of the Buddhadharma to the West.

In November of the Water Bird Year the Great Thirteenth summoned the photographer of the Nepalese mission and asked him to take a formal portrait of him for his disciples. The Tibetans took this as a sign that soon he would pass away, for it was an act that the Dalai Lama had never before done. Then suddenly in mid-December he fell ill with a strong cold. Within the space of a few days the cold developed into pneumonia and he passed away. Shortly afterwards the Ra-deng Tul-ku was appointed to serve as regent. One of his first deeds was to form a committee to search for the Dalai Lama's reincarnation. As Ven, Tak-tsen Rin-po-che so poignantly puts it in the Foreword, eventually the search for the Fourteenth Dalai Lama led to a small farmhouse in Am-do far to the east of Lhasa, beside which the Great Thirteenth had picnicked and meditated in 1909, and to which he had commented he would one day like to return.

Je Rinpoche Tsongkhapa

1 Heart of the Enlightenment Teachings

The peerless Buddha-son and spiritual guide Shantideva wrote[1],

> This human life endowed with freedom and opportunity
>   is most rare
> And has the capacity to fulfill every purpose.
> If it is not used to accomplish the meaningful,
> How will such an auspicious conjuncture come again?

Over the countless rebirths that we have experienced since beginningless time, we ordinary beings have been born again and again in the lower realms of samsara. But now as a result of our good karma we have achieved a human rebirth endowed with tremendous freedom and opportunity, a possession more precious than a wish-fulfilling gem. In addition, we have met with the sublime enlightenment teachings. Therefore no matter what temptations and distractions we meet with, we should not allow ourselves to become diverted from spiritual goals.

Instead, contemplate the shortcomings of cyclic existence and be inspired by the Bodhisattva ways. Apply yourself intensely to the spiritual practices and accept responsibility to accomplish enlightenment for the benefit of all living beings, each of whom has been a mother to you in some previous lifetime.

In order to achieve this illustrious ideal, study the essence of the ocean of enlightenment teachings under a qualified spiritual master.

Then engage in true practice, which means taking every point of the teachings as a tool for the taming of your mindstream. Steadily strengthen the qualities of transcendence and insight within yourself by means of applying yourself to study, contemplation and meditation as indivisible elements of the path.

If instead of going this way we opt to chase after the eight worldly dharmas and the ephemeral distractions limited in scope to this one short lifetime, the spiritual opportunities afforded by having gained a human rebirth are rendered meaningless. Then after death we will again fall back to the lower realms of samsara. Our precious human potential, rather than acting as a source of higher being, liberation and enlightenment, just becomes a source of further darkness, confusion and suffering.

When this is our direction, the prospects for our future seem dim indeed. Let alone ever again having the blessings of meeting with enlightened beings or the enlightenment teachings, it will be difficult even to achieve a human rebirth. This is clearly stated in both the sutras and tantras.

Rather than waste our time and energy on meaningless samsaric pursuits we should dedicate ourselves to the enlightenment path.

The path that is to be accomplished consists of the 84,000 teachings of the Buddha. There are numerous ways to categorize these, such as into the Hinayana and Mahayana, or into the Sutrayana and Vajrayana, etc.

Another manner of subdivision is to speak of the wisdom and method aspects of the teachings. This refers to the transcendent wisdom teachings (*prajnaparamita*) of the Great Mother sutras, which are the direct teachings on the meaning of emptiness as transmitted through Manjushri, Nagarjuna and so forth, and are known as "The Lineage of the Profound Instructions"; and the hidden, interpretative method teachings on the clear realizations (*abhisamaya*) as transmitted through Maitreya, Asanga and so forth, and are known as "The Lineage of the Vast Activities Instructions".

These two oral traditions came down in unbroken lineages as the "profound" and the "vast" transmissions. Eventually both were received by Lama Atisha[2], who joined them into a single stream and brought them to Tibet.

Atisha outlined the essence of this combined legacy in his classical text *A Lamp for the Path to Enlightenment* (*Lam-sgron*). Later on, Lama Tsong-kha-pa collected together the various lineages of instruction coming from Atisha and then, by means of intensive meditational application, achieved a vision of the Bodhisattva Manjushri in which Manjushri gave him the ear-whispered oral instructions on the principal themes of Atisha's teachings.

Using these visionary teachings he embellished Atisha's exposition of the three levels of spiritual application as outlined in *A Lamp for the Path to Enlightenment*. Tsong-kha-pa[3] then wrote his three famous *Lam Rim* treatises, that reveal the methods for quickly and easily traversing the path leading to peerless enlightenment.

These peerless *Lam Rim* treatises collect together hundreds of thousands of lineages of the Buddha's teachings, like Lake Manasrover collects together hundreds of thousands of mountain streams. They are like refined gold that has been burned and examined three times as a test of purity and authenticity; and like the essence of the milk of a cow fed only on milk that was taken from a cow fed only on milk that was taken from a cow fed only on milk, and so on for a thousand lines of cows.

Thus when we find ourselves at the bank of a river flowing with clean, pure water endowed with the eight qualities of excellence, there is no reason to allow ourselves to die of thirst.

This is our situation. We have arrived at the riverbank of the teachings of Buddha that were transmitted and refined as described above. We should drink deeply of the stream and experience the relief of liberation and enlightenment.

The method of drinking the teachings is outlined as follows in *The Condensed Sutra on the Perfection of Wisdom (Sher-phyin-sdud-pa)*,

> The Buddhas of the past, present and future
> Take the perfection of wisdom as their path,
> For there is no other way leading to enlightenment.

As Buddhists our main concern should be to practice the teachings well. And what is the purpose of this practice? To generate the qualities of transcendence and insight of the Sugatas. This is accomplished by means of the path of the perfection of wisdom.

If our objective is to accomplish the state of liberation and enlightenment, we should recollect that all Buddhas of the past traveled the path of the perfection of wisdom; all Buddhas of the present are traveling it; and all Buddhas of the future will travel it. There is no Buddha in any of the three times who does not have to rely upon the perfection of wisdom.

Therefore we should think, "If I wish to achieve the state of the four Buddha *kayas*, I too must practice like that." Then we should train accordingly.

Wishing for enlightenment is important, but it is not enough in itself. For example, if some people from a remote area want to visit Lhasa, the wish alone will not get them there. They also need the faith or confidence that they are able to make the journey. In addition, they need provisions for the journey, a map of the way, and the stamina and effort necessary in order to complete the long and arduous trip. The mere wish to come, divorced of these other factors, will not accomplish much.

Similarly, if we wish to arrive at the city of enlightenment we must first have the aspiration. Then on top of this we must have the map for how to get there, and also the stamina, energy and intelligent awareness necessary in order to be able to translate the map into effective action.

In the *Lam Rim* tradition of Atisha, there are three basic levels or stages in the training on the path leading to full enlightenment. These three are known as "the stages of the three types of spiritual aspirants."

Atisha describes the first of these three as follows in his *A Lamp for the Path to Enlightenment*,

> Someone who by the various methods
> Seeks to further himself
> By cultivating higher samsaric happiness
> Is known as the spiritual aspirant of initial scope.

He then describes the second stage,

> He who with the aim of nirvana for himself alone
> Strives to turn his back on samsaric happiness
> And attempts to utterly reverse all negative karma
> Is known as the spiritual aspirant of intermediate scope.

As for the third stage, Atisha writes,

> He who sees suffering in his own life
> And, realizing that others suffer likewise,
> Wishes to put an end to the misery of all,
> Is known as the spiritual aspirant of supreme scope.

In other words, the initial practitioner attempts to establish himself on the paths and practices leading to higher rebirth. The intermediate practitioner concerns himself with nirvana, or liberation from *samsara*. Finally, the practitioner of highest scope gives birth to the altruistic thought of achieving full Buddhahood as a supreme method of benefiting others.

As for the third of the above persons, here one's immediate aspiration is to be of the greatest possible benefit to others; but one realizes that this aspiration can only be fulfilled by first personally achieving full enlightenment. Therefore one engages in the Bodhisattva practices leading to omniscient enlightenment as the supreme method of working for others.

The full range of Buddha's teachings can be subsumed under the above three themes. To fully understand the three is to fully understand all factors to be cultivated and elements to be transcended on the paths leading to higher being, liberation and enlightenment.

It was because he perceived the importance of a correct understanding of the practices associated with these three phases of spiritual application that Lama Tsong-kha-pa wrote his three *Lam Rim* treatises.

Concerning the greatness of Atisha's essential *Lam Rim* tradition, Lama Tsong-kha-pa wrote,

> Through it one perceives all doctrines as non-contradictory,
> All teachings arise as personal advice,
> The intent of Buddha is easily found,
> And one is protected from the cliff of the greatest evil.
>
> Therefore the wise and fortunate of India and Tibet
> Have thoroughly relied upon this excellent legacy
> Known as "the stages in the practice of the three spiritual
>   beings."
> Who of powerful mind would not be intrigued by it?

The heart of Atisha's *Lam Rim* lineage is the twofold cultivation of wisdom and method, with wisdom referring to the techniques for cultivating an understanding of the ultimate level of truth, or the emptiness of inherent existence, and method referring to all other spiritual practices, and being linked to the conventional level of truth.

Thus under the topic of method is found a wide range of spiritual techniques. Yet of all these, the principal element is the cultivation of the altruistic bodhimind, the Bodhisattva spirit, the sublime aspiration to achieve the enlightenment of full Buddhahood as a supreme means of benefiting others, together with the practices for fulfilling that aspiration.

The importance of the bodhimind is described as follows in Atisha's *A Lamp for the Path to Enlightenment,*

> Were the meritorious energy of the bodhimind
> To manifest as a material object,
> All of space would become filled
> And still more would remain.

The bodhimind is the very root of the peerless Mahayana, and one should continuously hold it in the forefront of all activities. Especially, make it the basis of any study or practice that you engage in.

The correct manner of engaging in spiritual training is aptly described in the following verse,

> In the beginning, listen to many teachings.
> In the middle, take all teachings as personal advice.
> In the end, practice day and night without let.
> Throughout these three stages, dedicate the merit
> To the continuation of the enlightenment tradition.

The sign of having listened correctly is that the meaning of all the teachings heard will begin to arise as personal advice. Then when this second step becomes firm, one naturally inclines toward intensely practicing day and night without let.

The three main activities on the Buddhist path to enlightenment are study, contemplation and meditation. Meditation is of two types: analytical (i.e., cursive, reflective) and fixed (i.e., non-cursive, formal). It is a mistake to practice only the latter of these two types.

It is not necessary to retreat to a remote cave in order to practice meditation. Any quiet place will do.

Je Lang-dol Rin-po-che[4] once said, "An intermediate scholar meditator is equal to a great hermit meditator." What he meant by this is that it is best to have study and contemplation as the basis. Then meditation becomes really powerful.

While pursuing our studies we should train in the vast and profound oral instructions that constitute the fundamental Buddhist path. On top of that we should cultivate the samadhi that combines meditative serenity (*shamatha*) with insight (*vipashyana*), and thus accomplish the two final perfections: meditation and wisdom.

Then for those who are not satiated with these Sutrayana trainings there remain the Four Classes of Tantras: *kriya, charya, yoga,* and *maha anuttara yoga.*

The quintessence of these four is the *maha anuttara* yoga tantras, or 'great highest yoga tantra division,' through which the full enlightenment of final Buddhahood can be achieved in this one short lifetime.

In order to achieve complete Buddhahood one requires a path uniting both method (energy) and wisdom (insight) aspects of the path. This produces the state of the great union of evolved body and mind, which is the ultimate attainment. In the anuttara yoga tantras, 'method' refers to the illusory body yogas and 'wisdom' refers to the clear light yogas.

The anuttara yoga tantra system most clearly elucidating the path of the illusory body yogas is that of the *Guhyasamaja-tantra,* or 'Tantra of the Secret Assembly.' The system most clearly elucidating the clear light yogas is the *Heruka-chakrasamvara-tantra,* or 'Tantra of the Heruka Wheel of Bliss.' The essential points of both of these systems is skillfully combined in the *Vajrabhairava-tantra,* or 'Tantra of the Diamond Terrifier,' a tradition also known as the *Yamantaka-tantra,* or 'Tantra of the Destroyer of Death.'

Therefore these three anuttara yoga tantra systems—*Guhyasamaja, Heruka Chakrasamvara,* and *Vajrabhairava*—work very well together as a unified method bringing quick and easy enlightenment.

For this reason the Bodhisattva Manjushri advised Lama Tsong-kha-pa, "You should use the combined yogic techniques of the tantric traditions of Guhyasamaja, Heruka and Vajrabhairava as an inseparable method in the quest for enlightenment."

The above summary of the stages in study and practice outlines the basic steps in training followed by the great masters of the past. Through accomplishing this path they achieved the highest realization. If we ourselves wish to accomplish the same exalted states of knowledge and enlightenment, we should climb up the same staircase without mistaking the order of the steps on the path.

It is important that we take our Dharma practice into every moment of our lives. Otherwise, living foolishly while talking about colossal Dharma plans for the future produces no results. Through correct daily practice, this precious human rebirth is gradually turned to the meaningful and the essence of life is extracted. Then even if we do not achieve enlightenment in this one lifetime at least we have set ourselves in the right direction and in future incarnations will be able to continue along the way.

There was a time when each of the Buddhas was an ordinary being just like ourselves. At that time they too experienced confusion, anxiety and suffering, just as we do now. They too had been born many times in the lower realms of samsara. But because they applied themselves to the enlightenment teachings and to the process of cultivating wisdom and meritorious energy, they eventually achieved the state of omniscient Buddhahood. We, on the other hand, chose to follow the impulses of negative karma and delusion, and therefore have remained behind in samsara. We chose distraction rather than the path to enlightenment, and thus have gained samsara rather than Buddhahood.

We should take our inspiration and direction from the enlightened ones, and resolve to go the way they have gone. Then we too will experience the fruits of the spiritual path.

Other than by taking personal responsibility for our own spiritual training, there is no way that we can move toward enlightenment. The compassion of the Buddhas and Bodhisattvas is great, but it can only benefit those who respond to it. The Buddhas may point out the way to enlightenment for us, but we travel the path solely by means of our own efforts.

As is said in the scriptures, "The Buddhas cannot wash away our negativities with water, nor remove our sufferings by touching us with their hands, nor can they transfer their wisdom to us in the manner of giving us a material object. All they can do is show us the paths and practices." Whether or not we achieve spiritual liberation depends entirely upon whether or not we apply ourselves to the practices.

Therefore *An Ornament of the Clear Realizations (mNgon-rtogs-rgyan)* states,

> Although the king of gods sends forth rain,
> Infertile seeds do not sprout.
> Similarly, although the Buddhas manifest
> Those without merit experience no benefit.

As a result of the positive collective karma of all beings, the celestial forces of goodness send forth rain; and from this come rich harvests, prosperity and well-being. However, seeds that have been burned in fire or damaged in other ways will not sprout nor produce a crop.

Similarly, although the Buddhas come into the world the people of poor karmic instincts take no interest and therefore are not benefited. They are like Buddha Shakyamuni's cousin Devadatta, who even though he intellectually comprehended the Dharma was unable to really appreciate it. Consequently he was unable to put it into correct practice. The compassion of the Buddha was the same for him as for anyone else; but because Devadatta was obstructed by the negative preconceptions and the instincts of darkness, the Buddha was unable to get through to him.

Thus we play the fundamental role in our own spiritual growth. Nobody can achieve enlightenment for us; we must cultivate the realizations within ourselves. We are our own witness and our own navigator. The enlightened beings can only point the way for us and urge us on. The real power lies in our own hands.

It is said that whether the enlightenment teachings increase or decline in strength depends to a great extent upon the efforts of the spiritual practitioners. Therefore if we rank ourselves in the assembly of practitioners we must remember that we carry some degree of responsibility to live and practice well.

If anything in the above is useful to you and to your practice, I urge you to try and implement it.

> Should any meritorious energy arise
> As a result of this brief work,
> May it contribute to the happiness and enlightenment
> Of all the living beings, and also
> To the longevity of the precious Buddhadharma.

Chösum Altar

2 Sermons at the Great Prayer Festival

SERMON ONE: THE WATER DOG YEAR—1922

The incomparable Lama Tsong-kha-pa once wrote,

> Study the many stainless scriptures.
> If from now until Buddhahood is attained
> We look to the profound instructions
> That point the way to enlightenment,
> And if we internalize their meanings,
> Then all the words of Buddha and the later masters
> Will arise as personal advice to us.
> Whoever does just that is called "a sage."

Although we claim to apply ourselves intensely to the path of learning, contemplation and meditation, our merits seem small and both our inborn and cultivated powers of determination weak. For this reason it is difficult for us to apply the teachings to our own life experience in an effective way. Correct practice seems to elude us.

Lama Tsong-kha-pa, a spiritual master who had himself achieved the state of great union and who wished to guide others to the liberated state of the three Buddha *kayas*, therefore said,

The holy masters see the Dharma as being
The source of every goodness and happiness.
Thus they offer prayers that it thrive for long.
But merely to know the teaching
Without generating realization within one's mindstream
Will not accomplish this prayer.
One [i.e.,learning] without the other [i.e., realization]
Will not fulfill the aspirations of the sages.

The sages of the past, perceiving that the holy Dharma is a supreme source of goodness and happiness, made great efforts to preserve the precious teachings in both aspects of scriptures and insight. They offered the prayer that the Dharma remain forever in the world without degenerating. Thus we ourselves today, who proudly claim to follow in the footsteps of Buddha and the previous Buddhist masters who upheld the enlightenment teachings by means of pure vision and action, should generate a deeper sense of commitment to the fulfillment of the prayers and aspirations of these holy beings. In brief, we should sacrifice our petty self-interests and should cultivate a deeper sense of universal responsibility. Otherwise, how else can we accomplish spiritual purposes?

In order to preserve the enlightenment teachings one must first oneself realize their meaning.

A Treasury of Abhidharma (Chos-mngon-par-mdzod) states,

The Dharma taught by Buddha
Has two aspects: scriptural and insight.
The first of these is upheld
By means of study and teaching;
The second is upheld by practice and realization.

As said above, the doctrine of the Buddha dharma has two facets: scriptures and insight. We preserve the former of these by means of studying and later teaching the words of the *Tripitaka*, or Three Baskets of Scriptures, the sources explaining the nature of practice. We preserve the latter, or Insight Dharma, by means of intensive application to the three higher trainings: discipline, meditation and wisdom, the principal themes elucidated in the *Tripitaka*.

Some people say that studying and contemplating the great scriptures does nothing but increase the powers of the intellect and the conceptual mind. They loudly pronounce that, to accomplish the ultimate purpose, we must engage in a practice quite separate from those discussed in the great scriptures. They think that solely by pursuing some solitary meditation technique, without any supportive study, Buddhahood will eventually be accomplished.

However, unless one analyses in depth the nature of what is to be cultivated and what transcended in the quest for Buddhahood, the mind will be dominated by vagueness and unclarity, and will have no certainty concerning the precise points in the training.

The effects of meditating in mental darkness ignorant of the nature of the practices produces a Buddhahood as valid as the horn on a rabbit's head. It is an attainment devoid of all meaning. The path to enlightenment begins by attempting to weaken the delusions and mental factors that are to be transcended, and by increasing the mental and spiritual factors to be cultivated. With persistent application, all negative factors become replaced by enlightenment qualities; the state of perfect Buddhahood is achieved, and the mandala of the qualities of transcendence and insight waxes, to become like the refreshing full moon. The obscurations of delusion and the obscurations to knowledge, together with all negative instincts, are thus gradually purified and Buddhahood is achieved.

On the other hand, to meditate intensely with a dark mind for a year or an aeon is as effective as shooting an arrow into the darkness of night at a target one cannot see. It produces results about as spectacular as a star at mid-day.

Therefore the incomparably kind Lama Tsong-kha-pa, lord of the sutra and tantra teachings, founder of the Yellow Hat tradition, strongly emphasized that we should study the vast scriptures in the lineages of Nagarjuna and Asanga, the two great Mahayana forefathers. The impact of study and contemplation of, together with meditation upon, the themes of their ocean-like scriptures is extremely powerful, and produces quick spiritual progress unequalled by other simpler methods. Thus if we call ourselves followers of Tsong-kha-pa's Yellow Hat tradition, a lineage of pure practice combined with faultless philosophy, it is important that we make great effort to understand the nature of the points and levels in training, and to fully internalize these.

On the other hand, if one does not have the capacity to enter into study and practice based upon the great scriptures, then one should search for a living oral transmission teaching coming in an unbroken ear-whispered lineage.

As stated in (*Ashvagosha's*) *Fifty Verses on the Guru* (*bLa-ma-lnga-bcu-pa*), in order to quickly accomplish the path to enlightenment it is expedient to rely upon a spiritual friend who is qualified in learning, practice and experience, and who possesses the various fundamental and subsidiary qualities of a true spiritual master. Here it is important that the disciple proceed by means of correct attitude and action and apply himself/herself intensely to the key points in the teachings by means of diligently maintaining the instructions orally received.

The Ka-dam-pa master Ge-she Zung-jug Rin-po-che[1] wrote in his *Advice* (*Zhal-gdams*):

> We have taken birth again and again
> From time without beginning,
> But have not yet achieved liberation.
> This indicates that we have never met with a guru,
> Or [if we met with one] did not recognize him;
> Or, even if we met with and recognized a guru,
> We did not respond with skill.
> Thus we continue to wander in *samsara*.
>
> These days there are many qualified masters
> Whom we can meet and recognize.
> Do not run to many;
> Rather, search for one qualified master
> With whom you have a strong connection.
> Then, having found him, devote yourself correctly
> Without giving thought to worldly considerations.

As said here, we cannot fix any particular previous reincarnation as being the beginning of our rebirths in *samsara*, for time and previous births are without a beginning. Yet we have never managed to achieve spiritual liberation, and therefore continue to wander in *samsara*.

What is the root cause of our continued wandering? Simply this: We have not met with a spiritual master capable of showing us the path to liberation; or even if we met with a teacher, we did not recognize him/her as a source of all goodness and happiness; or even if we experienced this recognition, at the time of the encounter our minds were spiritually immature and we were unable to take advantage of the situation by engaging in correct practice under his/her guidance, and any spiritual efforts we made were but superficial reflections with no real strength. Consequently we have been unable to achieve higher knowledge, and have had to remain under the power of delusion and compulsive karmic patterns.

However, now we have achieved a human rebirth endowed with the freedom and potential for development of higher spiritual knowledge, and can meet with a spiritual master. We have a body and mind unhindered by faults, and possess the precious human intelligence capable of realizing the meaning of Dharma. We should take advantage of our auspicious situation and search for a guru qualified to teach the unmistaken path leading to spiritual liberation. Having found such a master, we should devote ourselves correctly by means of attitude and action, sacrificing all lesser purposes in order to achieve the highest purpose. The person who does exactly that gives birth quickly and easily to all the excellent qualities and realizations of the paths and stages leading to enlightenment.

Some practitioners study with just a few gurus; others study with many. In the histories of the early Ka-dam-pa masters it is said that the Ka-dam-pa forefather Lama Drom Ton-pa[2] relied upon only five gurus. On the other hand, Ge-she Song-phu-pa[3] studied under almost every guru with whom he ever happened to meet. Once when traveling from Kham to Lhasa, Ge-she Song-phu-pa encountered a lay *ngak-pa* and immediately asked him for his lineages of Dharma. The *ge-she's* attendants rebuked him, saying that the *ngak-pa* was neither particularly learned nor realized; but the *ge-she* shrugged off their objections, replying that regardless of their opinions, he felt that every teacher he met with was able to benefit him in one way or another.

Once Lama Gom-pa Rin-po-che and Ge-she Po-to-wa[4] were discussing these two approaches—to devote oneself to just a few gurus or to train under many. They both agreed that the former approach, that of Lama Drom, is better for most people, and particularly for those at basic levels of training. This, I think, is the meaning of the above quotation by Ge-she Zung-jug, in which he says, "Do not run to many; rather search for one qualified master...."

Once one has found a qualified teacher with whom one has a strong karmic connection, in what manner should one rely upon him/her?

Here it is said that one should rely in ten ways. The first of these is given as follows in Ge-she Zung-jug's *Advice*:

Rely with confidence free from apathy.

That is to say, one should devote oneself tirelessly to the guru, appreciating the opportunity as a source of great benefits.

Maintaining the correct attitude of faith and confidence is one's own responsibility. Therefore the yogi Je-tsun Mi-la-re-pa[5] once sang,

Most people keep their faith in their mouth.
I, a yogi, keep mine in my heart.

As said here, one's faith and confidence must be heartfelt, and not a mere vocal expression.

Ge-she Zung-jug's *Advice* lists the remainder of the ten modes of correctly relying on the guru as follows:

Rely by means of unattached generosity.
Rely by means of the stainless, special attitude.
Rely by means of unclouded wisdom.
Rely by means of respect free from pride.
Rely by means of unhesitating service.
Rely informally and without stiffness.
Rely patiently without short-temperedness.
Rely sincerely without hypocrisy.
Rely with divine pride free from the mundane vision.

Follow the examples set by
The youthful Bodhisattva Sudhana,
The constantly weeping Saraprarudita,
Atisha, Lama Drom Ton-pa, and Chen-nga-wa.
Befriend the guru and stay tirelessly with him.
Then, whether or not you formally study,
You will automatically generate spiritual qualities,
Like a cloth wrapped around incense
Naturally absorbs the aroma of the incense.
Carefully guard your relationship with your guru
As you would guard a precious gem.

These are the ten ways in which one should cultivate the guru-disciple relationship.

For inspiration in practice, one should look to the accounts related in the scriptures.

For example, the story of the youthful Bodhisattva Sudhana's insatiable devotion to his numerous gurus is wonderfully presented in the *Avatamsaka Sutra*. Also, the *Prajnaparamita Sutra* relates the inspiring manner in which the constantly weeping Sadaprarudita devoted himself to his guru Dharmodgata. And the early Ka-dam-pa literature is rich in stories of how Lama Drom Ton-pa trained under Atisha.

We should read and contemplate these various accounts, and model our relationship with our own guru upon them.

The great sage Je Tsong-kha-pa once wrote, "In cultivating our relationship with our personal gurus we should consider the biography of Shon-nu-od." Tsong-kha-pa then proceeds to praise Shon-nu-od's manner of relating to his guru as being exemplary of pure devotion.

This refers to the young monk who later became the great Ka-dam-pa master Ge-she Cha-yul-ba.[6]

Shon-nu-od had been born in To-lung. He became a monk while still a young child, and was placed in the care of the Ka-dam-pa teacher Ge-she To-lung-pa. One day the two of them—teacher and disciple— went to visit the renowned Ka-dam-pa master Chen-nga-wa.

Chen-nga-wa inquired about the boy, whereupon To-lung-pa replied, "He is a child who has been placed in my care and is traveling with me as my attendant."

Ge-she Chen-nga-wa observed, "He seems to have a brilliant mind. You are fortunate indeed to be attended to by such a brilliant young monk."

Taking this as a sign that the great guru was impressed with the boy's character, To-lung-pa placed a white silk scarf over the child's shoulders and pushed him forward, saying, "If you wish to have him with you, I can entrust him into your care."

From that day on, the young monk stayed with Chen-nga-wa. Eventually he became his chief attendant, devoting himself to the elderly guru with all his heart.

After some years had passed and he was old enough to go beyond the status of a novice monk by taking higher ordination, he refused, thinking that he would prefer to remain a novice so that he could continue to serve the old guru and personally carry his food to him every day (for it is the monastic tradition that only the novice monks serve food to the elders). Therefore he remained a novice. But whenever the great guru would teach, his faithful attendant was always present and thus came to hear countless discourses from him.

One day the attendant heard some monks from Kyi-sho discussing him, saying that it was sad that, with his genius, he had spent his life as an attendant and therefore had not been able to devote himself to intensive study. "Had a person with his intelligence been able to give himself solely to study and meditation," they were saying, "he would have become an incomparable sage."

The attendant interrupted their conversation, informing them that he disagreed with their view of the Dharma. "I have served as the guru's servant for many years. To my mind, this was the best way to learn and practice the Dharma. Although I had no wealth or possessions to offer, this impermanent body of mine belongs to me. Therefore I offered it in the service of the guru. I have done this without regard for whether or not it would perish like a water bubble on the river. And I have no regrets."

Shon-nu-od served his guru for many years in this way. Then one day he was performing the daily task of sweeping the guru's room. As he walked out of the room to discard the dust, a direct experience of the nature of ultimate truth suddenly arose within his mindstream. He immediately sat down and entered into the *samadhi* that realizes the non-dual nature of emptiness and manifest diversity.

He sat like this at length, totally absorbed in the enlightenment experience. Many hours later his friends found him sitting beside the road. Only with repeated attempts did they manage to rouse him from his absorption.

Eventually the boy Shon-nu-od became famed throughout the length and breadth of the land as the great master Ge-she Cha-yul-pa, whose life and enlightenment is recorded and acclaimed in so many of the histories of the early Ka-dam-pa adepts.

The lives and deeds of this and the other Ka-dam-pa masters reflect magnificence and the achievement of high states of enlightenment. They gained these exalted spiritual stages because they knew how to behave toward the guru in both thought and action. They understood well that practicing correct guru yoga is the root producing both high states of mind and ultimate realization.

If you have met with a qualified spiritual master with whom you feel a strong karmic connection, do not let the opportunity slip away. As human beings we have a mind capable of achieving anything, even the state of perfect Buddhahood within our lifetime. Do not let your life pass into meaninglessness.

We all know that each of us must die, yet most of us live under the delusion that our own death is something very remote. This dominating sense of permanence constantly deceives us, and under its power our mind loses sight of higher spiritual values. The things that are limited to this one short lifetime, such as social status and material possessions, come to be regarded as the essence and ultimate purpose of our existence. It is as though we walk around with our head on backwards.

The *Advice* states,

> We do no spiritual practice for a day.
> Days, months and years pass like that,
> And soon an empty life has passed.
> Then death catches us by surprise.
> We hold our head in sorrow
> And clutch at our chest in fear;
> But by then it is too late to change.

As said here, most of us pass our entire lives without ever getting around to spiritual training, the source of generating the eternally beneficial within the mindstream. Morning, afternoon, evening and night pass like that, and soon a complete day has gone. However, it does not merely pass into nothingness; for the mind, when not tempered by spiritual training, quickly accumulates negative habits, and this causes the body and speech to also fall under the influence of negativity. Thus a day passes in the service of darkness; days become months, and months become years. A lifetime soon evaporates in this way, with spiritual thoughts becoming as rare as a star at noon.

Then one day the face of death appears before us. The elements of the body begin suddenly to dissolve, and our limbs lose their power of motion. Our mouth dries and a dreadful sense of thirst sets in. We want to speak, but we haven't the strength to give voice to a single word. A strong sense of the vanity of our life wells up within us, and regret at our failures and shortcomings arises. Filled with apprehension, we clutch at our chest in fear and call out to the objects of refuge for help. However, although we once held in the palm of our hands the opportunity to benefit both this and future lives, we threw it away. Now it is too late to do anything. Our life has passed in negativity, and there is nothing at this late date that the refuge objects can do to save us from the karmic patterns that we ourselves have woven.

The power of the refuge objects and the power of the karma of liv-

ing beings are equal. If during our whole life we accumulate only negative karma, there will be no value in calling upon the refuge objects
at the time of death.

What the refuge objects can do is to guide and inspire us in spiritual training during our lifetime. In particular, the refuge object of the
Dharma, or the teachings, must be learned and internalized during
our life. Then at death it automatically benefits. But it is simply wishful
thinking to live in ignorance and negativity, avoiding spiritual practice and pursuing only materialistic goals, and then at the time of death
to hope for a savior.

This is illustrated by the story of Mon-dro Cho-drak. He was greatly admired for his charisma and intelligence, and everyone constantly
praised him. Eventually the people of his village elected him as their
chieftain. However, he only used his position of power for his own
personal benefit, and as a result his positive qualities became causes
of negative karma.

One day he became very ill and realized that he was dying. At the
time he was lying on a bed in a corner of his room, with the sun shin-
ing in on him. One of his admirers entered the room and, seeing him
lying there, jokingly said, "Everyone praises you for your intelligence,
but it isn't very clever of you to sleep in the sun when you have a high
fever."

Mon-dro Cho-drak replied, "All my life everyone has had only praise
for me. Now my life is almost finished, but when I look back over
the years I can see that I have done everything with it except practice
Dharma. Now the day of my death has come before me, but when
I analyze my accomplishments I cannot find anything of any significant meaning. Everyone praises my intelligence, but am I not the
greatest fool in the three worlds!"

Most of us are very much like Mon-dro Cho-drak, passing our lives
in the sphere of meaningless activities, being deceived and misguided
by flattery and materialistic allurements. With our heads thus turned
in the wrong direction, very little of what we do produces anything
positive and worthwhile.

Therefore we need a guru to help us keep our mind in focus, a
spiritual friend who is able to point us in the right direction, someone who can keep us on the pure paths leading to higher states of being and even to perfect enlightenment.

If you have found such a spiritual friend, regard him as an emanation of the Buddhas. Cultivate unfeigned confidence in him. Medi-

tate on the extraordinary kindness that the guru can perform, and on the many ways in which he benefits the living beings of the world. Constantly maintain awareness of the value of the guru to one's life, and respond correctly in body, speech and mind. The disciple who pleases the guru by making the offering of intensely practicing the teachings gains the inspiring blessings of the Buddhas of the past, present and future.

When a field is moist and fertile, any seed planted in it will quickly sprout and grow. Similarly, if one's stream of being is ripe any spiritual practices one engages in will produce rapid results.

For this reason it is important that we train according to the correct stages, beginning with fundamental themes such as guru yoga, the preciousness and rarity of human life with its eight freedoms and ten endowments, the nature of impermanence and death, the manner of taking refuge in the Buddha, Dharma and Sangha, the karmic laws of cause and effect, the vicious nature of samsaric existence, and so forth. Only when basic meditations such as these have produced some results within our mindstream should we go on to the higher meditations of love, compassion, the altruistic bodhimind that aspires to enlightenment as a means to benefit the world, the methods of cultivating the wisdom of emptiness, the various tantric yogas, and so forth.

It is said that to meditate for years on the higher subjects without having first achieved the fruits of the basic meditations will produce no results whatsoever. The example is given of a person who concentrates on the interior decoration of a house before the foundations of the house have even been laid. His activities are meaningless.

Therefore the ancient Ka-dam-pa masters had a saying, "Before going on to the next step in meditation, repeat the step you are on." This is the effective way to practice.

Guru yoga is the first step in the Mahayana trainings; but it does not stop there. In fact, all practices up to the final step before full Buddhahood can be subsumed under the topic of guru yoga. This is because every practice that we engage in at whatever level is an offering of correct practice. Thus the meditations on death, karma, the four noble truths, refuge, love and compassion, the wisdom of emptiness, the two yogic stages of the tantric path, etc., all collect into the theme of guru yoga.

The Ka-dam-pa master Lama Drom Ton-pa once said, "A boy travels through many countries. In each place he is known by a different name. Yet although the names are many, they all collect upon the one boy. Similarly, there are many names for the various subjects and techniques of meditation, yet all of these are collected within the topic of relying correctly upon the spiritual friend. None of them pass beyond guru yoga."

Therefore if you have encountered and are cared for by a spiritual friend, regard him as an emissary sent by the Buddhas in order to tame and cultivate your mindstream. When one relates to the spiritual friend correctly in both thought and action, all spiritual qualities are automatically achieved by association with him in the same way that incense wrapped in cloth automatically transmits its aroma to the cloth in which it is wrapped.

However, when one's attitude and behavior are undisciplined and inappropriate, mere association with the guru will be of no avail. The example is given of a bee and a frog. Both live at the side of the lake in a garden of lotus flowers, but only the bee daily drinks the honey of the lotus. The frog gets no benefits whatsoever from the lotus nectar. In the same way, only the person with the correct attitude and disciplined behavior will be able to extract the benefits of contact with the guru.

Moreover, there are some types of people whose minds are so distorted that contact with the guru just increases their accumulation of negative karma. Because of their own mental shortcomings, they just impute faults upon the guru and see the holy as unholy. They are like owls, for whom sunlight—an element that normally is only beneficial—causes eye problems. Because of their mental obscurations, a positive circumstance is twisted into something negative and only further compounds their confusion.

For this reason it is very important to gain an unmistaken vision of how to practice—of what has to be cultivated and what transcended in the course of traveling the path leading to enlightenment—and to constantly maintain this vision in one's mind, using it as a map and guide in each life experience.

It is said that the principal method of devoting oneself to the guru is by making the offering of practice. Primarily this means that one engages in meditation every day as the supreme means of pleasing the spiritual masters.

In the Ka-dam-pa tradition it was strongly recommended that each meditation session be begun with the six preliminary practices. These six deal with establishing a conducive environment, bodily posture and mental framework. When these three factors are present, meditation becomes extremely powerful and produces profound effects.

These six preliminaries are as follows: (1) cleaning the place of practice and setting up the altar; (2) arranging an attractive display of offerings; (3) sitting correctly in the meditational posture, and then taking refuge and developing the bodhimind; (4) generating the visualization of the field of merit; (5) offering the seven-limbed devotion, together with the symbolic offering of the universe; and (6) offering prayers and supplications to the gurus in the line of transmission.

Over the following years as part of my annual sermon at the Great Prayer Festival I will speak briefly on each of these six in turn. I will begin this year with a discussion of the first of the six—cleaning the place of practice and setting up the altar.

This first preliminary is spoken of in many sutras, tantras and shastras.

The *Prajnaparamita Sutra* in eight thousand verses relates the following story, in which the constantly weeping Saraprarudita prepared the place where the great guru Dharmodgata was to teach.

So obsessed was he with the wish to receive the teachings on transcendent wisdom, the constantly weeping Saraprarudita spent seven years unable to eat or drink. Throughout this time he could only sit thinking about when he would be able to find the wisdom teachings. Then one day from the sky came the words, "In seven days Guru Dharmodgata shall arise from his *samadhi* and teach the Dharma at the crossroads of town."

Saraprarudita instantly became extremely excited and, in order to serve the master and facilitate the teaching, rushed to the site to clean and prepare it.

After he had done this he thought to sprinkle water over the area in order to prevent dust from arising. However, an evil spirit manifested and caused him to be unable to find any water. Therefore he generated special courage, drained some blood from his own veins, and sprinkled this on the ground. Five hundred merchants' daughters appeared and each offered to donate some of their blood for his purpose. Thus the evil spirit was unable to hinder his work and went away in shame. The *deva* Indra then appeared and magically transformed the blood into sandalwood water, the exquisite scent of which spread into all directions for a hundred *yojanas*. This delighted the forces of goodness, and they released their blessings and harmonious energies.

Saraprarudita then adorned the site with flowers and arranged a seat for the master.

Because of the merits of his efforts, he eventually received the teachings on transcendent wisdom and, by its powers, achieved spiritual realization.

His sacrifice was obviously quite extraordinary. Most places of meditation and teaching do not have to be prepared with this intense an act of sacrifice. However, because in the above story the recipient of the teaching was already a high bodhisattva, it perhaps was necessary for him to make an extraordinary gesture. Also, as the teaching he was about to receive was extremely high and was obstructed by the forces of evil, an unusually austere effort seems to have been required in order to generate merit and to remove hindrances.

Another sutra describes how the *mahashtravira* Chudapantaka was instructed by the Buddha to clean the temple area. Through his practice of sweeping he attained the path of direct vision of reality, thus transcending all worldly delusions.

These and many other sutra references illustrate how the act of cleaning the place of practice or teaching produces significant results.

The same point is made in the tantras.

In general, the tantras are classed into four divisions: *kriya, charya, yoga,* and *maha anuttara yoga.* In the *kriya* tantras, the external activities of cleaning and washing are principal elements in the training, and are emphasized more than are the internal yogas. In the *charya* tantras there is an equal emphasis on the internal yogas and the external practices such as cleaning; thus here too cleanliness is stressed.

As for the *yoga* and *maha anuttara yoga* classes, here the internal practices are much more important than are the external methods, and in these tantric divisions there is no way to discern the level of the practitioner from his/her external manifestation. Nonetheless, practitioners on elementary stages of training are wise to follow the advice given in *The Ornament of Mahayana Sutras (mDo-sde-rgyan),* wherein it is stated,

> The practice site of a fortunate trainee
> Should have the following qualities:
> Convenience of acquiring necessities,
> A harmonious location, healthy,
> Being close to helpful friends,
> And having conditions conducive to yoga.

That is to say, the practice site should be endowed with five qualities. Firstly, from it one should be able easily to acquire food, clothing, medicines, and so forth that will be needed during the extent of the practice, a condition that is particularly important when choosing a retreat site. Secondly, it should be a harmonious place safe from dangers posed by humans and non-humans. Thirdly, it should have physical qualities conducive to health and that do not promote any diseases. Also, it should be near friends who are supportive, and who have disciplined behavior and positive attitudes. Finally, it should have conditions conducive to the practice of meditation, such as not having disturbances from humans during the day, nor having excessive noises at night.

As for the actual place of practice, the best is a traditional cave that has been used by the great meditators of the past. Otherwise, any retreat hut or even a quiet room in one's home is fine.

When you clean the practice place, imagine that the entire world is thus cleansed and purified.

There is a verse in Shantideva's *A Guide to the Bodhisattva Way* (*sPyod-'jug*) that is often recited at the beginning of our meditation sessions,

> May all the world become free from
> All harsh qualities, such as thorns.
> May it become as smooth as lapis lazuli
> And as tender as the palm of one's hand.

When reciting this verse, remember its meaning. This links the act of cleaning the practice site with the aspiration to produce our individual Buddhafield in the future when full enlightenment has been achieved.

The actual exercise of cleaning the place of meditation is in the category of methods for benefiting oneself. The exercise of imagining that thereby all the world has been purified is in the category of methods for benefiting others. These two factors—benefiting oneself and benefiting others—lay the imprints that contribute to the achievement of the two *kayas* of a Buddha: the *dharmakaya* (Wisdom Body) and *rupakaya* (Form Body).

The (Tibetan) word used for the practice of cleaning the meditation site is *chi-dor* (*byi-dor*). *Chi* means to clean or polish; and *dor* means to remove or discard.

Thus there are two aspects to the contemplation pursued while cleaning the place of practice.

In the first of these, that related to *chi*, while sweeping and dusting one contemplates that the negative karmic seeds, delusions and spiritual obscurations of both oneself and others take the form of the dirt to be cleared away. As the external dirt is swept one thinks that thus the inner negativities and obscurations fade away of themselves, and that in the place of these inner defilements one experiences the unobstructed wisdom that has the power to eliminate the obstacles to the individual stages of the path leading to enlightenment.

As for the second factor, that related to *dor*, when discarding the dirt one contemplates that the dust of the inner negativities is thrown far away, never again to return. This symbolizes the noble truth of the cessation of karma and delusion; and also the noble truth of the path of liberation, that possesses the powers which place the practitioner far above the forces of negativity.

Thus *dor*, or "discarding," represents the inseparable union of the truth of cessation and the truth of the path. The objects discarded i.e, the dust and dirt, represent the noble truth of suffering; and also the noble truth of the cause of suffering, which is contaminated karma and delusion.

In this way this first preliminary of cleaning the practice site becomes a contemplative exercise focussing on the four noble truths, the essence of the first teachings that Buddha gave after he had achieved his enlightenment.

When the site has been well cleaned and the dust thrown outside, one sprinkles the place with a few drops of scented water. This is done because during the practice one will imagine that all the gurus, Buddhas and Bodhisattvas are present as witnesses, and as an act of respect for them one wants the place to be clean and fresh.

If you cannot sprinkle water every day, at least do the cleaning meditation while visualizing that the inner pollutants that cause disease, and also the hindrances that cause unclear meditation, are swept away.

These are the correct contemplations and attitudes to be cultivated when performing the cleaning exercise. Otherwise, merely cleaning the practice site in order to impress visitors or patrons with one's fastidiousness will be of no significant spiritual benefit. The motivation and thought process involved are the important factors; the mere act of cleansing in itself has no intrinsic value.

The situation can be likened to two people who come from Eastern Tibet on a visit to Lhasa. One of them is on a pilgrimage and the other is on a business trip. Each step taken by the former becomes a cause generating spiritual energy, whereas the efforts of the latter have only a materialistic significance. Their physical movements of walking and riding may be identical, but because of the difference of their mental attitude and motivation the results produced are very different.

Although performed here as a preliminary, the practice of cleaning the meditation site is not merely a preliminary exercise. Every practice from guru yoga to the "yoga beyond training" can be linked to the contemplations involved in the sweeping practice. At each stage of development the contemplations involved may be varied somewhat in order to suit the specific situation, but the underlying theme is the same.

Once the place of meditation has been thus cleaned and purified, one should arrange an altar with representations of the body, speech and mind of the Enlightened Ones.

As a symbol of the body of the Enlightened Ones, at the center of the altar place an image of Buddha Shakyamuni, the monk who became the fourth universal teacher of this auspicious world cycle and set forth the vast and profound Dharma that has spread throughout the world and come down to us today. To the right of this image (his right, your left as you face the altar) place a Buddhist scripture to symbolize enlightened speech, and to his left (your right as you face the altar) place a stupa to represent the wisdom of the enlightened mind.

In addition to the Buddha image one may place images of the various Bodhisattvas, such as Maitreya and Manjushri, and of the gurus in the lineage of transmission.

It is also acceptable to place images of one's meditational deities and the Wisdom Dharma Protectors. However, do not include images of local divinities and worldly gods, as this would be in contradiction to the theme of Buddhist refuge. Also, as one's mindstream is prone to delusion it is possible that these worldly spirits would further agitate one's mind and create hindrances to meditation. It is acceptable to rely upon the worldly gods for worldly purposes, such as invoking them in order to gain wealth and prosperity, but to do so to an excess just places one outside the circle of those who follow the pure Buddhist tradition correctly.

There is no need for a complicated altar. If one understands that the various physical symbols are but reminders of the active enlightened wisdom, any simple Buddha image or picture of one's guru will do.

However, it is said that one's altar should be built in accordance with one's means. This contributes to a more powerful spiritual energy and to the accumulation of merit and wisdom. If one is of humble means, a simple rock or mound of grain will do. One simply imagines that the substance symbolizes the Enlightened Beings. The important thing is mental attitude.

There once was a great Tibetan yogi by the name of Je Kun-pang-pa.[7] He had renounced all worldly possessions. His altar had only a stone to represent the Buddha, and some clay bowls that he had made himself that he used in order to offer water. But his motivation was pure, and thus the merit of his altar and offering was great. The important thing is attitude and contemplation, not the physical objects that are used.

He (Je Kun-pang-pa) once wrote,

My imagination is my main Buddha image;
I place the Buddha in the presence of that imagination.

This is the correct way to practice.

On the other hand, there are some people who quote the life of Je Kun-pang-pa merely as an excuse to avoid spending their wealth on a decent altar piece. They are not renunciates; they just have cheap attitudes. Their problem is their priorities.

A beautiful altar is not merely a household decoration. It is an energy field meant to encourage mindfulness of the Dharma and the spiritual path. A beautiful altar is spiritually inspiring, but when it is just made in order to impress others with one's supposed religiosity, or as a status symbol, it merely becomes another cause of negative karma.

It is important that the sources of one's images, scriptures and so forth are pure. An image made by or purchased from a profit-monger is unacceptable. People who make religious images and print spiritual books should do so out of a pure motivation. As professionals they should make a reasonable living from their time and efforts, but their attitude should be to bring benefit to people and not merely to make a large profit. From our side we should take care that the artifacts we acquire are purchased from sincere people.

Hold the mind in the sphere of spiritual conviction, and regardless of whether you are walking, talking, lying down or whatever, maintain constant thoughts of the refuge objects. Continually recite the words of taking refuge in the guru, Buddha, Dharma and Sangha: *namo guru bhyah, namo Buddha ya, namo Dharma ya, namo Sangha ya.*

Whenever you eat or drink anything, first visualize making an offering to the Three Jewels. Constantly maintain the thought, "Every action that I create by means of body, speech and mind—be it positive or negative, wholesome or unwholesome—the guru and the Three Jewels are my witnesses. They never fail, and are always with me."

Thinking of them as omnipresent observers, generate a sense of conscientiousness and humble integrity. Rejoice in whatever spiritual practice you have cultivated, and strive diligently to further improve your mind.

As for those of you who have accepted the responsibility of teaching the Dharma, there is great merit in guiding others in study, understanding and practice. This is a supreme method of serving others and contributing to the world.

Once you have thus chosen and cleaned the practice place and have arranged the altar, it is customary to mark it off with mystic symbols. After that it should be kept private, and only one's gurus or those linked to the practice should be allowed to enter. Place a marker in each of the four directions and imagine that thus the four kingly protectors (*rGyal-chen-bzhi*) are present and that they serve to prevent all hindrances from entering.

Alternatively, simply place a marker above the doorway and imagine that it becomes Vaishravana. He then dispels all interferences and causes one's discipline to become especially strong.

If you are doing a lengthy retreat, regard the scriptures and instruction manuals as being embodiments of your guru, for it is they that now provide guidance and counsel. Think of their contents as being personal advice written directly for you. Keep several scriptures with you, and daily read from them and contemplate their meanings. Especially, refer frequently to one of the numerous *Lam Rim* treatises. It does not matter whether or not you are sufficiently learned to be able to fully understand what you read; even if you have no teeth, at least you can chew with your gums.

That is perhaps enough on the subject of the first of the six preliminary practices—cleaning the place of practice and arranging an altar.

The second preliminary is that of setting out elegant offerings to the refuge objects. I'll discuss that next year.

Our annual Great Prayer Festival is in commemoration of the time when Buddha entered into a competition of miracle performances at

Shravasti. The creation of the festival is said to be one of the four principal deeds of Lama Tsong-kha-pa. From his time it has been the tradition for the gurus, sages and scholars numerous as the stars in the sky to gather together, and on the fifteenth day of the festival for one from amongst them to read from Aryasura's *Jatakamala*, or *Garland of Birth Stories*. These relate episodes from the previous lives of Buddha Shakyamuni, when he was still a young Bodhisattva training in the practice of the six perfections.

Aryasura's *Jatakamala* contains thirty-four stories of this nature. The first of these describes how in a previous life the Buddha, practicing the perfection of generosity, gave his life to save a tigress and her four cubs from starvation.

> *His Holiness then read from*
> *the* Jatakamala. *Later he*
> *concluded his discourse as follows.*

Buddhism, which has survived as a spiritual tradition for more than two and a half millenniums, has benefited mankind in countless ways by bringing the messages of love, compassion, peace and harmony, and by setting forth a path whereby the mind of an individual practitioner can be trained and developed to the ultimate state of final enlightenment.

It is important that the Dharma be preserved for future generations, so that the enlightenment experience can continue on earth and the benefits that arise from it be enjoyed.

For it to continue, it is necessary for the Buddhist community to live in harmony undisturbed by sectarian rivalries, and that the individual members of the community live pure and disciplined lives. Dharma is not preserved by means of temples and monuments, but as a living experience within the mindstreams of practitioners.

In particular, those of us who are Sangha members [i.e., monks and nuns] have a special responsibility to dedicate ourselves to a pure life of study, contemplation and meditation. This must be based on the practice of observing the trainings in self-discipline, for discipline is the foundation on which is built the mental serenity necessary for successful meditative concentration. Meditative concentration in turn is the essential tool needed for cultivating the inner experience of wisdom. Thus the three extraordinary trainings of discipline, meditative concentration and wisdom are interdependent, and the higher cannot be achieved until the lower is made firm. Wisdom cannot be generated until meditative concentration has become strong, and there is no meditative concentration without a firm base of self-discipline.

The Sutra on Mindfulness (Dran-pa-nyer-bzag-gi-mdo) states,

> A flesh-eating vulture seems inappropriate
> In a beautiful lotus garden.
> Similarly in a spiritual hermitage
> A person with poor discipline is a bad omen.

According to folk belief, it is a bad omen for a vulture to appear in a place where there is no corpse to be devoured. And just as a vulture in a quiet lotus garden is inappropriate, a person with no self-discipline does not adorn a spiritual hermitage. Those of you who want to live as monks or nuns must reach up to the standards required by monastic ordination.

Especially, those of us who play out the role of being a spiritual teacher must be especially conscientious. Not to live up to our disciplines harms the general image of the Buddhist tradition.

The ill-disciplined monk not only harms himself. He harms the entire Sangha by damaging the image of the monkhood in the eyes of society.

A Treasury of Abhidharma (Chos-mngon-par-mdzod) states,

> This is a critical stage in the life
> Of the doctrine of the Enlightened Ones.
> Those wishing liberation should appreciate this
> And accordingly be especially mindful.

The decline and disappearance of the Buddha dharma will eventually be caused not by outside aggression but by the negative behavior, delusions and poor attitudes of the Buddhist practitioners themselves. Sectarian conflicts will play a significant role.

Therefore we should make special efforts to practice as purely and intensely as possible in order to reverse the pattern of decline. Especially, we should avoid all forms of sectarianism. If we want prosperity for our three great monastic universities and two tantric colleges, as well as for the smaller monastic communities and hermitages throughout the country, it is important that all of us individually check up on ourselves and make personal efforts to counteract any manifesta-

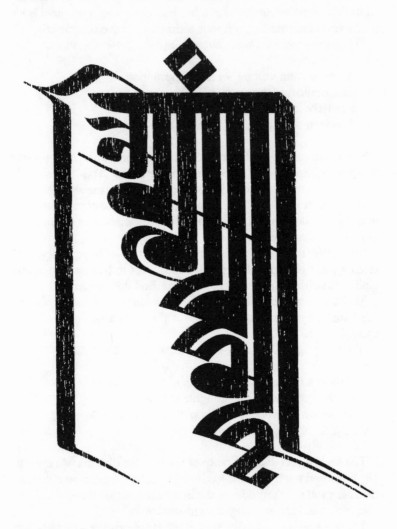

Cheresig mantra

tions of sectarian disharmony that we see.

The Sutra of Individual Liberation (So-sor-thar-pai-mdo) states,

> Harmony within the Sangha is joyous;
> The strict practice of harmony is joyous.

And also elsewhere the Buddha said,

> For some, discipline is a pleasure,
> For others it is suffering.
> Maintaining discipline is a pleasure,
> Transgressing one's disciplines is suffering.

This theme is repeated again and again in the scriptures. Therefore we who wish to achieve liberation and enlightenment should bear it in mind. If we ourselves don't take the responsibility to live and practice well, how can we expect anyone else to do so?

We should make firm our practice of the three extraordinary trainings: discipline, meditative concentration and wisdom. On that foundation any study of the Sutra and Tantra traditions that we pursue will immediately become beneficial.

It is important to mix the bodhimind, the altruist Bodhisattva aspiration, in with all our actions of body, speech and mind. This is the heart of the Mahayana endeavour. No matter what we are doing, using the bodhimind as the force behind the action transforms the activity into a Mahayana endeavour.

The character of the altruistic Bodhisattva aspiration was expressed succinctly by the illustrious *vinaya* master Kun-khyen Tso-na-wa She-rab Zang-po[8],

> However vast is the golden earth,
> May the altruistic bodhimind be as vast within me.
> However long is the Ganges River,
> May the stamina of my bodhimind be as long.
> However many medicinal herbs there are,
> May my bodhimind heal others in as many ways.
> And however spontaneous the creations of the wish-granting
>   tree,
> May my Bodhisattva aspiration be as automatically
>   beneficial to others.

Prostration

In general, the two goals of the Bodhisattva path are the benefitting of oneself and the benefitting of others. Benefitting oneself means achieving the Dharmakaya, or Wisdom-Truth Body which has realized the full transcendence and insight of enlightenment. However, one does not aspire to this attainment merely in order to gain the nirvana state of personal peace that is free from all-pervading samsaric suffering. Rather, one aspires to it in order to be of greater benefit to others. Only a fully enlightened being, a Buddha, is able to benefit others in a maximumly effective way, and therefore one aspires to the wisdom of Buddhahood.

The Bodhisattva Maitreya said,

The bodhimind is the aspiration
To achieve complete and perfect enlightenment
In order to be of greater benefit to others.

As said here, the Bodhisattva's aspiration has two facets: the wish to be of benefit to others; and the aspiration to achieve enlightenment oneself. These two must be kept together as complimentary forces, with the former being kept at the forefront.

Therefore the above verse of dedication by Kun-khyen Tso-na-wa is a supreme sentiment: May I constantly maintain the Bodhisattva aspiration with a strength as vast as the earth and as extensive as the Ganges River; may it always be like a medicine, healing others in countless ways; and may I be able to benefit others as effortlessly as does a magical wish-granting tree.

We ourselves should try to cultivate this auspicious aspiration.

I would like to close with the following verse for the dedication of meritorious energy:

If by giving or listening to this discourse
Any spiritual energy has been generated,
May it contribute toward the growth of wisdom
Within all living beings without exception.

SERMON TWO: THE WATER BOAR YEAR

The Indian master Acharya Vira, who was skilled in the five Buddhist sciences, once wrote,

From positive and negative actions
Come happiness and suffering, respectively.
As the results of karma are definite,
Avoid negativity and cultivate the wholesome.
As for those with no spiritual direction,
They simply do as they fancy.

The karmic fruits of positive and negative actions of body, speech and mind ripen as happiness and suffering, respectively. Therefore we should study the scriptures closely and gain an unmistaken understanding of the thoughts of the Buddha and the later Buddhist masters concerning the nature of what is to be overcome and what cultivated in the practice of the path leading to enlightenment.

Otherwise if we ourselves do not make some effort to learn the spiritual methods, there is nothing that anyone else can do to help us.

As the illustrious master Shantideva has said,

Countless Buddhas have manifested
And worked to benefit living beings.
But because of my own shortcomings
I did not become an object of their healing powers.

The countless Buddhas who have manifested in the world in the past have dedicated themselves exclusively to working for the benefit of the living beings afflicted by suffering. But many of us, overpowered by faults such as taking no interest in spiritual practice and being weak in both energy and wisdom, were too immature to profit from their presence. Unable to generate the strength to enter into the path leading to higher evolution and liberation—the path that the Buddhas came to reveal—we didn't become objects of their healing powers. Our lack of ability to cooperate with them rendered them unable to cure us of the sickness of compulsive karmic patterns and delusion. The fault lies on our side. The Buddhas themselves show no partiality in their compassion.

Now we possess all the circumstances necessary for Dharma practice. We should regard negative activity as being like poison and should avoid it; and we should look upon spiritual practice as being like medicine and cultivate it accordingly.

The above quotation says, "As for those of no spiritual direction, they simply do as they fancy." These words do not suggest that the Enlightened Ones abandon people who do not practice the Dharma, for the compassion of the Buddhas is as vast as the sky. But if from our side we make no effort at spiritual practice, we become unsuitable vessels for the teachings.

The situation is described as follows in *The Sutra of the Ten Dharmas* (*Chos-bcu-pai-mdo*),

> Those with no faith in the Dharma
> Rarely generate the white forces of goodness.
> They are like seeds scorched by fire
> That cannot sprout and grow.

As long as we entertain faults such as those described above, the Enlightened Beings can do nothing for us.

All beings carry within themselves the peerless seed of Buddhahood, the Buddha-nature, the root of goodness that, when it meets with the appropriate conditions, can ripen into the highest state of knowledge and liberation. The meaning of the above line, "...they simply do as they fancy," is that some beings are helplessly overpowered by karma and delusion, and we should offer prayers that, by hearing about, seeing, thinking of, or coming into contact with the refuge objects, the root of spiritual potential that they carry within themselves will become activated and will grow. For it is possible that, because of the power of instincts from previous lives, even those with no formal spiritual training can experience Dharmic thoughts when the appropriate conditions arise.

Appropriate conditions are important for the ripening of sentient beings. This is illustrated by the following anecdote from the life of Ge-she Po-to-wa.[9]

Po-to-wa often spoke on the Buddhadharma to large gatherings of disciples, their numbers sometimes counting into the thousands. There was an elderly man in the area, a grandson of Te-gu Na-gong, who was skeptical of both the Dharma and of Ge-she Po-to-wa. He often ridiculed them in public, saying things like, "The so-called teachings of Po-to-wa, are they true or not? That person called the Buddha, who even knows for certain that he ever existed? Who has ever seen him?" He would speak disparagingly like this at length to whomsoever he would chance to meet.

One day the old skeptic happened to meet Ge-she Po-to-wa while the latter was out taking his evening walk.

The old man asked him, "When you teach, whose tradition do you follow?"

Po-to-wa replied, "I follow the tradition of Buddha Shakyamuni."

"Who can know that Buddha Shakyamuni ever existed?" chided the old man.

"And whose tradition do you follow in speaking negatively and in giving your life exclusively to worldly activities?" returned Po-to-wa.

The old man answered, "That of my two parents, and of my grandfather Te-gu Na-gong."

Po-to-wa continued, "And how do you know that they ever existed?"

"I know they existed because, even though they have long since passed away and can no longer be seen, I am their son and thus my existence proves theirs. Moreover, even though I never met my grandfather Te-gu Na-gong, I know that he existed because he was my father's father and I can count the imprints of his various works. If he never existed I wouldn't be here now to testify for him."

Po-to-wa laughed and replied, "By that same logic I can say that I know that Buddha existed, because his spiritual sons were the Bodhisattvas Manjushri and Maitreya. Their spiritual sons were Nagarjuna and Asanga. Thus the teachings passed from generation to generation, until they came down to the incomparable Lama Atisha. Atisha's spiritual son was Lama Drom Ton-pa, the old man of Ra-deng Monastery. His son is none other than me, this bald-headed old monk. Therefore I am here to testify to Buddha's existence.

"Moreover, I can also count the imprints of the Buddha's deeds," Po-to-wa continued. "Buddha's father was King Suddhodhana, and his mother the beautiful Queen Mahamaya. He was born of this royal parentage and enjoyed the playthings of youth. He was fated to inherit a kingdom, but because he saw that worldly activity is essenceless he renounced his birthright and became a monk. Then he entered into austere practice in order to fulfill the merits that he had accumulated over many previous lives. Finally he subdued the forces of darkness and manifested full enlightenment. After this he turned the three wheels of Dharma and gave limitless teachings. Many of these from both the sutra and tantra vehicles have been translated into Tibetan, and I can list these for you if you like.

"Furthermore, we can perceive the numerous temples, *stupas* and monuments in honor of the Buddha that have been built by the Bodhisattvas, Shravaka Arhats, Pratyekabuddhas, pandits and *mahasiddhas*; and we can read the various commentaries to the themes of the sutras and tantras that have been written by the later Buddhist masters.

"In short, the marks and signs of the existence of Buddha are countless. They are inexpressible, so I can describe but a few.

"Conversely, if Buddha had not existed the lineages of gurus coming down from him would not exist; and I, this old monk called Geshe Po-to-wa, would not be here now to say all of this to you.

"But because Buddha Shakyamuni existed and showed the great kindness of teaching, we the followers of his spiritual legacy exist. In fact, we have become as numerous as the stars in the sky and the atoms of the earth."

When Po-to-wa had finished his exposition the old grandson of Te-gu Na-dong was filled with shame at the thought of the many times he had publicly ridiculed Po-to-wa and his teachings. Hanging his head in humility, he experienced profound faith in the illustrious guru and asked to be accepted as a disciple. From that time onward he dedicated himself intensely to the practice of the Buddhadharma, and by the time he reached the end of his life he had achieved a high state of spiritual realization. When he eventually passed away, his mind was firmly established on the path of liberation.

Thus it is said that spiritual confidence, or faith, is the mother that gives birth to every other quality on the path to enlightenment. From faith comes the wish to accomplish the path leading to liberation and enlightenment. Without faith we have no interest in spiritual practice, no inclination toward the path.

What are the causes of faith?

These are stated as follows in *The Questions of Karmavajra to Vajrapani* (*gSang-'dzin-las-kyi-rdo-rjes-gsang-bdag-la-zhus-pa*), "By relying on a spiritual friend and seeing him as a second Buddha, faith is naturally aroused. By spending time with spiritual friends, faith is aroused. By being mindful of impermanence and death, faith is aroused. By meditating on the karmic laws of cause and effect, faith is naturally aroused. By contemplating the shortcomings of samsaric existence, faith is aroused. . ." And so forth.

These are the factors that generate, strengthen and increase faith and spiritual conviction.

The lord of yogis Pa-dam-pa Sang-gye[10] in his *Parting Advice to the People of Ding-ri* (*Ding-ri-pai-zhal-gdams*) said,

> During life dedicate yourselves
> Unwaveringly to practice of the Dharma.
> Then at death the mind will naturally follow
> The path of truth. O people of Ding-ri,
> This is my parting advice to you.

And also,

> The path of the *bar-do* is long.
> Take the Dharma as your provision.
> O people of Ding-ri,
> This is my parting advice to you.

As said here, one must spur oneself on in the quest for enlightenment. The practice of the spiritual path is the supreme means of accomplishing the benefit of both this and future lives; but whether or not you practice is solely up to you. Nobody can drag you to enlightenment. You have to walk there yourself.

It is important to engage in spiritual practice from the present moment onward, without procrastinating. You must teach yourself to appreciate and maintain the attitude which realizes that now is the time for practice. Do not waste a moment.

In order to accomplish the path to enlightenment one needs to continually generate merit and purify hindrances. This twofold purpose is the point behind the daily practice of the six preliminaries. Last year I spoke on the first of these six: cleaning the place of meditation and arranging an altar with symbols of the body, speech and mind of the Enlightened Ones.

This year I would like to say a few words about the second preliminary, that of arranging on the altar a display of faultless offerings.

Here the word "faultless" refers to making the offering without contamination from faults in inner motivation, the actual substance, the nature of the offering, the manner in which the offering is made, and so forth.

Motivation is the most important factor in the practice of offering. The substances used as the basis of the offering themselves have no mindstream, so it is important that the practitioner see to it that the attitude within his/her own mind is pure. Just as food mixed with poison may look, smell and taste good yet will be inedible, similarly offerings made with the wrong mental framework become contaminated and are inappropriate.

The correct motivation is to approach the practice with the prayer that any energy thus generated will contribute to the attainment of enlightenment as a means of benefiting the world. Examples of incorrect motivation are to make offerings with the selfish hope of achieving personal happiness for oneself alone in this or future lives, or with a mind attached to samsaric perfection or to the thought of personal liberation. The fundamental attitude should be the altruistic Bodhisattva aspiration.

Thus after the first preliminary has been performed, that of cleaning the place of practice and arranging an altar with representations of the body, speech and mind of the Enlightened Ones of the past, present and future, one should generate a sincere motivation and set out a display of offerings. Not making offerings is a sign of lack of spiritual conviction, and a lack of spiritual conviction is a sign of weakness in Dharma practice.

Some people say that they do not like to rely upon the practice of setting up elaborate offerings to the Three Jewels, and that they prefer to rely exclusively upon the fruits of meditation. This is a mistake for both teacher and student alike.

Tsong-kha-pa's extensive *Lam Rim* states, "Saying that one does not like to rely on the practice of making offerings when engaged in the quest for enlightenment is a sign of limited understanding of the nature of the enlightenment path."

The daily practice of setting up offerings is a solid way of generating positive spiritual energy and dispelling obstacles. It prepares the way for successful meditation. As with the other supportive practices, it is not meant to be a substitute for meditation but rather as a supplement to it.

As for the actual things offered, it was the recommendation of Lama Atisha that we Tibetans mainly set out water bowls as symbols of the various sensory objects. Either seven or eight are used: one each for our own body, speech and mind, and then one each to represent the objects of the five senses. Atisha commented that water is one of the best substances to use, for it does not generate attachment in the mind of the practitioner; and although to us it is merely water, the Enlightened Beings regard it as ambrosial nectar.

It is said to be important to proceed with mindfulness when setting out the water offering. If the bowls are not completely filled, this becomes an omen that one shall become impoverished. If they are not all filled to a uniform level, this portends that one's meditation shall become unbalanced. If they are caused to overflow, this indicates that one shall fail in one's disciplines.

A variation on the water offering is to put out two water bowls for body and speech (water to wash the feet and to rinse the mouth), and a scented oil for the mind; and then for the five articles symbolizing the objects of the five senses, the water bowls are substituted with things related to the individual senses, such as flowers for the objects of touch, incense for the objects of smell, a butter-lamp for objects of sight, food for objects of taste, and a conch shell for the objects of sound.

In addition to the above, one should offer a small portion of one's food, placing it on the altar in a special dish. Here there is no need to make a large offering, as the act is symbolic; but it should be from the first and best portion. One should not offer leftovers, vegetable peelings, etc., nor rejected foods that one would not consider fit for one's own consumption. It is rather inappropriate to make offerings from old, unclean food and then to ceremoniously consecrate it with a flowery verse such as, "This delightful offering of food possessing a hundred flavors, etc...." One must always check to see that the words of one's prayers accord with the reality of what one is doing.

From the side of the refuge objects, the quality of the substance is insignificant. As Arya Maitreya says in *An Ornament of the Clear Realizations* (*mNgon-rtogs-rgyan*), "An unpleasant taste becomes pleasant [to the Enlightened Beings]." The Buddhas dwell in constant bliss, so for them there is no difference between good and bad. But from the viewpoint of the person making the offering there is a considerable difference. Therefore to offer something inferior and then to visualize that it is the best only undermines the act of offering and destroys the merit involved.

Even if the motivation, substance and nature of the offering are faultless, things can still go wrong when the manner of making the offering is mistaken. This is illustrated by the following anecdote from the life of Arya Nagarjuna.[11]

Nagarjuna had received his ordination from Saraha and was given the name of Bikshu Shri. Saraha foresaw that the district was about to be struck by famine and therefore he appointed Bikshu Shri as the food manager of Nalanda Monastery. He [Saraha] then returned to South India and entered into retreat on Glory Mountain.

The famine struck soon after his departure. It continued for twelve long years. Weak people gradually died off, and the strong moved away to other lands. The district thus became almost completely uninhabited.

Bikshu Shri, however, had previously mastered the occult art of alchemy and possessed the ability to turn ordinary metals into gold. Therefore he put his art to use and transformed several pieces of iron and copper into gold. He then used this gold to buy grain and other foodstuff from nearby areas not affected by the famine.

One day a group of pandits came to him and asked, "How have you managed to supply the Sangha with food when the rest of the area is afflicted so heavily by famine?"

Bikshu Shri answered then truthfully.

The pandits rebuked him. "You have manufactured gold without asking or informing the Sangha! Indeed, you have caused the monks to live by means of wrong livlihood." They then expelled him from the monastery and ordered him as a penance to build a million temples and *stupas*.

Thus even though his motivation was pure and his aim only to bring comfort and well-being to the Sangha, the manner of making the offering was in contradiction to the rules of monastic discipline; for monks are not allowed to indulge in exotic and diverse activities [such as alchemy] when residing in a monastery. Thus the manner of making the offering was inappropriate.

As for the offering vessels to be used, the best are made from gold or silver. Medium quality vessels are made from brass or copper. The simplest are made from clay or wood. The quality of the vessels does not matter, although it is said to be important to use the best that one can afford.

Whether or not the offering is small or large is of little concern, so long as the mind of the practitioner is not dominated by worldly considerations. The smallest offering made with a pure heart surpasses a large offering made impurely.

The practice of making daily offerings generates the merit that causes material prosperity to increase. This does not mean that one should engage in the practice in order to become wealthy as an end in itself; one should have the Mahayana aspiration of wanting to improve one's merit in order to be of greater benefit to the world. The main empha-

sis should be on the spirit of altruism. But if we are poor and can
only afford to make very small offerings, we should do so daily. Then
soon we will be in a position to increase the size and quality of the
offering.

This is illustrated by the biography of Lama Drub-khang Rin-po-
che Ge-lek Gya-tso.[12] In the beginning of his life he was so poor that
all he owned was a wooden tea bowl. From this he would eat and drink
whatever simple foods he could get. Then at the beginning of his meditation sessions he would wash the bowl out and fill it with water eight
times, each time placing it on the altar for a few moments. He also
had a piece of slate that he would use as a base for the mandala offering symbolic of the universe. After some time his merits increased
and his karmic obstacles were weakened. He no longer needed to use
his tea cup for offering bowls, and instead had bowls of engraved silver. The slate mandala base was replaced by an iron one, and then
by silver. The grain that he had been using for the mandala offering
was replaced by precious and semi-precious gems.

That lama himself once said, "In the beginning of my practice I
was dressed in rags. Often I did not even have plain barley flour to
eat. But I made my water offering every day. Then someone gave me
a Nepalese coin, which I used in order to buy butter. The temple in
my monastery had a special butter-lamp that when filled would burn
for two days. It was my plan to use half of my butter to fill this, and
to keep the other half for myself. However, when I melted the half-
portion of butter and poured it into the lamp, the vessel became only
half filled. Therefore I melted the rest and poured it in as well. I made
this offering at the time of the festival in celebration of Tsong-kha-
pa's birth, enlightenment and passing away. After that my fortunes
completely changed. Now I am able to make many hundreds of excellent offerings daily, and my resources never seem to become depleted."

We can find countless anecdotes illustrating how the practice of making daily offerings acts as a condition heralding material prosperity.
Je Nga-wang Cham-pa Kun-pang-pa relates how in his early life he
was very poor, but by means of making simple daily offerings he gradually increased his merits and removed obstacles. One day a patron gave
him two gold coins, which he immediately used to make an elaborate
offering. As a result his merits ripened, and thereafter material possessions came to him from every direction, like clouds gathering in
the sky.

The [Indian] master Acharya Ashvagosha wrote in his *Fifty Verses* on the *Guru*[13] (*bLa-ma-lnga-bcu-pa*),

> An offering placed on one's altar
> Becomes a constant offering to all the Buddhas.
> By that gift great merit arises, and with merit
> The supreme accomplishment is soon achieved.

Whenever you make an offering, imagine that the object to which the offering is made is a manifestation of the Three Jewels of Refuge. Then the offering becomes a gift to all the Buddhas of the past, present and future. By making offerings to all the Buddhas we generate a tremendous force of meritorious energy. This in turn acts as a cause for us to meet with conditions conducive to the realization of *mahamudra*, the supreme *siddhi*.

This is the correct way to practice. Otherwise, just sitting in a cross-legged position on a meditation cushion and pretending to enter into a deep *samadhi* uniting *shamatha* (meditative serenity) with *vipashyana* (higher insight) does not give birth to a state of consciousness free from the dominating forces of karma and delusion. Unless our spiritual conviction is deeply rooted and our meritorious energy made strong, there will be little spiritual progress. A fruit tree requires a firm root if it is to grow and produce well. When the root is healthy and free from defects, the branches and leaves will grow without any difficulties. Then when there are healthy branches the tree will naturally produce healthy fruit.

In the same way, in order for our practices to carry us to enlightenment it is important that we maintain the correct order and structure. Each meditation session should be initiated with these six preliminaries. Then follows the main body of the session. Finally, we should conclude with the dedication of the meritorious energy.

It is not easy to arrive at a level of understanding in which every aspect of the Buddhadharma can be seen as personal advice to ourselves. When we do, we can clearly see how the various aspects and stages of the training reinforce one another. This interdependence of the different teachings is lucidly described by Lama Tsong-kha-pa in his three *Lam Rim* treatises, and we should study these as much as possible.

I wish I could go into more detail on the subject of the interconnected nature of the various teachings, for an understanding of this topic really does help. However, we don't have a great deal of time today, and also my own understanding is limited. Besides, I think that perhaps many of you practice the Dharma more as a hobby than as a principal concern, and that you prefer the type of Dharma instruction that can be found in a small pamphlet and held in the palm of your hand rather than that found in the extensive scriptures. If I talk too much, you won't like it.

Next year I will continue with my discussion of the six preliminaries. We have now completed the first two, so next year we can move on to the third.

The Great Prayer Festival is our annual celebration in commemoration of the time when Buddha Shakyamuni met six Hindu extremists in a competition of miracle demonstrations. This festival, founded by Lama Tsong-khap-pa and honored by all the previous Dalai Lamas, culminates in the full moon ceremony of the fifteenth day of the festival, during which there traditionally is a reading from the *Jatakamala*, Aryasura's classical account of how the Buddha trained in the six perfections in his previous lives. I will now do this, continuing from where I left off last year.

> *His Holiness then read from*
> *the* Jatakamala. *Later he*
> *concluded his discourse as follows.*

Lama Tsong-kha-pa, who was like a second Buddha, once wrote,

> After you have studied the many scriptures
> Under a qualified spiritual master,
> Go alone to a solitary place
> And, abandoning all distractions,
> Enter into single-pointed meditation.

First we should study under a qualified teacher and learn the contents of the many scriptures. When this has been accomplished, we should leave distracting places far behind and take up residence in a quiet place conducive to meditation.

In particular, those of us who have taken the Dharma robes should try to avoid towns and cities, and instead live in a peaceful hermitage where we can dedicate our time to study and practice.

Especially, those of you who live in any of the three great monastic universities or two tantric colleges, or in any of the other distinguished monasteries throughout the country, should try to set a good example for others. Young monks should look to the elders for guidance and direction, and in general should emulate the ways of gentleness and self-control.

The gurus, *acharyas* and *mahashtaviras* should honor the ancient Ka-dam-pa precept of cultivating external behavior that accords with the Shravaka tradition of modesty and pure discipline, while internally cultivating the free spirit of renunciation, the altruistic bodhimind, and the two yogic stages of the *anuttara yoga* tantras.

It is especially important for novices to avoid distractions. If from the time they enter the monastic life they honor the traditions of their specific monastery, then before long they will have absorbed the various levels of learning and practice. Children who in the beginning cannot even read or write can grow up to become great spiritual masters if they dedicate themselves correctly to the training program.

Those of you who are teachers should dedicate yourselves joyfully to your work. The offering of a Dharma teaching far surpasses any material gift, for it brings lasting benefits to the mind. Wisdom is the most precious of treasures, but the continuation of the legacy of wisdom depends upon teachers being generous with their disciples, and upon the disciples dedicating themselves diligently to study and practice. Wisdom cannot be given from one person to another, but a guru can teach a disciple how to develop it.

The [Indian] master Nagarjuna wrote,

> If the disciple is without discriminating awareness,
> What benefit is the Doctrine to him?
> What value is a mirror
> To someone without eyes?

As said here, the guru can only teach effectively when the disciple cooperates. Conversely, when the disciple is ready the teacher should make every effort to see that the full and complete instruction is given. This may require time and energy, yet it is an indispensible condition to the process. If mighty beings such as the *tul-kus* (incarnate lamas) and *ge-shes* (learned spiritual friends) cannot take up the responsibility of upholding the Dharma by means of teaching and transmitting the various lineages, who can?

With this thought in mind the illustrious Fifth Dalai Lama wrote,

There are those who have not moistened their minds
With generosity and the free spirit of renunciation,
Yet who want to sit proudly amid
The four types of Buddhist Sangha.
They are like a donkey wearing a leopard's skin.

Some of us here are but partially learned and poorly trained, yet claim to be Dharma masters and like to sit proudly in the front seats at religious gatherings. For people like that to try and fulfill the role of a guru is like the blind leading the blind, and does not inspire a mustard's seed worth of confidence. If you carry some type of religious title, be sure that you are equal to it. The false guru just harms himself and others. You may be able to fool a few simple people in a remote mountain village, but at death there is no way to hide from the forces of your own karma.

A medicinal plant requires care from the time it is planted. Likewise, those of you who are dedicating your lives to the spiritual path should proceed with mindfulness from the very beginning, and give yourselves purely to study, contemplation and meditation. Then gradually the qualities of love, kindness and wisdom will grow within you. Eventually you will become a treasury of learning and insight, will begin to equal the mighty beings of the past, and will earn the names "Bodhisattva" and "sage". But you should read the biographies of the great beings of the past and see for yourselves how they trained and achieved their goals. Why should someone like me have to outline the details!

In general, it is very important to maintain constant mindfulness of the teachings and to try to integrate into one's life what has been learned. During the course of the day examine the nature and focus of the body, speech and mind. Relying on *satipatthana* meditation— disciplined mindfulness of the activities of body, speech and mind— is a key tool in gaining control over the continuum of one's being.

We must remember that the truth of karmic law is a constant witness to our every action. Be sincere and honest, and discriminate carefully between white and black ways.

The [Indian] sage Vasubandhu[14] wrote,

If we condense heavy karmic actions into categories,
They become subsumed within the ten paths of karma.

Study *The Sutra on Mindfulness* (Dran-pa-nyer-gzhag-pai-mdo) and gain a detailed understanding of the workings of karmic cause and effect and, in particular, the ten principal courses of action as mentioned above by Vasubandhu.

It is very important to understand the workings of karmic law in its various aspects: the ripening effects of an action; the results similar in nature to the cause; the main effect of a particular action; and so forth.

The doors through which we create any action, be it positive or negative, are the body, speech and mind. These are the three portals through which we release our energies into the world. Therefore the etymologists of the past correctly called them 'doors of karma'.

The [Indian] master Ashvagosha wrote in his *Revealing the Path of the Ten Negative Karmic Actions* (*Mi-dge-ba-bcui-las-kyi-lam-bstan-pa*),

> Concerning the ten negative courses of action,
> Three are counted as physical,
> Four are of the speech,
> And three are of the mind.

The three negative karmic actions created by means of the door of the body are destroying life, taking what is not given, and indulging in perverted forms of sexuality. The four created by speech are lying, slander, hurtful words, and meaningless talk. The three created by the door of the mind are covetousness, ill-will and superstitious beliefs.

We should contemplate the shortcomings of these ten negative courses of action and refrain from them by means of applying mindfulness, awareness, and conscientiousness.

The ten positive courses of action are the opposites of these: saving life instead of killing; being generous with others instead of stealing from them; and so forth. Because by cultivating these ten one automatically gains the fruit of higher rebirth, they are called "divine dharmas"; and because they are paths leading from happiness to greater happiness they are known as "the ten paths of wholesome action." Thus the Bodhisattva kings who in the early days introduced Buddhism into Tibet called them "the divine dharmas of ten wholesome ways." They are the basis of practice for monks and lay people alike.

On top of these, lay people in particular should cultivate what are known as "the human dharmas of sixteen wholesome ways": respect for the Three Jewels; practice of the holy Dharma; service to one's parents; respect for those of learning; honor for elders and those of high character; loyalty to friends; being friendly and helpful to everyone; sincerity; keeping one's eyes fixed on righteousness; being wise in the consumption of food and wealth; appreciating and returning kindness shown by others; being honest and non-deceptive in financial dealings; being impartial and without jealousy or envy; not listening to the advice of inferior people; speaking softly and only after deep consideration; and having perseverance and an open mind.

As these sixteen are practiced for the benefit of this life and are in accord with the ways of all civilized people, they are called "human dharmas". Because they are not stained by cruel or negative ways, they are called "wholesome ways". Thus they have become famed as "the human dharmas of sixteen wholesome ways." They were introduced into Tibet by the early Bodhisattva kings, and became the foundation and root giving birth to signs of happiness and goodness in this land of ours.

In general, any of you who are in positions of power and responsibility should be especially aware of the karmic laws of cause and effect. Daily contemplate "the divine dharmas of ten wholesome ways" and "the human dharmas of sixteen wholesome ways." Never abuse your positions of authority. Remember that the best way to administer is with the gentle power of love and compassion.

Recollect the advice of the [Indian] master Matichitra,[15] who wrote in his *A Letter to King Kanika* (*Ka-ni-kai-'phring-yig*),

> Cause all faults to fade away,
> Like the waning moon.
> Cause all good qualities to increase,
> Like the waxing moon.

If we follow that wise advice we will be benefited both spiritually and temporally.

During the rule of King Lha To-to-ri Nyan-tsen,[16] several sacred objects fell from space into the courtyard of Po-drang Yum-bu Langgang Castle [the oldest castle in Tibet]. Amongst these were the scriptures *Pang-kong-chak-gya-pa* (*sPang-skong-phyag-rgya-pa*) and the *Do-de-za-ma-tok* (*mDo-sde-za-ma-tog*). At the same time the following prophecy is said to have resounded from the sky, "After five generations have passed, the meaning of these texts will become known."

The appearance of these scriptures was a sign heralding the dawn of the Buddhadharma in this dark land. After that the Buddhist doctrines gradually were introduced and spread because of a hundred intense efforts on the part of the early Bodhisattva kings, *acharyas*, translators and pandits. The fact that the Buddhadharma now shines here as brightly as the sun and that we have a multitude of temples, monasteries and nunneries filled with countless saints, scholars and accomplished adepts is due to the efforts of these kind beings of old. Because of what they did for us, Tibet has become a holy land, a place of pilgrimage for peoples of many different countries. We should appreciate our situation. We hold a precious jewel in the palm of our hand, so it is important to appreciate its value and not to squander it.

Even amongst Buddhist countries our land is especially fortunate in that it is blessed by Avalokiteshvara, the Bodhisattva of Compassion. The recitation of his six-syllable mantra *om mani padme hum* brings liberation from the miserable realms of samsaric existence.

This mantra is unequalled in strength and wondrous qualities by any other. In the beginning it is learned without difficulty, and in the end it is never forgotten. In the middle it brings countless benefits to the practitioner, including the benefits of liberation and enlightenment.

Some people say that the way we Tibetans rely upon the six-syllable mantra is mere superstition. They argue that it is not easy to purify the mind of delusion and negative karmic instincts, for *samsara* and our previous lives are without a beginning, and throughout all of these lifetimes we have accumulated limitless negative instincts. The ripening effects of these even now are in motion, and it is only rarely that we apply the remedial forces by which negative karmic patterns are reversed. On top of that, even now the three psychic poisons are strong within us, causing us to continue to generate negativity. If we do not apply the opponents, then there is no means to escape the vicious cycle.

Such are their arguments, and much of what they say is quite true. However, the Bodhisattva of Compassion saw this predicament and, calling upon the Buddhas of the ten directions as his witnesses, he took the *vajra* pledge to directly help all those who would practice the Dharma and recite the six-syllable mantra. Therefore we should take advantage of his pledge and make our life meaningful by practicing accordingly.

A Letter to King Kanika states,

Even if beneficial advice is spoken harshly,
One should nonetheless cherish it.
And even if useless advice is spoken sweetly,
One should not become influenced by it.

It does not matter if the words I have spoken above are sweet or sour. It is the meaning of the words that counts. You should examine the meaning and see if anything is relevant to you and your life. If so, try and practice it.

It is important at the conclusion of any Dharma discourse to dedicate any meritorious energy that has been generated. A sutra states,

A drop of water flowing into the ocean
Is not exhausted until the ocean dries up.
Similarly, merit that is dedicated to enlightenment
Is not exhausted until enlightenment is attained.

Also, the incomparable master Lama Tsong-kha-pa wrote,

The merit generated from special endeavors
Stands out like the moon amidst a sky of stars.
May it cause beings to progress on the Great Way,
And may the deeds and prayers of Buddha Shakyamuni
  be fulfilled.

Ordinary merit is like the stars in the sky, whereas merit generated by giving or listening to a discourse on the Mahayana in a special place and on a special occasion is like the brilliant full moon of autumn. We should dedicate this merit to the aspiration that all living beings may traverse the paths and stages of the Mahayana, that so skillfully unites method and wisdom, and that thus the prayers and deeds of Buddha Shakyamuni may be fulfilled.

If by giving or listening to this discourse
Any spiritual energy has been generated,
May it contribute toward the growth of wisdom
Within all living beings without exception.

SERMON THREE: THE WOOD MOUSE YEAR

The incomparable Lama Tsong-kha-pa, a supreme teacher and peerless embodiment of the compassion, wisdom and power of all the
Buddhas, a Dharma lord with knowledge of the three worlds, once
opened the net of his vibrant voice by saying,

> Having the opportunity to hear the holy Dharma
> One should think, "Indeed I am fortunate."
> Then with a happy and smiling countenance
> Listen with a mind free from the three faults.

Most of us have very few positive karmic instincts from our previous lives. Carried along by the strong current of delusion, we rush
toward the dangerous cliff of negative ways. Waves of suffering strike
against us again and again, but still the horizon of the path to freedom does not come within our sphere of vision. Lost in a thick fog
of ignorance and ego-grasping, we fail to engage in the practice of a
spiritual path, which is the only means whereby we could reverse the
patterns of compulsive karma. Instead, we continue to be dragged along
by the river of afflicted emotions, sinking ever deeper as time passes by.

However, our position is not without hope. If we could but recognize delusion as the enemy and begin to apply the opponent forces
that counteract it, and especially if we could begin to cultivate the stainless wisdom that comprehends the non-inherent nature of both specific
phenomena and abstract generalities, eventually we would be able to
enter the state of consciousness that perceives the final nature of reality and uproots the dominating influence of the samsaric view.

From there we would be able to eliminate the two obscurations,
together with their instincts. Then through the force of understanding the extreme of samsara we would no longer remain in the ordinary world; and because of the compassionate aspect of understanding the suffering of living beings and the limitations of non-worldly
peace we would avoid the extreme of nirvana.

This is the meaning of "non-abiding nirvana," the Bodhisattva attainment. It has the wisdom that grants freedom from samsara, yet
possesses the great compassion that is not content to remain in personal nirvana. This is the enlightenment of full Buddhahood, the state
to which we ourselves as Mahayana practitioners should aspire.

In order to generate the wisdom that heralds this illustrious attainment we must first cultivate the state of clear, single-pointed *samadhi* able to hold the mind back from wandering and dullness caused by improper concentration and habitual negative thought patterns. This *samadhi* in turn depends upon the cultivation of pure self-discipline that guards the body, speech and mind against entering into agitating and distracting activities.

Thus wisdom, *samadhi* and discipline are interdependent factors. In turn, the successful implementation of all three depends upon a strong basis in study and learning, for without this we will not know how to begin and proceed in the various trainings. Lama Tsong-kha-pa, the omniscient Bu-ton Rin-chen Drub-pa, and all the other illustrious masters of the past therefore advised that we who wish to achieve liberation and enlightenment make special efforts to follow this type of approach.

To have the opportunity to study the sutras, tantras, shastras and so forth under the guidance of a qualified teacher is extremely rare. If we have the opportunity to do so, we should appreciate it and apply ourselves joyously. As an external sign of this joy, wear a happy face with a big smile rather than a pious, self-righteous, sober mask. Too many people seem to confuse spirituality with self-righteousness. The spiritual path is a happy experience. Reflect this happiness.

When attending a discourse on the Dharma we should try to hold the wild horses of the senses from running aimlessly. The body, speech and mind are to be brought under control by means of mindful awareness. Put pride and vanity far behind, and rely instead upon humility, appreciative clarity and attentiveness. Keep the mind clearly in focus on the meaning of what is being said, and avoid sleepiness, mental dullness, unnecessary talk, and all distracting activities. Otherwise, if we simply allow ourselves to fall prey to laziness, apathy and mental wandering, at best we will get but a rough impression of the contents of the teaching.

Also, no matter how profound a teaching may be it will be of little use to us if we do not remember it clearly and then apply it to the cultivation of our own mind. We may carry the name "practitioner," but it will be a mere label.

In addition, even if we gain a clear intellectual understanding of the words of a discourse we will not realize the desired benefits if this understanding is not combined with a deep sense of confidence in the teacher and the teaching.

It is important when approaching the Dharma to constantly remem-

ber that every teaching is meant only as a method to tame and cultivate the mind. The point of the Buddhadharma is not to make one
clever in argumentation or debate but to help one to overcome delusion and inner negativities, the sources of suffering and confusion.
Dharma is not an elite secret to be greedily shared with the guru, but
a personal instruction meant for inner practice and implementation.
We should study from this perspective.

Those of you who have difficulty in fathoming the meaning of the
great treatises should not become disheartened. As long as you maintain a persevering and inquiring attitude your understanding will continually increase.

Tsong-kha-pa's extensive *Lam Rim* treatise (*Lam-rim-chen-mo*) says,
"It is rare to meet someone who is able to practice all teachings that
are received. If you have difficulties in doing so yourself, then choose
your practices carefully." Rather than becoming overwhelmed with
daily commitments and practices, we should consult our personal
teacher and work out a schedule that is suitable to our own needs and
situation. It is best to take what is most essential for one's present
needs and to concentrate on that, rather than to take on more than
one can successfully apply. If we overload ourselves, nothing gets accomplished. It is better to be humble in one's adoption of practices,
and to accomplish what one engages in before going on to more.

Over the past few years we have been discussing the six preliminaries to be conducted at the beginning of every meditation session. So
far we have covered the first two of these: cleaning the practice site
and arranging an altar; and, secondly, setting up a display of offerings. This year I will begin a discussion of the third preliminary: sitting on one's meditation cushion in the full or half *vajra* posture, and
blending one's mindstream with thoughts of refuge and the
bodhimind.

The order of the six preliminaries differs somewhat in the various
Lam Rim treatises. Here I am following the structure outlined by Lama
Tsong-kha-pa.

It is important to have a good seat for meditation. This is illustrated
by the Buddha's own enlightenment. After he had spent many years
in intensive practice and he knew that the time of his enlightenment
was approaching, he began to search for the ideal place to sit for his
final *samadhi*.

First he sat on a large rock near a flowering fruit tree, but the *devas*
of the pure heavens came to him and said, "You must cross the Nairan-

jana River and go west to Vajrasana. There you will discover the perfect seat." Hence he left the hill that had been blessed by all the past Buddhas of this fortunate aeon, and walked westward. There he beheld a majestic bodhi tree that had the nature of the seven precious jewels and was surrounded by a natural flower garden rich with lotuses and many other types of exquisite foliage, and having every auspicious sign.

All past Buddhas of this auspicious aeon had achieved enlightenment while sitting upon a seat of grass. Knowing this, Indra gathered multi-joint grass that was as soft as cotton and induced bliss on mere contact. Manifesting as a grass-seller, he approached the Buddha and offered the bundle of grass to him.

Buddha accepted the gift, and carefully arranged the grass into a seat with the tips pointing inward.

As stated in *The Most Magnificent Drama* (*rGya-che-rol-pa*), he then took an oath,

> My body may dry up and
> My skin may fall from the flesh and bone,
> But I shall not rise from this seat
> Until enlightenment, difficult to attain in many aeons,
> Has finally been attained.

When these words had been uttered, the six great worlds shook. The devas who support goodness offered their assistance, and all the Buddhas and Bodhisattvas called on the forces of truth to bear witness.

That evening the master tamed Mara and his armies. All night he remained absorbed in meditation. Then at dawn he manifested full enlightenment.

We who train in accordance with the Buddhist tradition should therefore also give some importance to our place of meditation and to our meditation seat.

The manuals elucidating the twelve factors of intensive practice list two main purposes in having a proper seat: one will be able to remain absorbed in meditation for long periods of time without becoming tired due to discomfort; and also the seat itself will not disintegrate.

It is good to have a wooden platform as a base for one's seat. This prevents illnesses caused by earth dampness. There should be sufficient space between the boards to allow for some ventilation of the cushion. The platform itself should not be excessively high, ornate or expensive. It should not be more than five nor less than three cubits in width.

Sometimes it is said that on top of this one should place a drawing of either a *vajra*, a swastika, or a Dharma wheel. However, as the *vajra* is a tantric symbol and should not be stepped or sat upon by ordinary people, this is somewhat inappropriate; and as the swastika is a very popular symbol with the Bon-po magicians, its use is perhaps also inappropriate. This leaves the Dharma wheel.

Therefore on top of the platform place a drawing of an eight-spoked Dharma wheel. Above this arrange some kusha grass. Kusha is generally used in place of the multi-joint grass that Buddha favored. Kusha is an auspicious substance, for from its one stem come many strands and tips, each of which is straight and unentangled. Thus it symbolizes purity free from entangling faults.

Kusha grass is highly regarded in the Vajrayana, especially in the initiation process. A tantric scripture says,

> Then take kusha grass
> Free of all faults.
> Consecrate it with mantras
> And place it under the mattress and pillow.

This refers to the tradition of reciting the syllables *hum* and *dhih* on two strands of kusha grass. The former of these syllables symbolizes the Buddha-consciousness possessing the five wisdoms; the latter syllable symbolizes the wisdom of omniscient knowledge. The mantric syllables are used to empower the two pieces of kusha, and these strands of grass are then placed under one's mattress and pillow respectively. Because of the influence of this pure substance, the disciple's mind becomes clear and undistorted, and it is possible for him/her to have prophetic dreams concerning the effects of the initiation being received.

On top of the kusha grass one places the meditation cushion. If one is a monk or nun, one's monastic mat then goes on top of this. As for the meditation cushion, its back should be slightly higher than its front, so that one's spine will be somewhat raised.

The Root Text of Mahamudra (Phyag-chen-rtsa-ba) states,

> On a comfortable meditation seat
> Sit in the seven-point posture of Vairochana.

This means that after one has set up an adequate seat one should take one's place on it. The body should be established in the correct posture, which means the seven- or eight-point posture of Vairochana; the speech should be restrained with the breath stabilized; and the mind should be brought within the focus of a pure intention.

The main source of these teachings on meditation is Kamalashila's[17] *Stages of Meditation* (*sGom-rim*).

Also, Arya Asanga's *Shravaka Stages* (*Nyan-sa*) states,

> Whether you meditate in a hermitage,
> Whether you meditate under a tree,
> Or even in an empty house,
> The procedures are the same.
> First wash your feet,
> Place grass and a cushion
> On a large or small wooden platform,
> And sit there in the vajra posture.
> Keep the back perfectly straight
> And enter into closely placed mindfulness.

The Wen-sa-pa[18] ear-whispered tradition lists eight points for the Vairochana posture,

> Three concern the feet, hands and back.
> The fourth concerns the placement
> Of the teeth, lips and tongue.
> The positioning of the head, eyes,
> Shoulders and breath are four more.
> These are the eight points of the Vairochana posture.

The first point is the placement of the feet. This is explained as follows.

In the tantric view, the coarse and subtle karmic energies, which carry the conceptual mind of images and image retainers, must be prevented from flowing into the side channels. They should instead be redirected into the central channel. The supreme methods for doing this are found in the *anuttara yoga* tantras. These are of two types: male and female. When we sit in the *vajra* posture, folding the right leg on top of the left symbolizes practice of the male tantras; folding the left on top of the right symbolizes practice of the female tantras.

The second point concerns the hands. This is explained as follows.

By implementing the tantric yogas such as the vase breathing and *vajra* recitation methods in order to stimulate the various energy centers, the vital energies are caused to enter, abide and dissolve within the heart chakra. This process begins with stimulation of the energy center at the navel, and culminates in accomplishment of the impure and then pure illusory body yogas, together with realization of the semblant and and actual clear light yogas. Here the substantial cause of the illusory body is the five subtle life energies upon which ride the semblant and actual clear lights of the mind. Again, the principal techniques for accomplishing this process are found in the male and female *anuttara yoga* tantras. Of these, the male tantras emphasize the illusory body yogas and the appearance/luminosity aspect of the practice. The female tantras emphasize the clear light yogas and the emptiness/voidness aspect. Placing the hands just below the navel symbolizes the entire process, that begins with stimulating the navel chakra (four finger-widths below the navel). When the right hand is placed in the left palm, this indicates the practice of the male tantras. Conversely, placing the left in the right indicates the female tantras. This is the symbolism behind the meditation *mudra*.

In the practice of *Lam Rim* meditation, which is common to both the Sutrayana and Vajrayana, it is the tradition to place the right hand in the left.

The nature of meditation from the perspective of an understanding of the three doors of liberation as experienced at the time of accomplishment is expressed as follows in *The Root Tantra of Guhyasamaja* (*gSang-'dus-rtsa-rgyud*),

> As there are no "things"
> There are no objects of meditation.
> Thus there is no meditational process.
> Because there are neither "things" nor "no things",
> There is no thing called "meditation".

To symbolize this truth, the tips of the thumbs are touched together, causing the thumbs and index fingers to form a circle.

The third point in the Vairochana posture concerns the back. Here it is said that the backbone should be kept as straight as an arrow, with the twenty-one vertabrae like golden coins stacked one on top of another. This helps to bring the coarse and subtle energies into the central channel.

The fourth point deals with the mouth. The teeth and lips are held closed in a natural position, with the tip of the tongue placed against the upper palate. This permits one to meditate without the mouth either drying out or dribbling. It also symbolizes the purification of speech as accomplished by the correct intonation of mantra.

The next point relates to the head. When the head is held so high that the neck arches back, the mind becomes agitated and prone to wandering. To avoid this, the head is inclined slightly forward.

Now for the eyes. To prevent the energies which are a vehicle for the five sensory consciousnesses from running wildly, and at the same time to avoid falling prey to mental dullness and torpor, the eyes are cast downward at the angle of the nose, and are held partially opened.

Then, to reap the full benefits from the above six points, the shoulders should be kept at an even level, like the wings of an eagle in flight. The arms are relaxed with the elbows held slightly away from the body.

The above seven points of the Vairochana posture are common to the manner of sitting in both the Sutrayana and the Vajrayana.

Correct sitting is very important to successful meditation. Therefore Mar-pa the Translator used to boast teasingly by saying, "Although there are many oral transmission teachings in Tibet, nobody can rival the sitting tradition of Mar-pa Lo-tsa-wa."

The benefits of sitting correctly and the faults of not doing so, as well as the various alternatives, the symbolisms, etc., are explained in numerous sutras, tantras, oral transmission texts, contemporary practice manuals, and so forth. I need not go into the subject in detail here.

Kamalashila's *Stages of Meditation* (*sGom-rim*) and Asanga's *Shravaka Stages* (*Nyan-sa*) point out five excellent qualities of sitting correctly: the mind becomes supple and blissful; one is able to remain absorbed in meditation for long periods of time without tiring; the practice surpasses the techniques of the Tirthikas and argumentative Hindus; anyone who happens to see a person sitting correctly becomes deeply inspired; and the position was taught by the Buddha and continued by the Shravakas.

The above discussion deals with the standard seven points of the Vairochana sitting posture.

The ear-whispered tradition from the great yogi Wen-sa-pa mentions an eighth, namely, that of the breath.

As said earlier, correct body posture means correct sitting; correct speech posture means correct breathing; and correct mind posture refers to motivation and concentration.

In the Wen-sa-pa tradition it is said that after assuming the seven physical points of the Vairochana position one should stabilize the breath.

To accomplish this, first perform the nine-round breathing technique in connection with the meditation for purifying the distorted thoughts of the three psychic poisons: attachment, aversion and ignorance. One inhales through the left nostril and exhales through the right, visualizing that all attachments are thus expelled. This is repeated three times. Then one inhales through the right and exhales through the left, visualizing that all anger and aversion is expelled. Again, this is repeated three times. Finally for the three remaining cycles one inhales through both nostrils simultaneously, and when one exhales (through both nostrils) one visualizes expelling all ignorance and apathy. Because each of the three cycles is repeated three times, the process is known as "the nine-round breathing exercise." It is an excellent technique for stabilizing the breath.

One must then stabilize the mind. First observe the mental content to see the precise conditions of the moment. This means that we must determine if the peaceful nature of the mind is being disturbed in any way by deluded and distracting thoughts. Distractions rob meditation of power, so they must be counteracted by their specific opponents.

For example, if thoughts of lust and sexual desire are creating a distraction, these are easily eliminated by meditating upon the unpleasant aspects of the human body, such as blood, pus, urine, excrement, and so forth.

For problems of anger and ill-will, apply the techniques for developing equaminity, love and compassion.

When apathy and dullness predominate, meditate upon the twelve links of dependent origination.

To eliminate pride and arrogance, apply the antidote of meditating upon the various realms of worldly existence. No matter how high your pride may make you think you are, there is always someone in a better position. Reflecting in this manner eliminates pride.

To pacify mental agitation and the wandering mind, fix your attention on the coming and going of the breath.

The last of these techniques, that of fixing awareness on the ingoing and outgoing breath is particularly useful for people who live busy lives. It is an excellent way to calm the mind and prepare it for meditation.

However, when doing it you shouldn't breathe loudly through the nose or mouth, nor breathe heavily. Simply let the breath come and go as is natural, gently and without any special effort, with the mind placed casually on awareness of it. Remain absorbed in this way for seven, twenty-one, or a hundred or so breath cycles. Doing this calms the breath, which is the vehicle of the conceptual mind. Negative and distorting mental patterns are thus pacified and fade away of themselves; and the mind, an unspecified phenomenon [that by nature is neither positive nor negative, but adopts these qualities depending upon the mental content], assumes its naturally radiant qualities. From there it is easy to direct one's attention to any creative object of meditation.

Concerning the posture of the body when meditating, it is important to be physically comfortable. Therefore some people sit in the full *vajra* posture for only the first part of the meditation session, and then relax the legs into the half-*vajra* or even the *sattva* posture. Otherwise, it is also acceptable to sit in the easier half-*vajra* posture from the beginning. Because trainees are of a variety of natures and dispositions, Buddha taught a variety of approaches. In fact, he advised one of his first five disciples to meditate while lying down in bed, adding that it would be easier for him to attain *samadhi* in that way. The posture is intended to enhance meditation, not to create an obstacle to it.

After the body and the breath have been stabilized and the mind calmed, the motivation of the mind must be brought within correct focus.

Lama Tsong-kha-pa said,

If from within the mind we do not eliminate
The darkness of grasping at the extremes
Of "is" and "is not", reification and nihilism,
The sun of the clear light of the way things are
Will not be experienced.

If one does not follow the instructions
Of a spiritual friend, a wish-granting gem,
And does not become familiar
With study, contemplation and meditation,
No great fruit will be attained.

> At best one becomes an undiscriminating celestial,
> But more probably just some sort of animal.
> These are the dangers of wrongly practicing
> Meditation for days and nights on end.
>
> For those who wish to avoid this,
> I will briefly explain the correct way.
> If you don't agree with what I say,
> At least please don't take offense.

Some meditators think that they are practicing the profound meditative method of *shamatha* (meditative serenity) combined with *vipashyana* (higher insight) as taught in the sutras and tantras, whereas in fact they are applying the techniques incorrectly and have fallen into a blank-minded absorption. The results of this type of false meditation are that death is at best followed by rebirth as a mere samsaric god; but more probably the rebirth will be in the realm of animals. Meditators who make this mistake lose the fine line that divides meditation from non-meditation, following whatever arises in the mind and losing sight of the valid path to liberation and enlightenment. In their attempt to avoid the conceptual mind they miss the essential point of the teachings.

This topic is discussed in depth in Tsong-kha-pa's *The Uniquely Creative White Mind (Lhag-bsam-rab-dkar-ma)*, a text written in the form of questions and answers. Here he says, "No matter what the subject or technique of meditation, divide the day into meditation sessions and between-meditation periods. During the actual sessions, meditate with intensive mindfulness and awareness, using the spy of alertness to watch for mental wandering or dullness. Between sessions, keep the mind concentrated and engaged in supportive activities. In this way the two periods—meditation sessions and between sessions— complement each other."

Tsong-kha-pa then goes on to discuss numerous other subjects related to meditation, such as precisely what type of supportive activity should be engaged in, the number and procedure of the actual sessions, how to know when to break a session, etc.

The Pan-chen Lama Lob-zang Cho-gyen[19], who gained full realization of Lama Tsong-kha-pa's tradition and made a vast cloud-like offering of his accomplishments, wrote a text based on the themes of the above work by Tsong-kha-pa. He entitled his work *A Laughing Song on Lama Lob-zang's Questions and Answers (Dris-len-blo-bzang-bzhad-pai-sgra-dbyang)*. In this he writes,

> The Indian scriptures translated into Tibetan
> Always begin with the title being given in Sanskrit.
> Likewise, the door of every meditation session
> Is observation of one's own mind.
> This is the tradition of peerless Tsong-kha-pa.

As said here, all the sutras, tantras and *shastras* that were translated from Sanskrit into Tibetan begin with the title being given in the original Sanskrit. Similarly, we should begin every act of study, contemplation and meditation by checking up on our own mindstream. Our mind is an unspecified phenomena, being intrinsically neither positive nor negative; the quality it assumes depends upon how we direct it. Therefore we should use a part of it namely, the clear, quick, subtle wisdom aspect of consciousness that can distinguish specific qualities to check into the general contents of our mental continuum.

What precisely are we looking for? I and all sentient beings have been wandering in cyclic existence since beginningless time. Throughout all of these countless lifetimes our minds have carried the two thoughts of wanting to avoid suffering and wanting to acquire happiness. Yet we still have not gained the state of liberation and enlightenment. It is about time that we captured at least a glimpse of an experience of something from within the three vehicles taught by the Enlightened Beings.

But no! We continue to allow our mindstream to be dominated by negative karmic forces and delusion. So deeply accustomed are we to our samsaric ways that we constantly generate a steady stream of negativity without even noticing it. Not to speak of achieving a high spiritual state, we cannot be sure even to stay out of the lower realms. Living in habitual mindlessness, there is little hope for anything but regret in the end.

Even though we can intellectually see what is going on, it still seems difficult to turn the direction of the mind around, to replace interest in samsaric indulgence with interest in spiritual endeavour. Instead of delighting in the practice of Dharma, we delight in the false pleasures of worldly life. We grasp at permanence and security, and just further deepen our ocean of confusion.

Therefore in his *The Uniquely Creative White Mind* (*Lhag-bsam-rab-dkar-ma*) Lama Tsong-kha-pa writes, "Go to a quiet place of solitude. There, place the body upright in the meditation posture and focus the mind inward. We have lain in the deep bed of samsaric existence since beginningless time and as a result have repeatedly experienced suffering, confusion and pain. From now on we should make every effort to break this pattern of compulsive samsaric evolution."

We should generate the firm thought, "If I don't make some effort, surely my heart is empty." Our distaste for samsaric distractions should be as intense as our dislike for a pain in the kidneys.

This type of attitude is extremely rare. But if we do not generate it, then even if the guru teaches us the most profound method for gaining freedom from samsara and we intellectually understand his words perfectly, there will be very little transformative value.

Without the wish to drink water we will not engage in the actions whereby we create the circumstances for drinking. Therefore we should contemplate the nature of samsaric existence and develop a heartfelt aspiration to transcend it. Then apply the forces of mindfulness, awareness and conscientiousness in order to prevent the mind from flowing in negative ways. To make no effort to cultivate spiritual qualities and to transcend negativities, and instead just to live in acordance with samsaric conditioning and dark instincts, is to render one's human rebirth lower than that of an animal. Look closely at the writings of the ancient Ka-dam-pa masters. You will clearly see that this is their essential message.

Therefore we who are supposed to have attained the status of a human being and to possess the special human intelligence should use our opportunity wisely. Not to do so is to be like the person crazed by sickness who does not take the correct medicine, even though the doctor and medicine are readily at hand.

We are not alone in our samsaric plight. All sentient beings, each of whom in a previous lifetime has been a parent to us, share the same situation. Not only ourselves but also all living beings must be liberated from samsara.

The method for advancing personal and universal liberation is the practice of the enlightenment teachings. Do not postpone your efforts in practice. Time is the most precious commodity, and the need for your contribution in the spiritual quest is urgent. Think to yourself, "There is no alternative to spiritual endeavour. Other than by my own efforts, there is no way I can advance along the enlightenment path."

If we do not make some effort in this lifetime, what chance is there for us to again receive the same opportunity in the future? A human rebirth is not easily found, and those who waste one human life will not get another for a long time to come. Moreover, our life is short and is easily instantly destroyed. The body is an excellent example of impermanence. We should think, "How sad! All sentient beings wander helplessly in samsara in the same way that I do. Like me, they too are prone to confusion, suffering and the laws of impermanence. To benefit all living beings, I must immediately take responsibility for my own spiritual development, and must dedicate myself to the enlightenment path."

Concerning the third of the six preliminaries to be performed before each meditation session—that of sitting on one's meditation cushion in a correct posture and then taking refuge and generating the bodhimind—this year I have only been able to cover the aspect of correct sitting. Perhaps next year I'll be able to speak on the second aspect, that of taking refuge and generating thoughts of the bodhimind.

Now, our Great Prayer Festival is an annual celebration in commemoration of the time when Buddha met with the boastful and arrogant Tirthikas in a contest of miracles. At that time Buddha was in his fifty-sixth year. There are slightly different theories as to the specific month in which the contest took place. The Tirthikas, proudly flaunting their attachment to their false dogmas, had challenged the Buddha to public debate and were soundly beaten. Therefore toward the end of the Wood Hare Year they demanded that he meet with them in a contest of miracles. Buddha at first hesitated, not wanting to publicly demonstrate his occult powers; but in the end he was pressed into accepting. The contest eventually took place in the Fire Dragon Year.

When Lama Tsong-kha-pa was fifty-three years old he organized the first Great Prayer Festival of Lhasa in commemoration of these miracle demonstrations. It was the Wood Bull Year. During this festival he offered crowns to the two principal Buddha statues in Lhasa, thus transforming them into *samboghakaya* images. At the same time he made vast prayers for the long life of the Buddhadharma. Many thousands of monks and nuns participated in the festival.

As Buddha's contest had begun on the new moon and climaxed on the full moon, the Great Prayer Festival follows the same pattern.

In the early years of its existence the festival was largely confined to the Lhasa area. But gradually it spread throughout the country, until eventually it became an annual national celebration.

Shortly after Lama Tsong-kha-pa's death the tradition was somewhat weakened due to conflicts in Tibet.[20] Then the Second Dalai Lama Gyal-wa Gen-dun Gya-tso restored it to its original strength and purity, and from his time onward it has continued intact.

The Second Dalai Lama also greatly popularized the use of the six Ka-dam-pa classics, as well as *The Ka-dam-pa Father Dharmas and Sons Dharmas (bKa'-gdams-pha-chos-bu-chos)*. This is true both in general and also particularly as concerns the Great Prayer Festival. From his time on, at least one of the six Ka-dam works has been read from during the morning session of each day of the festival, with the *Jatakamala* being read on the full moon.

Today is the morning of the full moon session, so I will honor the tradition by reading from the *Jatakamala*.

> *His Holiness then read from*
> *the* Jatakamala. *Later he*
> *concluded his discourse as follows.*

The Ornament of Mahayana Sutras (mDo-sde-rgyan) states,

> In the beginning, rely upon study.
> Then internalize the meaning by meditation.
> From correct meditation arises
> The wisdom of correct understanding.

One should first study and contemplate the many scriptures, and then meditate intensely upon what has been learned. Otherwise, to study one thing and then to ignore this and go on to practice an unrelated meditation technique, such as a minor oral transmission teaching, is to mistake the path leading to enlightenment.

The great Ka-dam-pa forefather Lama Drom Ton-pa once said, "Studying many teachings and then looking somewhere else for what to practice is a sign of erroneous understanding."

In his extensive *Lam Rim* treatise Lama Tsong-kha-pa discusses the stages of meditation by using many illustrations and examples to clarify this point.

We should take study, contemplation and meditation as supplementary factors on the path.

Divide the day into meditation sessions and post-meditational periods. During the sessions, proceed as instructed in the standard manuals on the specific technique being applied. Begin the session with analytical meditation, engaging the wisdom of discriminating awareness in order to eliminate confusion and apathy. Once familiarity with the overall structure of the subject has been established, engage in formal [fixed] meditation. Cultivate faultless *samadhi* to create an inner transformation within the mindstream. Proceeding in this way, one goes from high to higher on the enlightenment path.

Between sessions, blend the Bodhisattva spirit with everything that you do.

Je Tsong-kha-pa wrote,

It is not enough for the practice to be Mahayana;
The practitioner must also be Mahayana.

That is to say, every activity should be initiated on the basis of the Bodhisattva spirit, the motivation of performing the action in order to achieve enlightenment so that one can be of greater benefit to the world. During the course of the action, maintain thoughts of love and compassion. At the conclusion, dedicate the meritorious energy of the action toward the cause of enlightenment.

The Buddhadharma in its twofold aspect of scriptural and insight transmissions is a precious source of peace and happiness for living beings, pointing the way to liberation and enlightenment. Here in Tibet we have many lineages and orders of Buddhism as established by the sages of the past. All of these contribute to the spiritual vitality of our land. In particular, our three wondrous monastic universities and two tantric colleges of Lhasa, which have produced innumerable accomplished masters of marvellous insight and action, are special fields of merit and have been nurtured by all the earlier Dalai Lamas. Our government is also something very unique, encouraging and supporting the spiritual tradition in every way. This is really something very extraordinary in the present degenerate age. Because of these many blessings we have a very strong Sangha in our country, and with the exception of a few mountain bandits all of our citizens live in peace and comfort.

We are rich in accomplished spiritual masters and recognized reincarnate lamas who carry the load of upholding the enlightenment teachings. These great beings first gained inner experience by means of intensive study and practice, and now out of the wish to benefit others dedicate their lives to teaching the profound treatises, imparting the oral tradition teachings, giving tantric initiations and transmissions, performing rituals for the benefit of the living and the dead, and pointing out the paths whereby negative circumstances are avoided and enlightenment achieved.

As well, here in Lhasa we have the Jo-wo and Ra-mo-che temples, the two oldest religious buildings in Tibet. These buildings are especially wondrous sources of merit, and are amongst the holiest monuments in the world.

King Song-tsen Gam-po described the greatness of the Jo-wo Temple as follows. "Seeing it once closes the door to the lower realms. Seeing it twice brings rebirth as a human or celestial with instincts to achieve liberation. Seeing it a third time eliminates the activity of the three root delusions and plants the instincts to achieve the three Buddha *kayas*."

He continues, "If an animal hears the name of this temple it will be freed from the lower realms and will enter the path leading to liberation. A human or celestial being who hears its name will be placed on the path to enlightenment. To remember the qualities of the images in this temple purifies the negative karma collected over five thousand aeons. However many times one circumambulates it, one plants an equal number of karmic seeds for achieving the wisdom of omniscience. The merit of making pilgrimage to it is not surpassed by a pilgrimage to either Vajrasana or the secret *dakini* treasury of Oddiyana. Visiting and offering worship at this temple is equal to doing the same at either Vajrasana or Oddiyana."

These and many other such benefits are listed in the standard accounts of the religious sites of Tibet.

Last year I ordered some restoration work to be done on these two temples. I understand that there has been some controversy over this because of the superstitious belief that once a religious building has been consecrated it should never be tampered with. Some people of little learning and less understanding erronously quote the Fifth Dalai Lama's writings on *The Sealed Transmission of Most Secret Hayagriva* in order to assert that it is improper to renovate a consecrated temple. I assure you that I am very familiar with what the Fifth Dalai Lama had to say. In fact, during his lifetime he himself had a lot of reconstruction done. It is far better to restore and then reconsecrate a beautiful old temple than it is to let it fall into ruin. In particular, our Jo-wo temple is something very precious and wonderful, and we have a responsibility to maintain the condition of this and other buildings like it. It is rather sad that, when Buddha himself so strongly advocated the use of reason and the logical mind, some of our people seem to still be completely stuck in the mire of superstition and primitive thinking.

We should now dedicate any positive energy generated by today's discourse.

> May the qualities and aspirations
> Of the Buddhas of the past, present and future
> Be linked with the ripening effects
> Of my own activities.
>
> By skilful means may these reach fruition
> And then by releasing a rainfall
> Of the nectar-like holy Dharma
> Upon the beloved sentient beings,
> May I contribute to the freedom of all.

By opening the door of the vast enlightened activities that herald peace and happiness, may a steady rain of spiritual knowledge fall upon the vast lands of the living beings, placing them on the supreme stage of eternal joy. May I be an instrument for the fulfillment of the qualities and prayers of the Buddhas of the past, present and future. And like a wish-fulfilling gem and an inexhaustible magic pot, may I be able to help the living beings in every way.

Please try to maintain that type of altruistic attitude in all that you do.

If anything that I have said here today is of any practical use to you, try and integrate it into your lives.

> If by giving or listening to this discourse
> Any spiritual energy has been generated,
> May it contribute toward the growth of wisdom
> Within all living beings without exception.

7 point Vairochana posture

SERMON FOUR: THE WOOD OX YEAR

The Fifth Dalai Lama wrote,

> Abandon the faults of an impure vessel
> And listen to the sweet, supreme Dharma
> From the mouth of a qualified master.
> Gather together the essence of the merits
> Produced over the last aeons.

One should search for a qualified master and from him learn the essence of all the spiritual teachings, the nature of the path that has been traversed by all Buddhas and Bodhisattvas, the instructions by which fortunate trainees can quickly achieve spiritual maturity and liberation. Then one should apply oneself diligently to the methods that have been learned, and thus fulfill the cultivation of meritorious energy and wisdom.

It is important to have the correct attitude in all that one does. This means having the presence of three factors within one's mindstream: spiritual confidence; the Bodhisattva aspiration; and enthusiastic joy. These three are especially important when engaging in any study or practice of the Dharma. They should be fierce, as though competing with one another for predominance. One proceeds on that basis, without confusing the points in the training.

The Collected Teachings of the Ka-dam-pa Masters (bKa-gdam-be-bum) says,

> The essence of all the oral teachings
> Is not to abandon training under a guru;
> For the guru is a treasury of everything good.
> He is the source of every spiritual development,
> Such as the growth of faith and the bodhimind.

Whoever relies correctly upon the guru can ripen the positive energy generated over the past three aeons, and in this one short lifetime can achieve the exalted state of full enlightenment, the omniscient wisdom of Buddhahood. Thus those who practice guru yoga become automatically close to Buddhahood.

By relying upon the guru with correct attitude and action one pleases all the Buddhas of the past, present and future; for it is the guru who is their representative. Being pleased, the Buddhas of the three times accept one's threefold devotion and with the illusory manifestations of their three mysteries they bestow their transforming blessings upon one's three doors [of body, speech and mind]. As a result of pleasing the Buddhas and receiving their blessings, one will no longer be overcome by outer or inner *maras* or delusions. One will quickly generate spiritual knowledge, and all mistaken behavioral patterns will spontaneously fall away.

The result which accords with the nature of the cause [produced by correctly relying upon the guru] is that in future lives one will continue to meet with and be cared for by the holy gurus, will continue to receive unmistaken guidance, and will make steady progress along the path leading to spiritual liberation. One will never be cut off from spiritual friends and, dwelling in practice of the enlightenment teachings, will never again take rebirth in any of the realms of misery. The effect that accords with the nature of the cause in terms of activity is that one will easily traverse the paths and stages leading to enlightenment. Qualities such as spiritual confidence, the Bodhisattva spirit and enthusiastic joy will steadily grow.

In brief, all realizations from those that demark entrance into the first step of the path until those that demark attainment of the final stage of the great union of full enlightenment arise from the power of correctly relying upon a qualified guru. Therefore it is said that the essence of all the oral teachings is to rely with undivided attention upon the spiritual master who shows the way.

Over the last years I have been discussing the six preliminaries to be applied at the beginning of each meditation session. Last year I began the third of these, that of sitting on one's meditation cushion in the seven-point posture of Vairochana Buddha, and then taking refuge and generating the bodhimind. We have covered the first part of this preliminary, which deals with sitting in the correct posture. Therefore this year I'll speak on taking refuge and generating the bodhimind.

The traditions of both Lama Tsong-kha-pa and the Fifth Dalai Lama stress that in order to generate a confident appreciation of the topic of refuge, the meditations on taking refuge should be conjoined with a panoramic understanding of the subject in terms of both scripture and reason.

The principal source for the oral tradition teachings on the nature of refuge is *The Peerless Thread (rGyud-bla-ma)* by Maitreya/Asanga.

This work points to the door for entering into the Dharma and treats in depth the three refuge objects: Buddha, Dharma and Sangha. These three refuge objects are three of the seven *vajra* topics that constitute the body of *The Peerless Thread* .

Another work by Maitreya/Asanga, namely, *An Ornament of the Clear Realizationsé (mNgon-rtogs-rgyan)*, acts as the source for the oral tradition teachings on the methods of generating the bodhimind. This work extracts the hidden meaning of the *Prajnaparamita Sutras.*

Thus our discussion this year, which focusses upon the process of taking refuge and generating thoughts of the bodhimind as a preliminary to entering into a formal meditation session, is essentially rooted in the above two texts by Maitreya/Asanga.

There are many different manners of explanation of the subject of refuge found in the Sutrayana and Vajrayana traditions.

For example, the two Hinayana schools—Vaibashaka and Sautrantika—speak of refuge from the perspective of function and differentiation.

The Madhyamaka and Chittamatrin schools of the Mahayana have a more elaborate presentation. They speak of it in terms of the two levels of truth, its principal and subsidiary factors, the meaning of refuge, the karmic implications, the actual act of refuge in context of the path of the three levels of spiritual application, the etymology behind the words of refuge, and so forth.

The Peerless Thread (rGyud-bla-ma) states,

> The Teacher, the Doctrine and the Trainees
> Of the three Vehicles, together with their functions:
> By the power of admiration for these,
> The three refuges are established.

The text then continues to expand upon the subject by using six headings: the reasons for having a threefold refuge; the purpose of refuge; the nature of each of the three objects of refuge; the imputed distinctions; the meaning of the words of taking refuge; and the manner of actually taking refuge.

In the Vajrayana, the subject of refuge is treated somewhat differently. Here the discussion centers upon the outer, inner and secret meanings of refuge on both direct and interpretative levels.

As mentioned above, it is very important to gain an understanding of a topic by investigating it from the twofold perspective of reason

and scriptural presentations, and then applying the logical methods
of testing the conclusions for validity.

The Fifth Dalai Lama wrote,

> Ascertain the meaning of the scriptures
> By means of critical investigation.
> Then experiment with the practices
> With firm, clear concentration.
> Finally, adorn your experiences
> By referring them back to the original scriptures.
> Through following these three simple steps
> One arrives at true understanding.

That is to say, first gain an overall picture of the topic by means
of reason and scriptural study. Then practice what has been learned
and observe the experiences induced. Thirdly, refer these experiences
back to what was originally studied and compare the actual experience
with the words of the teaching. This threefold approach is the supreme
method for translating scriptural teaching into inner experience, and
then for bringing experience back within the framework of the overall presentation of the path. It ensures the growth of a deeply rooted
and well-balanced understanding.

Today I don't have time to go into a great deal of detail, so instead
will concentrate upon the general procedures of the refuge meditation.

The supreme [Indian] sage Vira wrote in his *One Hundred and Fifty
Verses of Praise* (*bsTod-pa-rgya-lnga-bcu-pa*),

> There is nobody
> Who inherently has faults;
> But there are some who in all ways
> Have become embodiments of every excellence.

By seeing the exceptional nature of the body, speech, mind, qualities and enlightened energy of the Teacher Refuge, which refers to the
guru as an embodiment of the Buddhas, one gains the confidence that
it is possible to transcend all faults and to achieve every excellent quality. This faith or confidence is one of the two principal causes of taking refuge.

The second cause is that one experiences dissatisfaction with the
suffering nature of cyclic existence and feels oppressed by the burden

of the two sources of samsaric experience: contaminated karmic instincts and the delusions that afflict the mind. Disgusted with samsara and apprehensive of suffering, one thinks, "May I gain freedom from experiencing the results of samsaric existence, together with all suffering."

The Sutrayana and Vajrayana traditions present various approaches to the subject of taking refuge. The exclusive approach taken by Lama Tsong-kha-pa and the masters of the ear-whispered lineage coming from Gyal-wa Wen-sa-pa is as follows. The basis should be an understanding of the Prajnaparamitayana philosophy of emptiness as presented by the Madhyamaka Prasangika school. The person going for refuge should be of the definite [Mahayana] or indefinite [basically spiritual] nature, on either ordinary or *arya* levels. He or she then turns for refuge to the Three Jewels, in the hope of eliminating the delusion of grasping at true existence and at a final identity in the self and phenomena; and also with the hope of eliminating the obscurations to knowledge, such as the instincts of grasping at duality.

In the context of the Vajrayana, the yogi practicing the two tantric stages turns for refuge because he sees, is apprehensive of and wishes to overcome grasping at the mundane appearances of the five aggregates, twelve sensory bases, and eighteen sources of experience. He sees, is apprehensive of and wishes to overcome grasping at the habit of perceiving energy and mantra as being of different natures; and also wishes to eliminate the habit of grasping at the subtle dual appearance of the three facets of experience [i.e., a doer, a deed, and the act of doing]. He wishes to overcome the hindrances to accomplishing the yogas of isolation of body, speech and mind, the yogas of semblant and actual clear light experiences, the yogas of impure and pure illusory bodies, and the yoga of the stages of the two types of great union, that of a trainee and that beyond training.

The principal thought is that one takes refuge in order to be enabled to overcome the immediate obstacles to the stages of the path with which one is presently confronted, and that one will continue to do so until all faults and shortcomings have been transcended and all realizations achieved.

As for the manner of visualizing the refuge objects and taking refuge, this is discussed in depth in numerous treatises and therefore is well known to all of you.

The extensive and intermediate *Lam Rim* texts by Lama Tsong-kha-pa give only a general description of the methods for generating the mind of refuge. As the Fifth Dalai Lama's *The Sacred Instructions of Manjushri* (*'Jam-dpal-zhal-lung*) provides more detail on the subject, I will follow this latter tradition here.

One begins by generating a visualization of the refuge field. This can be as extensive or simple as is best suited to the individual practitioner. This refuge field is visualized in the space in front of the meditator, and then the words of the refuge formula are recited.

As said above, the visualized refuge field can be as simple or as complex as one likes. A simple Buddha image will suffice; or one can include all of the lineage gurus, meditational deities, and so forth.

One visualization technique is as follows. To symbolize the wisdom of bliss and void, a high and vast throne made from the jewels of the ten powers and upheld by the eight lions of enlightenment appears in the space before you. Its four sides symbolize the four miracle legs and four pure knowledges. Upon it is a seat made up of a multicolored lotus bearing sun and moon discs; these symbolize the illusory body, clear light and great union experiences produced by the wisdom of great bliss. Seated there is one's own root guru in the form of Buddha Shakyamuni. Lights emanate from his heart and then return, summoning with them the present and past lineage gurus, the meditational deities, Buddhas, Bodhisattvas, Shravaka Arhats, Pratyekabuddhas, dakas, dakinis and Dharma Protectors. These either dissolve into the image of one's guru in the form of the Buddha, or else they take up their places around him [depending on whether you wish to maintain a simple or complex visualization].

To expand the visualization one can imagine that the three principal lineages of transmission are seated above the figure of one's guru (who is seen in the form of a Buddha), and that below him are the four kingly protectors.

When envisioning the refuge field one thinks, "The guru's body is the Sangha; his speech is the Dharma; and his mind is the Buddha. His qualities and enlightened activities are symbolized by the other figures in the visualized assembly."

Alternatively one can think, "His realization of the illusory body yoga is the Buddha; his clear light realization is the Dharma; and his realization of the great union yoga is the Sangha."

These sorts of contemplations performed in conjunction with visualization are very useful.

One imagines that oneself and all sentient beings of the six realms of existence are sitting in front of this assembly. In the Sutrayana all of these sentient beings are seen as having the form of humans; in the Vajrayana the emphasis is on eliminating attachment to ordinary perception, so the beings of the six realms are seen as having the form of tantric deities. Here, however, one relaxes the divine pride concerning oneself, because the emphasis is on the act of taking refuge in order to transcend samsaric imperfection.

Then, without losing the vision of the refuge field before which are all the living beings of the six realms like a huge crowd in a busy marketplace, one recollects the two reasons for taking refuge and recites the four lines of the refuge formula: *namo Guru bhyah; namo Buddha ya; namo Dharma ya; namo Sangha ya* (I turn to the Guru; I turn to the Buddha; I turn to the Dharma; I turn to the Sangha.) This refuge formula is generally repeated seven, twenty-one or one hundred and eight times.

This is the general method of taking refuge as a preliminary at the beginning of the meditation session. In the exclusively Mahayana refuge one also recites the following verse three times. This verse combines the meaning of refuge with the act of generating thoughts of the bodhimind.

To Buddha, Dharma and the Supreme Community of Sangha
I turn for refuge until enlightenment is achieved.
By the merit of my practicing the six perfections,
May Buddhahood be gained for the benefit of all.

In conjunction with the recitation of the above mantric formula one visualizes that a stream of lights and nectars flow forth from the refuge objects. They come to oneself and all the sentient beings of the six realms, purifying obstacles and granting refuge.

The above verse, which links refuge with generating the bodhimind, should be recited in conjunction with the following thoughts. "All the sentient beings of the six realms are wandering toward the deep precipice of the sufferings of *samsara* and the limitations of personal nirvana. Overpowered by ego-grasping, they are unable to cut the overpowering influence of attachment, aversion and mental darkness. How sad! I must take some responsibility for helping them."

Then on the basis of that thought one engages in the seven-point bodhimind meditation, known as "the six causes and one effect of the bodhimind." This technique is taught in the Mahayana *Lo-jong* tradition and comes down from the oral tradition teachings of Asanga.

As a preliminary to the process one generates the mind of equanimity toward all sentient beings, the smooth mind that does not differentiate between friend, enemy and stranger. This smoothing of the mind is like tilling a field before farming it. One then scans through the six causes: seeing all beings as having once been one's mother in some previous life; recollecting the many ways in which the mother is kind; generating the wish to repay that kindness; engendering love, the mind that wishes to see all sentient beings have happiness and its cause; engendering compassion, that wishes to see them all be free from suffering and its cause; and then giving rise to the altruistic attitude of universal responsibility, that wants to personally contribute to the benefit of the world. Based on these six causes one gives birth to the bodhimind, the Bodhisattva spirit that understands that only a fully enlightened Buddha can really benefit others, and that therefore aspires to achieve enlightenment as the supreme means of fulfilling altruism.

As mentioned above, as a preliminary to contemplating these six causal factors and the resultant seventh factor of the bodhimind, one must first make the mind smooth by means of generating a sense of equanimity toward the three types of sentient beings: friends, enemies and strangers. One does this by recollecting that over the chain of previous lifetimes each of the sentient beings has changed places in the roles they have played with us. Sometimes we have been friends, sometimes enemies, and sometimes strangers. Even in this life the beings alter in these roles. The smallest conflict can turn a friend into an enemy, and a nicety can turn an enemy into a friend. We should therefore not exaggerate our relationships with others, but instead should learn to treat all living beings with an equal respect.

One thinks like this with intensity, and when a sense of equanimity has been engendered enters into the seven-point bodhimind contemplation described above.

Often in addition to reciting the refuge formula and the verse linking refuge to the bodhimind, both of which were stated above, one recites the verse of the four immeasurable thoughts:

> May all beings have happiness and its cause;
> May all beings be free from suffering and its cause;
> May all beings never be separated from that happiness
>   which is without suffering;
> May all sentient beings abide in equanimity which is
>   free from attachment for the near and
>   aversion for the far.

These are the aspirations of immeasurable love, compassion, joy and equaminity. They are inseparable from the Bodhisattva spirit.

In his *Lam Rim* treatises Tsong-kha-pa does not discuss any special connection between these four thoughts and the meditations for developing the bodhimind. Nor does the Fifth Dalai Lama broach the subject in his *The Sacred Instructions of Manjushri ('Jam-dpal-zhal-lung)*.

However, both *The Path to Joy (bDe-lam)* by the First Panchen Lama and *The Quick Path (Myur-lam)* by the Second Panchen Lama state that when reciting the verse of the four immeasurable thoughts we should meditate on the theme of exchanging self-awareness for awareness of others. Here the order of the four immeasurable thoughts is somewhat different: one begins with equaminity and then goes on to love, compassion and joy.

It is also suggested that to each of the four one applies intention, aspiration, and a sense of universal responsibility.

This then is but a brief explanation of the fourth of the six preliminaries to be performed at the beginning of each meditation session: sitting in a correct meditation posture and then taking refuge and generating thoughts of the bodhimind.

As said above, there are many different types of visualization and contemplation related to the subjects of refuge and generating the bodhimind. Here I have only dealt with the most commonly used techniques. You should adjust the practices in accordance with the instructions of your own personal guru and the traditions of his lineage.

Now, as today is the morning of the full moon session of the Great Prayer Festival I would like to perform the traditional reading from the *Jatakamala*.

> *His Holiness then read from*
> *the* Jatakamala. *Later he*
> *concluded his discourse as follows.*

The [Indian] master Asanga, who had achieved realization of the three grounds, wrote in his *A Summary of the Vehicles (Theg-bsdus)*,

> With the strength of goodness and prayer
> And the especially exalted motivation,
> The Bodhisattva strives for three countless aeons
> To fulfill merit and wisdom
> For the benefit of all living beings.

The Victorious Ones, as a condition for benefitting trainees, first generate the Mahayana attitude which has the great compassion as its root. From then until their accumulations of merit and wisdom reach fulfillment they work constantly in order to increase the strength and agility of the mind.

As *An Ornament of the Clear Realizations* (*mNgon-rtogs-rgyan*) explains by means of many examples and concepts, the Bodhisattva undergoes twenty-two levels of development of the bodhimind as he gradually evolves toward full enlightenment.

At the first of these he instinctively cherishes others more than himself. This stage is simply called "earth." It is given this name because it becomes the basis of all progress on the Mahayana path and acts as the foundation upon which the accumulations of merit and wisdom are grown, much in the same way that the earth acts as the basis and foundation for all life on this planet.

The twenty-second and final stage of its development is called "Dharma cloud," because at the last moment of the tenth Bodhisattva level the two obscurations are utterly destroyed by means of the *vajra*-like *samadhi*, and the bodhimind becomes like a mighty cloud releasing an unceasing rain of Dharma on the living beings.

The Sutra of Unceasing Wisdom (*bLo-gros-mi-zad*) states,

> In the beginning, unceasing bodhimind;
> In the middle, unceasing ten strengths;
> In the end, unceasing skilful means.

This is further expanded upon by means of numerous illustrations in *An Ornament of Mahayana Sutras* (*mDo-sde-rgyan*) and also in *The Bodhisattva Stages* (*Byang-sa*). Later, Lama Tsong-kha-pa and his disciples wrote various texts in order to synthesize the meaning of these scriptures and to further clarify the nature, meaning and stages of the Bodhisattva experiences.

These are the principal scriptural sources of the oral tradition teachings on the methods of generating the bodhimind. We should study and contemplate them in depth, and then apply ourselves to the actual meditations that give birth within the mindstream to inner experience. Whoever possesses the bodhimind in any of its twenty-two levels of development is counted as a Bodhisattva of that particular level. We should aspire to achieve at least the first of the twenty-two levels.

In order to be effective in our attempts at developing the bodhimind it is useful to train under a qualified master. Khe-drub Ge-lek Pal-zang-po[21] once wrote,

> Not having the guidance of a qualified master
> And instead chasing after worldly goals,
> Then no matter how much one strives at activities
> Like study, contemplation and meditation,
> One's efforts remain but a reflection of real practice.

In order to achieve the exalted states of realization demonstrated by the masters of the past, we should train just as they did. Without exception they all trained under qualified masters, so we would be wise to do the same.

A spiritual master should be endowed with the three qualities of sagacity, nobility and sublimity. These three are described as follows by the great guru Chang-kya Rol-pai Dor-je[22],

> One is called a sage when
> Study and contemplation are not unbalanced,
> All teachings arise as personal advice,
> And one can communicate one's understanding.

> One is called noble
> When one's delusions have been subdued,
> One is able to calm the minds of self and others,
> And one has vision and meditation free from confusion.

> One is called a sublime being
> When one's knowledge doesn't harm one's humility,
> One's humility doesn't obstruct expression of one's
>   knowledge,
> And one's works benefit truth.

In brief, like the great gurus of the past we should make self-discipline our foundation, and on that basis should ascertain the essence of the Buddhadharma by means of study and contemplation. Then we should enter into intensive meditation on the key methods found in the sutras and tantras. In this way we will be able to accomplish the activities that bear the seals of wisdom, nobility and sublimity, and will be able to help goodness to grow and blossom.

I would like to close my discourse today with a short prayer by the illustrious Sa-kya-pa master Bu-ton Tam-che Khyen-pa,[23]

> By the truth of the Three Jewels of Refuge,
> The blessings of the glorious gurus
> And the strength of the Bodhisattva aspirations,
> May all auspicious wishes be fulfilled.

We should gather together the positive energy that we have generated today, link it with the root of goodness of all beings of the three times, and dedicate it to the peace, happiness and well-being of the world.

May the Buddhadharma be like the sun in illuminating the world. May it shine for long and light up the three realms with a hundred rays of enlightened activity.

As for the various ideas we have discussed today, please try to practice those of them that are useful to you.

> If by giving or listening to this discourse
> Any spiritual energy has been generated,
> May it contribute toward the growth of wisdom
> Within all living beings without exception.

SERMON FIVE: THE FIRE DRAGON YEAR

Lama Tsong-kha-pa commented,

> One session of listening to or teaching
> This tradition embodying the essence of all Buddha's words
> Collects waves of merit equivalent
> To listening to or teaching all the Buddhadharma.

The body of the eighty-four thousand doctrines taught by the Buddha is contained in the thousands of scriptures found in the *Kan-gyur*

(Collected Translations of Buddha's Words) and *Tan-gyur* (Collected Translations of Later Treatises). The quintessential themes from these two collections as organized for systematic practice were gathered together by Lama Atisha and structured for trainees successively of initial, intermediate and advanced capacities. Applying oneself to this tradition fulfills both the conventional purpose of immediate happiness and the higher purposes of liberation and enlightenment. One session of listening to or teaching this supreme spiritual legacy produces beneficial effects equivalent to hearing or studying the entire corpus of Buddhist scriptures.

Our Great Prayer Festival is an annual event in commemoration of the occasion when Buddha Shakyamuni was challenged by the six Hindu extremists to a public contest of miracle exhibition. At first Buddha declined, but the demand was pressed upon him again and again, so in the end he was forced to acquiesce.

According to legend the contest continued for fifteen consecutive days. The traditional accounts of the miracles are elegant and beautiful, and over the next years I would like to relate them to you in brief as part of our full moon session. I will follow the style of presentation of them as listed in the short verse work *In Praise of Buddha's Miracles (Cho-'phrul-bstod-pa)*[24].

Concerning the first of the fifteen miracles, *In Praise* reads,

> On the first day of spring King Prasenajit
> Made offerings and requests.
> Buddha tossed his toothbrush to the earth,
> And it instantly became a wish-granting tree
> Fulfilling the aspirations of humans and divinities.
> Homage to Shakyamuni, fulfiller of wishes.

The six Hindu extremists had been defeated in public debate. Angered and humiliated, they demanded a contest of miracles. Buddha agreed to meet them at Shravasti on the first day of spring. King Prasenajit acted as the sponsor of the event and offered a lavish meal to all who came.

After the meal Buddha threw his wooden toothbrush to the earth. It immediately transformed into an enormous wish-fulfilling tree adorned with the seven precious gems. Its foliage spread for five hundred *yojanas* into all directions. It had flowers the size of cartwheels and fruit the size of barrels with an incomparable taste and aroma that induced virtuous thoughts within the minds of all those present. When any part of the tree was touched it would resound with sweet words of the Dharma. The tree was so enormous that it cut off the light of the sun and moon.

In Praise describes the second miracle as follows,

> On the second day King Udrayana
> Made offerings and requests.
> Immediately to Buddha's right and left
> There appeared magnificent mountains of jewels.
> On them grew every type of delicious foods,
> And gentle animals ate from their tender grasses.
> Homage to Shakyamuni, master of all powers.

As stated above, on the second day of spring King Udrayana came to Buddha, made offerings and requested that he perform a miracle.

Instantly a jewelled mountain appeared on each side of the assembly. These were towering and extremely solid, and radiated forth multicolored lights. Many varieties of trees with exquisite flowers and fruits grew upon them, and from the trees came forth sweet sounds of the Dharma. On the right mountain grew every type of delicious food able to satiate all the assembly, and on the left mountain many varieties of gentle animals grazed peacefully on rich, lush grasses.

In Praise then describes the third miracle,

> On the third day King Sochinadi
> Offered food and made requests.
> After eating, the Buddha rinsed his mouth.
> The discarded water magically transformed
> Into a lake with water of eight excellences
> Beautified with a net of lotuses in bloom
> Radiant with exquisite lights.
> Homage to Shakyamuni, lord of light.

King Sochinadi sponsored the gathering of the third day and offered the assembly a lavish meal. After the Buddha had eaten he rinsed out his mouth, and the discarded mouth rinse transformed into a lake two hundred *yojanas* in width. Its waters possessed the eight excellent qualities and resembled lapis lazuli. On its surface floated powders of the seven precious gems, and from its depths manifested multicolored lotus flowers the size of cartwheels. These flowers radiated forth lights so bright that the entire earth and sky were filled with a magical hue. Everyone who had gathered to witness the contest of miracles beheld this and were amazed.

Thus on each day the Buddha manifested wondrous miracle demonstrations. This continued for fifteen days. At the end of each day he would speak on the Dharma in accordance with the capacities of those in the audience who had been moved by faith, and many beings were placed on the path of one or another of the three vehicles.

Next year I shall continue to relate the legendary accounts of the miracles exhibited by Buddha Shakyamuni at that time.

Over the past years I have been speaking on the six preliminaries to be performed at the beginning of each meditation session. So far we have completed three of them: cleaning the practice site and arranging the altar; setting up an attractive display of offerings; and then sitting on one's cushion in the seven-point posture of Vairochana, taking refuge and generating the bodhimind.

The fourth preliminary is the visualization of the field of merit.

The tradition of Lama Tsong-kha-pa and his disciples is to first ascertain the nature and validity of a teaching by means of both critical reason and scriptural analysis. Then if it passes this twofold test it should be put into practice and internalized.

A glance at the sutras, tantras and shastras reveals that the core of the Bodhisattva practices in both the Prajnaparamitayana and the Vajrayana is concerned with advancing the twofold accumulation of meritorious energy and wisdom. It is to further this twofold accumulation that the practitioner visualizes the field of merit.

In the writings of Lama Tsong-kha-pa a special emphasis is given to this fourth preliminary of generating the vision of the field of merit. Therefore we can see that it has been regarded as an important practice for a long time.

Tsong-kha-pa's extensive and intermediate *Lam Rim* texts here give much the same advice, differing only on points of detail. They recommend that the central figure in the visualized field of merit be that of Buddha Shakyamuni. To Buddha's right sit the lineage gurus of the vast bodhimind teachings coming from Asanga. To Buddha's left sit the lineage gurus of the profound emptiness teachings coming from Nagarjuna. Surrounding this assembly are various Buddhas, Bodhisattvas, Shravakas, Pratyekabuddhas, and Dharma Protectors.

The Fifth Dalai Lama's *The Sacred Instructions of Manjushri* provides a more detailed explanation of the processes here involved, but limits its explanation to the Sutrayana presentation.

The process of generating the visualized merit field is much the same as was described last year with the visualization of the refuge field, except that here there is emphasis on the stages of summoning the Wisdom Beings, etc., as will be explained later.

At the center of the space in front, one visualizes a square palace with four gateways. At the center of it is a crossed *vajra*, and upon this stands a throne upheld by the eight lions of enlightenment. Bathing houses stand outside in each of the four directions. To the right and left of the throne are jewel thrones, and behind, in front, and all around are exquisite cushions.

The base [earth] on which the visualized assembly sits has four levels [for the beings to be summoned].

Then, just as when Queen Mahabadhri once requested Buddha to come from afar and he instantly appeared by means of his magical powers, one invites the beings of the merit field to come and take their places on the thrones that have been prepared for them.

Buddha Shakyamuni instantly appears on the central throne. One's principal guru appears on the cushion in front of him. On the thrones to Buddha's right and left respectively appear the Bodhisattvas Maitreya and Manjushri. The gurus of the sacred practice lineage appear in the sky above. The gurus of the vast bodhimind lineage and profound emptiness lineage appear on the upper level, with the other figures of the merit field in a circle outside.

Above the palace and also on its verandas are various Bodhisattvas, Shravakas Arhats, and Pratyekabuddhas. Some of them are teaching the Dharma, others are meditating, etc. In general, they are doing whatever activities are necessary in order to lead trainees along the paths suitable to their individual predispositions.

One invites the figures in the visualized assembly to accept the offering of bathing houses. They bathe, are annointed with oils, etc., and then magically return to their seats. One then generates the firm thought, "They will now remain as my field of merit."

The First Pan-chen Lama's *The Path to Joy (bDe-lam)* adds several tantric ideas to the above procedures. Whenever one meditates upon an object in the tantric vehicle, the mind apprehending the object and the object itself must be viewed as arising within the one nature of consciousness. This point is to be kept in the forefront when practicing the Vajrayana.

To return to the discussion of the difference between visualizing a refuge field and a merit field, the primary distinction is that the merit field is transformed by the invocation of the Wisdom Beings. This is done by imagining that brilliant lights stream forth from the heart of the principal figure—in this case that of the Buddha. These lights summon forth the Wisdom Being aspects of the visualized assembly, who come from the various directions and dissolve into the envisioned Symbolic Beings. Lights again emanate from the Buddha's heart and strike against all the other figures, empowering them and causing them to become especially luminous. One should think that now merely by fixing the mind on these figures they serve the function of a merit field.

Whether one is meditating upon the above visualized assembly in order to take refuge or to generate the merit field, it nonetheless is important in Mahayana practice to first give rise to thoughts of the bodhimind. For this one recites the prayer, "In order to quickly achieve enlightenment for the greater benefit of all living beings I will now engage in this practice of generating the merit field [or taking refuge, as the case may be]."

In the Prajnaparamitayana both aspirational and active aspects of the bodhimind are said to have the same nature. The Vajrayana is similar in this respect, although within it the emphasis is placed on achieving full enlightenment within this lifetime through the skillful means of the tantric path. In the Sutrayana (Prajnaparamitayana) it is said that many lifetimes are required in order to complete the quest for enlightenment; but in the Vajrayana one can rely upon the profound guru yoga techniques to achieve the enlightened state of the great union of full Buddhahood in one short lifetime of this degenerate era. In the tantric vehicle one takes this aim — enlightenment in one lifetime — as the basis for the aspirational aspect of the bodhimind, and connects it to the practice of purification by means of invoking the nectars, etc.

The word "profound" in the above phrase "the profound guru yoga" is not being used in the usual sense of "vast [bodhimind] and profound [wisdom of emptiness]." Rather, it refers to meditating upon the guru and the mandala divinities as being of one inseparable nature at all times and in all ways. Thus it is being used in the sense of a profound method of generating merit, eliminating obstacles and offering prayers while envisioning the guru and mandala divinities as being of one inseparable nature.

When the merit field is being utilized in conjunction with Vajrayana practice, one visualizes that above the central figure [Buddha Shakyamuni] is the lineage of gurus of whichever of the powerful tantric transmissions one is personally practicing. The main lineages here are Guhyasamaja, Heruka Chakrasamvara, Vajrabhairava, Kalachakra, the Sixteen Ka-dam-pa Heartdrops, etc.

As mentioned above, to the right of Buddha Shakyamuni sits the Bodhisattva Maitreya, together with Asanga and the Indian gurus in the line of transmission of the teachings on the vast bodhimind activities, up to Atisha and his Tibetan disciple Lama Drom Ton-pa. To their right and left are the masters of the Old Ka-dam School holding the oral tradition *(gDam-ngag)* and scriptural lineages *(gZhung-pa)*, respectively, with the holders of the pith instruction lineages *(man-ngag)* sitting behind. The masters of the New Ka-dam School, beginning with Lama Tsong-kha-pa, sit in front.

To the left sits the Bodhisattva Manjushri, together with Nagarjuna and the Indian gurus in the lineage of transmission of the profound emptiness teachings, up to Atisha and his Tibetan disciple Lama Drom. Again, they are surrounded to the right, left and behind by the three lineages of transmission of the Old Ka-dam School as described above, with the masters of the New Ka-dam, beginning with Lama Tsong-kha-pa, seated in front.

In general, the Buddha is seen in the stylized form having the 112 marks and signs of perfection. The remainder of the gurus are seen in their ordinary forms.

Some manuals also suggest that in front of Buddha Shakyamuni one should visualize a number of sutras, and in front of Vajradhara a number of tantras.

When the above visualization has been established one then performs the invocation by means of the three sheathed beings and the consecration of the five places. This is a speciality of the fifth preliminary.

An essential method for this process is given in *A Summary of the Five Stages (Rim-lnga-mdor-byas)*,

Meditate on the Wisdom Being aspect
Who resides at the center of the heart
   of the Symbolic Being.
As for the Absorption Being,
This is the syllable *hum.*

These are the three sheathed beings: Symbolic, Wisdom and Absorption. The first of these is the outer form of the visualized being [in this case, the various gurus]. The second is the Wisdom Being aspect, which is visualized at the heart of the first aspect. The third sheath is the syllable *hum*, visualized at the heart of the Wisdom Being.

As implied above, although the figures in the merit field are many and they appear in various forms, ultimately in terms of final nature they are all only symbols of the omniscient knowledge of non-dual bliss and wisdom. They all reduce into the common denominator of the Absorption Being, the syllable *hum*, that symbolizes the union of the most subtle aspects of body and mind, form and consciousness.

This in turn is the meaning of Buddha Vajradhara, emanator of the five Buddha families.

To take it one step further, Buddha Vajradhara is but a symbol of one's own root guru; or, to put it another way, one's own root guru is but a human embodiment of Buddha Vajradhara and the omniscient knowledge of non-dual bliss and emptiness wisdom.

Thus the entire merit field described above is only the sportive play of one's own root guru, a symbol of his nature, being and function.

The Guhyasamaja Explanatory Tantra (gSang-'dus-bshed-rgyud) describes the situation as follows,

All divinities of the mystic mandala
Abide within the body of the *vajra* master.

As said here, the various aspects of the guru's being are inseparable in nature from the mandala divinities. All Buddhafields appear within the guru, and he pervades all Buddhafields.

The merit field is radiantly luminous, and its emanated light consecrates the entire world, both animate and inanimate. This light manifests in accordance with the needs of those to be trained: as water in deserts, trees in remote places, bridges and boats to cross over rivers, food and drink for the hungry, friends and companions for the lonely, medicine for those suffering from illness, guides for those lost and wandering in confusion, wish-fulfilling gems for the impoverished, and so forth.

Furthermore, the Buddha figure at the center of the merit field acts in the twenty-seven mysterious ways to ripen and liberate the living beings. He sends emanations throughout the world to serve as befits the needs of living beings, revealing the 112 physical marks and signs of perfection and the sixty excellent qualities of speech. In this way he leads trainees to the paths of liberation and enlightenment.

Concerning the practice of offering the bathing houses, this is said to be an excellent way to purify obstacles to spiritual progress. The walls of the bathing houses are white, red and black, symbolizing the three states of consciousness preceeding the experience of clear light realization.

After offering the bathing houses one invites the merit field to partake of the baths. This is often done by imagining that the merit field is reflected in a circular mirror, and then pouring water over the mirror. This is symbolic of the act of removing the general and specific sufferings of the six realms of samsara. It also symbolizes the act of refreshing and healing the sentient beings.

Thus the practice of offering bathing houses and cleansing waters signifies the various Bodhisattva activities. To engage in the practice is to uphold the sublime ways of the mighty Bodhisattvas.

There are many variations in the details of how the merit field is arranged, empowered, and so forth. What I have said above is a brief sketch of the basic principles involved. You should adapt it to accomodate the specific lineages you are personally practicing. Precisely how to do that can be learned directly from your own root teacher.

Now I would like to honor the tradition of the full moon session of the Great Prayer Festival by reading from the *Jatakamala*.

*His Holiness then read from
the* Jatakamala. *Later he
concluded his discourse as follows.*

The form of the merit field described above is deeply connected with Atisha and the masters of the Old Ka-dam School. It may be useful to say something about this school, and about the way Atisha's chief disciple, the layman Lama Drom Ton-pa, divided the tradition into three different lines of transmission: scriptural, oral tradition, and pith instruction.

The character of the Old Ka-dam School is described succinctly by the following passage from *The Book of the Ka-dam-pa Masters (bKa'-gdams-glegs-bam)*,

Not allowing study and contemplation
To fall out of balance,
Building all practices on one firm base,
Using all teachings as methods to develop the mind,
And constantly meditating within this perspective:
This is the style of my Ka-dam tradition.
It does not fall from the way.

Atisha widely taught the essence of the Buddhadharma in Tibet. Later, his chief disciple Lama Drom Ton-pa organized his transmissions into the legacy known as "The Four Divinities and Three Dharmas," a tradition whereby an individual practitioner could perceive all doctrines of the sutras and tantras as non-contradictory and could personally apply them all as supplementary methods for the accomplishment of enlightenment. The lineage eventually came to be known as "Atisha's Ka-dam Tradition, the Marvelous Legacy of Seven Divine Dharmas."

Lama Drom Ton-pa transmitted the various lineages of Atisha by dividing them between 'the three Ka-dam-pa brothers.' To one he gave the scriptural traditions, to the second the oral teachings, and to the third the pith instructions.

The scriptural traditions were of two main types: those dealing with ultimate reality and the wisdom of emptiness; and those dealing with conventional reality and the vast bodhimind activities.

As for the former of these, or those dealing with the ultimate wisdom of emptiness, the principal texts stressed here were Nagarjuna's six treatises on emptiness philosophy, such as *The Root of Wisdom* (*Mulamadhyamaka-karika*) and so forth, together with the commentaries to them by the later Indian masters; and also Atisha's own commentaries on the middle view and on the nature of the two truths.

Six quintessential texts were used to elucidate the nature of the Bodhisattva's vast activities: *The Bodhisattva Stages (Bodhisattvabhumi)*; *An Ornament of Mahayana Sutras (Mahayanasutra-alamkara)*; *A Compendium of Bodhisattva Trainings (Shikshasamucchaya)*; *A Guide to the Bodhisattva Way (Bodhisattvacharya-avatara)*; *A Garland of Birth Stories (Jatakamala)*; and *Collected Sayings of the Buddha (Udanavarga)*. It is the tradition to read from the fifth of these, *A Garland of Birth Stories* (i.e., the *Jatakamala*), during the morning session of the Great Prayer Festival.

These were the principal scriptures studied in the Old Ka-dam

School.

As for the oral tradition teachings, these emanated from and were the essential practices taught in the above scriptures. These oral teachings are generally known as "the precepts for training the mind in the Mahayana tradition" *(Theg-chen-blo-sbyong-gi-gdams-pa)*. Atisha collected these from his three principal Indian gurus, and also from his Indonesian master Ser-ling-pa. He then secretly transmitted them to his chief disciple Lama Drom Ton-pa.

During the time of the three Ka-dam-pa brothers many of these oral teachings from Atisha's three Indian gurus were collected together and compiled into the text *Stages of the Doctrine (bsTan-rim)*. Yet at that time the lineages from his Indonesian master were still kept secret.

However, these too eventually were publically revealed when the times were sufficiently mature. First Ge-she Kham-lung-pa published *Eight Sessions for Training the Mind (bLo-sbyong-thun-brgyad-ma)*. Then Ge-she Lang-tang-pa wrote *Eight Verses for Training the Mind (bLo-sbyong-tshig-brgyad-ma)*. After this, Sang-gye Gom-pa composed *A Public Explanation (Tshogs-bshad-ma)* and Che-ka-wa wrote *Seven Points for Training the Mind (bLo-sbyong-don-bdun-ma)*.[25]

In this way the various *Lo-jong* oral tradition instructions gradually emerged.

Later all of these essential works were were brought together into the anthology *A Hundred Texts on Training the Mind (bLo-sbyong-brgya-rtsa)* and became widely disseminated.

As for the third lineage transmitted by Lama Drom — that of the pith instructions — this has its roots in the secret oral teachings of Atisha and his disciples as embodied in *The Great Book of the Ka-dam-pa Masters, A Jewel Rosary of Profound Words on the Bodhisattva Way (bKa'gdams-glegs-bam-chen-mo-zab-tshig-byang-chub-sems-dpa'-nor-bui-phreng-ba)*. Also of importance here is the two-volume esoteric work *Father Dharmas Son Dharmas (Pha-chos-bu-chos)*, which arose out of the private discussions between Atisha and Lama Drom Ton-pa.

All the key points concerning the emptiness philosophy and Bodhisattva activity that are found in the three lineages given to the three Ka-dam-pa brothers — scriptural, oral tradition and pith instruction — had in fact been outlined by Atisha himself in his *A Lamp for the Path to Enlightenment (Lam-sgron)*. This excellent work is a guide to both how to study and how to practice, and acted as the fundamental textbook of the Old Ka-dam School. Later Lama Tsong-kha-pa wrote his extensive, intermediate and concise commentaries to it; thus *A*

Lamp for the Path to Enlightenment also became the basis of the New Ka-dam School.

We have now had the good fortune to meet with this sublime lineage. At this auspicious time we should recollect the advice of Khe-drub-je,

Do not be satisfied with a fraction of the teachings.
Apply yourself to all of them
With a faultless mental attitude.
Otherwise, the results will be uncertain.

These days most trainees seem to approach their studies with the wrong attitudes. Rather than seek a complete understanding, they content themselves with partial learning and partial practice. They debate in order to ridicule their dialectic partners rather than to try to enhance mutual understanding. Even though their motivation may not be completely negative, it is not sufficiently pure to be able to induce the experience of enlightenment.

Test all the teachings by means of the four methods of critical analysis, and thus come to a correct understanding. Then internalize the teachings by means of intensive meditation. Cultivate your mindstream by training under the guidance of a qualified teacher. If you strive in this way the positive results are certain. At first the mind of Dharma will arise only with great effort, but eventually it will arise spontaneously and effortlessly.

I would like to conclude with a brief prayer written by Gyal-wa Gendun Gya-tso, the Second Dalai Lama,

May the world become filled with pure practitioners
Who uphold the three higher trainings, and who are
Engaged in constant study and practice of Dharma.
Until samsaric existence has been eliminated,
May there prevail signs of the presence
Of the enlightenment teachings in all times and places.

We should adorn all of our activities with auspicious thoughts such as these.

Today we have discussed a wide range of ideas. If you are able to put some of them into practice, please do so.

If by giving or listening to this discourse
Any spiritual energy has been generated,
May it contribute toward the growth of wisdom
Within all living beings without exception.

SERMON SIX: THE FIRE HARE YEAR

The illustrious master Lama Tsong-kha-pa wrote,

O fortunate beings who are not obscured
By an unbalanced view of the path,
Who have the wisdom able to discern
The difference between wholesome and unwholesome,
And who wish to render life meaningful,
Listen closely with a joyous mind.

In Buddhism there are two aspects to the path. On the one hand there is the activity of study and contemplation, of application to the great treatises by means of intellect and reason. On the other hand there is the activity of meditation, of application to the oral tradition teachings that emphasize internalization and actualization.

When these two factors in training are kept separate, there is no way that we can find certainty in the meaning and relevance of all the various doctrines of the Buddhadharma. Fortunate indeed are those practitioners who are able to take the intellectual wisdom which appreciates study and contemplation of every aspect of the vast and profound Dharma, and integrate this with formal meditation that engages in the *samadhi* able to give birth within the mindstream to the highest realizations.

This integrated approach is what is meant in the above verse by the words, ".... not obscured by an unbalanced view of the path."

It is for trainees of this nature that the Mahayana teachings of Atisha, that so skillfully condense all points of the Buddhist tradition, are intended.

Our annual Great Prayer Festival is in commemoration of the time

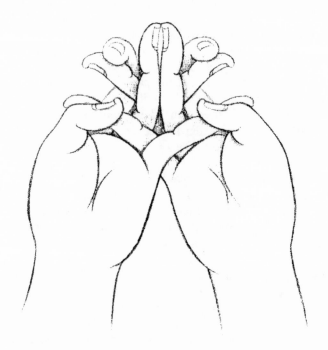

Mandala offering

when the Buddha defeated the six Hindu extremists in a public contest of miracles. Last year I related the first three of these to you. This year I will continue with three more.

In Praise of Buddha's Miracles (Cho-'phrul-bstod-pa) states,

On the fourth day King Indravarma made offerings.
Eight times four streams flowed forth from the magical lake.
These circled and then returned, their bubbling sounds
Revealing the teachings of the three vehicles.
Homage to Shakyamuni, a most wonderful teacher.

As said above, on the fourth day King Indravarma sponsored the event. In response, Buddha Shakyamuni caused eight streams to form from the magical jewelled lake that he had created the day before. These flowed into each of the four directions, circled and then returned to the lake.

The waters of these streams were endowed with the eight excellent qualities, and as they flowed the bubbling sounds that they made revealed inconceivable Dharmas: the five powers, the five strengths, the seven limbs of enlightenment, the noble eightfold path, the three doors of liberation, the various clairvoyances, the six perfections, the four boundless thoughts, and so forth.

Those who heard these sounds and who were mature vessels immediately gave birth to vast virtuous roots of higher being and final realization.

In Praise of Buddha's Miracles continues,

The next day King Brahmadatta made offerings.
From Buddha's face there emanated forth
A golden radiance that filled the 3,000 great worlds.
The minds of those in states of misery were purified,
And all beings were satiated with the bliss of *dhyana*.
Homage to Shakyamuni, he who brings joy.

On the fifth day King Brahmadatta acted as the principal sponsor. In response to his request, Buddha emitted countless rays of golden light from his face. These filled the skies of the great three thousand world systems. All the sentient beings touched by this light experienced immediate pacification of the three psychic poisons and the five obscurations, and attained a joyous ecstasy equal to that experienced in

the samadhi of the third *dhyana*. Thus they were placed in the sphere
of peerless faith.

In Praise then reads,

> On the sixth day the Licchavis offered delicious food.
> Everyone in the audience experienced clairvoyance
> And was able to know one another's minds.
> Seeing each other's black and white karmic seeds,
> They experienced deep faith and conviction.
> Homage to Shakyamuni, a source of inspiration.

On the sixth day of spring the Licchavis sponsored the gathering
and requested the Buddha to reveal his magical abilities. Buddha instantly caused everyone in the audience to have the clairvoyance able
to read the thoughts of others. Consequently they could see the forces
of karma at work in one another's minds. Deeply moved by this experience, they were placed in the field of firm faith.

It is said that when the Bodhisattva attains the tenth stage of the
path of meditation he is given the "initiation of great luminosity."
At that time he gains the power to manifest countless bodily emanations, each of which has limitless miraculous abilities. Each of these
bodies emanates boundless light rays, which pacify the suffering of
living beings and liberate them from the obstacles hindering progress
along the paths of the three vehicles. The lights also reveal to living
beings the magnificence of the Buddhafields. The Bodhisattva can
perform all of these wondrous deeds without even rising from his meditation cushion.

A sutra states,

> Just as space pervades everywhere,
> The form of an enlightened being does likewise.
> And wherever a Buddha's form pervades,
> That place becomes filled with light.

For as long as sentient beings are bound in delusion the compassionate Buddhas continue to send forth emanations to work for the
welfare of those sufficiently ripe to be trained, coming to each being
in accordance with need and capacity. Thus they continuously and
effortlessly benefit the world.

The various schools of Buddhist tenets have different ways of speaking about the nature, power, activities and so forth of a Buddha. These are not contradictory, but rather are intended to suit the predispositions of the various types of trainees. It is useful to study the different tenet systems so that the diverse interpretations of the points of doctrine come into a balanced perspective. Otherwise, there is the danger of misunderstanding and confusion.

As for the five obscurations mentioned above, these are listed as follows in Nagarjuna's *A Letter to a Friend (bShes-sbring)*,

> Distraction and apathy; harmful intentions;
> Dullness and sleepiness; desirous thoughts;
> And also hesitating doubt:
> These five obscurations are thieves stealing
> The gem of goodness and spiritual progress.
> Know them well.

Here, distraction and apathy are counted as one. Dullness and sleepiness are also counted together as one. These, together with harmful intent, desirous thoughts and hesitating doubt make up the five obstructions that hinder spiritual growth.

Over the last years we have been dedicating a part of each discourse to a discussion of the six preliminary practices to be performed at the beginning of each meditation session. So far we have covered the first four of these: cleaning the practice site and arranging an altar; setting up an attractive display of offerings; sitting on the meditation cushion in a correct posture, taking refuge and generating thoughts of the bodhimind; and generating the visualization of the field of merit.

The fifth preliminary involves the seven-limbed devotion. These seven limbs reflect seven themes: prostration, offering, confession of negativity, requesting the Buddhas to turn the Wheel of Dharma, requesting the Buddhas not to enter into *parinirvana*, and the dedication of merit.

Generally speaking, the basis to be purified by means of the practice of Dharma is nothing other than one's own mind. One's mind is also the basis within which the qualities of enlightenment are to be cultivated.

The role played by the seven-limbed devotion is threefold: the generation of meritorious energy; the purification of the mind; and the elimination of obstacles obstructing successful practice.

In addition, the seven limbs are a method for stimulating the Mahayana nature in trainees, for eliminating hindrances to the completion of the Bodhisattva deeds, and for amplifying the stamina of practice.

When a Bodhisattva comes into the presence of a Buddha, he always first mentally performs the seven-limbed devotion. This is his offering.

Sometimes in the scriptures we see mention of ten instead of seven limbs. When this is the case, three extra steps have been placed at the beginning of the process: arousing feelings of faith; taking refuge in the Three Jewels; and generating the bodhimind. But whether or not one speaks of seven or ten, the same basic process is being referred to. The latter form just includes three extra themes that here are covered in the earlier preliminaries.

The practice of the seven-limbed devotion is found in both the Sutrayana and the Vajrayana. For example, there is *The Sutra of the Seven-Limbed Rite (mDoi-yan-lag-bdun-pa)*; and also *The Tantra of the Seven Limbs (rGyud-kyi-bdun-rnam)*.

The purpose and function of the seven-limbed devotion are thus supported by both reason and scripture.

As Lama Tsong-kha-pa's extensive and intermediate *Lam Rim* treatises point out, the seven-limbed devotion is very powerful in generating the meritorious energy that ripens the conditions conducive to practice and to inducing realization within one's mindstream, and is also very effective in removing negative conditions and obstacles on the path. This is important, because even if we have the substantial cause for successful meditative endeavor, it will be extremely difficult to generate any solid progress when we lack supportive conditions. These supportive conditions are cultivated and reinforced by practice of the seven-limbed devotion.

In the practice of the six preliminaries, one engages in the seven-limbed devotion by means of reading a liturgy while contemplating its meanings. There are also ways to expand each of the seven limbs, and I will explain these in brief later in my discussion of each of the seven limbs individually.

One of the liturgies most commonly used as the basis for the seven-limbed devotion comes from the opening section of *The Prayer of Arya Samantabhadra (bZang-spyod-smon-lam)*[26]. This is recommended by both Lama Tsong-kha-pa and the Fifth Dalai Lama in their *Lam Rim* manuals.

The text for this is as follows:

(1) The Limb of Prostration.

> O Lions amongst Men,
> Buddhas past, present and future,
> To as many of you as exist in the ten directions
> I bow with my body, speech and mind.

> On waves of strength of this king
> Of prayers for exalted, sublime ways,
> With bodies numerous as atoms of the world
> I bow to the Buddhas pervading space.

> On every atom is found a Buddha
> Sitting amidst countless Bodhisattvas.
> I look with eyes of faith to the Victorious Ones
> Thus filling the entire *dharmadhatu*.

> Hail those with limitless oceans of excellences
> Endowed with an ocean of wondrous speech;
> I sing praises to the greatness of all Buddhas,
> A eulogy of those gone to bliss supreme.

(2) The Limb of Offering.

> Exquisite flowers, splendid garlands,
> And beautiful sounds, parasols,
> Butter lamps and delightful incense
> I offer to all Victorious Ones.

> Excellent food, the finest perfumes,
> And a mound of mystic substances high as Mt. Meru
> I arrange in special formations
> And offer to those who have conquered themselves.

> And all peerless offerings I hold up
> In admiration of those gone to bliss.
> With the strength of faith in sublime ways,
> I prostrate and make offerings to the Buddhas.

(3) The Limb of Acknowledging One's Weaknesses and Failings.

Long overpowered by attachment, aversion and ignorance,
Countless evils have I committed
With acts of body, speech and mind.
I now confess each and every one of these.

(4) The Limb of Rejoicing.

In the perfections of the Buddhas, the Bodhisattvas,
The Arhats in training and beyond training,
And in the latent goodness of every living being
I lift up my heart and rejoice.

(5) The Limb of Requesting the Buddhas to Turn
the Wheel of Dharma.

O lights onto the ten directions,
Buddhas who have found the passionless stage of
     enlightenment,
To all of you I direct this request:
Turn the incomparable Wheel of Dharma.

(6) The Limb of Requesting the Buddhas not to Enter into
Parinirvana.

O masters wishing to show *parinirvana*,
I request you to stay with us and teach
In order to bring goodness and joy to beings
For as many aeons as there are specks of dust.

(7) The Limb of Dedication of Meritorious Energy.

May any small merit that I have thus generated
By prostrating myself, sending forth offerings, confessing,
     rejoicing and
Asking the Buddhas to remain and to teach the Dharma,
Be dedicated now to supreme enlightenment.

Thus in the liturgy of the seven-limbed devotion as found in *The Prayer of Arya Samantabhadra* four verses are given to the first limb, three verses to the second limb, and one verse each to the five remaining limbs. There are also shorter liturgies for practitioners who have less time.

As I mentioned above, the method of engaging in the seven-limbed devotion is to read an appropriate liturgy, such as that given above, while contemplating the meanings.

The first of the seven limbs is prostration.

There is not much difference between the manner of offering prostrations in the sutra and tantra traditions, with the exception that in the former vehicle the prostrations are made daily in an informal way whereas in the latter vehicle there is the tradition of performing a hundred thousand prostrations as part of the five tantric preliminaries. As this aspect of the training is well known to all of you, I will not say more on it here now.

To offer prostrations, one first generates the visualization of the refuge field as described earlier. Make the image as clear in the mind as the things you see around you right now. Over the last two years I have spoken extensively on various ways of envisioning the refuge and merit fields. As I pointed out then, there are many variations on the basic theme. For beginners it is perhaps best to simply visualize a plain image of Buddha Shakyamuni. Think that this image is an embodiment of all enlightened beings, all teachings, and all spiritual friends of the past, present and future.

Whatever the merit field visualized, imagine that on every atom of existence there are countless such merit fields equal to the number of atoms in the world. Each of these are revealing the enlightened activities of the body, speech, mind, knowledge, compassion, and power of all the Buddhas.

Generate the thought, "From now until enlightenment I shall maintain constant mindfulness of the merit field and make it my object of appreciative awareness."

Then take refuge in the Three Jewels and single-pointedly establish firm conviction in their unfailing nature. As you make prostration, visualize that you are surrounded by sentient beings as numerous as the atoms of the world, all of whom are offering prostrations to the merit field while chanting verses in praise of the excellence of the enlightened beings. This is the essential method of offering prostrations simultaneously by means of mind, body and speech.

In addition, imagine that the images you are prostrating to are one with the actual Wisdom Beings that are being symbolized. Regarding the refuge objects in this way plants the karmic seeds for later being able to directly perceive the enlightened beings. At the moment we can only visualize the Buddhas; however, once the mind has become sufficiently trained and the obscurations sufficiently mitigated we will be able to directly perceive the real Wisdom Beings. The practice of visualization plants the seed for development in that direction. Thus it is a most profound path cultivated by those who wish to enter into the Bodhisattva experiences.

As for the merit field that is used as the object of concentration, one should imagine that each atom of the world contains merit fields as numerous as all atoms that exist.

We may think that this is an inconceiveably complex contemplation; but from the perspective of a yogi's understanding it is highly possible. As Nagarjuna has pointed out, the entire sky with its billions of stars can all be reflected in the water that collects in the footprint of a horse after a rainfall.

When the seven-limbed offering is being performed as the fifth preliminary step in a meditation session, the limb of prostration can be done either elaborately or else in brief.

The elaborate form would include reading the prayer to the gurus in the lineage of transmission of the teachings, beginning with the Buddha and coming down over the generations to the gurus of the present. Here one prostration to each name in the lineage would be made.

Otherwise, if the process is to be done in brief then it is sufficient to recite the first four verses of *The Prayer of Arya Samantabhadra* as given above, while contemplating their meanings. Instead of a full bodily prostration it is sufficient simply to make the hand gesture of prostration.

As for the actual physical prostration, these days there are two main forms: the half length and the full length. In the former of these, the five limbs — forehead, hands and knees — are touched to the earth. In the latter method, the entire body is stretched out on the ground, with the hands extended above the head. Je Tsong-kha-pa recommended full prostrations, suggesting that these should be done in conjunction with first collecting merit and purifying obstacles, and generating the profound view of emptiness within the mindstream.

When engaging in the practice of prostration it is important to avoid haste and carelessness. As is pointed out in *Stages of the Doctrine (bsTan-rim)*, if you wish to engage in the exercise of prostration you should make the effort to do so correctly. It is better not to do anything at all than to do something incorrectly.

The manner of offering prostrations, together with the symbolism and beneficial effects, were aptly described by Chu-zang Lama[27],

> By folding the palms of my hands together
> And touching the tips of my ten fingers,
> May wisdom and method enter into union
> And the ten Bodhisattva stages be crossed.
>
> By touching my folded hands
> To my head, throat and heart,
> And by touching my knees, hands and forehead
>   to the earth,
> May the negativities and obscurations
> Of body, speech and mind be purified
> And the various realms of suffering be emptied.
>
> By touching my two hands and two knees to the earth
> In either the half or full prostration,
> May the four magical activities spontaneously be
>   accomplished,
> And may I leave samsara far behind
> By quickly achieving Buddhahood.

When we make a prostration we first fold our hands together with the thumbs tucked inside, and then touch the joined hands to the crown, forehead, throat and heart. Touching the crown and forehead plants the karmic seeds to achieve the Buddha body endowed with the 112 marks and signs of perfection; touching the throat plants the karmic seeds to achieve the Buddha speech endowed with the sixty excellent qualities; and touching the heart plants the seeds to achieve the omniscient Buddha mind endowed with the 21 wisdoms.

Thus the benefits of performing even one prostration correctly are extremely powerful. They have been described in detail in *The Sutra which Distinguishes Karma (Las-rnam-'byed-kyi-mdo)* and also in *A Compendium of Bodhisattva Trainings (bsLab-btus)*. These benefits are innumerable, but if presented in summary it may be said that in general the practice of prostration purifies the mind of the five root delusions. In particular it is a direct antidote to faulty wisdom and the worldly view that manifests as pride, arrogance and disrespect for others.

This is all the time we have today for the discussion of the six preliminaries and the seven-limbed devotion. I will continue with them next year.

Today is the full moon session of the Great Prayer Festival, so I will do the traditional reading from the *Jatakamala*. As this is a Mahayana text, you should generate the Mahayana motivation of listening in order to progress along the Bodhisattva path to enlightenment as a supreme means of benefiting the world. For this it is important to listen closely with a clear mind, and to take to heart the meaning of the text.

*His Holiness then read from
the* Jatakamala. *Later he
concluded his discourse as follows.*

The Book of the Ka-dam-pa Masters (bKa'-gdams-glegs-bam) states,

Without being distracted by many activities,
Take up study of the *Tripitaka*.
This is the way to fulfill spiritual goals.
Enlightenment is difficult for the indecisive;
Practice with a single-pointed mind.

Atisha and Lama Drom Ton-pa were once having a discussion on the Dharma. Atisha advised Drom to avoid indecisiveness and the distractions caused by overextending himself and vacillating between too many activities.

Atisha added that, with the exception of a few select people having strong instincts from previous lives, practitioners should not be too eager to jump into the *Guhyamantrayana*, "the Tantric Path of Secret Mantras." The tantric vehicle is forceful and dangerous, and it is not definite that everyone can use it effectively. On the other hand, the *Tripitaka*, or threefold collection of Sutrayana scriptures, contains all the essential themes of the fundamental Buddhist teachings, and application to the three higher trainings of discipline, meditative concentration and wisdom—the central practices taught in the three scriptural collections—brings sure and steady progress on the path to enlightenment.

Atisha once received a vision of the four principal Ka-dam-pa mandala divinities (Buddha, Avalokiteshvara, Tara and Achala). In this vision he was advised,

> If you mainly teach the three higher trainings
> Of discipline, meditative concentration and wisdom,
> Countless accomplished practitioners will be produced.
> When the profound *Tripitaka* of Buddha is followed,
> There is goodness in the beginning, middle and end.

The ultimate goal of all Buddhists is the attainment of enlightenment. We who follow the Yellow Hat tradition of Lama Tsong-kha-pa do not differ in this respect. Moreover, in that our tradition unites the Sutrayana and Vajrayana methods, it should be our aspiration to achieve the full enlightenment of Buddhahood in this one short lifetime.

To achieve enlightenment we need to eliminate the mental delusions and negative karmic instincts from within our mindstreams. The method by which this is accomplished is the *samadhi* that combines *shamatha* (meditative serenity) with *vipashyana* (higher insight). This *samadhi* directly experiences the egoless nature of all phenomena, the deepest level of truth.

However, in order to prepare ourselves for the samadhi combining *shamatha* and *vipashyana* we must first ripen our mindstream by cultivating pure self-discipline through maintaining the three levels of precepts, the basis of all spiritual growth. In brief, the practice must be applied within the overall context of the three higher trainings, the essence of the experiential Dharma.

Lama Tsong-kha-pa wrote the following prayer,

> May I gain full realization of all
> Key points in the path to enlightenment.
> Then with skillful means led by great compassion
> May I remove darkness from within the world.
> May I contribute to the happiness of others
> And also contribute to the continued existence
> Of the sublime enlightenment teachings.

We should apply ourselves in body, speech and mind to intensive study of the *Tripitaka* under the guidance of a qualified guru. In conjunction with this study we should receive the living oral tradition teachings on the *Lam Rim* and *Lo-jong* systems of Sutrayana meditation, together with the ear-whispered instructions on the generation and completion stage yogas of the Vajrayana.

Through thus combining intellectual study with the practice of meditation, eventually our own mind will progress along the path of enlightenment. Then it becomes our responsibility to use our learning and enlightenment in order to remove darkness from within the world.

This is what is meant by becoming a Dharma master: first cultivating one's own mindstream, and then sharing the benefits with others. When this is done, trainees of deep learning, discipline, experience and activity increase and cover the earth. In this way one continues the tradition of upholding, preserving and transmitting the Buddhadharma.

As Mahayana Buddhists our two principal concerns are the benefiting of living beings and the preservation of the enlightenment teachings. These two are interrelated; for although our primary concern should be the benefiting of living beings, in fact it is the enlightenment teachings that are the source of lasting happiness for the living beings. Thus we have to accept some responsibility for the preservation of the teachings.

Therefore we should now dedicate any meritorious energy that has been generated today to the fulfillment of these two aspirations.

There is a wonderful verse for this, written by Dul-dzin Pal-den Zang-po,

> May any meritorious energy I have generated
> Benefit living beings and the Buddhadharma.
> Especially, may it contribute to the longevity
> Of the essential doctrines of Lama Tsong-kha-pa.

We should make the prayer that all our efforts contribute to the happiness and prosperity of all living beings, as well as to the continued existence and stability of all the various traditions of the Buddhadharma throughout the world. In particular, as followers of the Yellow Hat tradition we should offer prayers that the essential doctrines of Lama Tsong-kha-pa, that so skillfully unite all the central themes and practices of the sutras and tantras, flourish for many centuries to come.

As for the different topics I have discussed today, please make some effort to practice some of them.

> If by giving or listening to this discourse
> Any spiritual energy has been generated,
> May it contribute toward the growth of wisdom
> Within all living beings without exception.

SERMON SEVEN: THE EARTH DRAGON YEAR

The omnsicient Gyal-wa Gen-dun Drub-pa [the First Dalai Lama] once wrote,

> The qualities of a Buddha are vast as the sky;
> How could one possibly describe them all?
> Ah, but how fortunate I am
> To be able to express a few of them.

Any person attaining Buddhahood becomes a supreme being who has abandoned the obscurations to both liberation and knowledge, together with the instincts of these obscurations. The wisdom of his mind pervades all levels of reality, and becomes endowed with all qualities of both transcendence and realization. His speech, fully evolved in the ways of enlightenment, resonates with the sixty excellences and is able to teach living beings in accordance with their capacity and interests. And his body becomes adorned by the 112 marks and signs of perfection.

Thus the qualities of a fully enlightened being are beyond the powers of expression, and all one can do is describe a fraction of them.

Our Great Prayer Festival is an annual event in commemoration of the occasion when for fifteen consecutive days Buddha Shakyamuni publically exhibited miracles. Each year for the past few years I have been relating the legends of some of these as recorded in the brief text *In Praise of Buddha's Miracles (Cho-'phrul-bstod-pa)*. I shall continue from where I left off last year.

In Praise reads,

Then the Shakya clan made offerings.
Buddha caused everyone in the audience
To transform for a moment into a *chakravartin*
Possessing the seven precious endowments.
Homage to Shakyamuni, lord of emanation.

On the seventh day the Shakyas sponsored the gathering. Buddha instantly caused everyone in the audience to appear in the form of a *chakravartin* possessing the seven precious endowments and blessed with a thousand children. He then taught the Dharma to them. They were deeply moved by faith and gave birth to the root of goodness producing higher being and liberation.

In Praise continues,

On the eighth day Indra made offerings.
From Buddha's throne there emanated forth
Five *rakshas* and also Vajrapani,
Who destroyed the thrones of the six Hindu teachers
And liberated their ninety thousand followers.
Homage to Shakyamuni, who manifested limitless powers.

On the eighth day of spring Indra made offerings to the assembly. Buddha stamped his right foot, causing the six worlds to shake.

Each of the five hundred *rishis* that the six Tirthika teachers had brought with them then thought that Buddha indicated to them individually to come forth. They experienced deep faith and requested Buddha to give them ordination. Later they attained arhatship and took up residence together.

Several of Buddha's inner disciples, such as Maugalyayana, requested the master to permit them to act on his behalf and allow them to meet the Tirthikas in the miracle contest in his stead.

Buddha answered, "Who did the Tirthikas challenge?"

King Prasenajit stood up, placed his hands together and replied, "O Bhagawan, it is you whom they have challenged. Therefore it is you whom we want to see perform miracles."

The Buddha instantly caused himself to become invisible, and from the four directions came the sound of his voice teaching the Dharma. He reappeared, and Brahma and Ishvara approached him from the right and left simultaneously, and made extensive offerings.

Again Buddha asked, "Who has asked that I perform a miracle?"

A second time King Prasenajit repeated his request.

Buddha touched his right hand to the ground. From within the earth the *nagas* sent forth lotus flowers the size of cartwheels, each having a thousand golden petals and having *vajras* for stamens.

He then caused his body to emanate countless replicas, until the entirety of space was filled with them. Everyone, even children, was able to perceive this.

All the onlookers were amazed and stood staring with eyes agape. They prostrated and offered garlands of flowers.

The emanated replicas of the Buddha then simultaneously pronounced,

> Make efforts to accomplish the spiritual path
> And to abandon meaningless ways.
> Enter into the enlightenment doctrine,
> For soon the Lord of Death will destroy you
> Like an elephant destroys a bamboo hut.

Having said this, the emanations instantly disappeared.

The six Tirthikas looked sheepishly at one another. Each nudged the one next to him, saying, "It's your turn to do something now." But none of them rose to the occasion, and they all sat there despondently.

Buddha then touched his lion throne with his hand. A terrifying sound like that of a charging bull resounded. At the same time, five *rakshas* emanated forth from his throne and smashed the thrones of the five Tirthikas. Vajrapani also appeared. He was brandishing a *vajra* blazing forth with flame. A strong wind arose and the sky turned dark. The six Tirthikas were filled with fear. Overcome with shame at their inability to equal Buddha in a contest that they themselves had demanded, they threw themselves into a nearby well. Their ninety thousand followers embraced the Dharma and became monks. In fact, they all eventually attained arhatship.

Then from the eighty thousand pores of Buddha's body came forth radiant beams of light. At the tip of each beam was a tiny Buddha sitting on a lotus seat and preaching the Dharma. The Buddha caused everyone to be able to hear and see this.

The ninth miracle is described as follows in *In Praise of Buddha's Miracles,*

The next day Brahma made offerings.
Buddha caused his body to increase in size
Until it reached to the top of the Brahmaloka.
Homage to Buddha, an all-pervading master.

Not to mention the powers of the *rishis*, who have attained the *dhyana* of pure form, even the Shravaka Arhats, Pratyekabuddhas, and Bodhisattvas of the pure stages nowhere approach the power and abilities of a fully enlightened being. Therefore Buddha Shakyamuni was easily able to vanquish the six Tirthikas in a competition of miraculous exhibitions.

Each year we have also been discussing the six preliminary practices that are to be applied at the beginning of each meditation session. To review these, in the first preliminary we swept the place of meditation and arranged an altar. In the second we set up an attractive display of offerings. The third entailed sitting on our meditation cushion in a correct posture, taking refuge in the Three Jewels, and generating thoughts of the bodhimind. The fourth involved generating the visualization of the merit field. This brings us to the fifth preliminary, which is the offering of the seven-limbed devotion. This is where we arrived last year, when we discussed the first of these seven limbs, namely, the limb of prostration.

Last year we completed the first limb of the seven-limbed devotion.

The second limb is that of mentally presenting the actual offerings that had been arranged in the second preliminary above, and also sending forth countless imaginary offerings. As this subject is well known to all of you I do not need to say much on the subject. Also, most of what was said in the discussion of the second preliminary will also apply here. But it may be useful to touch on the key points.

Firstly it is important to check up and see that one's motivation is correct. Our intent should be to engage in the practice of offering as a means of fulfilling the meritorious energy of self and others in order to achieve enlightenment for the betterment of the world. When this is the attitude of the practitioner, the practice of offering becomes a direct antidote to the delusions in general and the delusion of miserliness in particular.

The best manner of offering to the visualized merit field is to make the offering while recollecting that the merit field is merely a symbol of the guru.

This is said in *The Tantra of the Mystic Bond (rGyud-sdom-'byung)*,

Devotion to a single hair on the *acharya's* body
Is greater than devotion to all the Buddhas
And Bodhisattvas of the ten directions.
Therefore all Buddhas and Bodhisattvas
Praise devotion shown to the *acharya* as supreme.

In addition, the practice of offering must be done on the basis of the awareness that all manifest phenomena are inseparable from their emptiness nature. This means that we must retain an awareness of the non-truly existent nature of the three circles: oneself who is making the offering, the objects being used as the basis of the offering, and the act of offering. None of these three has even a speck of inherent existence.

Making offerings furthers the practice of the accumulation of meritorious energy. Doing so on the basis of an understanding of the emptiness of the three circles furthers the accumulation of wisdom. It is important to always keep these two factors closely linked.

In fact, as is said in *The Great Commentary to the Prajnaparamita Sutra in Eight Thousand Verses (brGyad-stong-'grel-chen)*, all of our Dharma practices should be executed on the basis of the Bodhisattva armor. This refers to the tradition of placing every practice within the context of the six Bodhisattva perfections: generosity, discipline, patience, enthusiastic effort, meditative concentration, and wisdom.

In other words, each limb of the seven-limbed devotion must be practiced as an expression of these six perfections. For example, when we engage in the first limb, or that of prostration, the six perfections would be incorporated as follows.

Offering the prostration is the perfection of generosity. Doing so correctly and in a disciplined manner is the perfection of discipline. Not being discouraged by physical difficulties, pain, interruptions, etc., is the perfection of patience. Taking joy in the practice is enthusiastic effort; maintaining single-pointed concentration and clear visualization is the perfection of meditative concentration. Finally, maintaining awareness of the non-inherent, empty nature of the three circles of prostrator, prostration and act of prostrating is the perfection of wisdom.

The six perfections must be applied to each of the seven limbs in the same way. This point is also emphasized by Lama Tsong-kha-pa in both his extensive and intermediate *Lam Rim* treatises.

As for the offerings themselves, these are threefold: material things;

service; and the practice of the teachings. Of these, the last is by far the best. In particular, the supreme offering is the practice of meditation upon the subjects that lead the mind through the three levels of spiritual application.

The Bodhisattva Stages (Byang-sa) lists ten types of offerings. These are quoted by Ge-she Dro-lung-pa in his *Stages of the Doctrine (bsTan-rim)*,

> Actual and imagined images and *stupas*,
> Offerings made oneself or that one inspires others to make,
> Service, respect, undeluded offerings,
> And the offering of practice of the teachings:
> These are the ten types of offerings to be made.

This passage quite succinctly sums up the different types of offerings to be made, and Lama Tsong-kha-pa personally praised it. It includes all ordinary and peerless offerings, as well as the ten aspects of Dharma activity, and special kinds of offerings such as those of study, contemplation and meditation.

As mentioned last year, in the liturgy of *The Prayer of Arya Samantabhadra (bZang-spyod-smon-lam)* three verses are given to the limb of offering:

> Exquisite flowers, splendid garlands,
> And beautiful sounds, parasols,
> Butter lamps and delightful incense
> I offer to all Victorious Ones.
>
> Excellent food, the finest perfumes,
> And a mound of mystic substances high as Mt. Meru
> I arrange in special formations
> And offer to those who have conquered themselves.
>
> And all peerless offerings I hold up
> In admiration of those gone to bliss.
> With the strength of faith in sublime ways,
> I prostrate and make offerings to the Buddhas.

A Guide to the Bodhisattva Way (sPyod-'jug) suggests that, as well as the offerings of owned things, we should also imagine offering all unowned things, such as mountains, forests, rivers, lakes, the light of the sun and moon, and so forth.

Both the Fifth Dalai Lama's *The Sacred Instructions of Manjushri* (*'Jam-dpal-zhal-lung*) and the First Pan-chen Lama's *An Offering to the Guru (bLa-ma-mchod-pa)* recommend that at this point in the preliminary procedures one should perform the offering of the mandala symbolic of the universe. This may be done in accordance with either the long or short liturgy.

The short liturgy is as follows,

On a base resplendent with flowers, incense and scented water
I offer Mt. Meru, the four continents, and the sun and moon
To this field of supreme Awakened Beings.
May all beings delight in this pure sphere.
Idam guru ratna mandalakam niryata ya mi.

A contemplation often practiced in conjunction with the limb of offering is as follows.

Visualize a large lotus flower having a thousand petals. You are sitting at the center of this lotus, your physical body in the form of the Bodhisattva Samantabhadra. On each of the thousand petals of the lotus is a smaller replica of yourself, each also in the form of Samantabhadra.

Your hands are folded together at your heart, with the thumbs tucked inside to symbolize the wish-fulfilling gem.

From this gem you emanate forth countless offering substances, such as those described above, until all the world is filled with them.

Send forth the prayer, "Although enlightened beings have no attachment to the things of the world, please accept these humble offerings in order to help fulfill the merits and wisdom of both myself and others."

This is a Sutrayana method of making offering.

In the Vajrayana, the offering substances are imagined as being in nature the wisdom of bliss and void, and in form offering substances having the special ability to induce the experience of great bliss. The offering here becomes fivefold: special substances; mantras; *mudras*; *samadhi*; and accomplishments. In another way of speaking it becomes fourfold: outer, inner, secret, and suchness.

Those holding Vajrayana precepts of the Five Buddha Families [i.e., anyone with initiation into *yoga* or *maha anuttara yoga* levels] are required to make offerings six times a day.

Therefore most of the daily six-session guru yoga prayers include a verse of offering in order to fulfill this commitment.

That is all the time we have at the moment for our discussion of the six preliminaries. We can continue with them again next year.

Today we commemorate the fifteen days of Buddha's public exhibition of miracles. In accordance with the tradition of the full moon session of the Great Prayer Festival, I will now read from Aryasura's *Jatakamala*.

> *His Holiness then read from*
> *the* Jatakamala. *Later he*
> *concluded his discourse as follows.*

The Sutra on Mindfulness (Dran-nyer-gzhag-pai-mdo) states,

> The basis supporting all the delusions
> Is the unfocussed mind of apathy.
> Whoever is afflicted by apathy
> Is kept from all spiritual progress.

Those who have not developed disinterest for samsara and are handicapped by attachment to sleep, distractions and meaningless endeavors will not be able to progress on the spiritual path. Even if they have the opportunity to practice Dharma they will always procrastinate.

Therefore abandon apathy, the principal obstacle to the path; and cultivate the strength of enthusiastic effort, the source of all progress.

This same advice was given by Atisha in his *A String of Gems (Nor-bui-phreng-ba)*,

> Abandon dullness, apathy, and attachment to sleep;
> And always dwell in enthusiastic energy.

The basis of all happiness and spiritual growth is the practice of the enlightenment path. These days qualified masters of the Buddhist tradition in general and the lineages of Lama Tsong-kha-pa in particular are as numerous as the stars in the sky and the atoms of the earth; but if from our side we fall under the hindering forces of dullness, apathy and attachment to sleep, it will be difficult to reap the potential benefits.

We should follow the example of how the constantly weeping Saraprarudita dedicated himself to Guru Dharmodgata, and should search for a spiritual master with whom we have a strong karmic connection. Once we have decided upon a guru we should approach him with correct attitudes and actions as is explained in the various scriptures. Then we should eliminate all confusion concerning study, contemplation and meditation, and cultivate inner experience by means of applying ourselves to the essential practices of the three higher trainings: discipline, meditative concentration and wisdom.

Many of us here think of ourselves as being highly accomplished in the Dharma. But there is not much need at this point to talk about performing the great deeds of the true Dharma masters, such as upholding, preserving and transmitting the various lineages of the doctrine through teaching, discussion and composition. At the moment we seem unable to keep together even a simple daily Dharma practice, and thus lose the very basis of the training. Externally we act as though we are spiritually mature and accomplished, but internally our mind is undeveloped and churns about in confusion. Thus we gain neither happiness in this life nor hope for the next.

Continuing in this way, we do nothing but drag down the image of the living masters in the eyes of the world. Instead of becoming objects of faith we become subjects of ridicule.

Rather than just degrade ourselves and our spiritual traditions, we should train from the beginning as did the great beings of the past. Then when we gain inner experience of the enlightenment path and can teach others wisely and with skillful means, we will have earned the name "Dharma holder."

Here in the Land of Snows we have the wonderful blessings of a uniquely strong spiritual culture. Our annual Great Prayer Festival is really something very special, and our three illustrious monastic universities and two tantric colleges, in which thousands of monks live, study and practice in accordance with the pure *vinaya* trainings, are sources of tremendous merit. Also, our lay people are highly conscious of spiritual values and dedicate strong energy to supporting and upholding our enlightenment traditions.

The ripening effect of these positive elements is that our country, compared to most other lands in this degenerate age, is something of a paradise. Famine and starvation are almost unknown to us, and natural calamities are extremely rare.

We should appreciate the uniqueness of our situation and do our part to sustain it. Mindfulness, awareness and conscientiousness in action are extremely important factors. Try to maintain constant awareness of all actions of body, speech and mind, and to live in accordance with the nature of karmic law. It does not matter if you are high or low in the eyes of society; when it comes to karmic law all beings are equal. Therefore each of us must accept responsibility for what we do. Try to avoid negativity and to cultivate goodness. All of us have to make this our principal concern.

Our Land of Snows is also especially blessed by Avalokiteshvara, the Bodhisattva of Compassion. He has often incarnated in order to bring the enlightenment teachings to us and to preserve their integrity here. In fact King Song-tsen Gam-po, the first Tibetan monarch to officially accept Buddhism into this country and who had our first two Buddhist temples constructed, was himself an incarnation of Avalokiteshvara. His work in Tibet had long ago been prophesied in *The Manjushri Root Tantra ('Jam-dpal-rsta-rgyud)*, wherein it is said,

> In the Land of Snow Mountains
> In a city called "Divine Abode" (Lha-ldan)
> Shall come a king, a divinity amongst men.
> He shall be of the Li-tsa-chi family (Li-tsa-byi)
> And shall accomplish the essence of the Mantrayana.
>
> He shall possess great power
> And also a wealth of knowledge.
> This illustrious leader of men
> Shall rule for eighty years.

This prophecy clearly foretells how Avalokiteshvara, lord of the twenty-four mystic places, upholder of the ten virtuous actions, would incarnate in Tibet as King Song-tsen Gam-po and establish the Dharma in this rough land.

Song-tsen Gam-po was but one of many emanations of the Bodhisattva of Compassion who would appear in the Land of Snows in order to work for the welfare of the living beings and the doctrine. The presence of the Dharma here and the high level of our spiritual culture is largely due to the kindness of this Bodhisattva.

Meditation upon the Bodhisattva of Compassion is extremely powerful. It is said that to meditation for a single day equals a hundred years of any other practice. Merely hearing the name of Avalokiteshvara produces merit equal to making offerings to and serving all Buddhas and Bodhisattvas of the ten direction. Recitation of his six-syllable mantra — *om mani padme hum* — is equal to reciting the *dharani* in praise of the hundred million Buddhas. Reciting the six-syllable mantra weakens the very root of samsara. It heals the effects of having broken any of the root or branch trainings.

Not to talk about those who dedicate themselves intensely to the tantric yogas of the Avalokiteshvara system, even casual practitioners receive great benefits. One transcends proneness to the harms caused by illness, evil spirits and hindrances. All the tantric powers, such as the four activities and eight *siddhis*, as well as the supreme *siddhi* of *mahamudra*, are easily and quickly attained. And one gains the ability to take rebirth in whichever of the Buddhafields one chooses.

These and many other such beneficial effects are extensively described in numerous sutras and tantras, including the *Do-de Za-ma-tok (mDo-sde-za-ma-tog)* and *The White Lotus of Compassion (sNying-rje-pad-dkar)*.

Avalokiteshvara himself took the vow, "If practitioners do not receive these beneficial effects, may I be withheld from the experience of enlightenment."

Recollecting this pledge of Avalokiteshvara, the Seventh Dalai Lama wrote the following prayer,

> Whoever hears the sacred name "Avalokiteshvara"
> Is instantly freed from all fears.
> Saying his mantra even once
> Produces meritorious energy equal to
> Worshipping all Buddhas of the ten directions.
>
> The truthful sages have testified to this.
> Therefore, O Lokeshvara, when beings appeal to you,
> Do not forget your vow of compassion;
> Act instantly to assist and protect.

We should make firm our spiritual conviction in the infallible nature of the Three Jewels, and should exert ourselves to generate the meritorious energy and wisdom that benefits this and future lives. Meditating upon and reciting the six-syllable mantra of the Bodhisattva of Compassion accomplishes great merit and purifies the negative karma collected over many aeons. We should take advantage of the vow of Avalokiteshvara and dedicate ourselves to practicing the tantric yogas associated with him.

I would like to close my discourse with a thought written in verse by Lama Tsong-kha-pa,

> Only with difficulty and intense spiritual effort
> Did Buddha Shakyamuni achieve realization
> And then teach the path leading to enlightenment.
> We should think day and night about his kindness,
> And about how to contribute to the longevity
>   of his legacy.

Let's take any positive energy that has been generated at this discourse and dedicate it to the upholding, preservation and transmission of the precious spiritual tradition that Buddha Shakyamuni established after completing his intensive training and accomplishing the path to enlightenment. May his doctrines thrive for long.

As for the various topics that I have discussed above, please try and implement some of them.

> If by giving or listening to this discourse
> Any spiritual energy has been generated,
> May it contribute toward the growth of wisdom
> Within all living beings without exception.

SERMON EIGHT: THE EARTH SNAKE YEAR

Lama Tsong-kha-pa wrote,

> You with no attachment to worldly concerns,
> Who yearn to accomplish the meaning of life
> By entering into the paths pleasing to the Enlightened Ones,
> O fortunate ones, listen with a clear mind.

Practitioners with aspirations to achieve liberation and enlightenment should not be attracted to the limited happiness of either samsara or nirvana. Don't be like the fly, that delights in the taste of excrement. Whether you are on initial, intermediate or advanced levels of training, guard against attachment to worldly indulgence, meditational bliss, and so forth. This precious human rebirth adorned with the eight freedoms and ten endowments is a most precious and rare gift. Dedicate yourself continually to extracting its essence by means of study, contemplation and meditation. Apply yourself in this threefold manner to the teachings of the sutras and tantras. Never become separated from the sublime paths that are pleasing to the Enlightened Ones. Instead, cultivate the aspirations and activities of the Bodhisattvas and apply yourself to the path with joyous enthusiasm.

Our Great Prayer Festival is in commemoration of Buddha's public demonstration of miracle powers. Over the past few years I have been relating the legendary accounts of these as recorded in *In Praise of Buddha's Miracles* (*Cho-'phrul-bstod-pa*). I would like to continue from where I left off last year.

In Praise reads,

> The next day the world guardians made offerings.
> The exquisite body of the Victorious One
> Pervaded the world like an enormous cloud.
> It extended to the peak of samsara
> And radiated forth thousands of golden lights,
> Then released a rain of beneficial joy.
> Homage to Shakyamuni, demonstrator of truth.

On the tenth day of the month the four kingly guardians, such as Vaishravana and so forth, made offerings and requested Buddha to demonstrate his powers. Buddha caused his body to increase in size until it extended to the limits of the four directions watched over by the four kingly guardians, until eventually it reached to the peak of samsara. Inconceivable lights blazed forth from his golden body. Countless living beings witnessed these deeds.

The Buddha then taught the Dharma in accordance with the specific nature and capacity of each listener. Some instantly gave birth to the Bodhisattva spirit. Others gave birth to the root of merit that produces exalted spiritual states such as those of a stream enterer, once returner, never returner, arhat, etc.

In Praise continues,

Then Anathapindika made offerings and requests.
Without leaving his lion throne the Buddha
Caused his body to become invisible.
From that state he taught the Dharma
With sweet and melodious words.
Homage to Buddha the teacher.

On the eleventh day of the month the layman Anathapindika sponsored the event. The Buddha instantly caused his body to become invisible. From the place where he had been sitting there shone forth a brilliant light, and from it came melodious sounds revealing the nature and substance of the Three Vehicles. Of those in the audience, some gave birth to the Bodhisattva mind of supreme enlightenment and achieved the state of no return. Others gave birth to the root of merit bringing rebirth as humans or celestials.

In Praise then says,

The following day the layman Cheta
Made offerings and requests.
Buddha entered into the *samadhi* of love;
A golden radiance filled the great 3,000 worlds,
Causing all living beings to have feelings of love
Toward one another, like a parent toward a child.
Homage to Buddha, messenger of love.

On the twelfth day the layman Cheta approached the Buddha with offerings and the request that he demonstrate the miracle powers. Buddha entered into meditation on love, and radiated forth golden light from his body until the entire world was filled with an amber hue.

The trainees touched by this light were instantly purified of the three psychic poisons. Their minds pacified of attachment and aversion, they looked upon one another with thoughts of love and affection, like parents lovingly regarding their children, and like brothers and sisters looking upon each other.

He then taught countless Dharmas. Those who were ripe were placed in the state of final understanding of the Three Vehicles.

Over the past few years we have been discussing the six preliminaries to be performed at the beginning of each meditation session. The fifth of these is the seven-limbed devotion. So far we have covered the first two of these seven limbs, namely, those of prostration and offering. This year we will look at the third limb, that of acknowledging negativities.

The sutras and tantras present various manners of explanation of the limb of acknowledging negativities. Here I shall say a little on the essence of the practice.

The subject is usually presented under three headings: (1) the object before which the acknowledging of negativities is performed; (2) the negativities to be acknowledged; and (3) the actual practice.

(1) The object before which the acknowledging is done is the visualized merit field symbolizing the guru and Three Jewels. This is to be clearly visualized as was described in my discourses of the previous years. It is in their imagined presence that one acknowledges the negativities.

(2) The negativities to be acknowledged are listed in the following verse from Shantideva's *A Guide to the Bodhisattva Way*,

All negativities created since beginningless time
Those done by me, those I have instigated
And those I have rejoiced in when done by others
In the visualized presence of the Compassionate Ones
I acknowledge, regret and resolve not to do again.

One should think: "From time without beginning I have wandered throughout samsara. There is nowhere I have not taken rebirth and nothing I have not experienced. Throughout these countless rebirths my mind has been dominated by the three psychic poisons of attachment, aversion and ignorance, and as a consequence I undoubtedly have created innumerable negative deeds of body, speech and mind on both coarse and subtle levels. If I do not apply the the four opponent forces in order to purify the karmic seeds of these countless negative karmas, then sooner or later these seeds will ripen upon me and unbearable misery will have to be experienced."

A Treasury of Abhidharma states,

From a karmic cause comes an according result;
This law is unfailing.
A good harvest does not grow from a poor field.

(3) The actual practice of acknowledging negativities is to be performed in conjunction with application of the four opponent forces:

(a) the force of reliance; (b) the force of regret; (c) the force of applying remedial practices; and (d) the force of resolve. One reads the liturgy of acknowledging negativity while contemplating these four forces. As given previously, the liturgy from *The Prayer of Arya Samantabhadra* (*bZang-spyod-smon-lam*) is as follows,

> Long overpowered by attachment, aversion and ignorance,
> Countless evils have I committed
> With acts of body, speech and mind.
> I now confess each and every one of these.

I would like to explain each of these four opponent forces in some detail, as they are extremely important. Without applying them, the act of acknowledging weaknesses and failings is powerless.

(a) The practice of the force of reliance begins by generating a sense of Mahayana refuge. One then generates the Bodhisattva motivation of wanting to engage in the practice of purification of negativities on the grounds that the purer one's mindstream the more useful one is to the world. On this basis—taking refuge and generating thoughts of the bodhimind—one proceeds to acknowledge the negativities to be overcome. This is not done as a mere vocal exercise but from the depths of one's heart, keeping in mind the purpose and key points of the practice.

(b) The creator of an action must personally experience the karmic effects of that action. These effects cannot ripen upon anyone other than the original perpetrator.

One should contemplate this aspect of karmic law until apprehension of negativity arises. Then transform the negativity into disgust with yourself for having created it, like a person becomes disgusted with himself for having ingested poison. This is the force of regret.

(c) The force of applying antidotes refers to engaging in various practices in order to purify the mind of stains of negativity. Numerous methods of this nature are outlined in the sutras and tantras.

Shantideva's *A Compendium of Bodhisattva Trainings* (*bsLab-bsdus*) lists the following: recitation of the scriptures containing the words of Buddha or the later masters; meditation upon the profound nature of emptiness; meditation upon the powerful *dharanis* and mantras taught in the various sutras and tantras; making images of the body, speech and mind of the Enlightened Ones; making offerings and devotions to the Three Jewels of Refuge; reciting the names of the Buddhas and Bodhisattvas; and so forth.

Especially for Sangha members who have transgressed the disciplines of their ordination there is the ritual for restoring the monastic precepts. And for those holding tantric precepts who have weakened their tantric disciplines there are the methods of restoration by relying upon self-initiation, re-taking the initiation, etc.

We should engage in these various techniques in conjunction with acknowledging negativities and purification.

Lama Tsong-kha-pa wrote,

> In the practice of purifying
> Karmic instincts and spiritual obscurations,
> Utilize the four opponent forces.

(d) The fourth opponent force is the mind of resolve, which determines to refrain from the negativities in the future. This is very important; for even though we acknowledge a failing and apply purification techniques we will again soon fall back into the habitual negative pattern unless a firm resolve of restraint is established. The example is given of a sick man who accepts to take medicine but will not apply behavioral therapy or dietary disciplines; he will not be able to gain freedom from his disease.

The degree of mental purification achieved is determined by factors such as how intensely the opponent forces are applied, whether or not all four are completely and correctly applied, the strength and duration of the application, and so forth. With strong and persistent application, even the karmic effects of the most serious negative karma are overcome and one gains quick liberation.

Nagarjuna's *Letter to a Friend* (*bShes-sbring*) says,

> Whoever in the past was unconscientious
> And in the future becomes conscientious,
> That person gains beauty,
> Like the moon freed from clouds.
> Examples are Ananda, Anguillamala,
> Ajatashatru and Udayana.

A prerequisite to effective application of the four opponent forces is a confident understanding of the nature of karmic law. This means understanding the four principal aspects of karma: (a) an action done

plants seeds on the mind that will definitely one day ripen on the perpetrator; (b) there is an increasing aspect, which means that every action causes an ever-increasing chain reaction; (c) each experience we
encounter has a karmic cause in some past action, for without a cause
there is no effect; and (d) every action done leaves a karmic seed on
the mind that is never exhausted until ripened or purified.

The three ripening aspects of karma are : (a) the effect similar to
the causal deed, i.e., killing leads to rebirth with a short lifespan,
whereas saving life leads to rebirth with a long and healthy lifespan;
(b) the effect similar to the cause in terms of experience, i.e., killing
breeds instincts for further killing; and (c) the principal effect, which
refers to the environment, body and so forth of the rebirth.

Every action is also measured by three degrees of intensity, and this
also influences the nature of the result. For example, killing a human
produces a more intense karmic repercussion than does killing an
insect.

The precise workings of karmic law are extremely subtle. Therefore one should try and read those scriptures that illustrate it, such
as *The Sutra on Mindfulness (Dran-pa-nyer-gzhag-pai-mdo), The Sutra
on the Wise and the Foolish (mDo-mdzangs-glung), Sources of the Vinaya
('Dul-bai-gleng-gzhi)*, and so forth. In this way one can gain a clear
understanding of the general manner in which karma and delusion
shape our existence.

An understanding of the nature of the four noble truths is also useful here. So is an understanding of the twelve links of dependent origination, together with how they evolve and how they are reversed. In
brief, one should make every effort to gain experience in the meditations that constitute the common basis of all the Buddhist paths.

When the four opponent forces have been applied correctly over a
long period of time, one often experiences signs indicating that a degree
of purification has been achieved. To dream of drinking milk or yo-
gurt, or of vomiting bad foods, is a positive sign indicating progress
in the purification practices. Also, to dream of seeing the sun or moon
rise into the sky, of meeting with the guru or with monks or nuns,
or of a blazing fire or of flying through the air: these too are strong
positive signs.

Concerning the third of the four opponent forces, that of applying
remedial practices to counteract negative karmic instincts, Lama Tsong-
kha-pa relied strongly upon the practice of offering prostrations in
conjunction with recitation of *The Sutra of Three Themes (Phung-po-*

gsum-gyi-mdo), also known as *The Sutra to the Thirty-five Buddhas of Confession.* In particular, when in retreat at Ol-ga Cho-lung he dedicated tremendous energy to reciting this sutra, together with the names of the thirty-five Buddhas of Confession. It is said that at that time he simultaneously offered a hundred thousand prostrations to each of the thirty-five Buddhas, and at the end of the practice he achieved a vision of the thirty-five Buddhas.

This is described as follows in Jam-yang Cho-je's[29] *In Praise of Lama Tsong-kha-pa's Secret Life (rJe-rin-po-chei-gsang-bai-rnam-thar-stod-pa),*

> When performing the seven-limbed devotion,
> You directly perceived the thirty-five Buddhas
> Together with their individual forms and mudras.
> Homage to Je Rin-po-che, Lord of Dharma.

The Seventh Dalai Lama also relied intensely upon recitation of *The Sutra of Three Themes* and the names of the thirty-five confessional Buddhas. He too received numerous profound visions.

Therefore these days there are two major traditions of how to visualize the thirty-five Buddhas when reciting *The Sutra of Three Themes*: the method based on the visions of Lama Tsong-kha-pa; and the method based on the visions of the Seventh Dalai Lama.

The tradition based on the visions of Lama Tsong-kha-pa is as follows.

Either the thirty-five Buddhas are used as a merit field in themselves, or else one first generates one's usual merit field [as was described in the fourth preliminary] and then emanates the thirty-five Buddhas from it.

In the latter process one first generates the standard merit field. Then from the heart of the central figure, who is in actual nature a symbol of one's personal guru, there radiates forth thirty-five beams of light. These come from the guru's heart and open out, like the strands of a whisk. On the tip of each ray is one of the thirty-five Buddhas. These take up their places in the space in front of you.

Guru Buddha Shakyamuni sits in the center on a throne supported by eight elephants, and on cushions of lotus and moon. To his right and left are sets of seven Buddhas, and in front of him are two rows of ten Buddhas each. Both the two sets of seven and the two sets of ten Buddhas sit on seats of a lotus and moon. Establish this visualization clearly, and then recite the names of the thirty-five Buddhas while offering prostrations.

The tradition of the Seventh Dalai Lama begins in a similar way, with the thirty-five Buddhas being emanated forth from the heart of the principal figure in the merit field. But here their placement differs slightly. In this tradition they are grouped in five sets of seven, with one set in the center and one set in each of the four directions.

In the central set, Guru Buddha Shakyamuni is the central figure and is golden in color. Buddha Nageshvaraja is also in this set; he has a bluish body and white head, and is showing the *samaya mudra*. The remaining five Buddhas in this set are blue in color, with their right hands in the earth-touching *mudra* and left in the *mudra* of meditation.

To the east [i.e., in front of them] is the second set of seven, beginning with Buddha Ratna Chandraprabha. They are white in color and show the *mudra* of supreme enlightenment.

In the south [i.e., to the right of the central set] is the third set of seven, beginning with Buddha Varuna. They are yellow in color, with their right hands in the *mudra* of supreme generosity and their left in the *mudra* of meditation.

The fourth set, beginning with Buddha Narayana, is in the west [i.e., behind the central set]. Red in color, their hands are in the meditation *mudra*.

The fifth set, beginning with Buddha Indraketu, is in the north [i.e., to the left of the central set]. Green in color, their right hands show the *mudra* of bestowing refuge, and their left show the meditation *mudra*.

One can use the method of recitation of *The Sutra of Three Themes*, together with offering prostrations to the thirty-five Buddhas, either as a part of the seven-limbed devotion in the fifth of the six preliminaries to be applied before each session of meditation, or one can use it as the basis of a purification retreat.

It is perhaps more common to use it as the basis of a retreat. When this is the case, one performs either four or six sessions daily, visualizing the Buddhas and reciting their names, together with recitation of *The Sutra of Three Themes* and the performance of physical prostrations. During the retreat one links the practice to application of the four opponent forces. Between formal sessions one strives day and night to keep the mind flowing in Dharma directions by contemplating guru yoga, the Three Jewels, the nature of karmic law, etc. This supports the practice and facilitates purification and spiritual progress. One can set the length of the retreat according to time [i.e., for a week, a month, three months, etc], a number of recitations of *The Sutra of Three Themes* [a thousand, ten thousand, a hundred thousand, etc], the number of prostrations offered [the usual number being 100,000], or until signs of purification are experienced [such as those described above in the general discussion].

In conjunction with these trainings it is usual to perform daily tantric meditations in accordance with the generation or completion stage yogas, linking the practice with meditation upon and recitation of the hundred-syllable mantra of Vajrasattva.

Other more esoteric methods of purification are to be found in Lama Tsong-kha-pa's *Golden Dharmas*. These are discussed in Khe-drub-je's[30] *Twenty-one Notes* (*Yig-chung-nyer-gcig*). Included in these are the methods of recitation of the Samayavajra mantra, the Vajradaka fire rite, etc.

Another unique and very powerful method of purification is that in the lineage of Lama Khe-drub Khyung-po. This method is renowned as "the yoga for eliminating obscurations in reliance on meditating on the guru and protector as inseparable." As is explained in the scriptures, it is a particularly effective method for purifying breaches of the root and branch tantric precepts.

This is all the time we have today for our discussion of the preliminary practices. Perhaps I'll be able to continue with them next year.

As today is the morning session of the full moon gathering of the Great Prayer Festival I will now do the traditional reading from the *Jatakamala*.

His Holiness then read from
the Jatakamala. *Later he*
concluded his discourse as follows.

The Sutra Requested by Rastrapala (*Yul-'khor-skyong-gis-zhus-pai-mdo*) states,

> Indulgence is like the blade of a sword,
> Bringing pain and much suffering.
> Be apprehensive of it, see it as an enemy.
> It increases every delusion,
> And it is like a poisonous plant on a footpath.
> Therefore the *aryas* always avoid indulgence
> And regard it like a pot of excrement.

Understand the dangers and shortcomings of clinging to and attachment for the inner and outer objects of indulgence. Use mindfulness, awareness and conscientiousness to tie the doors of the senses. Cultivate interest in achieving the state of peerless spiritual liberation.

Atisha himself once said,

> Constantly guard the doors of the senses
> With mindfulness, awareness and conscientiousness.
> Three times each day and three times each night
> Check up on the stream of your thoughts.

All teachings of the Buddha condense into the central theme of gaining control of one's own mind. As long as delusion and sensual attachments dominate our stream of thoughts, it becomes impossible to have any inner control. Control is only gained by heightening one's level of conscious awareness of what is going on inside the mind. Therefore Atisha advises that we perform *satipatanna* meditation three times each day and three times each night in order to increase awareness of our mental states.

In particular, those of you who are interested in pursuing the powerful tantric practices must first qualify yourselves by cultivating a controlled mind that has been subdued by the trainings that generate nonattachment, tempered by experience of the Bodhisattva spirit, and sublimated by meditation upon the meaning of emptiness. Without an inner basis of these three qualities, any attempts at the tantric yogas will only lead to disappointment.

The root and foundation of tantric practice is the guarding of the root and branch precepts of the Vajrayana. These days the times are very degenerate, and it becomes increasingly important to keep these commitments purely.

The Vajrayana is a very forceful path. In it, successful practice totally depends upon receiving proper guidance from a qualified guru. In the Sutrayana many of the practices can be performed without close supervision; but this is not the case in the Vajrayana, where the yogas are far more powerful and dangerous.

The guru from whom we receive initiation should be a holder of an unbroken lineage of transmission. He should be skilled in the tantric methods, and should have completed the retreat on the specific tantric mandala being imparted, together with the concluding fire rite. He also should have received authorization to give initiation.

In order to embark upon a difficult and dangerous journey one first takes great pains to find a qualified guide. Similarly, when searching for a tantric guru one should analyze and test him in every way. Only accept to enter into training under him after you have become fully convinced of his competence. This is very important. When practiced correctly the Vajrayana can bring enlightenment in one lifetime, but when entered incorrectly it leads only to *vajra* hell.

The Vajra Tent (rDo-rje-gur) states,

> Application to mantra and tantra
> Bestows bliss on the beings of the world.
> Therefore do not think lightly of
> The guru who gives tantric initiation.

Unfortunately these days there are many self-appointed gurus who lack the proper qualifications, and who search out disciples in the hope of gaining fame and profit. Their motives are selfish, not altruistic. They should remember the advice of Khe-drub Tam-che Khyen-pa,[31]

> False gurus who exchange a hundred tantric initiations
> For wealth and attractive offerings;
> Vain disciples who only run to the guru
> For divinations, astrological predictions and medical advice,
> But never listen to what is said!

> Both abandon the Vajrayana vows and precepts.
> Their meeting is but a reflection
> Of real tantric initiation,
> And leads only to *vajra* hell for both.

The sutras, tantras and *shastras* all unaminously agree that the person who is attached to material gain and who pretends to be a spiritual teacher in order to get wealth or worldly success merely robs himself and his unfortunate disciples of all happiness in this and in future lives. He destroys both himself and others. Therefore trainees should chose their gurus very carefully. This is particularly important when it comes to tantric training, and it is often said that the guru and disciple should test one another for as much as twelve years before accepting to enter into a guru-disciple relationship.

Another point I would like to mention today is that of sectarian-

ism. It is quite natural to have a strong admiration for one's own lineages; but it is equally important to respect the lineages of others. We
who follow the Yellow Hat tradition, that possesses the four greatnesses
and that tries to see all doctrines of the Buddha as complementary
and non-contradictory, should apply this attitude of non-sectarianism
not only toward the ancient Indian schools of tenet systems but also
toward the various old and new schools here in Tibet. To cling strongly
with attachment to one particular lineage while holding feelings of aversion and sectarian discrimination toward other lineages is a sign of
wrong understanding of the scriptures.

Concerning lineage holders who have entered into this mistaken path,
the Fifth Dalai Lama wrote,

> Dull people long acquainted with mental darkness
> Yet who claim to hold lineages of pure gold
> Are but cheap brass imitations.
> When they come before a gathering of sages,
> They quickly reveal their negativities
> And their lack of true knowledge.

Pretending to be pure as gold yet behind the facade being dominated by the eight worldly concerns automatically contaminates whatever
is undertaken.

If this is our condition and it leads us to sectarianism, our religious
practice becomes like cheap brass that is hidden behind a thin veneer
of gold.

The Yellow Hat tradition coming from Lama Tsong-kha-pa and his
immediate disciples possesses a philosophical view that is free from
the extremes of nihilism and eternalism. It has a system of meditation
that brings freedom from mental agitation and dullness. Its activity
is in perfect harmony with the teachings of the Buddha. Thus its
philosophy, meditation and action are free from all distortion, and we
can be proud and confident to be followers of this lineage. But this
pride and confidence must not be allowed to become inflated to the
point that we look down upon other Buddhist sects.

Lama Tuo-kven[32] wrote in his *A White Crystal Mirror (Shel-
dkar-me-long)*,

If we check with the scriptures of Buddha
And test with the strength of pure reason,
A confident understanding arises
Concerning the tradition of Lama Tsong-kha-pa.

Now that we have entered the tradition of Lama Tsong-kha-pa we should make firm our practice of pure self-discipline, which is the basis of the spiritual path and the source of all higher attainments. On that foundation we can enter into the universally beneficial Bodhisattva activities. Then, within the perspective of the Bodhisattva motivation we can take up the two yogic stages of the tantric path, that produces enlightenment in one short lifetime.

Until you leave this life behind, dedicate yourself day and night to the various spiritual practices. Guard the door of the senses by means of mindfulness, alertness and conscientiousness. Cherish the commitments of the path, and strive in every way to achieve realization.

We should now dedicate any merit that has accrued today from our meeting. If anything that I have said is relevant to you, please try and practice it.

If by giving or listening to this discourse
Any spiritual energy has been generated,
May it contribute toward the growth of wisdom
Within all living beings without exception.

SERMON NINE: THE IRON HORSE YEAR

Gyäl-wa Nga-wang Lob-zang Gya-tso [the Fifth Dalai Lama] once said,

The pleasures of samsaric indulgence
Are illusive as a lightning-fast dancer;
And the bed of samsara brings darkness and misery.
Give birth to the pure mind of moderation,
That heralds the dawn at the end of night.

The superficial pleasures of cyclic existence are like the movements of a dancer; they quickly pass and are forgotten. Yet in the end samsaric indulgence leads to a spiritual darkness that obstructs the growth of knowledge, goodness and wisdom. It creates a spiritual apathy that is difficult to dispel.

When the mind lies in the bed of samsara, we walk in darkness wherever we go. It is as though we walk around in a thick fog that obscures awareness of the way things really are.

What we need is to generate the free spirit of renunciation, that takes no interest in samsara and that regards the objects of samsaric indulgence as disinterestedly as a tiger regards grass. We need to give birth to the pure mind of self-discipline, that heralds the dawn marking the end of samsara's long night.

As was stated by Lama Tsong-kha-pa, we must always cultivate the three principal elements of Buddha's teaching: the free spirit of renunciation, that does not cling to anything in samsara; the altruistic Bodhisattva aspiration, that aims at achieving enlightenment in order to be of greater benefit to others; and the wisdom of emptiness, that understands the deepest levels of reality. Treasure the trainings in these three spheres, cherishing them as inseparable jewels that bring about happiness in both this life and the hereafter. Make the mind moist with experience in meditation upon these three subjects, for they cause the very root of samsara to become weakened.

Over the past years I have been relating the legendary accounts of the miracles performed by Buddha Shakyamuni when he was publically challenged at Shravasti by the Tirthika extremists. We have covered twelve of the fifteen great miracles that he performed at that time. Only three remain.

The first of these is described as follows in *In Praise of Buddha's Miracles (Cho-'phrul-bstod-pa)*,

On the thirteenth day King Shunjanadi made offerings.
Light rays emanated from Buddha's navel
And extended for seven spans.
On the tip of each ray was a Victorious One,
From whose navel emanated forth light rays,
And so forth, until all directions were filled.
To Shakyamuni, a wondrous sage, I bow down.

On the morning of the thirteenth day of the month King Shunjanadi acted as the sponsor of the gathering, offering food and lavish gifts to the assembly, and requesting the Buddha to demonstrate his powers.

Buddha sat upon his lion throne and emanated two beams of light from his navel. These extended a distance of seven spans. At the tip of each ray was a lotus throne, and upon each of these sat a small Buddha figure. From the navel of each of these two Buddhas emanated forth two beams of light. These also extended for seven spans. Again, at the tip of each ray was a lotus throne, each of which bore a tiny Buddha figure. Each of these Buddhas in turn emanated two beams of light. And so on *ad infinitum*, with the number of Buddhas doubling on each stage of emanation, until the entirety of space was filled.

Everyone in the audience was filled with wonder. Some gave birth to the peerless enlightenment thought, some achieved the stage of a never returner, and some became Arhats. Countless living beings were placed on the paths leading to higher being, liberation and enlightenment.

In Praise continues,

> The next day King Udrayana made offerings
> And strewed flowers before the Buddha.
> Buddha transformed them into 250 carriages
> Made from the most precious of jewels
> Found in the three worlds.
> To Shakyamuni, he who beautifies, I bow down.

On the fourteenth day of spring King Udrayana scattered flowers in front of the Buddha and requested him to demonstrate his miraculous abilities.

Buddha instantly transformed the flowers into two hundred and fifty carriages made from precious substances. These shone with a radiance so bright that they illuminated the great three thousand world systems. Merely on perceiving this light the minds of the living beings were freed from suffering. Many people immediately gave birth to the thought of enlightenment, others achieved the state of a never returner, and so forth. In brief, countless living beings were placed on the path leading to liberation and enlightenment.

In Praise records the final miracle as follows,

On the fifteenth day King Bimbisara
Gave birth to goodness and virtue.
All in the audience were satiated
With a feast of divine ambrosia.
A golden light shone forth from Buddha's hand
And revealed both the heavens and the hells.
To Shakyamuni, he who shows all, I bow down.

On the day of the full moon King Bimbisara acted as the chief patron of the gathering.

Buddha requested him, "O King, please bring me some empty food vessels."

When the time for lunch arrived, Buddha caused the vessels to be magically filled with foods of a hundred divine flavors. The quantity was sufficient to feed the entire assembly, and everyone who partook of it instantly experienced great bliss of body and mind.

Buddha then touched his hand to the earth. Instantly the hell realms became visible. The beings of the hells realized, "It was because of having previously created such-and-such a negative karmic action that I have fallen into this state of misery."

Those in the assembly who saw and heard this were deeply moved. Thoughts of compassion arose within them, as intense as those a mother feels toward her only child. They wept and the hair on their bodies stood on end, so touched were they by this vision.

Buddha then taught the Dharma in accordance with the predispositions and needs of those in the audience. Some gave birth to the peerless Bodhisattva spirit, others were placed on the stage of a never returner, and so forth. Countless living beings achieved the virtuous karmic root that produces rebirth as a human or celestial.

Thus our incomparable teacher Buddha Shakyamuni manifested various miraculous performances by means of his extraordinary powers of body, speech and mind. In this way he dispelled the false confidence of countless Tirthikas and revealed the excellence of the paths leading to higher being, liberation and omniscient enlightenment.

Our Great Prayer Festival is an annual event in commemoration of this public demonstration of miracles by the Buddha. It has been a pleasure and honor for me to have had the opportunity to speak on them to you. I have only touched upon them in brief; to explain the full implications and symbolism behind them would require far more time than we have at this gathering. I chose to follow the poetic accounts of these fifteen days of miracles as recorded in *In Praise of Buddha's Miracles*. This brief verse work is both succinct and beautiful.

Over the past years as part of my discourse at the full moon session of the Great Prayer Festival I have been speaking on the six preliminaries to be performed at the beginning of each meditation sitting. So far we have arrived at the fifth preliminary, that of the seven-limbed devotion. Last year I spoke on the third of these seven limbs. This year I will deal with the fourth, the limb of rejoicing in goodness.

Lama Tsong-kha-pa wrote,

> Rejoicing in goodness is said to be a supreme practice,
> For great results are produced by a small effort.

As stated above, the practice of rejoicing in goodness is extremely powerful. For beginners it is particularly useful, producing great results without any strong effort or hardship being required.

Rejoicing in one's own positive qualities and accomplishments causes the root of the merit of the object to increase in strength and never to degenerate. Rejoicing in the positive qualities and accomplishments of others causes us to share in and enter into communion with their greatness. However, it is extremely important that the former of these [i.e., rejoicing in one's own blessings] is kept free from pride and vanity, and that the latter [i.e., rejoicing in others] is free from envy and jealousy.

How does one rejoice in the goodness of self and others?

Rejoicing in one's own merit means meditating on and contemplating whatever spiritual efforts great and small that one has made in the past or is presently making, and then generating a sense of admiration for and satisfaction in these efforts. This joy must remain free from pride or else the practice will become distorted.

Rejoicing in the merits of others involves several subjects.

Firstly one rejoices in the goodness generated by the Buddhas and Bodhisattvas, who have great love and compassion for all living beings. Impartial in their mighty altruistic deeds, they can easily sacrifice their lives or the limbs of their bodies for the benefit of others, and in order to help others can engage in austerities that ordinary people cannot imagine even in dreams.

Secondly one rejoices in the goodness of the Shravaka Arhats and Pratyekabuddhas, both those in training and those beyond training, who out of renunciation of and distaste for *samsara* have entered into the paths that pacify suffering by bringing freedom from the delusions of attachment and aversion with which the mind has been accustomed since beginningless time.

Thirdly one rejoices in the goodness of ordinary beings, who are still bound in the chains of *samsara* yet are attempting to reverse attachment to worldly existence and in order to achieve the eternally beneficial have taken refuge in the Three Jewels and are applying themselves to the practices of cultivating the wholesome and eliminating negativity.

Fourthly one rejoices in whatever root of goodness any sentient being may have collected in any past life since time immemorial, is collecting now, or will collect in the future.

The practice of rejoicing means that one reflects joyfully on these various levels of goodness found in both oneself and others. While contemplating in this way one recites a liturgy such as that found in *The Prayer of Arya Samantabhadra (bZang-spyod-smon-lam)*,

> In the perfections of the Buddhas, the Bodhisattvas,
> The Arhats in training and beyond training,
> And in the latent goodness of every living being
> I lift up my heart and rejoice.

Especially, those of you who have entered into intensive training under a qualified master and have the opportunity to study and contemplate the great scriptures should appreciate and rejoice in how fortunate you are. Do not allow your study to become merely a means to criticize others of lesser learning. Instead, strengthen the spiritual instincts within your mindstream by practicing every teaching you receive. The act of rejoicing in the merits of self and others helps to keep one's training within this perspective.

As for the beneficial effects of rejoicing, *The Mother of the Victorious Ones (rGyal-bai-yum)* states, "Given an appropriate scale, one could even measure the size of this universe made up of countless world systems; but one cannot measure the merit produced by rejoicing in the Bodhisattvas on the beginning stages, on the stages of intense application, and on the stages of never returning."

We should appreciate the tremendous value of the simple practice of rejoicing, and should cultivate it at all times.

Now, as today is the full moon session of the Great Prayer Festival, I would like to honor the tradition of reading from the *Jatakamala*.

*His Holiness then read from
the* Jatakamala. *Later he
concluded his discourse as follows.*

The Great Fifth [i.e., the Fifth Dalai Lama] once wrote,

The teachers who pretend to be pure gold
But in fact are only cheap brass imitations
Are like merchants in a marketplace.
When the Dharma falls into the hands of people like that,
This signifies the beginning of the era
When the Buddhist teaching will exist in name alone.

The teachers of the various Buddhist doctrines, and especially the holders of the Yellow Hat order, should be qualified and able to live up to their names. Their minds should be far beyond the eight worldly concerns: pleasure and pain, gain and loss, praise and criticism, fame and obscurity. Ordinary beings are dominated by concern with these eight worldly factors, but those who have found themselves in the position of teaching the holy Dharma should be far beyond them.

Teachers of the spiritual path have a special responsibility to follow in the footsteps of the sages of the past and not to disgrace their traditions. They should dwell in the ways of wisdom, nobility and goodness, and should dedicate themselves purely to upholding, preserving and transmitting the enlightenment teachings.

The Great Fifth also wrote,

Speaking falsity in elegant ways
Is like taking an unclean human body
And decorating it in precious jewels.
The false dance only deceives others
And produces illusory results.

Some gurus spread false teachings and erroneous, distorted practices in the name of true Dharma, clothing their wrong views in sweet, elegant words. Motivated principally by self-interest and the eight worldly concerns, they try and pass themselves off as qualified masters and their teachings as the true doctrine when in fact they themselves are poorly trained and their teachings meaningless garble. Through clever oration they spread their deceptive dance into the ten directions, deluding those unfortunate enough to be taken in by their sweet talk and cunning ways. These false teachers act with great confidence, as though they had captured the essence of spiritual knowledge; but they are merely deceiving both themselves and others. Their efforts produce empty results, and are but a futile, pathetic waste of time and energy.

The Great Fifth likened their situation to an Indian fable,

> Ravana once manifested as a beautiful animal
> In order to deceive the world.
> He led many living beings into the wastelands
> Of confused existence, and then stole
> The beautiful Sita, symbol of prosperity and joy.
> There are many false gurus who
> Deceive the world in this same way.

Feigning righteousness in order to attract the devotion of others merely adds to human confusion. A guru should be a spiritual friend whose only concern is to benefit others; but these days there are many false gurus whose aim is only to benefit themselves at the expense of others.

Therefore check out and test anyone whom you are considering to accept as a spiritual teacher. Be sure he really is qualified. Only accept a teacher after you have examined him in every way. Be skeptical and suspicious, like an analyst buying gold. Only accept him as your personal teacher when you are fully convinced of his integrity and depth of both learning and experience.

Another point I would like to make concerns our way of viewing both ourselves and others. The correct attitude is described as follows by Atisha,

> The superior person exposes his own faults,
> But hides his good qualities like a treasure.
> He never notes mistakes in others,
> But only notes their good qualities.

The true spiritual practitioner makes no attempt to hide his personal shortcomings; but he hides his learning, realization and good qualities like one would conceal a precious treasure. And although he may perhaps occasionally correct others out of altruistic reasons, he never searches for shortcomings in others out of a motivation of attachment or aversion. Instead of bringing attention to faults in others and trying to criticize them, he looks for their good qualities and tries to bring them praise, respect and honor.

This is the way of the Bodhisattva hero, the way we should try to follow. Rather than make others feel guilty over their faults, we should help to increase their strengths by encouraging and praising their good qualities.

Now let's dedicate any meritorious energy that we have generated today. An appropriate verse for this is found in the writings of the Fifth Dalai Lama,

> By any merits in this string of words,
> A rosary spun from the teachings of the Buddhas and
>   Bodhisattvas,
> May all beings come to equal in goodness
> The omniscient Buddhas themselves.

Today I have spoken on a variety of Dharma subjects. Let's dedicate the energy to the prayer that all Buddhist traditions in general and the Yellow Hat order of Lama Tsong-kha-pa in particular may endure for long with strength and purity, and may continue to bring the benefits of higher being, liberation and omniscient enlightenment to the world.

> If by giving or listening to this discourse
> Any spiritual energy has been generated,
> May it contribute toward the growth of wisdom
> Within all living beings without exception.

SERMON TEN: THE WATER MONKEY YEAR

(In the Iron Sheep Year His Holiness was in poor health and therefore was unable to preside over the Great Prayer Festival. However, the following year he continued to uphold the tradition. A summary of his discourse on that occasion is as follows.)

Khe-drub Ge-lek Pal-zang-po³³ once wrote,

> Speaking on the wondrous Bodhisattva ways
> Captures the attention of the wise.
> It delights those of good fortune
> And is praised by all the *munis*.

To speak on the mighty Bodhisattva ways, that are difficult for an ordinary being to conceive of even in dreams, captures the attention of the wise. A medicine for the ears of fortunate trainees, it is a vast offering cloud to the Victorious Ones.

Our Great Prayer Festival is an annual event in commemoration of the time when Buddha Shakyamuni met with the six Tirthika extremists and their followers in a contest of miracle demonstrations. Shakyamuni completely defeated them, bursting the bubble of their vanity and arrogance. The flag of Mara was brought down and the forces of goodness were delighted, causing the victory banner to fly high in the ten directions.

To honor this illustrious occasion Lama Tsong-kha-pa was carried on the rising tide of inspiration and, as a method for increasing the meritorious energy of living beings, conceived of and established the Great Prayer Festival of Lhasa. This exquisite festival eventually spread throughout the length and breadth of our land.

The Fifth Dalai Lama wrote a verse in praise of Tsong-kha-pa's work in creating this festival,

> In the Central Temple of Lhasa
> You ushered in a golden age of glory
> For the living beings of this land
> By honoring the oceanic sign of goodness
> Signalled by Buddha, the son of Suddhodana,
> When he defeated the Tirthikas at Shravasti
> In a public contest of miracles.
> O Tsong-kha-pa, this wonderful creation of yours
> Indeed was wisely conceived and designed
> And caused the strength of goodness in the world
> To grow like the waxing moon.

Over the past years as part of my discourse at the morning session of the full moon gathering of the Great Prayer Festival I have been speaking on the six preliminaries to be performed at the beginning of each meditation sitting. We have been working with the fifth of these six preliminaries, namely, that of the seven-limbed devotion. So far we have covered three of the seven limbs. This year I will speak on the fourth, the limb of requesting the Buddhas of the ten directions to turn the Wheel of Dharma.

The liturgy for this is given as follows in *The Prayer of Arya Samantabhadra (bZang-spyod-smon-lam),*

> O lights onto the ten directions,
> Buddhas who have found the passionless stage of
>   enlightenment,
> To all of you I direct this request:
> Turn the incomparable Wheel of Dharma.

The Buddhas are like lights of the world, for they eliminate the spiritual darkness from within the minds of living beings in all the ten directions of the universe. These Buddhas were once just ordinary beings like ourselves, but through their own personal efforts they achieved the state of complete enlightenment and thus gained the omniscient wisdom that possesses the ten powers, four fearlessnesses, six clairvoyances, and so forth. Therefore they are now in a position to be of great benefit to the living beings.

Yet although they have innumerable means with which to bring benefits to living beings, the supreme method at their disposal is the work of teaching, the act of turning the Wheel of Dharma.

Hence it is said that the principal deed of a Buddha in the world is the deed of speech, or teaching. This far surpasses any deed of body or mind, such as the exhibition of miracles or of clairvoyant powers.

After Buddha Shakyamuni achieved enlightenment he uttered the verse,

> Profound, at peace, free of distortion, clear light,
>   unproduced:
> I have found the nectar-like truth.
> But I shall remain in the forest and not teach it,
> For there is nobody who would be able to understand.

It is said that for some weeks after his enlightenment the Buddha did not teach, for he wished to generate greater interest within the living beings and to cause them to create greater merit by having to request the Dharma many times.

Then Brahma approached him and offered a golden wheel with a thousand spokes, requesting him to turn the Wheel of Dharma for the benefit of living beings. Buddha accepted and left for the *rishi* forest of Varanasi, where he knew that his first five disciples awaited him.

There he turned the First Wheel of Dharma, which centered on the teaching of the four noble truths and was mainly for those of Hinayana nature. After that he traveled to Vulture's Peak, Rajgir, where he turned the Second Wheel of Dharma. This centered on the *prajnaparamita* teachings and was mainly directed at those of Mahayana nature. Then he went to Shravasti and turned the Third Wheel of Dharma, that centered on teachings in clarification of the doctrines taught at the first two turnings. This third phase was directed equally at both those of Hinayana and those of Mahayana natures.

In this way he turned the golden Wheel of Dharma three times. In total he taught for some forty-five years, yet all of his discourses can be subsumed under these three themes. And just as a *chakravartin's* wheel flies into the four directions and destroys the four types of armies, these three Dharma Wheels spread throughout the four directions of the world and destroyed the four types of *maras*.

Thus Buddha Shakyamuni brought countless living beings onto the spiritual path of the ten wholesome ways and placed them in joy.

The reason why the teachings of a Buddha are called a "Wheel of Dharma" is that the words and realizations are transmitted in completeness from one mindstream to another. On the one hand there are the teachings born from the omniscient wisdom of an enlightened being's experience; and on the other there is the trainee's application to these methods by means of study, contemplation and meditation. When these two conditions come together, the experience of enlightenment is transformed from one mindstream to another. As long as the chain of transmission is not broken from one generation to the next, the Dharma Wheel can continue to turn and bring benefits to the living beings.

The way to practice the limb of requesting the Buddhas to turn the Dharma Wheel is as follows. One imagines that in every pore of every figure of the merit field are as many Buddhas and Bodhisattvas as there are atoms of the world. One requests them to turn the vast and profound Dharma Wheel. They are pleased by the request and cause limitless rains of Dharma to fall. These cause the practitioners of initial, intermediate and advanced capacities to be placed on the paths leading to higher being, liberation and enlightenment.

If one can pursue this type of contemplation, then in all future lives one will continue to be cared for by the Buddhas and Bodhisattvas, and will meet with the supreme Dharma.

When doing the above practice of requesting the Buddhas to turn the Wheel of Dharma there is the tradition of visualizing oneself in the form of Brahma holding up a golden wheel as an offering.

It is not enough just to request the turning of the Dharma Wheel. In addition, one should generate determination to listen carefully to that turning and to practice according to the teachings that are given.

The beneficial effects of requesting the Buddhas to turn the Dharma Wheel are described in *The Sutra Maintaining the Root of Goodness (dGe-bai-rtsa-ba-yongs-su-'dzin-pai-mdo)*, "One should request Buddhas equal in number to the sands of the Ganges River to turn the Bhagavan Dharma Wheel. One should request them to turn the Sugata Dharma Wheel. For by requesting them to turn the Dharma Wheel one will never again be reborn in an impure Buddhafield, only in pure Buddhafields. One will never again be reborn in a samsaric womb. And in whatever Buddhafield one takes rebirth, in that place the forests, trees, bushes and foliage will emit sounds of the teachings. They will emit sounds revealing the meaning of impermanence, suffering, emptiness and egolessness."

Also elsewhere we read, "In all future births one will meet with spiritual masters, and will never be separated from the wisdom that appreciates the holy Dharma. In the future when one achieves Buddhahood one will be asked to turn the Dharma Wheel oneself, and no hindrances to the effectiveness of that turning will occur."

That is all the time we have today for our discussion of the six preliminaries. I'll continue with the subject next year.

Now I'd like to perform the traditional reading from the *Jatakamala*. As it is a Mahayana text, you should listen with a Mahayana motivation.

> *His Holiness then read from*
> *the* Jatakamala. *Later he*
> *concluded his discourse as follows.*

The Fifth Dalai Lama wrote,

The great sages of the past, such as
Mi-la-re-pa, Atisha and the Ka-dam-pa masters,
Severed all contact with worldly activity.
Unlike them, today the teachers of all traditions
Seem to simultaneously carry the weight of
Both spiritual and secular affairs.

The masters of the old Ka-dam-pa tradition, who maintained the legacy of the Seven Divine Dharmas, turned their backs on all activities connected with worldly affairs.

Although in some ways spiritual and secular concerns are as opposite to one another as hot and cold, the Dharma in this country has developed in such a way that most lineage holders in all our traditions are required to take some responsibility in both these spheres.

No doubt there are some dangers involved in this development, but there are also many benefits. For example, secular life becomes enriched by having more religious values brought into it; and spiritual life gains the advantage of having a stronger and more materially stable Sangha.

As a sign of these benefits we have a unique form of government that unites both spiritual and secular elements of our society. We also have our two tantric colleges, two illustrious monasteries [Se-ra and Dre-pung], the wonderful Gan-den Monastery, and countless other monastic institutes of the various sects and traditions. The Sangha in our country has become as plentiful as the stars in the sky. High and low alike, all of our people seem to enjoy an atmosphere of peace, harmony and prosperity. Although this is said to be a degenerate stage in world evolution, somehow we have escaped much of the disease, conflict and hunger with which the outside world has been afflicted. Our reliance on the enlightenment teachings and the Three Jewels of Refuge has kept our spiritual energy at a sufficiently high level to allow us to come into the present era with our ancient traditions somewhat intact.

But whether our situation improves or degenerates depends very much upon the successful and efficient efforts of our government. In turn, the efficiency of the government depends upon those who serve in it. Therefore if you are in government service please remember that a lot is riding on your shoulders. It does not matter whether the level of your service is high, intermediate or low; keep the forces of karmic law as your constant witness. Your words and actions should be equal.

What you do in front and what you do behind should be the same.

Although your work commitments may be such that you have little time for intensive formal Dharma practice, at least you can try to bring basic Buddhist values to work with you. Qualities like honesty, sincerity, integrity and industriousness can greatly contribute to the efficiency and meaningfulness of your efforts.

Let's take a cabinet minister as an example. You have Saturdays off from work, so take your rest then and not during the week when you should be working. Otherwise, if you unnecessarily take days off, come in to the office late and leave early, and spend your days making false lists of fictitious activities merely in order to pass time, not much gets accomplished. We should aim at improving every year, not at becoming more lax and inefficient. If during work hours you have some spare time, look for something that needs doing rather than wait for a project to force itself upon you.

We should appreciate the value of our work and try to do it well. Instead of looking for easy alternatives and avoiding anything of any responsibility, look for what really needs doing. Otherwise, the river becomes polluted at its source.

Although in general our culture and political system have been quite successful in the past, these days an alarming level of apathy and corruption seems to have crept in. Government workers, both monks and lay people alike, seem to care little for the image that they create for our government. Dominated by petty self-interests, they disregard the laws and legal procedures in the administration of their offices. They use every means possible to please higher-ups in the hope of personal advancement, and out of jealousy try to hinder anyone doing creative work. This trend must be reversed, and each of you must begin the reversal with yourselves. Cause and effect are unfailing witnesses, and if we betray the trust placed in us the spiritual consequences will be severe. And what is most pathetic is that most of us know and accept this, yet like a moth drawn toward a flame continue to live in weakness and falsity.

We should care for our responsibilities as much as we care for our eyes. If not, all we do is collect causes of a rebirth in one of the hell regions. The wheel of time continues to turn day and night as we continue to spend our time and energy just creating problems for people we don't like and favoring those we like. Meanwhile, our actual work never gets done. We cannot keep even our own house in order, let alone doing anything useful for the country.

In this way our precious human rebirth become little better than that of an animal. Each individual day is passed fruitlessly, and before long an entire lifetime has been wasted. Nothing beneficial for this life or the next is accomplished, and in the end all we have is a decayed brain. The Three Jewels of Refuge and the Protective Divinities become saddened with us, and our hearts corrode from within. There isn't much distance between that and hell.

We should remember the words of Tvo-kven Cho-kyi Nyi-ma,[34]

When all we do is pass our time by frivolously
Decorating the body in fancy clothes and jewels,
Indulging in gluttony, gossip, sleep and gambling,
Then even if no *mara* or hindrance comes to harm us
We gradually make ourselves into one.

This means that those in government service should abandon distractions and should think day and night about how they can be more useful and efficient in their work. As was pointed out by the three early Bodhisattva kings, we should hold in our hearts an unmistaken vision of what is to be accomplished and what overcome, and then strive to realize this vision.

If we proceed in this way on a basis of mindfulness of the teachings of Buddha and awareness of our every action, we will be able to accomplish immediate and long-lasting happiness for both ourselves and others. Living and working within society like this is equal to renouncing society and following the lifestyles of Mi-la-re-pa, Atisha and the early Ka-dam-pa masters. If we all work hard, then well-being and prosperity are achieved in this life; and when the time of death comes there will be no need to fear the experiences of the *bar-do* and the lower realms. Our land is blessed by Avalokiteshvara, the Bodhisattva of Compassion, so we can have confidence that strong results will ensue if we live and practice well.

The Seventh Dalai Lama wrote,

One should turn the forces of selfishness
By practicing the sublime bodhimind,
Essence of the oral tradition of the perfect gurus,
The one path all Buddhas have followed,
The focal point of the Mahayana scriptures.
The mind becomes filled with eternal delight.

In other words if we apply the spirit of the teaching on cultivating the bodhimind and bring this spirit into our every action, then our work takes on a spiritually meaningful perspective. We should regard ourselves and our efforts as being essentially directed at the benefiting of others. When altruism is the motivating factor, all work becomes spiritual practice.

Personally I have few inborn or acquired qualifications. And although from my childhood I have been cared for by numerous excellent teachers, I have managed to make but little progress. It is my responsibility to maintain the Dharma here in this Land of Snows, yet unfortunately much of my time has been lost to the eight worldly concerns. Not much has been left over for real Dharma activity. I hold the external signs of being a monk, but inside am not much different than a layman.

You are therefore probably asking yourselves: How can this old uneducated imitation of a monk sit here today amidst an assembly of pure Sangha numerous as the atoms of the earth, and in front of a mighty sea of distinguished ministers and government officials, and scold us in this way?

Actually, sweet and flattering words are pleasant for awhile, but their results quickly fade. Also, future lives are more numerous than this one short life, and I thought that if I were to lie to you I would probably regret it later. I felt that it would be better to be kind enough to speak frankly.

The Fifth Dalai Lama once wrote,

> With students and followers
> Sweet words and niceties are good for awhile;
> But the results quickly fade.
> It is better to be straightforward
> And truthful from the very beginning.

I took this advice of the Great Fifth seriously and have spoken according to my knowledge and experience. Please don't take offence.

We should now dedicate any meritorious energy that has been generated by our gathering here today. A beautiful verse of dedication comes from the writings of the Fifth Dalai Lama,

May any meritorious energy thus generated
Act as a kingly wish-fulfilling gem
Fulfilling all needs of living beings.
May it cause goodness and prosperity to flourish
And completely pervade all realms of the world.

If any positive energy has been created by this gathering in honor
of Buddha Shakyamuni's demonstration of miracles, may it transform
into a magical gem able to cause a rainfall of all things needed by living beings. May it contribute to the birth of a golden age on earth,
ushering in an atmosphere of peace, happiness and prosperity throughout all regions of the earth.

If by giving or listening to this discourse
Any spiritual energy has been generated,
May it contribute toward the growth of wisdom
Within all living beings without exception.

SERMON ELEVEN: THE WATER BIRD YEAR

Gyal-wa Nga-wang Lob-zang Gya-tso [i.e., the Fifth Dalai Lama] once
wrote,

With appreciation for the Doctrine and love for living beings,
Listen to the teachings and meditate on their meanings.
Then when an inner experience has been achieved
Transmit the liberating methods to others.
This is the root that produces benefit and joy.

The Buddhadharma is a medicinal plant bringing both immediate
and lasting happiness to living beings.

Buddha Shakyamuni himself was accomplished in inner realization,
skilled in the means of maturing the world, and had great compassion for the living beings. He understood the diverse natures and capacities of those to be trained, and in acordance with these predispositions he taught the various *yanas*.

Of the teachings that he gave, all of them directly or indirectly point at the theory of relativity, the interdependent nature of phenomena. All of his instructions are exclusively methods for pointing disciples to that truth, and thereby of guiding them along the unmistaken paths leading to higher being, liberation and enlightenment.

Lama Tsong-kha-pa wrote,

> All the teachings given by you [the Buddha]
> Begin and end with dependent origination.
> This in turn leads to nirvana.
> Ultimately, your purpose in teaching was always
> Nothing other than to show the way to inner peace.

As said in this quotation, all teachings in both the sutra and tantra traditions are methods for cultivating an inner experience of peace. The diversity of these methods exists because of the diversity of the predispositions of practitioners. When one applies oneself to these methods by means of a unified approach of study, contemplation and meditation, lasting benefits are easily accomplished. These benefits are not limited to this one lifetime alone, but reach forever into future lives. There need be no doubt of this.

The Great Fifth wrote,

> A body adorned with the signs of perfection,
> Speech made rich with the sixty qualities,
> And mind understanding both the oneness and
> The diversity of all objects of knowledge:
> Such was the nature of Buddha Shakyamuni.
> When practiced well, his teachings yield lasting benefits.

Over the past years we have been discussing the six preliminaries to be performed before each meditation sitting. We have been working on the fifth preliminary: the seven-limbed devotion. Last year we completed the fifth of these seven limbs, or that of requesting the Buddhas of the ten directions to turn the Wheel of Dharma. This year I will concentrate on the sixth, the limb of requesting the Buddhas of the ten directions not to enter into *parinirvana*.

The nature of a Buddha's passing is described in the following verse,

> The Buddhas never enter parinirvana,
> And the Dharma never disappears.
> But in order to train those to be trained,
> The Buddhas sometimes pretend to pass away.

The fully accomplished Buddhas have vowed to remain in samsara for the benefit of living beings until the very end of cyclic existence. Therefore they can never actually pass out of samsara into parinirvana. Yet they occasionally withdraw their physical manifestations and pretend to pass away in order to tame trainees. Consequently there is the need to request them to remain and not to enter *parinirvana*.

The manner of making the request is as follows.

Begin by recollecting the Buddhas of the merit field as previously explained. As well, recollect all the millions of emanations of that merit field, together with all Buddhas in all the Buddhafields throughout the ten directions.

Then visualize that you emanate countless forms of yourself. These all simultaneously in one voice chant the verse from *The Prayer of Arya Samantabhadra (bZang-spyod-smon-lam)* requesting the Buddhas not to pass into *parinirvana*.

> O masters wishing to show *parinirvana*,
> I request you to stay with us and teach
> In order to bring goodness and joy to beings
> For as many aeons as there are specks of dust.

An alternative is to place a mandala base in the visualized presence of the merit field. Imagine that it is a *vajra* seat, complete with a lion throne. Then offer it to the Buddhas of the ten directions, dedicating it with the force of the meritorious energy collected by yourself and others over the three times.

Send forth this thought to the Buddhas: "In the beginning you generated the supreme altruistic thought of enlightenment. In the middle you accumulated meritorious energy and wisdom over the period of many lifetimes. In the end at Vajrasana you achieved the complete enlightenment of perfect Buddhahood.

"Throughout this process your main objective was to become of greater benefit to living beings. Therefore until both temporary and ultimate happiness have been brought to all living beings, please do not withdraw your physical manifestations. Remain in the world for as many aeons as there are atoms of the earth."

After this request has been fervently offered, imagine that the Buddhas of the merit field become delighted, and that they agree to remain in the world and turn the Wheel of Dharma. Also, imagine that you gain the karmic connection to become their direct disciple, that in future you will never be reborn in places lacking freedom, and will always meet with the holy Dharma.

As well as the above types of visualization practices it is also good to frequently request your personal guru to sit on a Dharma throne, to turn the Wheel of Dharma, and not to pass away.

The benefits of the practice of requesting the Buddhas and also one's personal gurus not to pass into *parinirvana* have been described as follows in *The Most Magnificent Drama (rGya-che-rol-pa)*, "If you place the master on a Dharma seat and request him to teach, you will come to possess eight seats. What are these eight seats? The seat of a caravan leader; the seat of a master layman; the seat of a *chakravartin*; the seat of an Indra; the seat of a Brahma; the lion seat of a never-returning Bodhisattva on his way to the heart of enlightenment; the lion seat which destroys all maras; and the throne of a Buddha who has accomplished full enlightenment and will turn the Wheel of Dharma."

Also, *The White Lotus of Excellent Dharma (Dam-chos-pad-dkar)* says, "Day and night hold only admiration for the Buddhas. Having aversion for a Bodhisattva for a single moment has terrible consequences, whereas having appreciation for a Bodhisattva produces a hundred great benefits. The results of disrespecting or admiring a Buddha are far more powerful."

In brief, the appearance and transmission of the true Dharma depends entirely upon the work of the Buddhas and the gurus. Therefore appreciate them from the depths of your heart. Practice their teachings to the best of your ability. In this way you will be able to purify your own inner negativities and obscurations, which are the factors hindering you from directly experiencing the manifestations of the Buddhas.

This is all the time we have today for our discussion of the preliminaries.[35]

Now to read a few passages from the *Jatakamala*.

> *His Holiness then read from*
> *the* Jatakamala. *Later he*
> *concluded his discourse as follows.*

A verse from the oral tradition states,

> The golden rosary of Ka-dam-pa precepts
> Contains all three baskets of Buddha's teachings
> And structures them into the oral instructions
> For the three types of practitioners.
> Whoever takes up this rosary
> Achieves the meaningful for this and future lives.

The supreme doorway for those wishing to achieve liberation is the legacy of the *Tripitaka*, the three baskets of Buddha's teachings: *vinaya*, *sutra*, and *abhidharma*.

The entire contents of the *Tripitaka* condenses into Atisha's tradition of *Lam Rim* instruction, which is structured for successive practice for trainees on the three levels of spiritual application. By means of the *Lam Rim*, an individual practitioner learns how to take all teachings of the Buddha as personal advice and how to put all teachings simultaneously into practice, seeing them all as supplementary and non-contradictory elements of the path. The thought of the Buddha is easily discovered, and one follows in the footsteps of the great Bodhisattvas of the past. Such are the excellent qualities of the wondrous lineages coming from Atisha.

The combined scriptural and insight transmissions of the Dharma are a source of tremendous goodness and joy in the world. This is true about the Buddhadharma in general and also about the individual traditions and sects of transmission. For example, most of us here follow the stainless Yellow Hat tradition of Gan-den Monastery, that maintains the powerful lineages of Atisha as clarified by Lama Tsong-kha-pa and that so skillfully unites all the teachings of the sutras and tantras. For us personally this specific tradition has brought tremendous spiritual benefits.

Every Buddhist should appreciate these two elements: the Buddhadharma in general; and also the specific lineage with which he or she as an individual is karmically connected.

On the basis of this appreciation we should individually make some effort to preserve both Buddhism in general and our own tradition in particular. This is done by means of the threefold application of study, contemplation and meditation; the threefold character building by means of wisdom, nobility and goodness; and the threefold activity of teaching, debate and writing.

Monks, who have vowed to follow the path of purity and simplicity, should avoid the distraction of preoccupation with the things of this life, such as fame, excessive food, and expensive clothing. Instead, they should dedicate themselves intensely to the four Dharma activities and should ignore all the hardships that arise during the long and arduous training, studying and meditating day and night until an unmistaken understanding is induced.

If strong efforts at Dharma practice are made, there is no doubt that lasting benefits will be achieved, benefits that not only improve the quality of this life but that also reach far into the future. Immediate and lasting happiness is achieved, and the benefits are experienced by both self and others.

This is the supreme way to contribute to the well-being of the Buddhadharma and the happiness of living beings.

All of you, both Sangha and lay people alike, should do all that you can to help preserve the unique spiritual heritage of our country. In turn, the stability of this heritage depends upon the strength and well-being of our unique form of government. If our government remains strong, our heritage can be maintained without degeneration. Whether or not this can be achieved depends very much upon the strength and integrity of the individual people working in the various government positions. The present international atmosphere is not very good for us. A number of our neighbors are building strong armies and seem to be motivated by hostile and aggressive attitudes. Their actions do not encourage confidence in a peaceful future. We have to come up with a strategy whereby we can avoid being invaded and taken over.

Unfortunately we seem to be of a situation internally wherein everyone working in the government is motivated solely by self-interests. Monks and lay officials alike, both high and low, everyone with any government position seems to be concerned more with personal gain than in how to contribute to the well-being of the country. Falsity, flattery and deceptiveness seem to have become integral features of political life.

We should try and cultivate the qualities listed in the following proverb,

> Not harming others, avoiding non-Dharmic ways,
> Not being feeble in one's responsibilities,
> And taking the initiative to do what is needed
> Without having to be told. . . .

Be constantly mindful of your personal gurus, the Three Jewels of Refuge, and the laws of cause and effect. What we do in front and behind, openly and in secret, should all be equal. Look to how the elder ministers have served, and follow their good examples. If you carry the load of responsibility for spiritual and secular affairs [i.e., if you serve in the government], do so to the best of your abilities and try to work as I have described above. Should you do that, good results will definitely ensue and prosperity will automatically be produced.

Otherwise, if we just continue with the present trend of chasing self-interests alone and competing with one another for who can set the worst example, the future can only bring disaster. This is being unkind to both oneself and others. It is self-deception, and is a great weakness bringing harm on both immediate and long-term levels. There is no greater failure, nor any greater disappointment for the gurus, mandala divinities and Dharma Protectors. When that is our way, the results are always undesirable no matter how strong the efforts we make.

The Fifth Dalai Lama wrote,

> The Bodhisattva way is as vast as the sky,
> And final reality is more subtle than an atom.
> For someone like me to attempt to describe these subjects
> Is like trying to measure the ocean with a mango seed.

Here the Fifth Dalai Lama is just being modest. But the quotation quite aptly fits my situation.

Therefore it is perhaps not right for me to confidently stick out my neck and speak to you as I have above. But I thought that if I were to say these things to you there may be some amongst you who would listen. I have set out these ideas as reminders and as material for reflection. The decisions concerning them are up to you. I really hope that you don't make the wrong choices.

Now let's dedicate any positive energy that has been generated today through our participation in this gathering.

A verse of dedication found in the writings of the Fifth Dalai Lama reads,

> May the lights of any goodness thus created
> Bring joy and radiance to the living beings and the Doctrine.
> May the door to an ocean of virtue be opened,
> And may glory spread into all directions.

If by participating in this Dharma event any merit has been collected, may it contribute to the longevity of the Buddhadharma in general and the peerless tradition of Lama Tsong-kha-pa in particular, a tradition uniting all essential elements of both the sutras and tantras. May all signs of the five degenerations disappear from this cool land blanketed in medicinal herbs and surrounded by snow mountains. May signs of temporary and lasting happiness manifest throughout all corners of the earth.

Should anything that I have said today seem relevant to you, please try to integrate it into your lives and practices.

If by giving or listening to this discourse
Any spiritual energy has been generated,
May it contribute toward the growth of wisdom
Within all living beings without exception.

Mandala of the 5 Jina

3 A Brief Guide to the Buddhist Tantras

I. A GENERAL INTRODUCTION

The incomparable Lama Je Tsong-kha-pa wrote,
For traveling to complete Buddhahood
There are two Mahayana vehicles:
The *Prajnaparamita* and the profound *Vajrayana*.
Of these, the latter greatly surpasses the former.
This is as well known as the sun and moon.

There are many people who know this fact
And pretend to carry the tradition of the sages
Yet who don't search for the nature of the profound
    Vajrayana.
If they are wise, who is more foolish?
To meet with this rare and peerless legacy
And yet still to ignore it:
How absolutely astounding!

The Vajrayana is to be practiced in secrecy and is not to be revealed to the spiritually immature. Therefore it is known as "the secret path."

It is a special method for protecting the mind from the subtle instincts of the three appearances, in which one meditates in the mode of the resultant stage. This means that in the Vajrayana one conceives of oneself and all others as sharing in the four pure qualities of a fully accomplished Buddha: perfect body, speech, mind and activities. Therefore it is also called "the resultant vehicle."

On this path one applies the yogas of non-dual method and wisdom in order to achieve the transcendental results of the secret mantra. Thus it is known as "the path of secret mantra."

This is the nature of the esoteric Vajrayana, the Diamond Vehicle that brings quick and easy enlightenment.

There is no difference between the exoteric Prajnaparamitayana and esoteric Vajrayana in terms of the Buddhahood that is attained, the Bodhisattva attitude used as the basic motivating factor, nor the nature of the view of emptiness that is experienced. In these respects the terms superior and inferior do not apply.

Nonetheless, the Vajrayana is superior in four ways:

(a) Its manner of generating the experience of emptiness is implemented by the peerless means of inducing the wisdom of semblant mind isolation which arises through working with the coarse and subtle energies of the body and causing them to enter into, abide and dissolve within the central channel. Thus the Vajrayana method of cultivating insight into emptiness is uncontrived.

(b) It has a more vast reservoir of methods, such as the meditation on a causal form that is in accord with the nature of the *rupakaya* to be attained.

(c) Its path is quickly accomplished without hardship. On the Prajnaparamitayana many lifetimes of intense effort are required in order to attain the state of enlightenment, whereas on the Vajrayana full enlightenment can easily be achieved within this one short life.

(d) Finally, it is fashioned especially for those of sharpest capacity, who are able to make quick progress along the path.

The Vajrayana teachings appear only very rarely in this world. They are more rare than even the Buddhas themselves.

The nature of the Vajrayana path is fourfold, the division being made according to the four classes of the tantras. This fourfold classification is symbolized by the four levels of engaging in passionate communication with the mystical Knowledge Lady as methods of achieving the path to enlightenment.

The four tantra classes are named as follows: *kriya, charya, yoga,* and *anuttara* yoga.

In the first of these, great emphasis is placed on external rituals, such as washing and physical purification. In the second tantra division there is an equal balance of external activity and inner yoga. In the third division the inner yogas take precedence over the outer activities. Finally, in the fourth tantra division the emphasis is always on the inner yogas.

II. THE KRIYA TANTRAS

Concerning the *kriya* tantras, Lama Tsong-kha-pa wrote,

> One may say that the *anuttara yoga* tantras
> Are supreme amongst the four tantra classes;
> But if when saying this one does not understand
> The paths of the three lower tantra divisions,
> One's words fade into meaninglessness.
>
> Understanding this to be the case,
> I first familiarized myself with the *kriya* tantras,
> Both general and specific, of the three *kriya* families.
> These included *The General Tantra of Secret Knowledge*,
> *The Tantra of Susiddhi*,
> *The Tantra of Questions by Subahu*,
> And *The Subsequent Absorption Tantra*.[1]

The three families of tantras in the *kriya* division are: the supreme family of Vairochana, also called the Tathagata family [which includes mandala deities such as Manjushri, Ushnisha Vijaya and Sitatapatra, etc.]; the intermediate Padma family [which includes Avalokiteshvara, Tara, etc.]; and the fundamental Vajra family [e.g., Vajrapani, Vajravidarana, etc.].

One should enter into whichever of these is suitable to one's personal karmic predispositions, receiving initiation into either a chalk, cloth or meditation mandala. The initiation begins with the claiming of the place of the rite. The mandala deities are invoked, the initiation vase is empowered, the disciples are enhanced, and so forth. Then follows the flower garland, water and crown initiations, together with the concluding procedures.

The disciples are thus ripened and matured by these processes, and are authorized to enter into practice of the kriya yogas.

Concerning the actual yogas, firstly there is the *dhyana* of four branches of recitation:

(a) The self-basis, or generation of oneself as a mandala deity. This involves meditation upon the six deities [or stages of arisal as a deity]: suchness, mantric sound, mantric letters, emanated forms, mudras, and symbol (i.e., the actual deity).

(b) The other basis, which means generating the supporting and supported mandala and deities in front, sending forth praises and offerings, etc.

(c) The mental basis, in which one meditates that one's mind rests on a moon disc at one's heart.

(d) The audial basis, wherein one concentrates upon the seed syllable and mantra rosary on that moon disc, and then does the mantra recitation.

Next there is the *dhyana* of abiding within fire. Here one visualizes oneself as the chief mandala divinity, envisioning that at one's heart is a radiant, blazing fire in the nature of emptiness. One fixes the mind upon this fire.

The sound of the mantra emanates from within the fire. Focussing the mind upon this is the *dhyana* of sound.

These are the practices known as "the yoga of symbols," the first stage of the *kriya* tantra yogas.

These methods are complemented by "the yoga beyond symbols," in which one engages in *shamatha* (meditative serenity) and *vipassana* (higher insight) meditation propelled by physical and mental ecstasy. This is the *dhyana* bestowing liberation at the end of sound.

By relying on these various *dhyanas* in conjunction with the yoga of symbols and yoga beyond symbols, one gains highest, intermediate or basic *siddhis*, and by becoming a knowledge holder of life achieves supreme accomplishment.

The tantric systems in the lower division are of two types: general and specific. In total there are said to to be thirty-four thousand of them in number.

Of these, Lama Tsong-kha-pa and his immediate disciples accepted the following as being the most significant.

The most important of the specific *kriya* tantra treatises include: *The Tantra Establishing the Three Pledges (Dam-tshig-gsum-bkod-kyi-rgyud)* in nineteen chapters; *The Healing Discourse in Eight Hundred Themes (sMan-mdo-brgyad-brgya-pa)*; *The Inconceivable Mansion of Vast Jewels (Nor-bu-rgyas-pai-gzhal-med-khang)*; *A Hundred Thousand Enlightenment Ornaments (Byang-chub-rgyan-'bum)*; *The Secret Relics (gSang-ba-ring-bsrel)*; and so forth.

As for general kriya tantra treatises, the most important of these are: *Fundamentals of the Empowerments of the Three Families (Rigs-gsum-dbang-gi-rnam-gzhag)*; *The General Tantra of Secret Knowledge (gSang-ba-spyi-rgyud)*, which explains in detail the mandala constructions in the four tantra classes; *The Tantra of Susiddhi (Legs-grub-kyi-rgyud)*, which mainly deals with retreat procedures, rituals and commitments of the kriya tantra mandala of Susiddhi; *The Tantra of Questions by Subahu (dPung-bzang-gis-zhus-pai-rgyud)*, which deals with topics left unclear in the above two treatises, and teaches in detail the knowledge mantras and especially the retreat procedures of the kriya system; the final section of *The Vajra Ushnisha Tantra (rDo-rje-gtsug-gtor-rgyud)*, which elucidates the four *dhyanas* common to both *kriya* and *charya* tantra divisions; and *The Subsequent Absorption Tantra (bSam-gtan-phyi-mai-rgyud)*, of which there are four fundamental versions.

The two great Indian elucidators of the tantric treatises in the *kriya* and *charya* divisions were Acharya Buddhaguhya and Acharya Varabodhi. They were as well known as the sun and moon.

From amongst their writings, *The Commentary to the Subsequent Absorption Tantra (bSam-gtan-phyi-mai-'grel-pa)*, *A Summary of the Tantra of Questions by Subahu (dPung-bzang-gi-rgyud-kyi-don-bsdus)*, and so forth are superb.

III. THE *CHARYA* TANTRAS

Concerning the *charya* tantra division, Lama Tsong-kha-pa writes,

> The second tantra class is called *charya*.
> The principal *charya* tantra system
> Is *The Vairochana Abhisambodhi Tantra*.
> By training in that system I gained definite experience
> In the supreme points of the *charya* tantras.

The Buddha, manifesting in the Akanista Pure Land, took the form of Tathagata Vairochana Abhisambodhi and expounded this supreme *charya* tantra.

The path of the *charya* tantras begins with receiving initiation. Here one enters into the mandala from the western gate, which is the direction into which the main mandala divinity is facing. There are various names for the four vase initiations and the bases of purification associated with this process. In brief, one partakes of the water, headdress, *vajra*, bell and name initiations, together with the concluding procedures, and thus is authorized to take up practice of the *charya* tantra yogas.

As in the *kriya* division the actual practice of the *charya* tantras is twofold, consisting of the yoga of symbols and yoga beyond symbols.

The body of the *charya* path, together with the results attained, is much the same as in the *kriya* systems. However, here in the practice of the generation of the mandala of oneself as the divinity it is not necessary to have the complete six deity stages [as was the case in the *kriya* yogas explained above]. Also, here the *dhyana* of four branches of recitation is applied in both inner and two outer aspects [which was not the case in the kriya tantras].

The two principal texts in the *charya* tantra tradition are *The Vairochana Abhisambodhi Tantra (rNam-snang-mnong-byang-gi-rgyud)*, which is in twenty-six chapters, and *The Subsequent Tantra of Vairochana Abhisambodhi (Dei-rgyud-phyi-ma)* in seven chapters. The text entitled *Tantra of the Vajrapani Empowerment (Phyag-rdor-dbang-bskur-gyi-rgyud)*, which belongs to the Vajra family, is also said to be of great significance, but unfortunately it was never translated into Tibetan. We only know of it through the many references to and quotations from it that appear in the treatises of the later commentators.

Buddhaguhya's *Abbreviated Commentary to the Vairochana Abhisambodhi Tantra (mNgon-byang-bsdus-'grel)* is perhaps the most important of the commentaries by later Indian masters.

IV. THE YOGA TANTRAS

The third division of the tantras is that known as "the *yoga* tantra class." Lama Tsong-kha-pa refers to this division as follows,

> Foremost amongst the principal traditions of
> The third tantric division, known as the *yoga* tantras,
> Are *The Glorious Compendium of Principles*
> And *The Vajra Highest Peak Explanatory Tantra*.
> By training in systems such as these,
> I experienced a *yoga* tantra feast.

In the *yoga* tantras it is said that the four elements arise with the strength of the four basic delusions—the three root delusions of attachment, aversion and ignorance, together with miserliness. These are transformed into the resultant four pristine wisdoms — distinguishing wisdom, the wisdom of equanimity, the accomplishing wisdom, and the mirror-like wisdom — by means of relying upon the yoga of non-dual profundity and radiance in union, together with the Mahayana bodhimind and the perfections of generosity, discriminating awareness and enthusiastic perseverence.

These four pristine wisdoms manifest in the four Buddha family aspects: Tathagata "Diamond Sphere" (*vajra-dhatu*); Vajra "Victory over the Three Worlds" (*trilokya-vijaya*); Padma "Tamer of the Living Beings" (*jagad-vinaya*); and the Amoghisiddhi nature of "Accomplishing Feats" (*siddhartha*), that unites both *Ratna* and *Karma* families.

One gains initiation into whichever of these five Buddha families is appropriate to one's individual character.

The basis of the initiation ceremony can be a chalk, cloth or meditation mandala.

The preparatory stages are much the same as in the two lower tantra classes. As for the actual initiation itself, here one takes the Bodhisattva vow, the pledges of the five Buddha families, the pledge of secrecy, the five knowledge initiations and also the *acharya* initiation, and then concludes with the verses of appreciation, etc.

When the disciple is thus ripened and matured by means of receiving initiation, he/she is authorized to enter into the yogas of the two stages—those of symbols and those beyond symbols.

By means of the mandala and the supremely victorious activities being performed in either extensive, medium or abbreviated forms one cultivates the coarse yoga of symbols. Firstly one visualizes oneself as the mandala divinity and then generates the divinity in front, incorporating both supporting and supported mandalas in the meditation.

After this has been accomplished the subtle mandala is generated at the tip of the nose of oneself envisioned as the divinity. The signs and symbols of the family with which the mandala is linked are similarly visualized. The mind is then held on this subtle image, and by forcefully engaging the methods common to all three lower tantra classes one accomplishes the subtle yoga of symbols.

Next one engages in the yoga beyond symbols by absorbing the mind in the sphere of purification in emptiness, the objects purified including the self-generation and frontal generation mandalas, deities, mantras and so forth.

In this way the ordinary aspects of body, speech, mind and activities gradually acquire the visible and tangible characteristics of the supported and supporting divinity forms. This is "the body *mahamudra*."

The sound of the mantra is spontaneously heard. This is "the speech *dharmamudra*."

The wisdom of non-dual profundity and radiance, which is maintained by *shamatha* and *vipashyana* combined, is "the mind *samayamudra*."

The appearance of impure activities automatically ceases and the four tantric activities of pacification, increase, power and wrath are accomplished merely by means of *dhyana*. This is "the activity karmamudra."

In our tradition it is said that when the seal of these four *mudras* is applied by a Bodhisattva holding the form of a Buddha and who is a knowledge holder on the tenth *bhumi* abiding near the end of cyclic existence, the all-pervading Buddhas are inspired to arise from their *samadhi*. They then reveal the empowerments and knowledge mantras, by means of which the Bodhisattva experiences the five actual purifications and achieves final enlightenment.

As for the precepts that are taken by the trainee who enters into practice of the *yoga* tantras, generally these are much the same as those taken in the *anuttara* tantra division [to be explained later], wherein there are fourteen root and eight secondary [branch] downfalls to be guarded against. However, there are some differences. For example, here the thirteenth root downfall is incurred by not relying upon tantric dance and hand *mudras*. Also, the fourteenth root downfall is incurred by underestimating the importance of the practice of the four *mudras*.

As for the textual traditions of the *yoga* tantra class, the most important of these are as follows.

Firstly there is *The Glorious Compendium of Principles (dPal-ldan-de-nyid-bsdus-pa)*, which is in four sections and reveals the purpose of maintaining the *samaya* of the yoga tantras. Then there is *The Very Nature (bDag-nyid-can)* in five chapters. To this latter work there is *A Subsequent Tantra (Dei-rgyud-phyi-ma)* and also *A Later Subsequent Tantra (Phy-mai-phy-ma-rgyud)*.

Other important texts include *The Vajra Highest Peak Explanatory Tantra (bShad-rgyud-rdo-rje-rtse-mo)*; *The First Supreme Glory (dPal-mchog-dang-po)*; *Victory Over the Three Worlds ('Jig-rten-gsum-rgyal)*; and *The Tantra which Purifies the Realms of Misery (Ngan-song-sbyong-rgyud)* in both the original form *(rTags-pa-dang-po)* and the reorganized form *(rTags-pa-phyogs-gcig-pa)*.

The three greatest Indian elucidators of the *yoga* tantra systems were Acharya Buddhaguhya, Acharya Anandagarbha, and Acharya Shakyamitra.

Buddhaguhya's main treatise in this area was his *The Extensive Avatarana Commentary ('Grel-chen-a-wa-ta-ra-na)*, that unpacks the meaning of *The Root Tantra (rTsa-rgyud)*, or *The Glorious Compendium of Principles*. Anandagarbha's *An Extensive Treatise ('Grel-chen)* elucidates the meaning of *The First Supreme Glory*. Finally, Shakyamitra's most significant text here is his *A Silken Ornament (Ko-sa-lii-rgyan)*.

V. THE *ANUTTARA YOGA* TANTRAS

A. A General Survey

Lama Tsong-kha-pa then describes the *anuttara yoga* tantras as follows,

> Amongst the sages of holy India,
> The two *anuttara yoga* tantra systems
> Famous as the sun and moon
> Were the male tantra of Guhyasamaja and
> The female *yogini* tantra of Heruka Chakrasamvara,
> Both of which have root tantras, explanatory tantras
>   and so forth.

The cause which accords with the nature of a Buddha's form body, or *rupakaya*, is the impure and pure illusory bodies. The principal sources explaining the methods for realizing this illusory body are the male tantras, foremost of which is the Guhyasamaja tantric tradition.

The causes which accord with the nature of a Buddha's truth body, or *Dharmakaya*, are the semblant and actual clear light consciousnesses. The principal sources explaining the methods for realizing this clear light are the female tantras, foremost of which is the Heruka Chakrasamvara tantric tradition.

The trainees who wish to engage in these profound paths must first complete the according generation stage yogas. After these have been accomplished, then in order to gain the common attainments such as the eight *siddhis* they must rely upon one of the four types of ordinary consort — red lotus, white lotus, utpala, and sandal. Otherwise, in order to achieve supreme *siddhi* in this very lifetime they must rely upon the supreme jewel-like consort.

B. Initiation

The door to *anuttara yoga* tantra practice is the receiving of complete initiation from a qualified *vajra* master. To be more specific, to enter into the path of the *anuttara yoga* tantras one must receive initiation using one of four types of mandala as the basis: chalk, cloth, *dhyana* or body mandala.

The initiating master should be endowed with the ten inner qualities, and should have a mindstream that has been purified by accomplishing the retreat and maintaining the *samaya* of the system being transmitted.

The disciples receiving the initiation should have completed the preliminary trainings of the Sutrayana and thus have prepared their mindstreams by laying a firm spiritual basis. Only then can the tantric yogas be successfully engaged in.

All of the *anuttara yoga* tantra initiations begin with the master analyzing, claiming and purifying the place of the rite. He then establishes protection and consecration. This is followed by the rite for the earth divinity, the mandala divinities, consecration of the initiation vase, enhancement of the disciple's stream of being, and so forth.

As for this last phase [i.e., enhancement of the disciple], this includes the instruction on establishing correct motivation, taking the inner initiation, the disciple's act of making requests and asking to be cared for until enlightenment is attained, establishing the pledges, blessing the three doors [body, speech and mind], tossing the divination stick, drinking of the vase waters, being given the kusha grass and mystical armband, giving birth to appreciative joy, and being instructed how to observe one's dreams.

Concerning the methods for entering into the mandala, there are three basic forms of doing this: performing self-generation and frontal generation separately but entering in one movement; performing self-generation and frontal generation non-separately but entering separately; and, lastly, performing the self-generation and frontal generations separately and entering separately.

Following whichever system is appropriate to the specific tradition, one enters into the mandala and takes the initiations.

The disciple here makes the request to be granted initiation. He is given a blindfold, the deity costumes, and a flower garland. Next he is asked about his character and purpose, takes the Bodhisattva vow and the precepts of the five Dhyani Buddhas, is instructed to generate the all-encompassing yoga mind, and is given the oath of secrecy.

This all occurs outside the mandala curtain. He then enters inside the curtain. To establish external merit he circumambulates the mandala, offers prostrations, and is placed in the *samaya*. For inner merit he meditates on receiving a rainfall of wisdom nectars. The master pronounces the words of truth, and the disciple throws the prophetic flower into the mandala. He is then given the flower garland initiation.

This is the stage of entering the mandala while still blindfolded.

Next the disciple is instructed to remove the blindfold. He has now acquired the spiritual maturity necessary in order to be allowed to see the supporting and supported mandalas.

He now proceeds to receive the four initiations: vase, secret, wisdom and sacred word.

The first of these is the vase initiation. This includes the five common initiations of the [five] Dhyani Buddhas, and also the exclusive *vajra acharya* initiation. As each of these stages are completed with the sprinkling of water from the initiation vase, they are all called "vase empowerments."

Almost all the *anuttara yoga* tantra systems contain these six fundamental stages of the vase initiation [i.e., the initiations of the five Buddhas and of the *vajra acharya*]. However, some *anuttara* initiation manuals further subdivide these processes, and in these alternative traditions the vase initiation sometimes includes as many as nine and even eleven phases.

By receiving these six, nine or eleven vase initiations, the disciple experiences purification of all coarse and subtle bodily obscurations, such as grasping at mundane appearances. He is empowered to meditate upon the generation stage yogas and to perform the various mandala activities, etc. The potency for accomplishing the *nirmanakaya* of a Buddha is established.

Then follows the secret initiation. Here the disciple relies upon the use of the special secret substance, and experiences purification of all coarse and subtle speech obscurations, such as grasping at energy and mantra as being separate. He is authorized to cultivate the illusory body, the conventional reality, and to meditate upon the yogas that accomplish this body, namely, the yogas of isolation of body, speech and mind. The potency for accomplishing the *samboghakaya* of a Buddha is established.

The third of the four *anuttara yoga* tantra initiations is called "the wisdom initiation." By means of it the mind is purified of all coarse and subtle obscurations, especially the obscuration hindering the perception of all appearance [i.e., all reality] as arising as the sportive play of bliss and emptiness. One is authorized to meditate on the semblant and actual clear light yogas, the highest reality. The potency of the *dharmakaya* of a Buddha is established.

Fourthly is the sacred word initiation. Here the wisdom of the third initiation is used as a tool to point out the nature of the state of Great Union. All coarse and subtle stains of the body, speech and mind are simultaneously purified. Especially, the instincts of the distortion caused by grasping at duality are removed. One is authorized to meditate upon the completion stage yogas of the inseparable two levels of truth, i.e., the inseparable nature of the illusory body and clear light. The potency is established to actualize the state of Buddha Vajradhara, wherein one becomes a revealor of the festival of great bliss.

Once one's continuum has been matured by these four initiations, one should carefully protect the root and branch precepts of the tantric path and should enter into the generation and completion stage yogas that mature and liberate the mind.

This is the general picture of the overall structure of the *anuttara yoga* tantra systems. Now I'd like to say something about each of the principal individual *anuttara* traditions.

C. Guhyasamaja: A *Male* Anuttara Yoga *Tantra System*

Concerning the Guhyasamaja system Lama Tsong-kha-pa wrote,

> The *anuttara yoga* tantras are
> The highest teachings given by the Buddha.
> From amongst these the most profound is
> That of glorious Guhyasamaja, the king of all tantras.

And also elsewhere,

Understanding the sublime path of Guhyasamaja
Bestows fearless, confident understanding
Of all the teachings of the Buddha.

As said above, once one understands the *Guhyasamaja Tantra* this comprehension can be used as an infrastructure for the understanding of all other tantric systems.

(1) The Generation Stage Yogas
Here by relying upon a mind mandala, a most wondrous field of merit, one is empowered to enter into the practices that purify the mind by means of engaging in the activities that accumulate vast stores of merit.

The mandala meditations, or generation stage yogas, proceed as follows.

To symbolize the time when the universe previously was destroyed and became nothing, one meditates with wisdom on the emptiness of the three doors of liberation.

Later the universe again began to reform, and the elements once more began to reappear. This process is symbolized by the arisal of the protection wheel, the *dharmadayo*, the four elemental mandalas, the crossed *vajras*, the inconceivable mansion, and so forth.

After our universe had once again become developed, the sentient beings began to reappear in it. This was a golden age on earth, and the sentient beings at that time took birth miraculously. To symbolize this, the thirty-two deities of the mandala are visualized as suddenly manifesting simultaneously in a single moment.

Then there are the activities of emanating out from and withdrawing back into the mandala, and the invoking of the Wisdom and Commitment Beings.

There is the entering from above the mandala: the Wisdom *Vajra* Being enters; the entering from below: *Vajra* Strength enters; the unhindered simultaneous *Vajra* Being entrance from above, below, and both the cardinal and intermediate directions; and the entering of the *Vajra* Disciple from the eastern gateway. These are the four manners of entering.

Next follows the invocation beginning with Vairochana and culminating in Sumbharaja. These tantric divinities are arranged on the body of the principal figure in the mandala. One meditates that they become inseparable in nature from the *skandhas*, elements, and so forth.

This establishes the basis of the deity visualization.

The sentient beings with the karma to experience birth from a womb on this planet and whose bodies are composed of the six impermanent substances must eventually meet with death. At the time of death they experience the dissolution of the twenty-five coarse substances: the five *skandhas*, such as form and so forth; the five basic wisdoms, such as the mirror-like wisdom, etc.; the four elements; the six gates of perception; and the five sensory objects.

At each phase of this dissolution there is the external sign of the respective sensory power losing its capacity of apprehension, and also the according element failing in strength. Simultaneously there occur inner signs, such as the mirage-like vision, smoke, fireflies, and the flickering of light like that of a butter-lamp.

When the elements have thus dissolved there is the threefold phase of absorption of the vital energies. These three are "appearance," "increase," and "near-attainment." The signs of these occur, and the "near-attainment" experience melts into the clear light. A sense of luminosity arises, like the vibrant radiance of a clear dawn free from the three obstructions, just before sunrise.

With this clear light level of consciousness acting as a simultaneously present condition and the flowing energy which is the vehicle of this consciousness acting as the substantial cause, the dying person emerges from the clear light experience and prepares to enter into the *bar-do*, or "in-between" state.

The three phases (mentioned above) of "appearance," "increase" and "near-attainment," as well as the visions of mirage, smoke, and so forth now once again arise. However, this time their order of appearance is reversed. In this way the dying person leaves the clear light and enters into the *bar-do*, acquiring a *bar-do* body.

To symbolize the above process, in the *sadhana* there are now five phases of unfoldment. These are known as "the five clear enlightenments": suchness, seat, symbol, syllable, and complete deity body. By means of these five unfoldments one arises as a samboghakaya deity.

The *bar-do* being then enters into a womb and eventually takes rebirth. To symbolize this the samboghakaya deity transforms into the nirmanakaya deity Vajrasattva.

The meditations on the processes of formation, disintegration, birth, death, *bar-do*, and so forth of the world and its inhabitants as described above and symbolized by the various phases beginning with purification in suchness until the offering of suchness is known as "the perfect accomplishment of one's own purpose." It is the *samadhi* of the first application.

To symbolize the physical deeds of the resultant stage of Buddhahood, the deities of the space mandala together with the consorts of their individual families are summoned to the heart. Clouds of emanations are sent forth and withdrawn in order to purify the world and its inhabitants.

The stage from emanating via the seven doors until the emergence of the wrathful deities is known as "the perfect accomplishment of the purpose of others." It is also called "the supremely victorious mandala."

The mental deeds of the resultant stage of Buddhahood are symbolized as follows. To arrest mental wandering and torpor one visualizes mystical hand implements, tiny in size, at the tip of the nose. Alternatively, one generates a coarse single-pointed recollection of a drop the size of a mustard seed, within which is envisioned the complete deity mandala. This is performed together with the processes of emanation and absorption, and is known as "the yoga of subtle realization supported by *shamatha*."

The Buddahood deeds of speech are symbolized by mental and also verbal mantric recitation. This latter has five aspects: pledge, cyclical, flowing, forceful, wrathful, and diamond.

The main steps in the process are as follows:

The principal mandala deity melts into clear light. The four indescribable goddesses offer songs of inspiration, and the deity reappears from the light. Then there is the offering, the praise, the experience of blissful ambrosia, and so forth.

In brief, from the phase of meditating on the mystical hand implements at the upper door until the phase of establishing *siddhi*, there are forty-nine steps to be cultivated.

There are the three *samadhis*, such as that called "the first application"; the four branches, known as "propitiation," "proximate attainment," "attainment" and "great attainment"; four yogas to be cultivated, called "yoga," "beyond yoga," "intense yoga," and "great yoga"; four *vajra* stages, known as "emptiness enlightenment," "seed absorption," "form completion," and "mantric syllable placement"; and so forth.

These are the processes of the Guhyasamaja generation stage to be cultivated as a preliminary to entering into the completion stage yogas.

(2) The Completion Stage Yogas
The subjects taken as the focal points in practice of the completion stage yogas are the general and individual natures of the body and mind on coarse, subtle and extremely subtle levels.

Here the three topics of energy channels, vital energies and mystic drops become very important.

By understanding these topics well, one can successfully enter into practice of the various completion stage yogas: body isolation, speech isolation, mind isolation, illusory body, the clear light, and great union.

The yoga of body isolation is explained as follows.

The basis of this isolation is comprised of the aggregates, elements, entrances, and sensory objects. Each of these is fivefold, making a total of twenty factors. The five Buddha families are then applied to each of these twenty, making a total of one hundred supreme natures to be explored.

Here the four elements, together with consciousness, constitute the "five thatness natures" to be meditated upon. Body, speech and mind envisioned as being deities of the three *vajras* are the three secret natures. Finally, the practitioner possessing the three doors is envisioned as being Buddha Vajradhara, which is "the great secret solitary nature" to be meditated upon.

One seals these various factors with the mark of bliss and void, and isolates them in the nature of a *devakaya*, or "deity body."

Moreover, when one meditates on the yoga of the subtle drop at the tip of the jewel—an element possessing the four factors of substance, time, energy and object—mind and energy flow together into the central channel. Signs arise to indicate that the vital energies enter, abide and dissolve at the heart. The yogi achieves absorption in the sphere of bliss and void, and attains the *samadhi* of the *vajra* body isolation in which the hundred natures and so forth [described above] appear as *devakaya*.

The basis of the second isolation, or that of speech, involves the root and branch energies in coarse and subtle aspects, and especially the life-sustaining energy at the heart, together with the undying mystic drop.

This, the basis of all expression, abides as a short syllable *ah*, symbol of the ultimate profundity. The yogi engages the *vajra* recitation while appreciating the inseparability of energy and mantra, and experiences yogic isolation in the nature of the illusory body. He moves the undying drop to the various places of the body, such as heart, head, secret place, and so forth. Also, he engages in the vase breathing yoga, taking as objects of concentration the undying drop, together with the mantra wheels, the energies in the nature of five radiances, the substances of white and red [i.e. male and female] sexual fluids locked in mystical union and formed into a drop the size of a mustard seed, and so forth.

In this manner all the root energies, with the exception of the all-pervading energy, are brought under control.

The yogi then applies the *vajra* recitation methods and ignites the mystic heat. The vital energies are absorbed into the undying drop, and the knots in the channels at the center of the heart are released.

This is the process of the yoga of speech isolation, the *samadhi* of *vajra speech*.

The basis of the third isolation is comprised of the three appearances and the eighty conceptual minds. By relying upon the two *dhyanas* as well as upon conducive inner and outer conditions, the yogi isolates [i.e., withdraws] into the sphere of semblant clear light that sees all as emptiness. He relies upon the external condition of a *karmamudra* and/or a *jnanamudra* to induce the four joys of downward showering and upward rising energies. As an inner condition he focusses the *vajra* recitation method upon the all-pervading energy.

He then dissolves his body from above and below into the clear light at the heart. The entire world and its inhabitants are in the same manner gradually dissolved into the vision of clear light.

In this way the yogi performs the absorption by means of the two *dhyanas*. The dissolution of the eighty natural conceptual minds is experienced: thirty-three in the nature of appearance; forty in the nature of increase; and seven in the nature of near-attainment.

These eighty natural conceptual minds that are carried by the coarse and subtle contaminated energies thus dissolve just as at the moment of death. The wisdoms of the three appearances arise, leading the mind to the experience of the semblant clear light.

This is the process of the yoga of mind isolation, the *samadhi* of *vajra* mind.

When these three isolations have been taken to fulfillment, the yogi is given the actual precept on how to generate the illusory body, and also the oral instructions of the nine points in blending and transference.

The basis for producing the illusory body is explained as follows.

The semblant clear light acts as a simultaneously present condition, and the vital energy of five radiances which is the vehicle of that clear light acts as the substantial cause. It is this [vital energy] that produces the illusory body described by the twelve similes and having the fifteen qualities, the form which substitutes for the merit generated in the exoteric Sutrayana by means of three aeons of practice.

Such is the completion stage yoga of the illusory body, which in the Vajrayana represents the conventional level of truth.

The clear light yoga is explained as follows:

The external time for the experience of clear light is dawn, when neither sun nor moon is in the sky and yet darkness has passed. The internal time is after the subsiding of the three appearances [i.e., appearance, increase and near-attainment], just as at the moment of death. These are the two moments for the manifestation of clear light consciousness.

At a time when these two are possible, the yogi relies upon inner and outer conditions to manifest the clear light, which in the Vajrayana represents the ultimate level of truth and is the remedy that eliminates at once the nine circles of obscurations to knowledge.

The final completion stage yoga is that of great union. It is described as follows:

The yogi reverses the processes whereby he entered into clear light consciousness, pulling back into the consciousness of near-attainment and so forth. Simultaneously he experiences the path of freedom, the "great union of transcendence" which is produced from non-contaminated mind and energy.

Arising from that absorption he realizes the inseparable nature of the body and mind. This is the "great union of a trainee."

That practitioner then intensifies his experience by engaging in the three methods known simply as "contrived," "uncontrived," and "utterly uncontrived." Training in this way he experiences the clear light at the fulfillment of training, thus eliminating all obscurations to omniscience and attaining the "great union of no-more-training" which is enriched by the seven mystical qualities.

(3) The Five Paths to Enlightenment

How are these various *anuttara yoga* tantra practices linked to the categories of the five paths to enlightenment—accumulation, application, vision, meditation and no-more-training?

"The path of accumulation" is comprised from the period beginning with the time when one acquires the four complete initiations until by the power of meditation one achieves a glimpse of emptiness through dissolving the vital energies into the central channel.

"The path of application'" is experienced from then until the attainment of the impure level of the illusory body yoga that directly perceives emptiness by means of the wisdom of great bliss.

From the first experience of the actual clear light until the attainment of the great union of a trainee is "the path of vision," the first Bodhisattva *bhumi.*

"The path of meditation" is comprised of the period beginning with the moment after that until the first moment of the attainment of the stage of the ultimate clear light of the great union at the end of training.

The yogi then crosses the tenth Bodhisattva *bhumi*, and in the second moment of that experience achieves complete enlightenment, "the path of no-more-training."

Everything that has been said above about the Guhyasamaja system can be abbreviated into the mystical syllable *Eh-vam*, which is spoken of in terms of path, fruit and signs.

It can also be abbreviated into the threefold category of the tantras of basis, path and fruit.

(D) *The Three Types of Male* Anuttara Yoga *Tantras*

The *anuttara yoga* tantras are of two main types: male and female. Of the male *anuttara yoga* tantras, there are three basic types: those that work with lust, those that work with anger, and those that work with ignorance.

The principal male *anuttara yoga* tantra working with lust as the basis of the path is that of Guhyasamaja, the yogas of which have been described above.

The Indian textual traditions of the Guhyasamaja system are as follows.

Firstly there is *The Root Tantra (rTsa-rgyud)* in seventeen chapters.

Then there are "The Six Great Explanatory Tantras" *(bShad-rgyud-chen-po-drug).*

The first of these is *The Subsequent Tantra (rGyud-phyi-ma)* in eighteen chapters, which explains the six facets of *The Root Tantra* by means of the four modes. These six facets are: direct, indirect, obvious, non-obvious, literal and alternative. The four modes are: meaning of the words, the general ideas, the hidden meanings, and the ultimate significance.

The remaining five explanatory tantras include *The Vajra Rosary Tantra (rGyud-rDo-rje-phreng-ba)*; *Revealing the Intent of Buddha (dGongs-pa-lung-ston)*; *A Synopsis of Vajra Wisdom (Ye-shes-rdo-rje-kun-btus)*; *Questions of the King of Celestials (Lhai-dbang-pos-zhus-pa)*; and *Questions of the Four Goddesses (Lha-mo-zhis-zhus-pa)*.

Numerous commentarial traditions appeared later in India, including those of the Aryas [i.e., Nagarjuna and Aryadeva], Jnanapada, Anandagarbha, Shantipada, and so forth. Of these, the first two are the most complete [i.e., that of the Aryas and that of Jnanapada].

The Indian commentary most clearly elucidating the generation stage yogas of the thirty-two deity Guhyasamaja mandala of Akshobya is Nagarjuna's *The Summary (mDor-byes)* and also his *A Brief Synopsis (mDo-bsred)*.

Some of the more important Indian commentaries elucidating the completion stage yogas are: Nagarjuna's *The Five Stages (Rim-lnga)* and also his *A Commentary to the Bodhimind (Byang-chub-sems-'grel)*; Aryadeva's *Stages of the Self-Blessed Illusory Body (sGyu-lus-bdag-byin-brlab-kyi-rim-pa)* and also his *A Compendium of Practices (sPyod-bsdus)*, which is a commentary to Nagarjuna's *The Five Stages*; Nagabodhi's *Steps in the Generation Stage (sKyed-rim-rnam-bzhag-rim-pa)*, his *Twenty Mandala Rites (dKyil-chog-nyi-cshu-pa)*, and also his *Explanation of the Completion Stage Activities (rDzog-rim-las-mtha'-rnam-'byed)*; Shakyamitra's *Supplement to the Two Stages (Rim-pa-gnyis-pai-kha-skong)*; and Shrichandra's *Generation Stage Vajrasattva Method (bsKyed-rim-rdor-sems-sgrub-thabs)*, his *Six Applications on the Completion Stage (rDzogs-rim-sbyor-drug)*, and also his *A Lamp to Illuminate the Tantric Scriptures (rGyud-'grel-sgron-gsal)*.

As for how these lineages came to Tibet, it is said that Manjushrimitra, an incarnation of the Bodhisattva Manjushri, once appeared to Acharya Simhabhadra's disciple Buddhajnana. He manifested in the form of the lord of the Manjushrivajra mandala, initiating Buddhajnana into the *dhyana mandala* and also bestowing upon him the complete instructions. Eventually the venerable Atisha received this secret lineage, brought it to Tibet, and in turn passed it on to his chief Tibetan disciple Lama Drom Ton-pa.

Another important lineage of instruction is that of the translator Gos Lotsawa *('Gos)*, who collected the various Indian traditions listed above and brought them to Tibet, passing them on to the Sa-kya and Zha-lu lineages.

A third important lineage was brought to Tibet by Mar-pa the Translator and passed on through the order of Kar-gyu gurus.

Lama Tsong-kha-pa collected together these various lines of transmission and united them into one stream. Later he went into retreat at the Ol-kha mountains for a number of years, where he achieved insight. Here he received numerous direct visions of Manjushrivajra and was given special oral instructions. These included the instruction of the three *samadhis* of the generation stage practice of the nineteen-deity mandala. They also included the completion stage precepts such as the instruction on the body isolation yoga involving the undying drop at the heart, the speech isolation yoga involving the secret drop at the jewel, the mind isolation yoga involving the mantric drop, and also the three higher yogic stages of illusory body, clear light and great union, which are linked to the drop of suchness.

The yogic stages of these four drops — undying, secret, mantric and suchness — is the subject of numerous treatises by Buddhajnanapada. Included here are his *The Four Hundred Points Concerning the Mandala Rite (dKyil-chod-bhyed-bcas-bzhi-brgyad-pa)*; *The Always Sublime Generation Stage Method (bsKyed-rim-sgrub-thabs-kun-bzang)*; *The Liberating Drops in the Completion Stage Yogas (rDzog-rim-grol-thig)*; and *The Sacred Instructions of Manjushri ('Jam-dpal-zhal-lung)*, that explains both generation and completion stage yogas.

Lama Tsong-kha-pa collected and united all of these oral and scriptural lineages, thus preserving them for future generations. It is due to his kindness that the Guhyasamaja tradition still exists today in such completeness.

The principal male *anuttara yoga* tantra using anger as the basis of the path is that of Vajrabhairava, also known as Yamantaka.

The complete root tantra of this system, or the *Vajrabhairava Root Tantra ('Jigs-byed-rtsa-rgyud)*, is known as *The Three Hundred Topics (rTog-pa-sum-brgyad-pa)*. However, it was never translated into Tibetan. Only those sections dealing with the methods of accomplishing enlightenment and those dealing with the activities of the wheel of emanation were translated.

The sections dealing with the methods for accomplishing enlightenment were translated in two different forms: *The Seven Topics (rTog-bdun)* and *The Four Topics (rTog-bzhi)*. As for the sections dealing with the methods of engaging in the activities of the wheel of emanation, these were compiled into *The Three Topics (rTog-gsum)*.

Other important Indian classics in the Vajrabhairava tradition include *Vision of the Practitioner Teu-lo-pa (Las-mkhan-teu-lo-pai-rtog-pa)*;

Tantra of the Black Warrior (dGra-nag-gi-rgyud) in eighteen chapters; and *The Tantra of the Red Opponent (gShed-dmar-gyi-rgyud)* in nineteen chapters.

Three basic forms of the mandala are presented in these various texts: red, black and extremely fierce. Of these, the last is the most important in general practice.

The Vajrabhairava generation stage yogas usually consist of cultivating the three *samadhis* on one of the mandalas associated with this last form of Bhairava: the forty-nine deity mandala, the seventeen-deity mandala, the thirteen-deity mandala, the mandala of eight *vitali* deities, and the mandala of the Solitary Hero.

As for the completion stage yogas, the Vajrabhairava system arranges these into four categories. Here the phases of body isolation and speech isolation combine as Mantra Yoga. Mind isolation becomes Commitment Yoga. Both impure and pure phases of the illusory body trainings combine as Form Yoga. Finally, semblant and actual clear light phases become the Wisdom Yoga.

The principal Indian commentators on these four completion stage yogas were the *mahasiddhas* Lalitavajra, Shridhara, Amoghavajra the First, and Amoghavajra the Second.

The various Indian lineages of the Vajrabhairava system were brought to Tibet by yogis such as Rva Lo-tsa-wa, Nyo Lo-tsa-wa, Kyo-od-jung, and so forth.

The most authoritative early Tibetan commentaries are those by Rva Lo-tsa-wa and the Dri-kung Kar-gyu master Pal-dzin.

The third type of male *anuttara yoga* tantra is that working with ignorance as the basis of the path. Here the principal system is *The Tantra of Vajra Arali (rDo-rje-a-ra-lii-rgyud)*.

Other important related texts are *The Peerless Miracle Net (bLa-med-sgyu-dra)* and *The Vajra Essence Ornament (rDo-rje-snying-po-rgyan)*.

(E) Heruka Chakrasamvara: A Female Anuttara Yoga Tantra

As for the *anuttara yoga* tantras that belong to the female category, Lama Tsong-kha-pa writes,

It is said that the female *anuttara yoga* tantras
Are inconceivably numerous;
But of all of these the central and supreme
Is that of Heruka Chakrasamvara,
A tantra like the ornament
On the very tip of a victory banner.

The essence of all the female *anuttara yoga* tantras is the tantra of Heruka Chakrasamvara, "the Wrathful Lord of the Wheel of Supreme Bliss."

The canonical sources of this tradition are *The Concise Samvara Tantra (bDe-mcog-nyung-ngui-rgyud)* in fifty-one chapters; *The Peerless Expression (mNgon-brjod-bla-ma)*; *Source of the Mystic Bond (sDom-'byung)*; *Tantra of the Vajra Space Warrior (rDo-rje-mkha-'groi-rgyud)*; and so forth.

Three principal Indian lineages of transmission of the Heruka Chakrasamvara system developed, namely, those of the *mahasiddhas* Luipada (Lui-pa), Krishnacharyin (Nag-cho-pa), and Gandhapada (Til-bu-pa).

In the first of these three systems [i.e., that of Luipada], the generation and completion stage practices are applied by means of the four daily sessions of yogas.

Here the generation stage of practice consists of the five purifications, which are associated with the threefold process of yoga, beyond-yoga, and intense yoga [as listed earlier].

As for the completion stage practices, here the yogi fixes his mind at the sound cluster at the navel. The karmic energies are brought into the central energy channel and the four downward showering and upward rising joys are induced. He then relies upon the meditations of the *dhyanas* of *vajra* recitation and systematic absorption. In this way on the emptiness side he gains an inconceivable experience of semblant and actual clear light; and on the appearance side he achieves the impure and pure levels of the wondrous illusory body. He then manifests the inconceivable state of great union, both that of a trainee and that beyond training.

As for the lineage of Gandhapada (Til-bu-pa), in the generation stage practices the outer and inner mandalas are cultivated by means of the three yogas.

In the completion stage practices [of the Gandhapada tradition], the yogas of the three isolations, the illusory body, the clear light and great union are collected into five stages of yogic application. These five are called "self-consecration," "crossed vajra," "the filled jewel," "*jalandhara*," and "the inconceivable."

The fundamental commentaries in these various Heruka lineages are the two generation stage manuals by Luipada, known as *The Great* and *The Small; The Seven Treatises* by Gandhapada; and the six texts of Krishnacharyin.

Another very important tradition in the Heruka cycle of mandalas is that of the *Hevajra-tantra*. Here there is *The Root Tantra (rTsa-rgyud)*, also known as *The Tantra in Two Forms (brTag-gnyis)*; *The Explanatory Tantra (bShad-rgyud)* known as *The Vajra Tent (rDo-rje-gur)*; *The Subsequent Tantra (Dei-phyi-ma)* known as *The Drop of Mahamudra (Phyag-chen-thig-le)*; and *The Later Subsequent Tantra (De-yang-phyi-ma)* called *The Essence of Wisdom (Ye-shes-snying-po)*.

All of these principal lineages of root, explanatory, and subsequent tantras in the Heruka cycle, as well as the commentarial traditions, were transmitted in the form of the "Path and Fruit" *(Lam-'bras)* line of transmission [coming into Tibet through the Sa-kya Order]. Lama Je Tsong-kha-pa praised this transmission as being supreme.

(F) Kalachakra: A Clarified Anuttara Yoga *Tantra*

Another important *anuttara yoga* tantra system is that of Kalachakra, a tradition that presents the *anuttara* path in a manner markedly different than the presentation found in all the other *anuttara yoga* tantras.

Concerning the Kalachakra system Lama Tsong-kha-pa writes,

> Another important *anuttara yoga* tantra system
> With a quite unique manner of presenting the path
> Is that of Kalachakra, 'The Wheel of Time,'
> Which is based upon *The Abbreviated Tantra*
> Together with its commentary *The Stainless Light.*

The clarified tantra of the Kalachakra tradition is usually mentioned separately to the other *anuttara yoga* systems, for its infrastructure is considerably different than those of the mainstream traditions such as Guhyasamaja, Vajrabhairava, Heruka Chakrasamvara, and so forth.

Kalachakra, or "The Wheel of Time," is spoken of in three aspects: outer, inner and alternative.

Outer Kalachakra is comprised of the six elements of earth, water, fire, air, space and wisdom; the world of Mt. Meru, the four continents, and the eight sub-continents and so forth, together with everything above, below and in all the directions; and also all objects of smell, sight, taste, touch, sound and dharma.

Under the topic of Inner Kalachakra are included the three realms of living beings, the sixteen worlds, the ten planets, the twenty-eight principal heavenly bodies, the five places of rebirth, the six types of living beings, the time cycles of years, months and days, the six energy centers of the body, the ten vital energies, the eight drops that carry the instincts of the two obscurations, and so forth.

In other words, included here are the living beings and the world as understood in an astrological context.

Alternative Kalachakra is the actual practice of the yogas of the Kalachakra system whereby the world and its beings are purified.

The actual basis of the purification is the person possessing the six elements with the karma to be born from a human womb here in this world.

The process begins by taking initiation into a mandala made from colored powders.

This initiation begins with the nine preliminary steps of invoking the earth *deva*, consecrating the vase, the conch of great victory, the action lines, *vajra*, bell, enhancing the disciple, establishing the seat, and the analysis of the divinity.

The seventh of these preliminary steps above involves placing the disciple within the six families, invoking Vajrasattva, and so forth.

The actual initiation process is constituted of three phases: the seven called "entering like a child"; the four higher initiations; and the four higher-than-higher initiations.

When a child is born into this world he undergoes seven experiences: being washed; having his hair cut; having his ears pierced; learning to laugh and speak; using the sensory objects; being given a name; and learning to read and write.

Accordingly the Kalachakra initiation begins with seven processes that are likened to these seven steps in childhood.

To receive these the disciple in turn stands before each of the four faces of Kalachakra—white, red, black and yellow in color—and is given the seven initiations: water, headdress, silk ribbon, *vajra* and bell, activity, name, and permission.

By means of these initiations the disciple experiences purification of the five aggregates, ten energies, right and left energy channels, ten sensory powers and their objects, the activities of the five bodily functions, the three doors, and the element of wisdom.

As for the *samaya* taken during this process, there are seven root vows in common [with other *anuttara yoga* tantra systems], together with seven further root vows exclusive to Kalachakra.

In addition, there are the twenty-five special precepts of the Kalachakra system, five each relating to the five topics of negativity, killing, the sexual substances, and desire.

During this phase of the initiation ceremony these are introduced and one is advised to guard against them.

Next one receives the four conventional higher initiations, also known as "the four worldly initiations." Here the disciple is established in the path of the four joys by means of the vase waters, tasting the secret substances, experiencing melting and bliss, and being introduced to the innate bliss and void.

Finally there are the four higher-than-higher initiations, also known as "the four beyond-worldly initiations." Here the disciple is introduced to the consciousness which directly perceives emptiness while abiding in supreme unchanging great bliss, a consciousness that is of one taste with the empty body arising in the form of Kalachakra and consort in sexual union.

By gaining these initiations the disciple is introduced to the real meaning of being a layman, a novice, a fully ordained monk, a Sangha elder, and a leader of living beings.

Also, during the rite the significance of each of the steps in initiation is pointed out.

Thus by receiving the empowerments of the three *vajras*, being shown the commitments, and gaining the initiation of a great *vajra acharya*, the mindstream of the disciple is ripened and is prepared for entrance into the actual yogic practices of the Kalachakra tradition.

As for the various mandalas that can be used as the basis of the generation stage yogas, *The Root Tantra* (rTsa-rgyud) speaks of the mandala of glorious moving stars containing 1,620 divinities.

The Abbreviated Tantra (bsDus-rgyud) speaks of 722 divinities in the mandalas of body, speech and mind.

Other alternatives are the mind mandala of thirty-six divinities and the mind mandala of thirty-two divinities. Then there are the smaller mandalas of twenty-five, twenty-three, nineteen, thirteen and nine divinities. Finally, there is the mandala with only Kalachakra and consort, and also the mandala of Solitary Kalachakra.

In the generation stage the yogi contemplates one of these various mandalas by means of the three *samadhis*, engaging in the four-branched propitiation, maintaining the four *vajra* points, and cultivating the four enlightenments.

In the completion stage the meditator engages in the six yogas: sense withdrawal, meditative stabilization, energy concentration, retention, post-recollection, and *samadhi*.

These six abbreviate into the four branches: the branch producing form, the branch producing energy, the branch producing bliss, and the branch of great accomplishment. The first branch is linked to the first two yogas, and the second branch to the third and fourth yogas. Finally, the third and fourth branches are linked to the fifth and sixth yogas.

By means of these six yogas the disciple achieves the *mahamudra* of the empty body. The energies enter the central channel, and the drops of red and white sexual forces flow down from the crown *chakra* above and flow up from the *chakra* at the secret place below. Twenty-one thousand and six hundred of each of the two sexual drops [male and female] are gathered together in this way, giving rise to an experience of great bliss understanding emptiness. Each occasion of experience of this great bliss dissolves an according amount of karmic wind and atomic bodily matter. The obscurations of the four occasions, such as the waking state and so forth, are thus destroyed, and one travels to the twelfth stage of attainment, the enlightened state of Kalachakra's great bliss.

This is the system of the Kalachakra initiations, generation stage yogas, and completion stage yogas that produce the four *kayas* of a fully enlightened being.[3]

Buddha Shakyamuni originally taught this tradition at the Great Rice-Heap Stupa in Southern Jambudvipa. The teaching had been requested by King Suchandra of Shambala, who was an actual emanation of the Bodhisattva Vajrapani. Emissaries from six different kingdoms were also present.

On that occasion Buddha transmitted *The Root Tantra (rTsa-rgyud)* in twelve thousand lines, and shortly thereafter King Suchandra composed his *The Great Commentary ('Grel-chen)* in sixty thousand lines.

However, the only section of *The Root Tantra* to survive is that known as *The Treatise on the Initiations (dBang-mdor-bstan-pa)*.

Later Manjushrikirti, who was the first of the twenty-five knowledge holder kings of Shambala, wrote a summary of *The Root Tantra* that came to be known by the title *The Abbreviated Tantra (bsDus-rgyud)*, which is in five chapters. Two different translations of the commentary to this, *Essence of the Abbreviated Tantra (bsDus-rgyud-snying-po)*, exist in the Tibetan canon.

Another important text is *The Great Commentary to the Abbreviated Tantra (bsDus-rgyud-kyi-'grel-pa)*, perhaps better known in association with the title *Three Commentaries on the Mind (Sems-'grel-skor-gsum)* by the second of Shambala's knowledge holders, Acharya Pundarika.

Also of significance is the Bodhisattva Vajragharba's *Commentary to the Vajra Essence (rDo-rje-snying-'grel)*. This work unpacks the themes of *The Tantra of Two Forms*, which is the root tantra in the Hevajra system; however, it comments upon Hevajra in a manner consistent with the Kalachakra presentation, so often is read in conjunction with a study of the Kalachakra tradition.

Acharya Vajrapani's *Commentary to the Song of Vajrapani (Phyag-rdor-stod-'grel)*, which explains the essential points of *The Root Tantra of Heruka Chakra-samvara (bDe-mchog-rtsa-rgyud)* in terms compatible with the Kalachakra system, is also important.

Also, *The Subsequent Tantra of Guhyasamaja (bSang-'dus-pai-phyi-ma)* presents the path in a manner consistent with the Kalachakra structure and therefore is often read in conjunction with the Kalachakra literature.

Kalachakrapada's extensive and abbreviated commentaries to the Kalachakra generation stage yogas are also fundamental reading, as are the writings of the two Dro ('Bro) brothers.

The Three Rosaries (Phreng-skor-gsum) by Acharya Abhayakara are worthy of mention: *The Vajra Rosary (rDo-rje-phreng-ba)*, which contains forty-two mandala rites from all four classes of tantras; *The Rosary of Complete Yoga (rNal-'byor-rdzogs-phreng)*, which is a *sadhana* collection; and *A Rosary of Sunbeams (Od-kyi-nye-ma)*, which is a collection of fire rite practices.

Finally, there is *A Compendium of Purification Practices (Kri-ya-kun-bsdus)* by Acharya Jagaddarpana.

(VI) THE TANTRIC PRECEPTS

In the Resultant Vajrayana—even more so than in the Causal Sutrayana—it is said to be extremely important to train under the guidance of a qualified tantric master, to avoid wrong attitudes toward him and to cultivate positive attitudes, and to remain within the framework of the vows and commitments of the tantric path. In order to be able to do this it is useful to know the beneficial effects of conducive attitudes and the shortcomings of faulty attitudes, how to regard the guru's entourage and possessions, the nature of correct and incorrect practice, and so forth. All of these topics are discussed in detail in *The Root Tantra of Guhyasamaja (bSang—dus-rtsa-rgyud)*, *The*

Peerless Miracle Net (bLa-med-sgyud-dra), *The Tantra of Two Forms (brTag-gnyis)*, *The First Supreme Glory (dPal-mcog-dang-po)*, and other such texts.

The general themes on how to correctly rely upon the vajra guru were gleaned from these early source works and collected into fifty quintessential verses, entitled *Fifty Verses on the Guru (bLa-ma-lnga-bcu-pa)*, by Acharya Vira, who was also known by the names Aryasura and Ashvagosha.

Although all four classes of tantras involve some type of *samaya*, the two lower tantra classes do not require the taking of the nineteen *samaya* of the five Buddha families.

The method for acquiring these *samaya* is expounded in *The Vajra Space Warrior (rDo-rje-mkka'-'gro)*, *The Perfect Union (Yang-dag-'byor-ba)*, and so forth.

The general samaya of the anuttara yoga tantras include topics like the commitment of consumption, such as the vow to rely upon consumption of the five meats and five drinks; the commitment to uphold the sacred materials, such as *vajra*, bell, the six tantric ornaments, and so forth; the commitment of protection, meaning the *samaya* to protect the root and branch vows; and so forth.

The root vows are fourteen in number, and transgressing them is known as "the root downfalls." By understanding their individual natures, what constitutes each, and being apprehensive of the shortcomings of transgression, one guards against the stains of a root downfall.

Should a root downfall occur, there are numerous methods of restoring the strength of one's disciplines. These are expounded in *The Tantra of the Red Opponent (gShed-dmar-gi-rgyud)*, *The Tantra of the Black Warrior (dGra-nag-gi-rgyud)*, *The Vajra Essence Ornament (rDo-rje-snying-po)*, and so forth.

In brief, based on these numerous canonical works Acharya Ashvagosha compiled the list of fourteen root tantric downfalls, and Acharya Nagarjuna compiled the list of the eight secondary precepts.

The tradition of Lakshmikara emphasizes a number of alternative precepts. Here it is said that engaging in the various mandala activities without first completing the formal retreat is a root downfall. Also, included in the secondary precepts are the three commitments to cut off self-interest, arrest attraction to mundane appearances, and abide within the three vows (*pratimoksha*, Bodhisattva and Vajrayana).

This tradition also lists as a secondary tantric precept the commitment to respect holy images, tantric implements such as *vajra* and bell, tantric substances such as even old and discarded ritual materials, and so forth. As well, it mentions the commitments to engage six times a day in the practice of recollecting the mind of spiritual determination, to meditate four times daily upon the yogas of the tantric system into which one is initiated, to make a food offering (*tor-ma*) during the last daily session of meditation, and to strive between meditation sessions to maintain the special tantric attitudes [such as seeing oneself as a mandala divinity, the world as a mandala, all sounds as mantra, all thoughts as the interplay of bliss and void, etc].

Practitioners of the female *anuttara yoga* tantras are instructed to observe a number of additional precepts, such as beginning all activities with the left side of the body, performing a tantric feast (*tsok*) on the tenth day of each lunar cycle, and so forth.

Should either the root or secondary tantric precepts be transgressed, the strength of the disciplines can be restored by means of taking the initiation again, or else by means of performing the self-initiation practice.

To prevent negative effects arising from any downfalls that have been created it is useful to practice the meditations and mantric recitations associated with the tantric systems of Vajrasattva or Samayavajra, and also to engage in the Vajradaka fire rite.

These methods of purifying transgressions of the tantric precepts are taught in the various scriptures listed earlier.

(VII) CONCLUSION

The omniscient Sa-kya master Bu-ton Rin-po-che, who understood and elucidated all the teachings of Buddha, greatly contributed to the preservation and dissemination of the vast range of the Buddhist tantras here in Tibet. Lama Tsong-kha-pa and his immediate disciples continued his legacy.

My own root guru Pur-chok-pa received the complete tradition coming from them, analyzed it with pure reason, and internalized its meaning through intense meditation. He thus crossed the vast ocean of study, contemplation and meditation in the tantric tradition.

It was under his kind guidance that I myself ventured into the Vajrayana. And although I cannot boast of spectacular personal accomplishments, I must say that I feel very honored to have trained in this vast and profound system under the guidance of such an accomplished master.

Monogram of Kalachakra

Thus is complete my brief presentation
Of the main points in the Vajrayana system
Of four classes of tantras,
The essence of Buddha's teachings
As collected by the omniscient Bu-ton Rin-po-che,
Elucidated by the incomparable Lama Tsong-kha-pa,
And [given to me by] my kind root guru Pur-chok-pa.

May any small merits that it possesses
Be dedicated toward the cause of enlightenment;
May the Vajrayana teachings last for long,
And may living beings continually abide
Within the golden rays of peace and joy.

4 Poems Pointing Out the Nature of Correct Practice

A. A SONG TO STRENGTHEN ONE'S PRACTICE OF THE PATH

1. Kye-ma-hoh !
   I bow to the feet of the root and lineage gurus,
   Embodiments of the objects of refuge,
   Essence of the kindness of the *Aryas*.
   I call to you from the depths of my heart:
   Reach out with the hook of your compassion
   And care for living beings until *mahabodhi* is achieved.

2. In this coarse age marked by five great degenerations,
   The living beings are weak in spirit and
   Are firmly held in the prison of samsara.
   Their minds are of limited understanding, and
   They are bound by the noose of the five psychic poisons.
   Therefore the compassion of the Buddhas
   Manifests especially strongly at this time.

3. Hence it is also a time of opportunity, and
   It becomes important to apply ourselves with joy
   To the Dharma methods that accomplish the purpose
   Of this life, the *bar-do*, and all future births.
   Make clear in your mind with precision
   The steps on the supreme path that leads
   To the states of liberation and omniscience.

4. To give a single day to the cultivation of goodness
   Without mixing in any negativity
   Is as rare as a midday star.
   The eight worldly concerns and the activities
   That benefit this one lifetime alone
   Seem to totally dominate us,
   Cheating us out of lasting joy.

5. Then, because of the instincts collected
   By constant familiarity with the superficial,
   We come to possess the prejudiced mind
   That rejects the truth of karmic law
   And mistrusts the three supreme Refuge objects
   Like we cynically doubt a magican's act.
   Thus controlled by misconcepion,
   Our mind becomes accustomed to bad habits
   And we collect a mass of negative karma
   By ridiculing and disparaging the holy beings.

6. This burden of misconception is heavy,
   And even further clouds the mind.
   Then, living a life contradicting truth,
   We procrastinate in doing anything worthwhile.
   Indeed, it is sad to witness those
   Who thus misuse the jewel-like human potential
   And turn their backs on responsible living.

7. Human life is rare and precious,
   And is possessed of limitless capacity for growth.
   Yet it is short and fragile;
   And although we constantly see others
   Die without respect to their youth or age,
   We continue to act with the false confidence
   That somehow our own death is far away.
   O Jewels of Refuge, inspire us now to turn
   Our minds toward spiritual practice, so that at death
   We need not clutch at our chests in fear and regret.

8. For, living under the illusion of our own permanence,
   We generate vast stores of black karma
   That after death will ripen as lower rebirth.
   Then we will have to face great suffering,
   And will not hear words of truth for many aeons.
   Such is the reality clearly described
   In the sutras, tantras and other scriptures.

9. There are many people who have heard these teachings,
   But whose minds are blocked by arrogance
   And they excuse themselves from acting accordingly
   On the grounds that the Bodhisattva or tantric yogin
   Can behave unconventionally due to the power
   Of his insight and great compassion.

10. However, these sophists are not governed by compassion,
    And this we can clearly discern when we observe
    The distance between their words and their ambitions.
    It would seem that their foolhardy habit
    Of boldly contradicting karmic law
    Will do little for them but bring them
    Into the flames of the hot hells.

11. The Three Jewels of Refuge are unfailing protectors,
    And their power and compassion flow ceaselessly
    Without discrimination for friend or foe.
    May they send forth their inspiring blessings,
    That by the strength of their boundless excellence
    All beings may realize the highest path,
    And that our spiritual journey need not be long.

12. In order to help the unfortunate beings of this age
    And lead them to the sublime stage of bliss,
    Buddha taught the vast and profound Dharma,
    That includes the six perfections, egolessness,
    Emptiness, and the three higher trainings.

13. Such is the purpose and content of all the scriptures.
    As for the beings who reject this sublime Way,
    What can one possibly say for them, other than that
    An evil spirit has captured their minds.
    May the objects of Refuge release their blessings,
    That these people may be turned by truth
    And may follow in the footsteps of the holy ones.

14. These days there are many charlatans who profess
    To carry the weight of upholding
    The theory and practice of Buddha's tradition.
    They pretend to be of great learning and insight;
    But to settle upon an interpretation of the Dharma
    Without first examining the teachings in depth
    By means of reason and analysis of the scriptures
    Produces very little valid understanding.
    And on that basis they praise their own lineages
    While disparaging the traditions of others!
    Are they not simply Dharma businessmen?

15. And this is their spiritual focus!
    May the inspiring blessings of the Three Jewels
    Enter deeply into their hearts,
    That they may bring their minds under control
    And joyfully practice the real meaning of Dharma.

16. We must eliminate all signs of entanglement
    In the web of mistaken understanding.
    The Indian and Tibetan masters of the past
    Composed innumerable holy scriptures
    In order to benefit future generations,
    And it is through application to these
    That we should enter into the Great Way.
    Study and master the five principal themes
    Of the wondrous teachings given by the Buddha:
    *Prajnaparamita, madhyamaka, pramana, abhidharma and
        vinaya.*[1]
    This is the true means of contributing
    To the preservation of the scriptural and insight
    Transmissions of the Dharma.

17. As for the members of the Sangha,
    They should try to live in mutual harmony
    And always be helpful to one another.
    They should constantly maintain with purity
    The vows entailed by their ordinations,
    Abide in the ways of Dharma and,
    By means of cherishing the eight excellences,
    Be sources of inspiration for living beings.

18. Their basis should be the free spirit of renunciation,
    The mind of non-attachment. On this foundation,
    The vows of the sevenfold restraints can be received.
    Not allowing the stain of a transgression
    In either the natural or prescribed disciplines,
    They should joyfully practice the three foundations—
    Fortnightly purification, annual rainy season retreat,
    And the special retreat concluding procedures—
    And thus make firm the victory banners
    Of discipline and spiritual liberation.

19. As for lay practitioners of the Dharma,
    The source of happiness and well-being for both
    Those maintaining the five lay vows
    And those not formally maintaining any commitments
    Is to avoid all forms of negative karma—
    Such as killing living beings—
    And to apply themselves purely to cultivation
    Of the ten wholesome courses of action.

20. O Three Jewels, release your blessings, that
    The living beings may turn their backs on
    Following useless and misdirected ways,
    And instead may strive continually
    To accomplish the always white truth.

21. The uncontrolled consumption of alcohol
    Strengthens the root of every weakness,
    And the use of tobacco is a weakness in itself.
    We should examine our activities of mind, speech and body,
    And regard negative habits as similar to poison.
    May we learn to be disgusted with our failings
    And resolve to avoid them from now on.

22. There is no need for me to list
    The detrimental effects of consuming alcohol,
    For Buddha himself spoke explicitly on the subject.
    As for tobacco, it is said to be a weed
    Born from the blood of a demon.
    When tobacco is smoked, the stench first rises
    And disturbs the celestial beings;
    It then descends and pollutes the
    Hundreds of thousands of [[naga]] lakes.
    This in turn leads to sickness, want and conflict,
    And the root of inauspicious conditions grows strong.

23. This is my summary of the advice found
    In the sutras, tantras, and precepts of the gurus.
    By means of it may trainees on the various levels
    Gain a more clear idea of what is to be cultivated
    And what abandoned in the practice of the path
    That produces goodness, liberation and enlightenment.

24. May trainees strive single-pointedly to accomplish
    The Dharma as explained in the sacred writings
    Of the Buddhas, Bodhisattvas and masters of the past.
    May they complete the six perfections
    And four ways of ripening trainees,
    The means of crossing over to the supreme ground
    Of victory, the jewel isle of Buddhahood
    Possessed of the three perfect *kayas*.

25. Some disciples from Eh-chil of Kham repeatedly
    Requested that I compose some verses of advice
    On how to live in correct practice of the Dharma.
    Therefore I, a Buddhist practitioner called Tub-ten,
    In the hope of providing useful guidance to others
    Have here taken up my pen and transcribed
    A few of the thoughts that arose in my mind concerning
    The many instructions received from my kind teachers.
    May it cause goodness and correct practice to increase,
    And may the living beings of the world
    Apply themselves joyfully to spiritual endeavor.

The colophon: In the Iron Mouse Year of the fifteenth sexantry, my philosophy instructor Go-mang Lob-zang Nga-wang approached me on behalf of some disciples of the Lower Kham area. It was their sincere wish that I write them a short verse work of spiritual advice on the nature of correct and incorrect Dharma practice, in order to inspire them in the cultivation of the wholesome. Therefore I have done so, with the prayer that the Doctrine and the living beings may benefit from it in some small way.

B. THOUGHTS TO BE HELD IN THE HEART

1. Homage to the spiritual masters and meditational deities
   Who are inseparable from Avalokiteshvara,
   The Bodhisattva of Compassion,
   Lord of the Potala Pure Land,
   In nature an embodiment of the ocean of Buddhas.
   With concentrated attention I call to you:
   Send out waves of your compassionate energy.

2. When stability in training has been accomplished,
   One can easily transform into aids on the path
   All negative conditions and unpleasant events
   That arise to disturb the mind,
   Such as illness, hindrances and problems.
   Cultivate the ability to implement correctly
   This essential oral instruction.

3. After birth, there is no possibility other
   Than eventually to meet with death.
   Death is constantly approaching us,
   And there is no method for turning it away.
   Therefore cultivate the ability to dedicate yourself
   Constantly to goodness from the depths of your heart.

4. At the moment apathy, sleep and laziness
   Seem to exert an insurmountable influence.
   But consider the misery of the lower realms,
   And think about when this misery will be yours.
   Cultivate the strength able to eliminate
   The tendencies of apathy, attachment and aversion
   That arise toward the the objects of perception.

5. Although involvement with the eight worldly concerns
   Can bring some immediate superficial benefits,
   In the long run it only harms us
   And hinders our chances for enlightenment.
   Generate the attitude that is disinterested in
   Activities that bring only temporary pleasure,
   And instead strive to attain the stage
   Of enlightenment's lasting joy.

6. Our lifespan is indefinite; no one
   Can prophesy exactly when we shall die.
   Therefore practice the enlightenment teachings.
   Find a quiet place of meditation
   Far from the hustle and bustle of the world.
   Take your example from the rhinocerous,
   Who is always content to live alone
   Without the company of distracting friends.

7. Tie the mind firmly with the rope
   Of the three supreme trainings, and guard these
   As carefully as the skull of your head.
   Become skilled in the spiritual trainings
   And wise in the ways of karmic law,
   That the paths leading to the lower realms
   May be cut off and closed forever.

8. There are those of us who have entered deeply
   Into the Doctrine by taking monastic vows,
   And who should live by the Dharma precepts.
   Yet we do not maintain our disciplines purely,
   And behave little better than pigs and dogs
   As we wander about town in search
   Of distraction, amusement and pleasure.
   Do not allow yourself even for a moment
   To engage in vain and fruitless activities.

9. Although the great meditator owns no wealth
   Nor property gained through cunning means,
   He will never die from hunger or cold.
   Try to follow his sublime example,
   And be able to live as a beggar
   Rather than accumulate wealth unscruplously.

10. We may obtain worldly property,
    But if our level of consciousness is coarse
    It is difficult to achieve the stage
    Even of a mere *chakravartin*.
    At death we must go on alone,
    Leaving behind all friends and possessions.
    Therefore cut off all compromise
    With samsara from this moment onward.

11. There is no need to cultivate a vast retinue
    Of friends and attendants who just increase your wants,
    And who care for you only out of selfish reasons.
    Instead, may your friends and attendants be spiritual qualities
    Such as wisdom and skillful effort,
    And may you always dwell untiringly
    In the essential practices of the teachings.

12. The blind beings wandering in samsara try
    To deceive others by claiming wrong as right;
    But the gurus and the enlightened beings
    Have eyes that see truth without obstruction.
    Hence always try to abide in correct practice
    Without being misled into mistaken paths.

13. Dedicate all your actions to the benefit
    Of the living beings and also the Doctrine.
    Strive in every way to accomplish
    The purpose of this and future lives.
    Constantly meditate and cultivate your mindstream
    Just as is described in the writings of the gurus.

14. Thus is concluded this brief text of advice
    Written according to my personal understanding
    Of the important points in training the mind,
    And from what I could remember
    Of the instructions of my gurus.
    May any white energy it possesses
    Act as a cause to inspire in practice
    People of a disposition similar to me.

15. If we can attune our minds
    To the teachings of the holy masters,
    Then we will be able to transcend the limits
    Of both samsara and nirvana,
    And attain the peerless state of Buddhahood.
    Of this there need be no doubts.
    Therefore I urge those of you with intelligence
    To make every effort to accomplish the path.

The colophon: This brief text of spiritual advice, entitled "Thoughts to be Held in the Heart," was written at the repeated request of Lob-zang Jang-chub Ten-pai Dron-me, who asked me to compose a verse work of spiritual advice in accordance with my personal experiences. Therefore when I was in Tha-khu-ral [of Mongolia] and was residing in the "Hermitage of Undying Joy" in Gan-den She-drub-ling Monastery, I wrote out the above reflections. May they contribute to goodness and spiritual happiness.

C. A MIRROR TO REFLECT ONE'S FAULTS

1. Om svasti!
   O Buddhas and Bodhisattvas, manifest your compassion
   That I might utterly uproot the faults and shortcomings
   Of both temporal and spiritual aspects of my life.
   O Avalokiteshvara, Bodhisattva of Compassion,
   Grant me your attention for a moment.

2. These days there are many false practitioners
   Who pretend to maintain the three higher trainings.
   They should hold their thoughts from wandering,
   And heed these words of mine.
   To benefit from a conversation
   There must be understanding; so pull in the puppy
   Of the mind's intellect, and listen well.

3. From beginningless time until this present life
   We have possessed countless samsaric bodies
   Born from the forces of ripening karma.
   But the opportunity to receive the scriptural
   And insight Dharmas of the Buddhas
   Has come to us only now.

4. By the force of previous good karma
   We have gained this jewel-like human body;
   Yet because of our deep attachment
   To mundane daily routines,
   It is very rare for us to meet
   With a qualified spiritual master.

5. And even when we try to devote ourselves
   To a teacher of the Great Way,
   Our confidence in the guru-disciple relationship
   Seems to be limited to mere words.
   Then, due to our negative attitudes,
   We do little but open even further
   The door to the lower realms.

6. Thus although we hold in our very hands the means
   To benefit both this and future lives,
   Due to our own stupidity we throw it away
   And instead wander after the false images that appear.
   An entire human lifespan passes like that!

7. This easily lost body produced from the elements
   Will not possess the puppy of consciousness for long;
   And if we do not contemplate the four great sufferings—
   Birth, sickness, old age and death—
   We will certainly go empty-handed
   From this life into the next.

8. We have no ability to proclaim
   How long we will remain in this life
   Nor where we shall go in the next.
   And even if we make a hundredfold effort
   To satisfy the spirit through materialistic ways,
   Not the slightest fruit is attained.

9. We see that the bodies of the old,
   The young and the in-between become
   Nothing but food for dogs and vultures,
   Yet somehow we don't sense that our own body
   Will soon share this identical fate.
   When our natural condition leads only to death,
   How amazing that we sit casually
   As our time steadily ebbs away.

10. The words of the Buddha clearly describe
    The nature of the hot and cold hells;
    But we fail to grasp their significance,
    And even now continue to make plans
    For more meaningless worldly works.
    It is as though our mind has fallen
    Under the spell of the agents of darkness.

11. Many of us have had the excellent opportunity
    To receive the vows of the *brahmacharya* trainings[3]
    In the presence of an abbot and *acharya*;
    Yet we do not maintain our commitments, and instead
    Transgress both natural and prescribed precepts.
    We are but shameless imitations of the Sangha
    Falsely enjoying offerings made by the faithful.

12. With a mind burdened by the weight
    Of these many failings and downfalls,
    We listen to a few discourses
    On the vast and profound Dharma.
    But although we pretend to be counted
    In the fold of pure practitioners,
    The basis of our inner motivation is only
    Jealousy, pride and the competitive spirit.

13. The compassionate energy of the enlightened beings
    Is present in all times and places;
    But the Buddhas cannot remove our negativities
    By washing us with water,
    Nor can they eliminate our sufferings
    Like extracting a thorn with their hands.

14. It is only by means of their teachings
    That they are able to be of benefit to us;
    But their teachings we ignore!
    Thus we wander weak and protectorless
    Under the dark powers of karma and delusion,
    And are about to stagger over the cliff
    Falling into the three lower realms.
    May the great gurus look upon us,
    And hold us in their compassion.

15. May we maintain constant awareness
    Of the shortcomings of worldly indulgence,
    And not become distracted by ephemeral works.
    May we purify the stream of our being
    By means of the three higher trainings,
    And take to completion the deeds
    Of the stages and paths of enlightenment.

16. In this and in all future lives,
    May we dwell on the pure and sublime paths.
    May we manifest the state of supreme liberation,
    And become spiritual guides to the countless beings.

17. The mindless prattling in this poem
    Written by a mad irreligious beggar
    May become an object of jest to scholars.
    Indeed, I must openly confess
    That all I have really done here
    Is list all of my own faults
    And attribute them to others.

The colophon: This brief advice, intended as a spur to inspire the mind in the practice of the Mahayana *lo-jong* (mind-training) tradition, is entitled "A Mirror to Reflect One's Faults." It was written at the request of the Tong-khor Tul-ku, Ho-tuk-tu Lob-zang Jik-me Tsul-trim Gya-tso, who asked me for a verse work of this nature.

These days most practitioners are guided largely by negative influences. They reverse the trainings in karmic law, cultivating evil rather than goodness and abandoning goodness rather than evil. Thus in general they destroy the very root of their trainings. The legacy of using the teachings of the sutras and tantras for the cultivation of one's own mindstream rather than as a prop for one's ego has become as rare as a daytime star. Therefore I composed the above in order to try and straighten out those who are prone to the same failings as I, and with the hope of creating a more clear understanding within the community of Buddhist practitioners.

D. ESSENCE OF THE SPIRITUAL INSTRUCTIONS
(A poem of advice to benefit the mind)

1. Namo!
   Homage to the spiritual masters, embodiments of all Refuges.
   Homage to the Buddhas and Bodhisattvas, and also
   To the holders of the ear-whispered lineages.
   O holy gurus, vast fields of merit,
   Release your blessings here and now.

2. From beginningless time until this very life
   We have been tormented by the evil demon Delusion.
   Propelled by a distorted mind, the door of aversion
   And attachment to worldly concerns has been held open,
   And we have been made to wander in cyclic existence.

3. Even now, those of us of rough character
   Continue in the ways of negativity.
   If we consider the results of bad karma,
   We see that it produces only states of misery
   From whence it is difficult to evolve to joy.

4. But now we have achieved a rare human rebirth,
   Have met with the precious holy gurus,
   And live in a time when Dharma flourishes.
   Thus it would be most appropriate now
   To apply ourselves intensely to the path.

5. This life, like dew on a blade of grass,
   Can be lost at any moment.
   We should strive immediately to accomplish Dharma,
   That benefits both here and hereafter.
   Not practicing now will later bring regret,
   And what good can regret produce?

6. It is easy to boast and say, "I practice Dharma well,"
   And easy to flaunt one's so-called righteousness;
   But if one's days and nights are pervaded
   By attachment to the eight worldly concerns,
   Religion just becomes a nest for faults
   That will be difficult to sweep away.

7. Seeing the imperfect nature of humanity,
   The Enlightened One was deeply moved by compassion.
   In order to lead to the highest eternal joy
   The protectorless beings of this degenerate age,
   He expounded the vast and profound Dharma.

8. Should we apply ourselves correctly
   And make intense efforts to accomplish this path,
   We too can achieve final Buddhahood.
   And a Buddha, having taken to completion
   The qualities of transcendence and insight,
   Has no need to rely upon direct or indirect advice.

9. Therefore search out the numerous teachings,
   And apply their meanings to the cultivation
   Of your own body, speech and mind.
   Then, having gained realization, it is befitting
   To give unmistaken teachings to others
   In order to share your benefits with the world.

10. The study of *pramana* is the door releasing
    The lucid energy of the mind's intellect.
    Having done this, learn in detail
    Both the *madhyamaka* and *prajnaparamita* scriptures.
    Also, cherish the precious *vinaya* teachings,
    And master the seven divisions of the *abhidharma*.[4]
    These five subjects constitute the wing of learning,
    The scriptural basis of the Mahayana tradition,

11. As for the practice instructions that extract
    The essence of these many scriptures,
    These are outlined in the legacy called *Lam Rim*,[5]
    Which is also known as "Stages of the Path to Enlightenment
    Through the Three Levels of Spiritual Application."
    This is the one road traveled by all the Buddhas,
    The faultless tradition of the great masters of the past.
    Accomplish the meditations of this transmission
    And extract the essence of Buddha's thought.

12. The *Lam Rim* outlines the fundamental trainings,
    The practices common to both the Sutra and Tantra Vehicles.
    Having generated mastery of them within your mindstream,
    Apply yourself to the two yogic stages of the tantric path,
    That eliminates the mundane perception of the world
    And causes all that manifests to arise within
    The vision of continual bliss and void.

13. In order to accomplish the tantric path by achieving
    The *vajrakaya* possessed of the two perfections,
    Guard well the tantric vows and commitments.
    Then the four initiations that ripen one's stream of being
    Will reach fulfillment, to produce quick enlightenment
    And the power to accomplish the good of self and others.

14. Like the sun, the compassion of the Enlightened Ones
    Shines equally on all living beings;
    But those who are spiritually ripe
    Are able to reap the greater benefit from it.
    The difference lies on the side of the trainees;
    The Buddhas themselves do not discriminate.
    Therefore try to cultivate spiritual maturity.

15. In brief, in accordance with your capacity,
    Apply yourself in every way to realization of
    The scriptural and insight aspects of the Doctrine,
    And to the benefit of the living beings.
    These indeed are praiseworthy pursuits.

The colophon: These verses of advice for the cultivation of the mind, entitled "Essence of the Spiritual Instructions," were written at the request of Ge-she Nga-wang Tsul-trim of Kum-bum Monastery of Eastern Tibet, who expressed his need for a brief text of quintessential precepts. Therefore I have summarized the instructions that I myself received from my own spiritual teachers, and have herein arranged them as a gnomic poem.

I wrote the piece while residing in the hermitage "Radiance of Enlightenment" at Ra-deng Monastery, a Dharma seat upholding the tradition uniting the streams of the three Ka-dam-pa lineages.

May any merits it contains act as a cause of goodness and inspiration for living beings.

E. HUM OF THE SIX-LEGGED BEE
   (A poem of spiritual advice, together with a prayer to be cared for by the compassionate gurus)

1. Homage to the Buddha, an incomparable teacher,
   He of the sugarcane garden;
   To the scriptural and insight Dharmas,
   A treasury of precious realization;
   And also to the three types of Sangha,
   Upholders of the Three Vehicles.
   And homage also to Lama Tsong-kha-pa,
   Supreme emanation of Manjushri, the Wisdom Bodhisattva.

2. You have met with the glorious unbroken lineage
   Of Lama Tsong-kha-pa, that so skillfully unites
   All teachings of the sutras and tantras,
   A most rare and opportune encounter.
   How wonderful that you have thus entered
   Through the door of the Dharma
   And are cared for by a Mahayana guru
   Accomplished in both learning and practice,
   And possessing the four spiritual qualities.

3. But remember that this illusory body is impermanent
   With no certainty of when it shall perish.
   To squander it on worldly goals
   Will benefit neither this nor future lives.
   There are many people who ignore spiritual values;
   Without exception, they die with an empty heart.

4. Take control of your mind right now.
   Do not lose this opportunity to the apathy
   That says, "Tomorrow or the next day."
   Now is the time to meditate on the teachings.
   Then there will be no cause for regret
   When you become a guest of the Lord of Death.

5. Most of us dedicate our lives solely
   To the pursuit of fruitless, worldly activities.
   Our lifespan constantly drains away
   As day after day is given to meaningless purposes
   And we bicker with others and chase selfish ends.
   Thus we dwell in opposition to karmic law
   And lose touch with the rays of compassion
   Of the holy objects of Refuge.

6. Then, cut off from spiritual inspiration,
   Our rare and precious human life,
   A product of tremendous merit,
   Becomes lost to unconscious living.
   Nothing but negative karma is generated,
   And we fall deeply into states of misery
   Far from the paths leading to joy.

7. The nature of karmic law is infallible;
   The fruits of white and black action are certain.
   Therefore do not confuse the practices
   Of eliminating negativity and cultivating goodness.
   Be confident of your ability to fulfill
   The purposes of this and future lives,
   For the compassion of the Enlightened Ones
   Is with you, and is measureless.

8. Make efforts to accomplish within yourself
   The stages of the path to enlightenment
   Through the three levels of spiritual application.
   Do not mistake the trainings;
   Transcend what is to be transcended
   And cultivate what is to be accomplished.
   Do not ignore the advice of Buddha.

9. At this auspicious time when you have met
   With the Yellow Hat tradition, that
   Does not confuse coarse or subtle points
   In the practices leading to enlightenment,
   And that presents the sublime teachings of Buddha
   With the full force of the rational mind,
   Try to live an exemplary lifestyle
   Of philosophy and meditation worthy of this legacy.
   Strive unerringly at the supreme methods
   That lead from joy to higher joy.

10. Offer the prayer that, by practicing thus,
    You may never be separated in this life,
    The *bar-do*, and in all future incarnations
    From the holy masters who embody the realizations
    Of the lineage of mighty Tsong-kha-pa;
    And may you always dwell within their compassion.

11. As is prophesied in the *The Root Tantra of Manjushri*,
    We who live in this Himalayan nation of Tibet,
    A land adorned by valleys of medicinal herbs,
    Are especially blessed by Avalokiteshvara;
    For when the flower of the Tibetan people
    Was tossed into the initiation mandala,
    It fell to the quarter of the Bodhisattva of Compassion.

12. Thus it is through the strength of the merits
    Generated over many previous lifetimes
    That we have been reborn as humans in this land
    Where Dharma thrives with such strength.
    We are vessels very capable of fulfillment
    And realization of the enlightenment teachings,
    And have a legacy of many holy gurus.
    We stand on the threshold of greatness;
    Our life is a unique conjunction of events.

13. Therefore detach yourself from superficial activities
    And abide within the sublime tradition
    Of cultivating the spiritual path
    That is based on the ten wholesome ways.
    Also, strive day and night to generate
    The sixteen qualities of a noble human being.

14. Make these your constant aspirations:
    "May I study the profound and holy teachings
    And, not mistaking their meanings,
    Take their themes as personal advice.
    May I apply myself with all my strength
    To practice of the ear-whispered instructions
    And thus fulfill the legacy of the masters.

15. "May I first purify my stream of being
   By means of the exoteric Sutrayana teachings.
   Then may I enter into the secret Mantrayana,
   Accomplish both coarse and subtle tantric yogas
   Of the generation and completion stages,
   And in one short lifetime arrive at the end
   Of the path leading to peerless Buddhahood
   Having the nature of the five Tathagata families.

16. "But should this final attainment not be achieved
   Before I meet with death, then in my future lives
   May I always achieve positive rebirths
   And continue my practice of the Mahayana.
   May I be cared for constantly by Avalokiteshvara,
   And become one of his chief spiritual sons
   Upholding the mysterious ways of a Bodhisattva.

17. "May every creative effort I make
   Act as a cause of peerless enlightenment.
   May the holy gurus, embodiments
   Of everything good and powerful,
   Hear this request of mine
   And accept responsibility to guide me
   From now until enlightenment is achieved."

The colophon: This poem of spiritual advice, together with a prayer to be cared for by the compassionate gurus, is entitled "Hum of the Six-legged Bee."

It was written at the request of Ah-rong Tul-ku from Kham, who strongly upholds the threefold tradition of study, contemplation and meditation, and has caused the sun of the Buddhadharma to shine with brilliance in the east during this degenerate age. He had sent me a letter requesting me to write a verse work of advice to him, together with a prayer to be cared for by the holy gurus.

Therefore I looked over various works of this nature found in the writings of the masters of the past, with the thought to just send him one. It seemed to me that one of these would suffice, and that it would be unnecessary for me to compose anything new.

But then I hesitated, not wanting to disappoint him; for indeed he seemed to have asked out of genuine faith and because of the strength of our spiritual relationship.

However, I am not possessed of the pure white vision of a man caught in the middle of a snowstorm, and confess that I write from the perspective of my own personal limited understanding. Nonetheless, may those of a perspective similar to mine find some meaning in it.

Fifth Dalai Lama

5 The Most Secret Cycle Of The Mystical Mandala of Hayagriva

(Ritual manuals of initiation and the consecration of medicines, in accordance with the occultly revealed lineages of Gong-pa Zil-non Zhe-pa Tsal,[1] the Fifth Dalai Lama)

PART ONE: A LONGEVITY INITIATION

Homage to the immortal guru Tso-kye Dor-je,
Embodiment of the three Buddha *kayas*,
He born magically from a lotus;
And homage to the nine Heruka deities
Of the most secret Hayagriva mandala.
With reverence I bow to them
And request their inspiring blessings.

(I) The Preamble

Here, from among the many lineages of the Pure Visionary tradition (Tib., *dag-snang*) of the Fifth Dalai Lama that are related to *Yang-sang Gya-chen*, or "The Sealed Transmission of the Most Secret Mandala of Hayagriva," is a ritual text on longevity initiation and the consecration of medicines in accordance with the mystical tradition coming from Lama Tso-kye Dor-je Ku-sum Rik-du, the Lotus Born Guru who is an emanation of the three Buddha *kayas.*

The master who is leading the rite should begin the practice early in the morning. He commences with the usual procedures of taking refuge, generating the bodhimind, and so forth, as outlined in the standard texts. He then performs the self-initiation rite, together with the *tsok* (tantric feast) offering.

The disciples are invited to enter the room. They symbolically wash, flowers are given out and then offered, the *tor-ma* (sacrifical cake) for the removal of hindrances is offered, and the protection circle is established.

When these preliminaries have been completed, the master explains the Dharma in general and then in particular. [That is, he first explains the general nature of the the the Buddhist path, and then says something on this particular lineage.]

(II) A Survey of the Dharma in General and also of this Particular Tradition

Hark! In order to be of maximum benefit to the countless living beings, whose number is as vast as the extent of the skies, one must first gain the state of peerless, complete, perfect Buddhahood. It is with this thought in mind that one receives initiation, the root of the Vajrayana path, and then engages in the various tantric yogas.

Contemplate this theme, and by means of it generate the sublime bodhimind as the motivating factor. Also, cultivate the correct attitudes that are to be maintained when listening to the Dharma, as is explained in the many sutras and tantras, and thus listen correctly.

The Buddha, who himself achieved complete enlightenment, and who possessed profound skill and great compassion, taught the nectarlike Dharma in accordance with the mental tendencies, capacities and karmic predispositions of those to be trained.

The doctrines that he taught may be categorized in various ways. An elaborate manner of doing so is to speak of the Nine Vehicles, or *Yanas.* Alternatively, these nine may be abbreviated into two: the Hinayana and Mahayana, or Small and Great Vehicles.

In turn the second of these, the Mahayana, is often subdivided into two: the exoteric Causal Prajnaparamitayana (Transcendent Wisdom Vehicle); and the esoteric Resultant Guhyamantrayana (Secret Mantra Vehicle). These two have the same basic focus (Tib., *don*), yet the latter is said to be superior to the former for four specific reasons: it is uncontrived; it has more methods at its disposal; its techniques are easier to accomplish; and it is especially designed for those of highest capacity. These four points are clearly outlined in *A Lamp on the Three Ways* (Tib., *Tshul-gsum-sgron-me*), wherein we read, "The Resultant Vajrayana is superior for four reasons...."[2]

As for the Resultant Secret Mantra Vehicle, it can be subdivided into two levels of practice: the External Vajrayana of three outer classes of tantras — *kriya*, *charya* and *yoga*; and the Internal Vajrayana, which refers to the *anuttara yoga* tantras, or "Highest Yoga" tantras. The transmission to be dealt with in this treatise belongs to this second category.

Furthermore, the Secret Mantra Vehicle lineages found in Tibet are of two distinct types: those transmitted through the Old School, or Nying-ma; and those transmitted through the New Schools, or Sarma [which refers to the Sa-kya, Kar-gyu and Ge-luk]. The Old School lineages of the Hayagriva Tantra are superior to those found in the New Schools.

Within the Old School, there are three different lines of transmission of this tradition: the "distant lineage" of the original instructions [i.e., *The Root Tantra*, or *rTsa-rgyud*]; and two "close lineages" — the "discovered treasure texts," and the "profound pure vision texts."

The system that is the subject of this treatise is from the pure visionary experiences of the White Lotus Holder Gong-pa Zil-non Zhepa Tsal, the Fifth Dalai Lama.

The outer, inner and secret biographies of the great lamas of the past speak of three types of pure visionary experiences: those received in dreams; those received in meditation; and direct mystical communications. This particular tradition belongs to the last of these, for Gong-pa Zil-non Zhe-pa Tsal was continually absorbed in the wisdom dance that experiences all appearances as pure vision, and was in constant communion with the oceanic deeds of the great *aryas* who are purified in spirit. Thus all his visionary experiences were pure direct cognitions.

The tantric lineages that he received in this way he later transmitted to those of his more advanced disciples who possessed conducive karmic predispositions. However, so that those who were not sufficiently mature would be unable to misuse these mystical teachings, he marked them with the seal of secrecy in the same way that the great guru Dharmodgata had sealed the *prajnaparamita* teachings seven times.

Therefore the tradition has come to be known far and wide as *Zab-cho Gya-chen,* or "The Profound Dharmas of the Sealed Transmission."

There are numerous scriptures in this "sealed" genre that were written by Gong-sa Zil-non Zhe-pa Tsal. That to be dealt with here belongs to those marked by the seal of the mystic knot. It should not be given to those practitioners who are dominated by indecisiveness or by negative preconceptions.

(III) *The Story of the Mystical Origins of this Profound Transmission.*

It was the eleventh day of the twelfth month of the Water Ox Year (late 1673 or early 1674). The Fifth Dalai Lama was performing various mystical rituals with the Nying-ma yogi Jang-ter Dak-po Rik-zin Chen-po Tul-ku. The fundamental structure of the procedures was based on the occult lineages of Guru Tso-kye Dor-je Ku-sum Rik-du, with *tor-ma* rites to remove hindrances in accordance with the *Lama Gomg-du* tradition and also longevity rites accomplished by means of sheep-shaped effigies, etc.

During the ritual, the Fifth Dalai Lama experienced the following vision.

In the space before him appeared Guru Tso-kye Dor-je, seated at the center of a vast sun disc and locked in sexual union with his consort. To his left appeared the yogi Cho-gyal Ta-shi Tob-gyal, seated on a thick cushion, dressed in white clothing, pressing down on the earth with his right hand, and holding his left at his heart in the *mudra* of supreme generosity.

To his [Guru Tso-kye Dor-je's] right, sitting slightly lower, appeared the yogi Cho-gyal Rik-zin Nga-gi Wang-po.[3] He was seated on a moon disc, was dressed in a mystical hat and occult shawl, and was wearing the robes of a monk. His right hand was at his heart, and his left, poised above his lap in the *mudra* of meditation, held a longevity vase.

During the phase of the ritual when the life energies of the five Buddha families are visualized as being summoned, light-rays suddenly burst forth from the heart of Guru Tso-kye Dor-je. The tips of the rays bore the five Dhyani Buddhas and five families of *dakinis,* each in the color of the respective direction of the light-ray. The *dakinis* were carrying longevity arrows with auspicious threads hanging from the tips, and as they waved them the Fifth Dalai Lama actually felt the threads caress the crown of his head.

When the ritual arrived at the phase when the *tor-mas* and sheep-shaped effigies are carried outside and discarded, Cho-gyal Wang-po De rose from his seat and, brandishing a mystic dagger, performed a wrathful tantric dance. His appearance was extremely forceful, and all hindrances and obstructing elements were immediately expelled.

At that point the life energies of the collection of the three Buddha *kayas* were drawn forth. The lama dressed in white then reached out. In his hand was a longevity arrow draped in threads, with which he made a summoning gesture.

The names of two lamas, Yol-mo Tul-ku and Zur-chen Cho-ying Rang-drol, resounded from the sky, and the Fifth Dalai Lama's attention moved over to Lama Wang-po De. Instantly Yol-mo Tul-ku appeared to his [Lama Wang-po De's] right. He was standing in the royal posture and was dressed in white. His long hair was tied back in a braid, and with his right hand he was turning a rosary made of *raksha* beads. To Wang-po De's left, sitting on a slightly lower cushion, appeared Lama Zur-chen Cho-ying Rang-drol [the Fifth Dalai Lama's root guru in the Hayagriva yogas]. He was dressed in the red robes of a monk, wore the pointed hat of a *pandit*, and was seated in the meditation posture.

Suddenly Lama Zur-chen stood up, folded his hands together at his heart, and spoke the following words, "Kye hoh! Pay heed. The longevity deities of the mandala of the three Buddha *kayas*..." and so forth, thus transmitting the oral instructions of this unique lineage.

When he had finished speaking, a stream of nectars flowed forth from the longevity vase in Guru Tso-kye Dor-je's hand. They came to the crown of the Fifth Dalai Lama's head and entered his body, completely filling it. He had the sensation that his central energy channel became as firm as an iron arrow, and had red half-*vajras* at the top and bottom. He later commented that this sensation continued for almost the entire day.

At the conclusion of the vision, the entire assembly of gurus, including Guru Tso-kye Dor-je, dissolved into Lama Wang-po De. Wang-po De then placed his hand on the Fifth Dalai Lama's heart and said, "Do not forget the instructions that have been transmitted to you." He then transformed into a ball of light and dissolved into the Fifth Dalai Lama. The Fifth experienced a strong sense of bliss and void united.

That then is the story of the origins of this unusual tantric legacy, a tradition born from auspicious conditions and the unfolding of a great mass of virtue, a wondrous and sacred transmission having the powerful blessings of the revealed "close lineage" of the omniscient Dor-je Tok-me Tsal [i.e., the Fifth Dalai Lama].

As for the procedures of performing the longevity initiation that is the central pillar of this tradition, these involve two topics: the activities to be performed by the guru alone; and the activities that involve the disciples.

(IV) *The Activities to be Performed by the Guru*

The preliminary activities to be performed by the guru have been explained above — taking refuge, generating the bodhimind, performing the self-initiation ritual, making the *tsok* offering, and so forth.

Beyond that, his functions involve the participation of the disciples and therefore will be explained below.

(V) *The Activities That Involve the Disciples*

The initiating master begins by instructing the disciples:

> In order to receive the blessings of the mandala divinities, who are to be seen as inseparable from the guru, you should first make the offering symbolic of the universe [i.e., the mandala offering].

The disciples do so. The master continues:

> You have performed the symbolic offering well. Now you should request the initiation. But in order to do so you should first generate the following mental image.
>
> This house that we are in is not to be regarded as an ordinary dwelling. Rather, see it as a mystical tantric mansion standing in the legendary pure land of Nga-yab-ling (rNga-yab-gling).
>
> The guru is sitting at the center of this tantric mansion. Although in nature he is your personal guru, visualize him as having the form of Guru Tso-kye Dor-je, the Lotus-Born Guru, embodiment of all the Buddhas of the past, present and future. Generate undivided conviction and make the following request:

Kye!!! O guru, embodiment of the three *kayas*,
Grant us the holy initiation.
Grant us protection from the dangers
Of sudden, premature death.

When this has been repeated three times, the guru admonishes the disciples to create the following visualization, and to take heartfelt refuge and to generate the bodhimind aspiration to highest enlightenment:

In the space before you appears the guru inseparable from the principal deity of the mandala. He is surrounded by myriads of Buddhas, gurus, meditational deities, dakas, dakinis and Dharma Protectors.

Generate the firm determination to practice in accordance with their instructions and not to transgress their words.

Fixing your mind single-pointedly on this image, repeat the following verses after me three times,

Dharmakaya Amitabha, lord of life energies,
Samboghakaya Avalokiteshvara, the Bodhisattva of
    Compassion,
And *nirmanakaya* Padma Sambhava, subduer of living
    beings:
I take refuge in these three supreme beings.

In order to be of maximum benefit to the living beings
Whose number is as vast as the extent of space,
I will practice according to the ways
Established by these three sublime beings,
Embodiments of the three *kayas*.

I will free all living beings
From the dangers of premature death,
And will lead them to the stage
Of supreme, peerless enlightenment.

When this has been said three times, generate the confidence that refuge and the bodhimind have been made firm. Then create the visualization of the field of merit:

> Guru, meditational divinities, *dakas* and *dakinis*,
> I summon you to come forth now
> And sit before me on these thrones
> Each of which is made from
> A sun, a moon and a lotus flower.
>
> I bow to you with body, speech and mind,
> Make outer, inner and secret offerings,
> Confess every weakness, negativity and obscuration,
> And rejoice in the practice of the Secret Mantra Vehicle.
>
> Pray, turn the Dharma wheel of the Secret Mantra Vehicle,
> That so matures and frees the mind.
> Do not pass away into *parinirvana*,
> But remain for the benefit of living beings.
>
> And all my merits of body, speech and mind
> I myself will dedicate with purity
> For the benefit of the world.
> May insight into the pure *vajra* knowledge arise.

Each of the disciples now must develop the vision of himself/herself as a mandala divinity. This is done by means of the following liturgy:

> From the sphere of the *dharmadhatu*,
> In the nature of great compassion,
> My mind appears as the syllable hrih.
> This transforms into a pure realm
> For both vessel and contents,
> The legendary Sindhu Lake, at the center of which
> Is a throne made from lotus, sun and moon.

There I sit as Guru Tso-kye Dor-je,
Having one face and two hands.
My appearance is that of a sixteen year old,
And my face is white tinged with red.
Above the top of my crown protrusion
Is a tiny green horse's head,
And above that, in nature Amitabha Buddha,
Is a small ball of radiant light.

My right hand holds a *vajra*,
My left a longevity vase,
And I sit in sexual union with the consort
Chandali, who is white tinged with red.
She holds a longevity arrow and vase,
And her arms are wrapped around me.
Both of us are draped in ornaments
Of jewels and human bone,
We wear silks and flower garlands, and
Are sitting amidst a halo of five hues.

The three syllables — *om, ah* and *hum* —
Stand at the male's crown, throat and heart,
And at the heart of the consort
Is a sun and moon disc surrounded
By the syllables of the life mantra.

Above the male's crown is a moon disc, and on it
Sits the *samboghakaya* form of Avalokiteshvara.
At his heart, on a sun and moon disc,
Is the *nirmanakaya* emanation Padma Sambhava.
Surrounding the male and the consort
Are countless *dakas* and *dakinis*.

The master then picks up the longevity arrow and calls forth for
the blessings of the field of merit:

HUM! HRIH! Guru Tso-kye Dor-je,
He complete with the three Buddha *kayas*,
Please empower this secret mandala.
Cause these substances which produce longevity
To glow with a special power.
Bestow the powerful initiations
And release the exalted *siddhis*.
Om ah hum hrih vajra guru ayur jnana siddhi phal abeshaya ah ah.

The master then touches the statue to the head of each of the disciples while saying:

HRIH! Guru Tso-kye Dor-je,
Embodiment of the three Buddha *kayas*,
Bestow the powerful blessings
Of the physical marks and signs of perfection
Upon these trainees of good fortune.
May they gain the life power
Of the immortal *vajra* body.
Om ah hum hrih vajra guru ayur jnana siddhi phal renra bhum hum jaka ah ah.

The master should recite this mantra three times, with the disciples repeating it after him. He then touches the rosary to the throat of each disciple while saying:

HRIH! Guru Tso-kye Dor-je,
Embodiment of the three Buddha *kayas*,
Bestow the powerful blessings of divine speech
Upon these trainees of good fortune.
May they gain the life power
Of pure, faultless speech.
Om a hum hrih vajra guru ayur jnana siddhi phal hum vamkha abhishiccha ah.

The mirror, symbol of the *vajra* mind, is touched to the heart of each of the disciples:

HRIH! Guru Tso-kye Dor-je,
Embodiment of the three Buddha *kayas*,
Bestow the powerful blessings
Of the mind of bliss and void united
Upon these trainees of good fortune.
May they gain the life power
Of an undistorted mind.
Om ah hum hrih vajra guru ayur jnana siddhi phal hum chitta ab-hishiccha hum.

The initiation vase is touched to the crown of the head of each disciple:

OM! This vase is the tantric mansion.
From it flows forth ambrosial nectars
Of the deities of the three Buddha *kayas*,
Which wash away the stains of delusion
And of grasping at the appearance of duality
From within trainees of good fortune.
May they gain the life power
Of the immortal *vajra* wisdom.
Om ah hum hrih vajra guru ayur jnana siddhi phal hum kalasha ab-hishiccha om ah hum hrih.

Thus by the power of the longevity initiation, the ambrosial nectars of immortality flow forth. They fill the body of each of the disciples, and overflow from the crown aperture. The overflow crystalizes above the crown of each disciple and forms into the shape of a horse's head, green in color and releasing neighing sounds. Above this is red Hayagriva, holding a club in his right hand and showing the threatening *mudra* with his left. Tiny *vajras* and sparks of flame emanate from Hayagriva's body, forming a ring of protection around the body of each of the disciples.

The master now places the longevity arrow in the hand of each of the disciples and says:

HRIH! Now you have a special body
Ablaze with *vajra* wisdom
Emitting sparks of flame as hot
As the fire at the end of time.
Thus you have gained protection
From the evil forces and hindrances
That wait in watch for the chance to harm.

Thus is complete the steps of the method for attaining the blessings and initiations that produce longevity by relying upon the Hayagriva lineages of Guru Tso-kye Dor-je as clarified and enhanced by the pure visionary experiences of Gong-pa Zil-non Zhe-pa Tsal, the Fifth Dalai Lama.

PART TWO: A RITE OF MEDICINAL CONSECRATION

Herein follows a healing and medicinal empowerment in accordance with the tradition of the nine deity mandala of *Tam-din Pad-ma Wang-chen*, or "The Powerful Lotus Lord Hayagriva."

(I) *Making the Request and Establishing the Correct Motivation*

The initiating master begins the rite by giving the disciples the following instructions:

If you wish to participate in the healing initiation and medicinal empowerment related to the mandala of the nine wrathful deities of the glorious, powerful Most Secret Lotus Lord Hayagriva, then repeat this request after me three times,

O Vajraraja, bestow blessings and initiation
Of the highest *siddhis* of body, speech and mind
Upon this supreme, secret mandala.
Manifest now from the sphere of Samantabhadra.

The master continues:

Ah! In order to be of full benefit to all living beings, you should try to attain in this very lifetime the enlightenment state symbolized by glorious Hayagriva. This should be your motivation in participating in this healing initiation and medicinal empowerment related to the tantric cycle of practice connected with the nine deity mandala of Most Secret Lotus Lord Hayagriva. Then, by means of using the mystical substances, one will be able to accomplish vast benefits for self and others.

This should be your fundamental motivation when listening to this profound Dharma.

(II) *A General Survey of the Dharma and of This Particular Lineage*

As for the Dharma that is to be transmitted, the original source is of course the Buddha himself. This wonderful friend of all living beings, who showed partiality to none, out of profound skill and great compassion taught the eighty-four thousand branches of the doctrine. All of these were but methods to cultivate the minds of the various types of trainees.

These eighty-four thousand branches of the doctrine all collect into the twofold division of sutras and tantras, or the Causal Sutrayana and Resultant Vajrayana. Of these two, the Resultant Vajrayana is the superior.

The Vajrayana itself is spoken of in various ways. One such way is to speak of the four classes of tantras. Of these, the fourth and supreme is the *anuttara* yoga class, or "highest yoga tantras." It is to this tantric division that the mandala of the Most Secret Lotus Lord Hayagriva belongs.

Guru Padma Sambhava, who was like a second Buddha, once wrote,

The Buddhas, fully understanding
The different stages of the mind,
Taught the Secret Mantra Vehicle.
Of all the various doctrines,
This vehicle is supreme;
For it contains all the essential points
Of all levels of training,
And produces quick enlightenment.

Also, *The Subsequent Tantra of Mystical Emanation (sGyu-'phrul-'gyi-rgyud-phyi-ma)* states,

> Because it is free from karma and delusion,
> Its powers of mantra, *mudra* and *samadhi*
> Purify and bless the five impure substances
> And transform them into the five nectars.
> The mystical syllables *ya, ham, na, bam,* and *wa*
> Transform the five meats into five luminosities.
>
> By arising in the form of a tantric deity
> And applying the methods of purification,
> Then merely by eating the consecrated substances
> Powerful *siddhis* are achieved
> And the *yogini* attainments are gained.
> There is no method more powerful than this.

And *The Directly Imparted Tantra of Glorious Heruka (dPal-he-ru-gah-mngon-pham-'byung-bai-rgyud)* states,

> Honey, vermillion and camphor
> Are mixed with red sandalwood powder.
> This is placed in with the *tsok* offering.
> The *vajra* is then taken up,
> And the *mudra* is shown.
> The yogi then proceeds with awareness
> And tastes the substances.
> The mere contact produces *siddhi*.
> The five filths become five pure substances
> And produce every powerful attainment.

Moreover, it is said that all accomplishments arise from ingesting the mystical substances. Even the immortal *vajra* body itself can be attained in this way. When one's own vision is pure, the entire universe is seen as a divine mandala and everything in the three worlds is seen as ambrosial nectar.

The Eight Volumes on Ambrosial Substances (bDud-rtsi-bam-brgyad) states,

Ultimately speaking, the three worlds
Are in nature constructed from the five nectars,
And all living beings by nature are perfect Buddhas.
The three times, three worlds,
And the body, speech and mind
Ultimately are only ambrosial nectars.
This truth is pronounced from the highest sphere.

Thus, as said above, the basis of everything in existence ultimately is only ambrosial nectar, and all living beings share in the nature of perfect enlightenment. But because of the distortions to perception caused by the impure prejudiced mind, we see the world as impure.

However, if we should come to be cared for and guided by a qualified tantric guru and should we practice correctly in accordance with his instructions, then by the power of being shown the central points of the path of the Secret Mantra Vehicle we come to directly perceive for ourselves the essential, pure nature of that which had previously appeared to us as impure. This is how being shown the conventional level of truth leads to an understanding of the ultimate. Thus it is important that we clearly understand the main points of how an appreciation of the conventional directs the mind to a higher knowledge of the nectar-like ultimate.

The Compendium Sutra (*'Dus-pa-mdo*) states,

Countless Buddhas of the past
Made these their main trainings.
Because they held them as supreme *samayas*,
They are famed as "classical disciplines."

Also, *The Tantra on Excellent Nectar* (*bDud-rtsi-mchog-gi-rgyud*) states,

Mainly there are five supreme nectars.
Eight root and a thousand branch ingredients
Are combined to make the ambrosial medicines
Which become *samaya* substances.
The syllables *ka, sa, ya,* and *na*
Transform these into great medicines;
And then by eating these substances
The common and supreme *siddhis* are achieved.

As for the authoritative scriptural sources on which this tantric tradition of achieving *siddhi* by means of relying upon mystical substances is based, these are as follows.

My treatise here follows the structure of *An Essential Sun Benefitting Others by Bringing Joy to the Three Worlds (Kham-gsum-bde-byedgzhan-phan-nyi-mai-snying-po)*, a ritual manual composed by the illustrious yogi Lama Pad-ma Zhe-pai Dor-je, a holder of many secret traditions. In structuring his text, this excellent master extracted the essence of all the earlier scriptures, both great and small, that were related to medicinal consecration, rearranging the materials for easy practice.

I have used his manual as my fundamental guide, and on top of that have brought in various themes from the special teachings on the Hayagriva tradition that are concerned with medicinal empowerment, structuring these to suit my purposes. Moreover, *The Root Tantra of Most Secret Hayagriva (Yang-gsang-rtsa-rgyud)* has numerous sections that deal directly with producing mystical nectar-like substances, and I have consulted these throughout.

I should perhaps also say something about the historical background of this particular tradition.

Originally taught by the Buddha himself, in the beginning the lineage was transmitted through an occult line of *dharmakaya, sambhogakaya* and *nirmanakaya* emanations, until it came down to the Bodhisattva Vajrapani. After this it was passed through the five *dra-ma* knowledge holders *(Gra-ma-rig-'dzin-lnga)*, and descended through the centuries as the undegenerated "Profound Instruction of the Seven Lineages."

Eventually the tradition was acquired by the great *acharya* and *vidyadhara Padmakara* (i.e., Padma Sambhava).

From Padmakara come two lineages: that of the original instructions *(bKa')*; and the tradition of treasure texts *(gTer)*.

The former was transmitted through a successive lineage of gurus, such as Vairochana the Translator, King Tri-song Deu-tsen, Gyal-wa Chok-yang, and so forth.

As for the tradition of treasure texts, these were written out by Padmakara himself and then hidden in a cave at Yer-pa to the northwest of Tibet's Vajra Abode [i.e., Lhasa]. There they remained, until the times had ripened sufficiently for their general propagation. They then were discovered and propagated by "the three treasure revealors": Wang-chen Gyal-tsen; Dre She-rab Lama; and Kyang-po Drak-pa Wang-chuk.

Thus the sacred and profound instructions uniting both the distant scriptural tradition with the close lineage of discovered treasure texts has come to Tibet, and has become renowned here as "The Combined Scriptural and Treasure Text Tradition of Profound Instruction of the Mandala of Nine Wrathful Divinities of the Cycle of Supreme Hayagriva, the Most Secret Lotus Lord."

(III) *The Actual Rite*

Hark! The method of practicing the consecration of nectar-like ambrosial medicines compounded from the eight root and one thousand branch ingredients by relying upon this exalted meditational mandala is as follows.

Begin the ritual as described in the standard manuals — taking refuge, generating the bodhimind, etc. Perform the self-generation and generation-in-front, creating the two mandalas as one. Then visualize the various transformations, such as those of the one hundred supreme families, the five Buddha families, the one most secret family, etc., consecrating the medicines in this way. Then generate the seven levels of the mandala, beginning with the level of physical bone until the level of the immortal *vajra* mandala., together with the Mystic Dagger *(Vajrakilaya)* methods of medicinal consecration.

Concentrate on this mandala of seven levels, constructed according to an oral tradition procedure received from holy gurus of the lineage, above which are the substances to be consecrated and transformed into ambrosial medicines.

Then summon forth the essence of all Refuge Objects, the forms of all good things in both samsara and nirvana, and the quintessence of all non-samsaric nectars. These come and transform into the great palace of medicines that bestow instant liberation merely upon being tasted, and that are the basis for the request for the profound initiations.

The method for requesting the initiations is as follows. The master says:

> In the sky before you visualize the kind Root Guru inseparable in nature from the meditational deity Powerful Lotus Lord Hayagriva. He is surrounded by great clouds of gurus of the seven lineages, the eight great classes of practitioners, the various mandala divinities, and also countless Buddhas, Bo-

dhisattvas, *dakas*, *dakinis*, Dharma Protectors, guardians, and
so forth.

Single-pointedly request the initiations from them by means of the verses having six lines beginning with the words
"the time has come," and four lines beginning with the word
"Bhagawan." [See the following pages, where these verses
are repeated.]

After the request has been made in this way, the master takes the
longevity arrow in his *vajra* hand and makes the summoning gesture.
The music of symbols, horns and drums is offered in order to invoke
the lineage blessings. In brief, the unfailing powers of the mystical
substances, mantras, the laws of interdependent origination, and the
strength of *samadhi* are applied in order to invoke the compassionate
blessings of the divine beings in the visualized field of assembly.

From their bodies there then flows forth nectars and lights of five
colors. Especially, from the body of Powerful Lotus Lord Hayagriva
there emanates forth countless replicas of himself, some large and some
small. These fall like rain upon the world and its inhabitants. They
also fall upon and melt into your body, speech and mind. The blessings of the body, speech and mind of the Mandala Lord become of
one taste with your own three doors. All negativities and obscurations
caused by body, speech and mind, together with all weakened *samaya*,
become cleansed and purified. The forces of your karma and awareness become blessed with the strength of longevity and wisdom. In
brief, all things in the world, including the earth, the mandala substances, all living beings, etc., gain the powerful blessings of the Lotus Lord Hayagriva and shine with a special radiance.

Especially, the medicine mandala achieves the power to induce all
siddhis both common and supreme merely upon being seen, heard of,
thought about, or touched.

Fix your mind upon this thought and do not mentally wander from
it. Then make the following request,

O supreme Aryas, grant me your attention.
The time has come to show your compassion.
The time has come to show your unique nature.
The time has come to use your powers.
The time has come to bestow *siddhi*.
The time has come to free [us from] enemies and hindrances.
The time has come to restore weakened *samaya*.

Bhagawan, give of your great powers.
Bhagawan, bestow the great initiations.
Bhagawan, please release your great blessings.
O Bhagawan, fulfill these requests,
And for all of us here
Ripen the fruit of our karma.

*Hrih! Vajra krodha Hayagriva hulu hulu hum phat. Kaya vak-
ka chitta vajra jnana abeshaya ah ah.*

This mantra is recited three times, together with an offering of forceful music. The master then says:
As is stated in *The Tantra of the Secret Cycle (gSang-ba-'khor-rgyud)*,

Each of the disciples should
Touch his/her head to the mandala.
Then with the appropriate procedures
The initiation should be performed.

When this has been heard, you [the disciples] should focus your
attention on the ambrosial medicine mandala and should develop a
firm aspiration to receive the initiation.

The blessings of the body, speech and mind of the Tathagatas flow
forth. Their nature is that of *vajras* but their form is that of brilliantly
white, red and blue nectars. These dissolve into your body, speech
and mind, purifying and cleansing you of all negativities and obscurations collected by means of body, speech and mind. The wisdom
of the threefold *vajra* (i.e., of *vajra* body, speech and mind) is attained,
and the supreme *siddhi* of *mahamudra* is achieved.

Imagine that these are gained even as you sit on your meditation
cushion.

Dharmadhatu, ultimately unborn and pure,
Free from concepts of pure and impure; and a form
That never fails to manifest in any of the three times
With a style blazing with the vibrance of all *siddhis*:
Whoever wants the initiation of this mandala,
Prepare to receive it now.

Like the sun rising from behind the clouds,
It eliminates the spiritual darkness
Generated over an aeon of lifetimes.
By receiving this initiation of kingly nectars,
May the stages of a kingly *vidyadhara* be obtained.

Om ah hum sarva panja amrita maha shri heruka padma nata khrid maha krodhi shvari stvam samaya abheshaya ah ah.

By the great initiation of a Wisdom Krodharaja,
All *siddhis* of body, speech and mind
Become of one nature with the stream
Of the body, speech and mind of the yogi/yogini.

Kaya siddhi om. Vakka siddhi ah. Chitta siddha hum.

(IV) *Enunciating the Benefits*

Hark! Hear now the inconceivable benefits that arise from having received this profound healing initiation.
A scripture states,

One gains the eight qualities:
Lifespan, meritorious energy and
Charisma are increased;
All hindrances are dispelled; and so forth.

Lob-pon Rin-po-che [i.e., Guru Padma Sambhava] said,

Ambrosial medicines to be offered to the Sugatas,
Nectars which delight the Gurus and meditational deities:
These are like the heart drops of the *dakinis*.
When they are ingested, the benefits are inconceivable.

One gains the qualities of a Buddha's five *kayas*.
Externally, all diseases and physical obstacles are destroyed;
Internally, the psychic poisons of five delusions are purified,
And weaknesses in *samaya* are overcome;
And secretly one gains the self-born wisdom.

Even a Shravaka Arhat or Pratyekabuddha
Who tastes this ambrosial medicine
Is transported to the tenth Mahayana *bhumi*
And becomes a Bodhisattva Mahasattva.

If one offers this medicine to the guru,
Great blessings are achieved.
If one offers it to the meditational deities,
Powerful *siddhis* are attained.
If one offers it to the Sugatas,
Their compassion is invoked.
And if one offers it to the *dakas* and *dakinis*,
They will deliver a prophecy.

Should a yogi or anyone at all even taste it,
The negative influences and obscurations
Of physical illness and obstacles are purified.
The internal quality of the *samadhis*
Of generation and completion stage yogas
Becomes firm and clear.
Secretly, self-awareness becomes *dharmakaya*,
And all shortcomings and excesses are made right.

Merely by holding this medicine,
The dangers of premature death are eliminated
And the strongest poison is counteracted.
By massaging it onto one's body,
All sicknesses and obstacles are dispelled.
If one burns it as incense,
Harmful spirits and hindering agents
are chased away.

The place where this rite is performed
Becomes equal to the mystical Cooling Wood Cemetery.
The area gains the blessings
Of countless *dakas* and *dakinis*.
Rains will be consistent and crops abundant.
Anyone who later uses the place for retreat
Will easily gain *samadhi*.

Should anyone who is about to die
Ingest a portion of this sacred medicine,
He/she will gain the state of a *vidyadhara*
Regardless of what kind of life was led.
Indeed, it is a supreme substance.

Also, *The Eight Volumes on Ambrosial Substances (bDud-rtsi-bam-brgyad)* states, "O Manjushri, should a person work for the benefit of living beings for a thousand aeons, the merits produced are not as great as those generated by this nectar-like medicine. For this medicinal substance even has the ability to lead beings from the eighteen great hells to the path of final liberation."

These and many other non-fallacious scriptural sources speak in detail on the wondrous benefits of the nectar-like medicines produced by this mystical ritual.

In brief, whoever relies upon this ambrosial nectar gains power over every *siddhi* of both samsara and beyond. It effortlessly fulfills the good of both oneself and others. Therefore do not doubt its efficacy.

PART THREE: THE CONCLUSION

This concludes the summary of two traditions of Hayagriva: the first being a longevity initiation in accordance with the lineage of transmission of Guru Tso-kye Dor-je, embodiment of the three Buddha *kayas*, as clarified by the pure visionary experiences of Kun-kyen Tok-me Tsal [the Fifth Dalai Lama], a legacy known far and wide as "The Sealed Transmission of Most Secret Hayagriva"; and the second being the healing empowerment, together with the rites for consecrating the *samaya* substances that become ambrosial medicines, in accordance with the nine-deity mandala of the Most Secret Powerful

Hayagriva

Lotus Lord, the Bhagawan Heruka Hayagriva.

At the end of the ceremony, the disciple should repeat the pledge to maintain all the vows and practice commitments taken during the initiation in the visualized presence of the Buddhas and Bodhisattvas.

> O masters, I vow to accomplish
> All that you have instructed me to do.

This is said three times. The *vajra* master and disciples then perform a *tsok* offering together, and offer prayers associated with the initiation tradition of Hayagriva. The disciples offer the mandala symbolic of the universe in order to express their gratitude at having received the initiations. The standard concluding procedures are then performed: sending out the excess *tsok* to the local spirits, offering prayers to the Doctrine Protectors, making the thanksgiving offering, and sending forth prayers and auspicious verses.

The Colophon: Zhab-gon Dro-dren De-kyi-ling Monastery of Nak-chu [in Eastern Tibet] maintains the tradition of annually performing the great consecration of ambrosial medicines as a method of contributing to the happiness of all beings.

In the Earth Bird Year of the Fifteenth Sexantry, the Thirteenth White Lotus Holder [i.e., the Thirteenth Dalai Lama] was on his way back to Lhasa after having visited the Empress of China in Beijing. The Tibetans were celebrating his return to the Land of Dharma [i.e., Tibet], and were filled with joy. He happened to arrive at Nak-chu while the monastery was engaged in the annual ambrosial medicinal rites. The presiding master was Drub-khang Tul-ku, whose mindstream had been ripened by study and practice of the hundreds of sutras and tantras over many previous lifetimes. He and the other practitioners requested the Thirteenth Dalai Lama to stay for some time and lead them in their meditations and rites. His Holiness consented, and wrote the two above texts in the form of notes arranged for his own participation in the ceremonies.

Thirteenth Dalai Lama with the 3 Bodhisattvas

6 A Vase of Ambrosia to Fulfill All Wishes

(A meditation upon the guru as being inseparable from the three essential Bodhisattvas)

> *Namo!* I pay homage and turn for refuge
> To the guru and the three essential Bodhisattvas.
> I offer them this prayer:
> Manifest your great compassion,
> And watch over me in all times and situations.

[Herein follows a guru yoga meditation written as a liturgy for daily practice. It takes as its theme the inseparable nature of the root guru with the three principal Bodhisattvas: Manjushri, Avalokiteshvara and Vajrapani, who respectively symbolize the wisdom, great compassion and power of all Buddhas of the three times and ten directions.]

(Begin with the usual preliminaries of cleaning the practice site, arranging an altar, etc., as described in the standard manuals. Place your body on a comfortable meditation seat, and then with a mind motivated by the altruistic thought of enlightenment commence the liturgy by taking refuge:)

With undivided attention I turn for refuge
To the Buddhas, who have evolved to perfection,
To the scriptural and insight Dharmas, that were so
      skillfully transmitted,
And to the Sangha community, who are endowed with
Wondrous qualities of knowledge and realization. (3X)

(Next one engenders the Bodhisattva attitude:)

In order to benefit the living beings
Wandering in the difficult realms of samsara
And to inspire them toward supreme liberation
I will enter into the ocean of Bodhisattva practices,
Just as have all Buddhas and Bodhisattvas of the past. (3X)

(Contemplating the four immeasurable thoughts:)

May all living beings have happiness and its cause;
May they be without misery and its cause;
May they never be separated from joy beyond sorrow;
May they abide in equanimity free from attachment and
      aversion. (3X)

(Generating the special Vajrayana attitude:)

In order to quickly achieve full enlightenment
As a method to benefit all living beings,
I now engage in this Vajrayana method of meditating
On the guru as being inseparable in nature
From the three essential Bodhisattvas:
Manjushri, Avalokiteshvara and Vajrapani,
Symbols of the wisdom, compassion and power
Of enlightened beings past, present and future.

(One then consecrates the world and its inhabitants, together with
the various offering substances:)

From within the sphere of understanding
The naturally pure nature of all phenomena,
I envision myself in the form of a tantric divinity.

Lights emanate forth from my body, purifying
The world and its inhabitants of all stains
And transforming the offering substances
Into non-samsaric ambrosial nectars.

(When these preliminaries have been completed, one begins the actual practice by building the visualization of the Merit Field:)

> *Om svabhava shuddho sarvadharmah svabhava shuddhoh ham.*
> All phenomena are seen in the nature
> Of emptiness free from having a self-nature.
> From within the sphere of emptiness
> In the space before me there appears
> A jewelled throne upheld by eight lions.
>
> Seated there on cushions made
> From a lotus, sun and moon
> Is my personal root guru,
> The wisdom, compassion and power
> Of all Buddhas manifest in human form,
> An ocean of Dharma knowledge, he of sublime mind.
>
> His body is white in color, and
> His face bears a tender smile.
> He wears the three robes of a monk,
> A heavier ceremonial shoulder robe,
> And also the golden hat of a pandit.
>
> His right hand is in the *mudra* of teaching Dharma
> And holds the stem of a white lotus.
> His left is in the *mudra* of meditation
> And supports a volume of holy scripture.
> His legs are crossed in the *vajra* posture.

Seated at the crown of the guru's head
On a lotus and a moon cushion
Is Manjushri, the Bodhisattva of compassionate wisdom.
His youthful body is reddish-yellow in color
And is embellished by the 112 marks and signs of perfection.
His right hand brandishes the sword of insight,
And his left supports a copy of
The *Prajnaparamita Sutra* in 100,000 lines.
His legs are crossed in the *vajra* posture,
And he wears divine silks and ornaments.

Seated at the guru's throat
On a lotus and a moon cushion
Is Avalokiteshvara, Bodhisattva of wise compassion,
His body white in color
And transparent like a stainless crystal.
He has one face and four arms, and is
Adorned by the 112 marks and signs of perfection.

His two inner hands are folded together at his heart;
His outer right hand holds a crystal rosary,
And outer left an eight-petalled lotus.
An antelope skin hangs over his left breast,
And he is adorned with the Bodhisattva ornaments.

Standing at the guru's heart
On a lotus and a sun cushion
Is Vajrapani, Bodhisattva of wise, compassionate power.
His body is dark azure in color,
His right hand brandishes a *vajra*,
And his left, poised at his heart,
Shows the threatening *mudra*
And holds the strings of a noose.
Adorned with jewel ornaments and snakes
And wearing a tiger skin as a loin cloth,
He stands amidst a ball of fire
With his left leg extended and right slightly bent.

The three places of the guru's holy body—
His crown, throat and heart — are also respectively
Marked by the syllables *om, ah* and *hum.*
Lights emanate into the ten directions
From the *hum* at his heart.
They summon forth the Wisdom Beings
Of the three Bodhisattvas, together with countless Buddhas.
Jah hum bam hoh! They merge into the Commitment Beings.

(One then offers the seven-limbed devotion, together with the mandala symbolic of the universe:)

Homage to the kind root guru,
Lord of truth, he of sublime wisdom,
Upholder of the ocean of Buddhadharma,
Fearless possessor of the eight powers,
He victorious over all inner negativity.

Homage to Manjushri, whose wisdom-sword cuts
The net of wrong understanding,
Bodhisattva symbolizing the wisdom of compassionate insight
Of all Buddhas of the three times,
The guru's *vajra* body, great bliss at the guru's crown.

Homage to Avalokiteshvara, symbol
Of the wise compassion of all Buddhas,
Bodhisattva who extends the hand of kindness
To guide living beings to peace and joy,
The guru's *vajra* speech, beatific joy at the guru's throat.

Homage to Vajrapani, symbol of the
Wise and compassionate power of all Buddhas,
Bodhisattva emanating in wrathful aspects
To suit the needs of practitioners,
The guru's *vajra* mind, Dharma wheel at the guru's heart.

From my heart I emanate forth goddesses
Who sing songs of praise and fill the skies
With delightful offerings of every variety
For the guru inseparable from these three Bodhisattvas.
And I also offer the mandala symbolic of the universe
As a sign of my commitment and dedication.

In the presence of the *gurudeva* I acknowledge
My every fault and shortcoming;
And I rejoice in every positive quality and potential
That exists within myself and others.

I request the guru: In order to dispel
The hundreds of sufferings found in the world,
Perform the supreme deed of releasing
A feast of vast and profound teachings.
Remain until samsara is ended; and manifest
In accordance with the nature and needs of trainees.

Whatever meritorious energy I have generated,
May it be dedicated as would please the guru.
O kind teacher, please accept my humble devotion
And bestow your powerful blessings.

(A prayer requesting guidance and inspiration:)

Navigator of living beings, treasury of compassion,
 Liberated one in the robes of self-discipline,
Upholder of the Bodhisattva Way,
guru absorbed in the dance of bliss and void,
I turn to you for guidance and inspiration.

Although the living beings desire only happiness
They constantly collect the causes of misery
Like droplets of rain falling in a rainstorm.
Out of compassion you have taken up the burden
Of working to strengthen the light of happiness.
My guru, I turn to you for guidance and inspiration.

Other Buddhas have overlooked this field,
But you, O treasure of kindness,
Have accepted to teach us the paths and practices.
My guru, I turn to you for guidance and inspiration.

From now until I achieve enlightenment
I place my hopes in you.
In this life, the *bar-do* and all future rebirths
Hold me with your great compassion.

When this prayer has been thus offered
Sincerely from the depths of my heart,
Light rays emanate forth from a syllable *hrih*
That appears at the guru's heart.
These purify the negativities and obscurations
From within the six realms of living beings
And automatically bestow *siddhis* both common and supreme.

(The special visualization to be performed during the mantra recitation is as follows:)

On a moon disc at the guru's heart
Stands a syllable *hrih*, white in color,
Surrounded by the guru's name mantra
Om a guru vajradhara . . . . . (Guru's name) . . . . . *sarva siddhi
      hum hum.*
Lights emanate forth from these syllables;
They make offerings to all the Buddhas and Bodhisattvas
And then summon forth the blessings of the
Body, speech and mind of all Enlightened Beings.
These come in the form of brilliant lights
And absorb into the guru's holy body.

Then from the guru a stream of nectar
Flows into the ten directions.
Merely on touching the world and its inhabitants
It purifies them of all faults.
All the living beings are thus placed
On the stage of a *gurudeva*.

(This is the basic meditation to be pursued while reciting the guru's name mantra. Do so as long as is comfortably possible, being careful to avoid mistakes such as are created by haste, laziness or unclarity.

Then recite the mantras of the three Bodhisattvas: *om vagi shvari muh*; *om mani padme hum*; and *om vajra pani hum*. These mantras may be visualized in a number of places: either in concentric circles outside the guru's name mantra described above; or each in a circle at the heart of the respective Bodhisattva; etc.

No matter which method is used, the contemplation of the light rays purifying the world and its inhabitants is done in a similar manner.

You should learn more on the specific details of the mantra visualization from your personal guru.)

(When the recitation has been concluded:)

O guru, embodiment of all refuge objects,
I offer this heartfelt prayer to you.
Grant your inspiring blessings,
That I may ripen my mindstream
By means of the four tantric initiations
And may quickly achieve the four Buddha *kayas*. (3X)

When this request has been heard
The Bodhisattvas at the guru's three places
Emanate forth brilliant lights,
First in turn from each Bodhisattva
And then from all three simultaneously.
These lights dissolve into me,
Purifying me of the four obscurations
And bestowing the four initiations upon me.
I gain the seed of the good fortune
To one day achieve the exalted state
Of Great Union, enlightenment possessed of four *kayas*.

(This is the meditation of gaining the blessings of the four tantric initiations.)

(Conclude the practice by briefly contemplating the stages of the complete path leading to enlightenment. A liturgy for this is as follows:)

The source of all spiritual growth is found
In relying correctly upon a qualified spiritual teacher.
This gives birth to everything wholesome
In both this world and beyond.
May I never be disturbed by negative thoughts
And preconceptions in my relationship with the guru
And may I enthusiastically apply his teachings.

I have found a rare and precious human rebirth
Enriched with the eight freedoms and ten endowments.
May I deeply appreciate the human potential,
And live in awareness of how easily it is lost.
May I appreciate the significance of impermanence and death
And, by dedicating my energies to lasting values,
Extract the very essence of being.

When only negative karma is collected in life,
Death becomes followed by lower rebirth.
May I turn now to the Three Jewels of Refuge
And dedicate myself to spiritual training.

Worldly accomplishments are meaningless,
And the real enemies are karma and delusion within.
Instead of rushing after samsaric perfection
May I cultivate the three higher trainings
And destroy the inner demon of ego-grasping.

Since beginningless time I and all others
Have experienced countless rebirths,
And thus every sentient being has many times
Been a parent to me and has shown me great kindness.
Therefore may I look with eyes of love, respect
And compassion upon all living beings,
And thus sever the habit of selfishness from its root.

Caring only for the happiness of others
Is the character of the Bodhisattva path.
May I have the courage to take to fulfillment
The practice of relinquishing personal comfort
For the happiness and well-being of the world.

And may I always practice the six perfections:
Generosity able to sacrifice even one's life
In order to be of benefit to others;
Self-discipline, the basis of all progress, that
Guards the trainings like one protects one's eyes;
Patience, the source of great benefits, that is
Easily able to bear all hardships;
Enthusiastic perseverence, that never becomes disheartened
With the effort required in spiritual practice;
Single-pointed meditative concentration,
That engages in deep contemplation
Without falling prey to torpor or agitation;
And, finally, the wisdom that distinguishes
The deeper nature of all phenomena
And understands the two levels of truth.
Also, may I dwell in the four ways
Of benefiting trainees, and thus ripen
The mindstreams of other sentient beings.

Having developed stability in these basic themes
That constitute the essence of the Sutrayana,
May I ripen my mind for Vajrayana practice
By receiving the four tantric initiations
From a qualified *vajra* master,
And by carefully guarding the vows
And commitments of the tantric path.

Then may I achieve the *samadhis* of
The coarse and subtle generation stage yogas,
And be able to engage in the five profound yogas
Of Vajrayana's powerful completion stage.
In this way may I in one short lifetime
Attain full enlightenment, the state of Great Union.

(Absorbing the blessings of the guru:)

When this prayer has thus been offered,
The guru smiles with delight
And comes to the crown of my head.
He shrinks to the size of a thumb
And enters my body through the aperture at my crown,
Descending into me via my central energy channel
And coming down to the center of my heart.
There he merges and becomes one with my mind, and
The potential to achieve all goodness and happiness
Is automatically strengthened and made firm.

The Colophon: Dar-han-pai Li-yu Drung-wang repeatedly requested me to write him a liturgical text that would serve as a practical guru
yoga manual for daily meditation upon the inseparable nature of the
spiritual master and the three essential Bodhisattvas. Although I am
not really qualified to do so, I felt that it would be equally inappropriate to refuse the petition of such a faithful disciple. Therefore in the
end I accepted the task, and offer the prayer that the work may in
some small way contribute to the increase of goodness and enlightenment in the world.

A History of the Fourteen Dalai Lamas

The office of the Dalai Lamas of Tibet is one of the truly unique institutions the world has produced. Shortly after a Dalai Lama dies, a committee is formed to find his reincarnation. Most Dalai Lamas have left mystical "clues" as to where they shall take rebirth, and these are always used as the basis of the search. In addition, oracles, famous lamas, clairvoyants and all the elements of Tibet's unusual society work together to locate and reinstate the young incarnation. Search parties are formed, likely candidates identified and then extensive tests are made. Each of the young candidates is shown items that belonged to the deceased Dalai Lama, such as rosaries, ritual implements, articles of clothing and so forth. These are mixed in with replicas, and the true incarnation is espected to choose correctly those articles that belonged to his predecessor.

The successful candidate is officially recognized and is enthroned with great regalia. He is then given to the best tutors in Tibet, and for the twenty or thirty years to follow is submitted to an intensive spiritual education in the Buddhist arts, sciences and humanities. At the conclusion of his studies he is expected to face examination by debating with dozens of Tibet's highest scholars before an assembly of some 20,000 monks and nuns from Tibet's greatest monastic universities. Only then is he invested with the powers of spiritual authority over the country. The present Dalai Lama is the fourteenth to hold this extraordinary office.

The name "Dalai" is in fact a Mongolian word, although the Dalai

Lama lineage is older than the title. The first to be known as a Dalai was So-nam Gya-tso, who converted the Mongolian king Altan Khan and his nation to Buddhism in 1578. Rather than call the Lama by his Tibetan name, Altan Khan translated the second part of it, or "Gya-tso," which simply means "Ocean," into Mongolian. The result was "Dalai Lama," or "Teacher [like the] Ocean." "Dalai" also is a term implying supremacy or greatness; consequently, an alternative translation would be "Supreme Teacher" or "Greatest Master." Thus the Mongolians were the first to use the title Dalai Lama. From them it spread through China and the Far East, and then to Europe and the Americas. It was never used by the Tibetans themselves, however, who preferred to call their spiritual leader by Tibetan epithets such as Kun-dun (the All-Purposeful One), Yi-shin Nor-bu (the Wish-fulfilling Gem) and Gyal-wa Rin-po-che (the Precious Adept). Because So-nam Gya-tso was considered to be a reincarnation of Gen-dun Gya-tso, and he in turn a reincarnation of Gen-dun Drub, Altan Khan's guru became known as the Third Dalai Lama. The two predecessors only posthumously came to be called the First and Second Dalai Lamas.

Although the Dalai Lamas are technically thought of as reincarnations of the same being, nonetheless each has manifested greatness in a unique way and has chosen his individual sphere of activity and attention.

The First Dalai Lama, Gyal-wa Gen-dun Drub, was born in Gur-ma of Zhab-to in 1391 as the son of nomadic peasants. Left fatherless at the age of seven, he was placed by his mother in Nar-tang Monastery (of the Ka-dam Sect) for education. He was to become the greatest scholar/saint to be produced by this monastery, and his fame spread like a victory banner over all of Tibet. In 1447 he established Ta-shi Lhun-po Monastery at Shi-ga-tse, which was destined to become Southern Tibet's greatest monastic university. In writing he focused on the Ka-dam-pa practice traditions and also the Five Themes of Buddha's Teachings (pramana, abhidharma, prajnaparamita, madhyamaka and vinaya), which had been popularized in Tibet by the Sa-kya Sect. He was particularly famous for combining study and practice, and spent more than twenty years in meditational retreat. He passed away while sitting in meditation in 1474.

The Second Dalai Lama, Gyal-wa Gen-den Gya-tso, was born in 1475 in Yol-kar Dor-je-den. The son of a renowned yogi of the Nying-ma Sect, he was recognized at the age of four as Gen-dun Drub's reincarnation. He studied and wrote extensively on practices from various of the Tibetan sects, but is particularly renowned for his writings on the lineages of the Nying-ma, Shang-pa Ka-gyu and Ge-luk Nyengyu traditions. His principal focus was the tantric tradition. He is particularly noted for "discovering" and consecrating the La-tso "Lake of Visions" and establishing Cho-khor-gyal Monastery beside it. He is also noted for constructing Gan-den Po-drang house in Dre-pung Monastery. He passed away in 1542 while sitting in meditation.

The Third Dalai Lama, Gyal-wa So-nam Gya-tso, was born in 1543 in Khang-sar of To-lung. Recognized at an early age as Gen-dun Gyatso's reincarnation, he was placed in Dre-pung for education. He rapidly became known for his wisdom and accomplishment, and was appointed as the Dre-pung Abbot. His name spread throughout Asia, and Altan Khan of the Tumed Mongols became his disciple. He traveled to Mongolia in 1578, where the Tumeds formally adopted Buddhism under him. Here he established Tek-chen Cho-khor Monastery. Later he traveled widely throughout Eastern Tibet and Western China, where he taught extensively and established many monasteries, the most important being Li-tang and Kum-bum. He was noted for combining the Nying-ma and Ge-luk lineages in his practice, and for bringing civilization to the wild borderlands of Central Asia. He passed away in 1588 while still teaching in the northeast.

The Fourth Dalai Lama, Gyal-wa Yon-ten Gya-tso, is the only Dalai Lama to have been born outside of Tibet. He took birth in 1589 in Mongolia. A direct descendant of Altan Khan, he fulfilled So-nam Gya-tso's promise to the Mongolians to return to them in his future life. Because he was born outside of Tibet, his official recognition and enthronement took longer than usual, and he was not brought to Tibet until he was twelve years old. Both he and his predecessor, the Third Dalai Lama, received opulent gifts from the Emperor of China and numerous invitations to visit the Manchu court; but both declined. The Fourth Dalai Lama did not write any significant works, but instead dedicated his time and energy to study, practice and teaching. He passed away in early 1617.

The Fifth Dalai Lama, Gyal-wa Nga-wang Lob-zang Gya-tso, popularly known as "The Great Fifth," was born in Chong-gye in the fire Snake Year, less than a year after the passing of Gyal-wa Yon-ten Gya-tso. This was to be the most dynamic of the early Dalai Lamas. He wrote as much as all other Dalai Lamas combined, traveled and taught extensively, and reshaped the politics of Central Asia. During his lifetime the three provinces of Tibet (Central, South and East) that had been divided into separate kingdoms since the demise of King Lang Dar-ma in the mid-ninth century, once again joined together to form a united Tibet, with the Great Fifth arising as the spiritual and secular ruler in 1642. He was invited to the Chinese court by the Ching Emperor to restructure the Buddhist monasteries. He visited Peking in 1652. He wrote on a wide variety of subjects, but is especially noted for his works on history and classical Indian poetry, and his biographies of eminent personalities of his era. His last great deed was to initiate the construction of the magnificent Potala Palace at Lhasa, which was not completed until after his death. He passed away in 1682 while engaged in a three year retreat. To ensure the completion of the Potala, he ordered that his death and the location of his reincarnation be kept secret until after the main part of the building had been secured. The Great Fifth is also remembered for establishing a national system of medical care in Tibet, and initiating a program of national education.

The Sixth Dalai Lama, Gyal-wa Tsang-yang Gya-tso, was the only Dalai Lama not to maintain the monastic disciplines. Born in the Chime Ling-pa family in Southern Tibet on the Indian border (today the birthplace lies within Indian territory), he was located two years later and in 1688 placed in Nang-kha-tse for education. This was all kept secret at the time, and not revealed until the Potala Palace was completed in 1695. The Second Pan-chen Lama was sent to ordain and educate him, and he was enthroned in 1697. But he preferred sports and social life to the monasteries, and when he turned twenty years of age he gave back his robes and moved out of the official residence in the Potala into a small apartment that he had had built at the foot of the hill. He is remembered and loved for his romantic poems, his merry lifestyle and his disregard for authority. However, tragedy was to overtake him. Some Mongolians were displeased with his lack of external discipline, and they invaded Lhasa and seized him in 1705. He died in 1706 while being transported to Mongolia. Tibetans nonetheless regard him as a true incarnation of the Great Fifth and interpret his unusual behavior as tantric wisdom manifested as a means of delivering a paranormal teaching to his people.

The Seventh Dalai Lama, Gyal-wa Kal-zang Gya-tso, was born in 1708 in Li-tang, East Tibet. He was located soon thereafter, but due to troubles with Mongolia could not be officially recognized. Eventually in 1720 he was brought to Central Tibet and enthroned, but not until persistent rebellion had managed to oust the Dzungar Mongolians from Lhasa. Unfortunately this was accomplished with the aid of the Manchus, who regarded Mongolia as their principal enemy and saw the conflict as an opportunity to further their interests in Central Asia. This alliance was to lead to later political complications. The Seventh Dalai Lama was to prove very important to Tibetan religious history, however, and his simple and pure life as a monk won the hearts of his people. He wrote extensively, particularly on what are known as "the popular Tantras": Guhyasamaja, Heruka Chakrasamvara, Vajrabhairava and Kalachakra. He is particularly renowned for his informal spiritual poetry and the many prayers and hymns he composed. He died in 1757.

The Eighth Dalai Lama, Gyal-wa Jam-pal Gya-tso, was born in Tobgyal of Tsang Province the following year. He was recognized and brought to Lhasa in 1762. It is this Dalai Lama who built the legendary Nor-bu Ling-ka in 1783 in the park to the west of Lhasa. Educated by the Third Pan-chen Lama, he exhibited wonderful spiritual qualities mixed with a distaste for political intrigue. During his lifetime, Tibet became, for the first time, very much aware of British colonial interests in Asia. It was due to this that she formed a defensive isolationist policy in 1802. Jam-pal Gya-tso passed away in 1804.

Each of the four Dalai Lamas to follow were to live short lives. There is speculation as to whether this was due to intrigue, increased disease due to an increased contact with the outside world, or simply lack of good karma on the part of the Tibetan people (the good karma of disciples being regarded by Tibetans as the primary cause for the long life of a high lama).

Be this as it may, the Ninth Dalai Lama, Gyal-wa Lung-tok Gyatso, who was born in 1805, died in the spring of 1815. It was prophesied that this Dalai Lama would have obstacles to his lifespan, but that should he live to old age would perform the greatest deeds of all the Dalai Lamas. When he passed away, all of Tibet mourned the loss.

The Tenth Dalai Lama, Gyal-wa Tsul-trim Gya-tso, born in 1816, was recognized and enthroned in 1822. He was in constant poor health and died in 1837 at the age of twenty-one.

The Eleventh Dalai Lama, Gyal-wa Khe-drub Gya-tso, was born the following year in Gar-tar, Eastern Tibet. He was enthroned in 1855, but died eleven months later.

The Twelfth Dalai Lama, Gyal-wa Trin-le Gya-tso, born a year later, was the only Dalai Lama whose selection was made on the basis of the "Golden Urn Lottery" decreed by the Chinese Emperor. Due to the fact that there had been no strong Dalai Lama for some time, Tibet's internal politics were becoming increasingly unstable. This Dalai Lama also died young, in the year 1875.

The Thirteenth Dalai Lama, Gyal-wa Tub-ten Gya-tso, was born of peasant stock in 1876 in southeast Tibet at Tak-po Lang-dun. Recognized in 1878 and enthroned a year later, he was to provide the strong spiritual and political leadership necessary to revive a Tibet that had become confused and entangled by the colonial age with its intrigues, conflicts and power struggles. Placed in power in 1895, he saw Tibet through the Anglo-Russian conflicts of the late nineteenth century, the British invasion of 1904 and then the Chinese invasion of 1909. The Tibetans managed to suppress this latter attack after three years of effort, and in 1912 all Chinese soldiers in Tibet surrendered and were deported. Unfortunately, he was unable to get Tibet admitted to the League of Nations. England, afraid that an independent Tibet would be an easy prey to expansionist Russia, insisted on Tibet legally being regarded internationally as being under the suzerainity (though not under the sovereignty) of China. Nonetheless, the Thirteenth banned all Chinese from Tibet, and this remained de facto throughout his life. This was the first Dalai Lama to have extensive contact with the West, and he was deeply loved by those who met him. Sir Charles Bell's *Portrait of the Dalai Lama* (London: Wisdom, 1987) testifies to the respect the British held for him. He completed his studies at an early age, and then in 1914 entered the three year meditational retreat. During the later years of his life he attempted to modernize Tibet, although his efforts met with considerable resistance from the powers that be. In 1932, he prophesied the future invasion of Tibet by China and urged his people to prepare themselves. He wrote extensively, although the demands of his era required him to dedicate much of his time to reviving and restoring his nation and the spirit of his people. He traveled to Mongolia, China and India, and spent many years on the road in his efforts to keep his country from being crushed by the ploys of the superpowers—England, Russia and China. He passed away in 1933.

The Fourteenth Dalai Lama, Gyal-wa Ten-zin Gya-tso, was born on July 6, 1935, in Tak-tser, East Tibet. Located and recognized two years later, he was brought to Central Tibet in 1939 and enthroned. This is the Dalai Lama whom we in the West have come to know and love. The Chinese invasion of Tibet in the 1950s and the mass exodus of

the Tibetan refugees that followed, although a terrible human tragedy, has had the effect of making the Dalai Lama and the high Tibetan Lamas accessible to the Western world for the first time. The Fourteenth Dalai Lama has now made numerous teaching tours of the West.
The depth of his learning, wisdom and profound insight into the nature of human existence has won him hundreds of thousands of friends
around the world. His humor, warmth and compassionate energy stand
as living evidence of the strength and efficacy of Tibetan Buddhism,
and of its value to human society.

The concept of the *tul-ku*, or Incarnate Lama, was an integral aspect
of Tibetan culture. The Dalai Lama was but one of the approximately one thousand such tul-ku incarnates; but he was somehow special
amongst them, a king of tul-kus, above and beyond the perimeters
of this or that sect of Tibetan Buddhism. The temporal ruler over all
of Tibet, he was in addition the spiritual leader not only of Tibet but
of all those lands where Tibetan Buddhism predominates, such as Mongolia, Western China, Northern India, and so forth. His devotees were
not limited to the six million Tibetans, but to the tens of millions of
Buddhists who inhabit these vast lands, a territory larger than the entirety of Europe. Now that Tibet no longer exists as an independent
nation, his secular position has diminished somewhat; but his spiritual
influence has only grown. Moreover, the respect of the international
community for the Tibetan Lamas and Tibetan Buddhism has increased tremendously.

The destruction of Tibet and its future resurrection were prophesied by the eighth-century Indian sage Padma Sambhava, who also
prophesied, "When the iron bird flies and horses run on wheels, the
Dharma will be carried to the land of the Red Man." Perhaps the
suffering of Tibet and the amazing dignity of the Tibetans in the face
of it was the necessary catalyst to bring the wealth of Tibetan culture
to the world's attention.

When asked about the above prophecy, His Holiness the Dalai Lama
XIV answered, "Prophecy or no prophecy, the Western world is showing strong interest in Buddhism. More and more universities are offering Buddhist studies, and hundreds of Buddhist meditation centers
have appeared around the world. I myself firmly believe that Buddhism is the property of mankind, not of any particular people or nation. It has a lot to offer to mankind in terms of understanding and
developing the mind. Through understanding the mind and increasing its creative qualities, we increase human peace and happiness. If

we Tibetans can contribute to this in any way, we are most pleased to be able to do so.... There are many elements in Buddhism that could benefit the world, many methods for cultivating higher love, compassion and wisdom. Everyone benefits by increasing these qualities.... People do not have to become Buddhist in the formal sense in order to use the Buddhist techniques. The purpose of the teachings is only to benefit living beings.... The world is deeply in need of peace, love and understanding. If Buddhism can make a contribution to this end, we would be happy to contribute what we can. We are all on this planet together. We are all brothers and sisters with the same physical and mental faculties, the same problems and the same needs. We must all contribute to the fulfillment of the human potential and the improvement of the quality of life as much as we are able.... Mankind is crying out for help. Ours is a desperate time. Those who have something to offer should come forward. Now is the time...."

Footnotes

1 Heart of the Enlightenment Teachings

1. The eighth century Indian master who wrote *A Guide to the Bodhisattva Way of Life*, or *Bodhisattva-chaya-avatara*.
2. Atisha: The eleventh century Indian master who came to Tibet in 1042 A.D. and founded the Ka-dam-pa tradition, to which the Dalai Lamas have been most closely affiliated.
3. Founder of the Yellow Hat Tradition and root guru of the first Dalai Lama.
4. The eighteenth century encyclopedia.

2 Sermons at the Great Prayer Festival

1. Twelfth century.
2. Lama Drom was Atisha's principal disciple. He is regarded as being an early incarnation of the Dalai Lamas.
3. Elevenh—twelfth century.
4. Both of these masters were important disciples of Lama Drom Ton-Pa.
5. The eleventh century Kar-gyu-pa forefather.
6. I don't have his exact dates at my disposal. He was, I believe, in the third or fourth generation.
7. A thirteenth century Ka-dam-pa master.
8. The classical Tibetan *vinaya* commentator, whose works form the basis of *vinaya* studies within the Ge-luk-pa tradition. His reincarnation today is a young monk of Dre-pung Monastery.
9. One of the three most important disciples of Atisha's successor, Lama Drom Ton-pa.

10. The eleventh century Indian sage who traveled and taught widely in Tibet. The Shi-je tradition descends from him.

11. The second century Indian sage often regarded as the father of Mahayana Buddhism. His numerous treatises on madhyamaka philosophy has earned him a lasting reputation as one of India's greatest thinkers.

12. The first Drub-khang Rin-po-che, who founded Drub-khang monastery in Eastern Tibet. The Thirteenth Dalai Lama spent considerable time in this monastery on his way back from China and became close friends with the Drub-khang reincarnate. He later wrote several poems and treatises at the Drub-khang's behest.

13. A disciple of Nagarjuna's successor Aryadeva.

14. The fourth century compiler of the *abhidharma* literature and the brother of Asanga.

15. Tibetans regard Matichitra as being another name for Ashvagosha, who has been quoted above.

16. Although his exact dates have not been established, it is known that he ruled Tibet several generations prior to the seventh century monarch Songtsen Gam-po.

17. Kamalashila was the principal Dharma heir of Shantirakshita. The latter came to Tibet in the mid-seventh century and established Sam-ye monastery. The former was brought to Tibet a generation later to meet the Chinese master Ho-shang in debate. This debate was a turning point in Tibetan history, for following it Chinese Buddhism was banned from within Tibet.

18. Wen-sa-pa is regarded as the predecessor of the line of Pan-chen Lamas. The first Pan-chen (seventeeth century) was his immediate reincarnation.

19. That is, the first Panchen Lama.

20. This refers to the fifteenth century war with the Kar-gyu-pas, when Geluk-pa monks were banned from attending the festival. The festival itself continued, with the rites being performed by the Kar-ma-pa Lama. During the Second Dalai Lama's lifetime the Lhasa ruler intervened and returned control of the festival to the Ge-luk-pa.

21. Fourteenth century.

22. The chief disciple of the Seventh Dalai Lama (eighteenth century), Chang-kya is perhaps best known for his work in getting the fundamental Indian Buddhist scriptures translated from Tibetan into Mongolian.

23. That is, Bu-ton Rin-chen Drub-pa, the twelfth century compiler of the *Kan-gyur* and *Ten-gyur* scriptural collections.

24. This work is attributed to the Indian sage Nagarjuna.

25. These are all early Ka-dam-pa masters.

26. This prayer, originally a brief passage in the *Avatamsaka Sutra*, has become something of a religious tradition of its own throughout Central Asia and the Far East. It is known by several names: *Mahayana-pranidana-raja*, or "The King of Mahayana Prayers"; *Arya-samantabhadra-pranidana*, or "The Prayer of Samantabhadra"; and *Arya-bhadra-charya-pranidana*, or "The Prayer of Ways High and Sublime." Here I have chosen the first of these forms.

27. A famous eighteenth century Ge-luk-pa monk.

28. The twelfth century Ka-dam-pa master.
29. The fourteenth century disciple of Tsong-kha-pa, who later founded Drepung Monastery.
30. Tsong-Ka-pa's chief tantric disciple.
31. That is, Khe-drub-je, who is referred to in note 30 above.
32. Lama Tuo-kven: A nineteenth century Ge-luk-pa monk.
33. Again, this is another way of refering to Khe-drub-je (see note 30 above.)
34. See note 32 above.
35. As the Thirteenth Dalai Lama passed away later the same year, he did not complete his exposition of the six preliminaries.

    However, not much material remained to be covered. He was well into the fifth preliminary, with only the last point of the seven-limbed devotion remaining, i.e., the limb of dedication. And in fact he had already touched on this particular limb every year in the conclusion of his discourse, as well as having given us the liturgy for it six years earlier when generally introducing all seven limbs (see pages   -   )

    As for the sixth preliminary, this involves reading a supplication for the blessings of the lineage gurus, beginning with Buddha up to and including one's personal guru of today. Thus the precise liturgy for this differs in dependence upon which particular lineage of transmission one is practising.

    One of my earlier books, *Essence of Refined Gold*, contains a prayer of this nature written by the Third Dalai Lama. The Seventh Dalai Lama composed a shorter version, which I included in my study of him, *Songs of Spiritual Change.*

    A concise presentation of all six preliminaries has been published by the Library of Tibetan Works and Archives, under the title *Jor-Cho*, 1984, prepared from the Tibetan by Losang C. Ganchenpa and Karma Lekshe Tsomo.

3 A Brief Guide to the Buddhist Tantras

1. Throughout the text the Thirteenth Dalai Lama first quotes Tsong-kapa's verses on each of the tantra categories, and then goes on to explain the meanings in detail. The verses mention numerous textual titles belonging to each of the tantra categories; however, as transliterations look terrible in the middle of a verse, I give the titles only in English when they appear in the individual verses, and reserve the Tibetan forms for the places where the texts are later again quoted in the commentary that follows. The texts quoted are in fact Indian scriptures; anyone wanting to know the Sanskrit forms of the names can easily find them by checking the Tibetan as I have given it against the indexes of one of the *Kan-gyur* collections. These indexes are readily available in most university libraries. I generally recommend the Suzuki (Tokyo) index, although the more recent work by Dharma Press, California, is also very good.
2. The completion stage practices of the five principal male and female tantra systems were united by the Indian *mahasiddha* Tilopada, and were passed

on by him in two forms: the Six Yogas of Naropa, and the Six Yogas of Niguma. For a detailed explanation of the latter, see my *Selected Works of the Dali Lama II: The Tantric Yogas of Sister Niguma*, chapter six. 3. These topics are discussed in more detail in my *Selected Works of the Dalai Lama I: Bridging the Sutras and Tantras* (Snow Lion, 1981), chapter six, 'The Two Yogic Stages of the Kalachakra Tantra.'

4 Poems Pointing Out the Nature of Correct Practice

1. These are the five classical subjects comprising the *ge-she* training program, that every Dalai Lama is expected to complete.
2. It is interesting to note the strong line the Great Thirteenth takes on tobacco, some fifty years before medical science understood the health hazards involved.
3. That is, the monastic ordinations.
4. See note 1 above.
5. I have included the Third Dalai Lama's famous *Lam Rim* commentary, *Essence of Refined Gold*, in my study of him, *Selected Works of the Dalai Lama III: Essence of Refined Gold* (Snow Lion, 1982).

5 The Most Secret Cycle of the Mystical Mandala of Hayagriva.

1. This is the Fifth Dalai Lama's Nying-ma-pa name.
2. This verse was earlier quoted in full by the Thirteenth Dalai Lama in the opening section of chapter III, "A Guide to the Buddhist Tantras,"
3. These are all eighth century Nying-ma masters.

6 A Vase of Ambrosia to Fulfill All Wishes

1. The procedure is to translate the name into its Sanskrit counterpart. As all traditional Buddhist names have a Sanskrit root, the matter is simple enough. The name of the present Dalai Lama, for example, is Nga-wang Lob-zang Ten-zin Gya-tso Pal-zang-po, which translates as Vagindra Sumati Shasana-dhara Samudra Shri-bhadra. This is somewhat longer than the ordination name given to an ordinary teacher; but then, the Dalai Lama is no ordinary teacher.

Bibliography

A. TIBETAN SOURCES

Lhar-bcas-srid-zhii-gtsug-rgyan-gong-sa-rgyal-bai-dbang-po-bka'-drin-m-tshungs-med-ku-phreng-bcu-gsum-pa-chen-poi-rnam-thar-rgya-mtsho-lta-bu-las-mdo-tsam-brjod-pa-ngo-mtshar-rin-po-chei-phreng-ba-zhes-bya-ba; or (in English) *A String of Wondrous Gems, A Drop from the Ocean of Liberated Life of the Great Thirteenth, the Incomparably Kind Lord of all Buddhas, He on the Highest Stage, Crown Ornament of Samsara and Nirvana* (which, throughout my introduction, I have referred to simply by the short title *A String of Wondrous Gems*). This is the principal Tibetan biography, being two thick volumes in length, and was composed by the Great Thirteenth's disciple Pur-chok-pa Tub-ten Jam-pa (Phur-lcog-pa-thub-bstan-byams-pa) from the Dalai Lama's personal diaries, as well as other immediate sources. Throughout my Introduction I quote the abridged Dharamsala edition of 1977, which was printed as a single volume of 736 pages.

rJe-sku-phreng-bcu-gsum-pai-rnam-thar; or, in English, *A Biography of the Thirteenth Dalai Lama* by mKhas-btsun-rin-po-che, from the collection *Biographical Dictionary of Indian and Tibetan Sages.*

rJe-btsun-rGyal-wa-sku-phreng-bcu-gsum-pai-ngo-mtsar-mdzad-pa; or, in English, *The Wondrous Deeds of the Victorious Thirteenth Incar-*

nation by Tak-dra Rin-po-che, from his introduction to the catalog to the Great Thirteenth's edition of the Kan-gyur.

rGyal-mchog-bcu-gsum-pai-gsung-'bum; or, in English, *Collected Works of the Dalai Lama XIII*, Sata-pitaka series, Volumes 283-289, New Delhi 1981.

B. WESTERN SOURCES

Avedon, John F.,
 In Exile from the Land of Snows, London, 1984.

Bell, Sir Charles Alfred—
 Tibet, Past and Present, London, 1924.
 Portrait of the Dalai Lama, Collins, 1946.

Candler, Edmund,
 The Unveiling of Lhasa, 1905.

Das, Sarat Chandra,
 Journey to Lhasa and Central Tibet, London, 1902.

Dhondup, K.,
 The Water Bird and Other Years, New Delhi, 1986.

Fergusson, W.N.,
 Adventure, Sport and Travel on the Tibetan Steppes, London, 1911.

Filippi, Filippo de,
 An Account of Tibet: The Travels of Ippolito Desideri of Pistoia S.J., *1712-1727*, London 1932.

Fleming, Peter,
 Bayonets to Lhasa, London, 1962.

Hopkirk, Peter,
 Trespassers on the Roof of the World: The Race for Lhasa, Oxford, 1983.

Kawaguchi, Ekai,
 Three Years in Tibet, Benaras and London. 1909.

Lama, The Dalai,
 My Land and my People, New York, 1967.

Lamb, Alastair,
 Britain and Chinese Central Asia, London, 1957.

Landon, Perceval,
 Lhasa, London, 1906.

Lhamo, Rinchen,
We Tibetans, London, 1926.

MacGregor, John,
Tibet: A Chronicle of Exploration, London, 1970.

Markham, Clements R.,
Narratives of the Mission of George Bogle to Tibet, and of the Journey of Thomas Manning to Lhasa, London, 1879.

Mehra, Parshotam—
The Younghusband Expedition, London, 1968.
Tibetan Polity, 1904-37, Germany, 1976.

Michael, Franz,
Rule by Incarnation, Colorado, 1982.

Norbu, Thubten Jigme, with Colin M. Turnbull,
Tibet: Land, History and People, New York, 1968.

Richardson, H.E.,
Tibet and its History, London, 1962.

Rockhill, W.W.,
The Dalai Lamas of Lhasa and their Relations with the Manchu Emperors, Leiden, 1910.

Shakabpa, W.D.,
Tibet: A Political History, Yale, 1967.

Tada, Tokan,
The Thirteenth Dalai Lama, Tokyo, 1965.

Taring, Rinchen Dolma,
Daughter of Tibet, London, 1970.

Teichman, Eric,
Travels of a Consular Officer in Eastern Tibet, Cambridge, 1922.

van Walt van Praag, Michael,
The Status of Tibet, Colorado, 1987.

Winnington, Alan,
Tibet, London, 1957.

Younghusband, Sir Francis,
India and Tibet, London, 1910.

Index